Cruise of the *Conrad*

Cruise of the *Conrad*

A Journal of a Voyage round the World,
undertaken and carried out in the Ship
Joseph Conrad, 212 Tons, in the Years
1934, 1935, and 1936 by way of Good Hope,
the South Seas, the East Indies, and Cape Horn

by

Alan Villiers

SEAFARER BOOKS
SHERIDAN HOUSE

First published 1937
This edition published 2006
© Nancie Villliers 2006

Published in the UK by:
Seafarer Books
102 Redwald Road
Rendlesham
Woodbridge
Suffolk IP12 2TE

UK ISBN 0 9547062 8 5

And in the USA by:
Sheridan House Inc
145 Palisade St
Dobbs Ferry
NY 10522

USA ISBN 1 57409 241 3

Library of Congress Cataloguing in Publication Data

Villiers, Alan John
 Cruise of the Conrad / by Alan Villiers.
    p. cm.
Reprint. Originally published: New York: Scribner's, 1937.
New introductory biography.
ISBN 1-57409-241-3 (alk. paper)
    1. Villiers, Alan John, 1903-1982—Travel. 2. Voyages around the
       world. 3. Joseph Conrad (Ship) I. Title.
    G440.V75 2006
    910.4'1—dc22

                  2006005849

British Library Cataloguing in Publication Data

Villiers, Alan John, 1903-
  Cruise of the Conrad
  1.Villiers, Alan John, 1903- - Travel 2.Joseph Conrad
  (Ship) 3.Voyages around the world
  I.Title
  910.4'5'092
  ISBN-10: 0954706285

Biography of Alan Villiers © William Facey and the Estate of Alan Villiers
Cover design by Louis Mackay
Copy-editing by Hugh Brazier
Typesetting by Julie Mayhew
Printed in Finland by WS Bookwell OY

CONTENTS

Foreword

Alan Villiers lived a seaman's life, but one that most true seaman could only envy. He jammed so much into his life, but as with so many great people, it is the early years that show us the character and provide the expectations of more to come. The first book of his I read was *Sons of Sindbad*, because I was serving on ships that traded from India to the head of the Persian Gulf and had become fascinated by the dhows that were still to be seen trading there and all the way to East Africa in those days. It gave me a far better respect for those Arab seamen we still saw sailing the traditional routes they had voyaged for more than a thousand years. Alan Villiers had taken a year out to go and join one of those dhows for its voyage from Arabia to Africa. He gave us an account of a way of life that has now disappeared, but thanks to him we do know how the Arabs sailed their dhows around the Indian Ocean for some 2,000 years.

Later, as Second Officer, I wrote to him and asked his advice about a plan two Third Officers and I had to sail back to England at the end of our contracts. I asked whether we could sail a dhow. He replied with a three-page handwritten letter that was full of sound advice, not least that we would never get back our investment as we would find it very hard to find a market for a dhow in Europe. The result was that we built *Suhaili* instead. For that I shall always be grateful to him.

Villiers had served before the mast in square rig, not as in these days in training ships, but on vessels that were still trading on the old classic around-the-world route from Europe to Australia. People look back on those days as a romantic period. It wasn't. These were the last days of commercial sail, when costs were being pared to the bone and stores and food were at a minimum level. It was a fantastic experience and the best possible training for what was to come. It turned him into a practical seaman. Seamen can always find a way to deal with shortage of stores – they adapt – but food is far more fundamental and most seamen finished a voyage tired, strained, and with little fat on them. Life at sea was never easy. Captains took on huge responsibilities, but the greatest of these was, as always, taking on nature – in the raw.

No piece of paper can give you this experience or ability – as Alan Villiers proved. But time spent on a square-rigger was considered the finest training for a seaman, and Villiers came in right at the end of this era. Steamers had taken over, but they could never provide the challenge to compare with climbing aloft in a gale to furl a sail. By the time I went to sea, sail training in the manner Villiers had experienced had disappeared. My apprenticeship was spent on a modern diesel cargo ship, albeit the crew had been removed so we manned the vessel and all had to qualify as Able Seamen. It was a good training, but some of us felt we had missed out on the ultimate training – in square rig.

Villiers finishes regretting the fact that sail training was becoming a thing of the past. He could not have foreseen that twenty years later the first Tall Ships Race would take place, open to sail training ships from a number of nations. That has grown now into a worldwide movement with an annual race in which vessels from large square-riggers to comparatively small yachts, crewed by young people from many nations, compete against each other in conditions that Villiers would have recognised. He helped to keep that spirit alive through the transition from commercial sail to sail training.

What I love about this book is the fact that Villiers was able to buy the vessel, recruit crews and sail around the world entirely without the piece of paper that said he could do it. This is what bureaucrats hate and usually stop. Today's rules would never have allowed Villiers to undertake the voyage, because we live in an age of paper rules. Bureaucrats cannot usually measure experience. To avoid the responsibility of judging a person by ability, they fall back on paper qualifications which absolve them from making a judgement.

This is a wonderful story. An adventure in the real sense. A young man, who has learned his trade the old fashioned 'hands-on' way, risks everything to buy a ship and sail it around the world. Short of money throughout, he overcomes all the problems and vicissitudes that can be thrown at him. But he perseveres to complete the voyage – and has left us with one of the great classics from the twilight of the age of sail. *Cruise of the Conrad* belongs to a time when adventurous people took on responsibility and dared. It could not happen today.

Robin Knox-Johnston

Alan Villiers

This short biography is based on an original text by William Facey, who has prepared a new edition of *Sons of Sindbad*, by Alan Villiers (London: Arabian Publishing, 2006). This will be followed by *Sons of Sindbad: the Photographs* (London: National Maritime Museum, 2006), a new book of Alan Villiers' photographs of sailing with the Arabs, taken from the archives of the National Maritime Museum, and previously unpublished – a unique contribution to our knowledge of the Arab way of life. We are grateful both to Mr Facey and to the National Maritime Museum for their kind permission to make use of this material in edited form. It is part of a renewed interest in the life and work of Alan Villiers as seafarer, writer, photographer, and chronicler of ships and the sea, who inspired a generation of sea-enthusiasts in his own life-time, and continues to do so after his death.

Alan John Villiers (1903–1982) was born in Melbourne, Australia, second son in a family of four sons and two daughters. His father, Leon Joseph Villiers, was a trade union leader and political activist, highly regarded in the Australian labour movement. In addition to his everyday work of driving a grip-tram though the Melbourne streets, his political activities, and bringing up a family of six children on a tiny income, Leon was also a poet, whose poems and essays were collected and published by his colleagues on his death.

The young Alan was thus exposed from an early age to the idea of writing, and inculcated with a very Australian egalitarianism and sense of fair play – although he was never to embrace the political activism of his father. Party politics may have not have appealed to him, but his empathy with the common working man in any part of the world shines through his work. The most important influence of his childhood, however, was the sea, and in particular the sailing ships that in those days before the First World War thronged the Melbourne docks like delivery vehicles parked in a busy transport depot – an irresistible magnet to the eyes and imagination of this highly intelligent and impressionable young Australian.

As he wrote in his autobiography, *The Set of the Sails*:

> Almost always then, there were a score or more big sailing-ships secured in Yarra berths and in the docks, at Williamstown and Port Melbourne. All these were in sight of the house on Spencer Street, and my earliest memories are of gazing at them for hours, before I could walk very much, with wonder and admiration … I kept a secret book in which I drew all the sailing ships I saw, as accurately as I could present them, and kept a list of all their names.
>
> It was my hobby and my delight to make friends aboard the sailing-ships in the docks. Timidly, I went aboard – first, the tiny brigantines and schooners lying in the picturesque Little Dock … and then, gathering courage, the great Cape Horners through whose great riggings the west wind roared. I liked Norwegian ships best, as they were the friendliest. [i]

At the age of eleven he attempted to join the crew of a Norwegian barque, and was only dissuaded by the mate, who warned him against romantic notions of life at sea drawn from books. But Villiers had fallen under the spell of old seafarers' tales, and all such attempts to put him off served merely to deepen the enchantment. He went to Essendon High School, where his natural aptitude ensured that he was an outstanding student in both English literature and mathematics. At the same time he worked to augment the family income, and exercised racehorses at the local racecourse. But his ambition remained to go to sea under sail, and he was determined to achieve it.

His father's untimely death of cancer in 1918 left the family almost destitute and, in 1919, they were hit by the great influenza pandemic, which closed the schools. Alan seized the opportunity and left formal education for ever. Not for him the path to university at the state's expense, provided that he paid his dues back by becoming a schoolteacher, as his youngest brother Lionel was later to do. Alan enrolled in a sail training school, and by the age of fifteen was serving as an apprentice on the *Rothesay Bay*, an elderly barque plying the timber trade between Australia and New Zealand. The harsh reality of life at sea, so far from undermining the lad's resolve, crystallized his credo:

> The great sound of the wind in the rigging was a threat no longer but a symphony of strength and power, and I knew that in a world beset by wars and mounting daily difficulties, the sailing-ship was still a triumph of man's seafaring genius. To be one of a band of men who conducted such ships upon their voyages was to me also triumph – it was a fulfilment of life such as I had dreamed on. Here in the battered barque all men mattered: by the sure efforts of our own hands we survived. [ii]

Alive to the prospect that wind ships, and the traditions of toughness and comradeship that went with them, were on the verge of extinction, Villiers began to keep a diary when he joined his next barque, the *James Craig*.[iii] By now even more deeply under the spell of life afloat, he wrote:

> It seemed to me that the fo'c'sle of a happy sailing ship at sea was one of the more pleasant abodes of labouring man, where the sailors of all nations had learned through the centuries to work and live amicably together. Here there was true democracy, true international co-operation. At least all were equal in their lack of possessions, their pride in their great calling and their skill, and their spirit of service to the ship. [iv]

When in 1920 the *Craig* was decommissioned, he joined a four-masted British 'lime-juicer', the *Bellands*, carrying grain to Europe. A harsh voyage round the Cape of Good Hope, under officers he despised for their arrogance and superior airs, brought him in 1921 to a Britain in the grip of post-War austerity, and in London he was unable to find another ship. Crossing to France as an illegal immigrant, he tramped from Nantes to Bordeaux, living rough, before at last finding a place as able seaman aboard the *Lawhill*, an old steel-hulled four-masted grain barque about to return from Bordeaux to Adelaide. The *Lawhill* belonged to Gustaf Erikson, of Mariehamn in the Finnish Åland Islands, the last big owner of sailing ships in the intercontinental grain trade from Australia.

Villiers found the openness and egalitarianism he so admired among the young Swedish-speaking Finns who made up the crew. (He was to find this same quality of instinctive teamwork and concern for one's crewmates on board the *Triumph of Righteousness*, a Kuwaiti dhow on which he later sailed in order to study and record Arab methods of sailing). But, as the *Lawhill* neared Adelaide, she hit a sandbank, precipitating Villiers from the rigging to the deck in a near-fatal fall. 'It seemed to me,' he wrote, 'in a last instant of consciousness, that the deck was surprisingly soft. It was not the deck that was soft. It was I.'[v]

His injuries led him to give up sailing and, after a series of odd jobs including a dispiriting spell on a cargo steamer, to begin life afresh in Tasmania. There a chance encounter with a journalist, which led him to the office of the *Hobart Mercury*, enabled him to discover his great flair for writing.

True to his instincts, he used his pen to get back to sea, persuading the *Mercury* to send him as special correspondent with an experimental Norwegian whaling fleet to the Antarctic. Here, on board the steam factory ship *Sir James Clark Ross* as a whaler's labourer at £4 a month, but with a fine new camera and a mission to report, he found his métier: seafaring combined with writing and photography. And on board the *Lawhill* he had already discovered a fourth talent, that of picking up a working language from scratch, which would later serve him well in sailing with the Arabs, the Portuguese, and other seafarers of many nationalities.

His Antarctic experiences of 1923–24 were published as articles, which he then expanded into his first book, *Whaling in the Frozen South*, published in 1925 with some success in Britain and the United States. By the time he was twenty-two, his journalistic talents had earned him promotion to senior reporter on the *Hobart Mercury*. He had also married his first wife in Hobart and was trying to settle down. But the siren-song of the sea ordained that he would use his way with a story to subsidize further sailing adventures.

In 1927, Villiers was in Melbourne on an assignment from the *Mercury* when he noticed a fine four-masted Erikson barque, the *Herzogin Cecilie*, discharging Baltic timber in the port. He went on board to find its captain, who turned out to be the very same Ålander, Ruben de Cloux, who had captained the *Lawhill* on the voyage to Adelaide. De Cloux's formidable sailing skills and perfectionism had made their mark on Villiers, who immediately set about persuading his paper to grant him six months' leave to sail for Europe on the *Herzogin Cecilie* as an able seaman and, once there, to report home on the fruit trade in Europe. The ship was to load grain and to race another, the Swedish four-master *Beatrice*, in one of the so-called 'Grain Races' to Britain via Cape Horn. Villiers got his permission and bought his own camera; the *Herzogin* made the 15,000-mile passage from Port Lincoln to Cornwall in 96 days and won the race, and a best-seller was born. *Falmouth for Orders* was published to acclaim in 1928, and went into several editions, creating a public appetite for Villiers' vivid accounts of the last days of the tall ships that would ensure a brisk demand for his future books.

The success of his investigations into the European fruit trade and the articles that followed made Villiers' name as a journalist, and even opened up the prospect of a political career in Australia. But, addicted to the sea as he was, he was busy contriving a saltier career for himself. His ambition now was to capture the twilight of sail on movie film before it was too late, to augment the still photographs he had already amassed. Teaming up in 1929 with a fellow journalist, Ronald Walker, he took ship as an able seaman on the ageing Finnish three-master *Grace Harwar*, the last of the full-rigged Cape Horners. She was notoriously under-maintained and undermanned, but her lack of modernization appealed to the two men as being well-suited to their theme. The choice turned out to be a tragic one. Villiers' decision to go effectively put an end to his first marriage, and of this ill-starred enterprise he later wrote:

> We were lucky to arrive at all. On the voyage Walker was killed [by a falling spar], the second mate driven out of his mind, the ship sprang a serious leak, and we ran out of food ... We were the last ship to sail and the last in the race. The whole voyage was a savage fight against the sea, in a ship which was seriously handicapped from the setting-out to the end. [vi]

Another passage shows how the voyage brought out all Villiers' remarkable combination of physical stamina and creative skills:

> I was one of a handful of able seamen in a heavy ship, grievously undermanned. I steered. I pumped. I worked aloft. I often sewed sails all day on deck, and worked with them in the rigging half the night. I did what I could to help the second mate. I filmed and photographed, for that could not be given up, and I tried to make as good a job as Walker would have done. When the weather was good,

I brought out my battered portable typewriter, and got on with my maritime history of Tasmania, for that had to be ready for the press when we came in. [vii]

Despite the discouragements of the *Grace Harwar* experience, Villiers had managed to shoot all 6,000 feet of film, and had collected material for his biggest-seller yet, *By Way of Cape Horn*. A job in Fleet Street, a lecture tour in America and a relationship with the *National Geographic Magazine* quickly followed. By 1931 he found himself with capital to spare, and went in with de Cloux in the purchase of the *Parma*, a 3,000-ton steel four-masted barque built in Port Glasgow. It turned out to be a shrewd investment. Villiers made two voyages on the *Parma* under de Cloux, transporting grain from Australia to Britain, in 1932 and 1933, and both turned in a very handsome profit. More best-sellers followed: *The Voyage of the Parma* (1933), followed by *Last of the Wind Ships*, a book of some 200 photographs of the *Parma*'s voyages.

As part-owner of the *Parma*, Villiers had sailed not as an able seaman but as understudy to the masterly de Cloux.[viii] With that experience behind him, he felt ready to command his own sailing vessel. He sold his share in the *Parma*, and in 1934 bought the Danish training ship *Georg Stage*, a three-master of just over 200 tons, 'a tiny full-rigged ship, a veritable miniature, perfect in every detail'.[ix] Renaming her the *Joseph Conrad*, in homage to that great maritime man of letters, he assembled a crew of experienced hands and invited 'all the young fellows who cared to come and there was room for' to make a voyage round the world, 'an ambling circumnavigation by way of Good Hope and the Horn, the East Indies and the South Seas'.[x] His route was inspired by the voyages of James Cook but, if Cook inspired Villiers the sailor, it was the 'convincing and stirring prose of the brooding Polish-English master mariner' Conrad that helped inspire him as a writer. Villiers pondered much on the effect sailing might have on a writer's style. 'The seaman,' he wrote, 'had time to think but not to write ... He had need to make decisions most clearly conveyed in minimal and incisive prose.'[xi] Villiers had literary contacts aplenty by now, and there was even some talk of T. E. Lawrence coming along on the voyage.[xii] This adventure took two years, 1934–36, and took him over some 57,000 miles of ocean. It was when he was in the Pacific, after the *Conrad* had left Australia, that his first wife finally divorced him – citing the sea as co-respondent![xiii]

Cruise of the Conrad, yet another best-seller, was published in 1937, but the venture had exhausted Villiers' funds and, on arrival in New York in October 1936, the *Conrad* had to be sold to clear his debts. By a lucky stroke, the ship was bought by an American millionaire who happened to see her in New York harbour, and she is now preserved in the Mystic Seaport Museum in Connecticut.

While Villiers was engaged in these voyages European sail had been steadily dwindling, and by 1937 many of the ships that he had known had been sold off as hulks or for scrap. His next big idea was to turn his attention to seafaring in other, pre-industrial cultures. He opted first for the Arabian dhow world of the western Indian Ocean because it seemed to him, 'having looked far and wide over a seafaring lifetime, that as pure sailing craft carrying on their unspoiled ways, only the Arab remained'.[xiv] But this choice was part of a larger vision:

> My sailing with the Arabs was part of a programme, to occupy at least five years, by which I hoped to acquaint myself with the sailing-vessels of the world … There were still large fleets quietly going about their share of the world's sea-borne trade in the Indian Ocean and the waters of East Asia … A life of wandering in sailing ships appealed to me, and I proposed to make an exhaustive survey of the types of ship and the trades I came across, and to photograph and make films as records.[xv]

Villiers chose Aden as his starting point. He was put in touch first with the captain of a little Yemeni *zarook*, setting off for the Red Sea port of Jizan. Having spent two weeks on that voyage, he made his way up to Jiddah before returning to Aden by ship. Then, in December 1938, he was introduced to the captain of one of the great Kuwaiti *booms* then frequenting the port.

This Kuwaiti *nakhoda*, Ali bin Nasr el-Nejdi, was making the age-old voyage from the Gulf to East Africa, coasting on the north-east monsoon winds, with a cargo of dates from Basra. The dates had been sold at Berbera, in British Somaliland, and Nejdi's ship, *The Triumph of Righteousness*, was continuing its voyage with cargo from Aden to pick up passengers on the Hadhramaut coast, to sail thence to the ports of East Africa down to Zanzibar. The return voyage to Kuwait would be made in early summer of 1939, on the early breezes of the south-west monsoon, with a full cargo of mangrove poles from the mosquito-ridden Rufiji Delta, south of Zanzibar.

From this voyage on the monsoon winds, made by Arabia's mariners from time immemorial, and regarded by Villiers himself as 'my most interesting sailing experience',[xvi] *Sons of Sindbad* was fashioned. Dashed off with his usual facility in the early weeks of the Second World War, he has given us one of the great classics of Arabian travel and, indeed, of travel writing in general.

Sons of Sindbad is the work not only of a naturally gifted sailor, writer and photographer, but also of an astute businessman. With his background in commercial journalism and nose for a business venture, Villiers was interested in the economics of the dhow and pearl trades and the social conditions of those engaged in them. In Kuwait he was able to interview people from every walk of life, from the ruler Shaikh Ahmad Al-Sabah to ministers, merchants, captains and homeless seamen on the waterfront. His analysis of the bonds of debt tying the sailors and divers to the *nakhodas*, and the *nakhodas* to the merchants, makes compelling reading. It also goes to the heart of the inequities of the old system, as it stood on the very threshold of being swept away by the wealth from oil that had just, in 1936, been discovered in commercial quantities.

Having spent the summer of 1939 in Kuwait and on the pearl banks of the northern Gulf, Villiers, who had been toying with the idea of buying and restoring one of the last three surviving Kuwaiti *baggalas*, decided in September to return to England to play his part in the war effort.[xvii] In London, he renewed his acquaintance with his future wife Nancie, a fellow Australian who had arrived to tour Europe in 1939. She worked for the publisher John Murray and then joined the Women's Royal Air Force. They married in 1940, by which time Alan Villiers had joined the Royal Naval Volunteer Reserve (RNVR). He spent most of the war on active service with Infantry Landing Craft in Italy, Normandy and the Far East, where he operated along the Arakan coast of Burma, at the landing in Rangoon and at the recovery of Singapore.[xviii] He reached the rank of commander and was awarded the Distinguished Service Cross (DSC) for his part in the invasion of France.

After the war he became master of the training ship *Warspite*. Meanwhile Kit, Katherine and Peter had been born,[xix] and the family made their home in Oxfordshire. In 1952 they moved to a house in North Oxford. Here in 'Dons' Alley', as he called it, Villiers would be based for the remainder of his life.

He quickly returned to his sailing activities, but in a new guise. Commercial sail had by now completely died out in the West, and his ventures were henceforth centred on survivals of sail in other cultures, on the re-creation of historic sailing voyages, and on the preservation of the records of sail. He had been appointed a Trustee of the National Maritime Museum in 1948, and would later help found its historic photograph collection with his friend, Basil Greenhill, Director of the Museum from 1967 to 1983.[xx] His own collection, of some 20,000 negatives and transparencies, constitutes an important part of the Museum's Historic Photographs archive. The Alan Villiers film collection, comprising footage from several of his voyages, has been on long-term loan at the National Maritime Museum since 1983. He also served on various committees, including the Society for Nautical Research (of which he was successively a vice-president, chairman from 1960, and president 1970–74), the *Cutty Sark* Preservation Society, and the *Victory* Technical Advisory Committee.

Alan continued to travel widely until the mid-1970s in search of new adventures, from which emerged a steady stream of books, as well as of articles for the *National Geographic Magazine*. 1950 found him sailing with the Portuguese cod-fishing fleet on the Grand Banks of Newfoundland and off Greenland. True to form, he embraced the rigours of life as a common fisherman, spending days alone paying out and hauling in long lines in a flimsy dory on a treacherous sea. Other explorations of traditional sail included voyaging on a Maldives *baggala* (1956), and a visit to the Brahmaputra (1960). His last major excursion was to the Philippines in 1975, to write an article on Magellan for the *National Geographic*. Latterly he was frequently accompanied by Nancie, who throughout was a great help with his work.

Growing fame also brought assignments of a more glamorous nature. He was called in as adviser on various films, including the Hollywood versions of the Melville classics *Billy Budd* and *Moby Dick*, in which he was master of the *Pequod*. In 1957 he commanded the *Mayflower* replica during its successful voyage to the United States, and in 1964 he recorded the Lisbon–Bermuda Tall Ships Race. He was much in demand as a broadcaster and lecturer on both sides of the Atlantic, and many still recall his idiosyncratic style. Capable of a quarter-deck delivery and endowed with a keen sense of the dramatic, he could electrify his listeners, whom he never failed to enthral.

In all he published more than forty books and innumerable articles, introductions and prefaces. Alan was one of the fortunate few authors who do not struggle with the act of creation – his first book was said to have been completed in just four days – and he also kept a regular diary, whether at sea or ashore. One of his greatest satisfactions came when his literary merits were recognized, just a few months before his death, with the award of a Doctorate of Letters by the University of Melbourne. His pre-war books had been mostly accounts of individual voyages, but he subsequently branched out into memoirs and history with books such as *The Set of the Sails* (1949) and *Monsoon Seas* (1952). A later volume of reminiscences, *Give Me a Ship to Sail* (1958), contains some of his liveliest writing. His last book, *Voyaging with the Wind*, a simple introduction to handling large square-rigged ships, returns to the essentials of his trade. It is testament to the deep reverence for the sea and the wind, and for those who by choice or necessity had learned to harness them, that had sustained and given purpose to his life. As he once said, 'I loved the sound of the wind in the rigging, because it seemed to be challenging and – music. It was music, and it was music that struck a chord somehow in me. But I didn't know I'd pick up the chord. I did, thank God, and I stayed with it.'[xxi]

During a life spent largely at sea, this remarkable man both lived and recorded the last days of sail. By combining his skills as seaman, writer, photographer, lecturer and adviser, he made a contribution to maritime history, research, training and public education that few others can claim to equal. In doing so, he built up a unique body of work on the world of commercial sail that vanished during the first half of the twentieth century, and amassed a huge amount of material. Its location today reflects the Anglo-Australian course of his career: his papers are held at the National Library of Australia in Canberra, the University of Melbourne holds his library of 5,000 volumes, while his film and photographic archive resides at the National Maritime Museum, Greenwich.

Notes

i Villiers, Alan J., *The Set of the Sails* (London: Hodder & Stoughton, 1949), p. 11.
ii Ibid., p. 47.   iii Ibid., p. 72.   iv Ibid., p. 73.   v Ibid., p. 123.   vi Ibid., p. 197.
vii Ibid., p. 201.   viii Ibid., p. 216.   ix Ibid., p. 219.   x Ibid., p. 223.
xi Villiers, *Of Ships and Men: a Personal Anthology* (London: Newnes, 1962), pp. 43–4.
xii Villiers, *Set of the Sails,* pp. 224–5. The connection with T. E. Lawrence was Bruce Rogers, his typographer friend, who was also a devotee of sailing and a friend of Villiers. See Lawrence, T. E., *The Letters of T. E. Lawrence,* ed. by David Garnett (London: Jonathan Cape, 1938), p. 843.
xiii Brett, Oswald L., 'Commander Alan John Villiers, DSC, FRGS, D.Litt.' *Sea History* 32 (Summer 1984), p. 20.
xiv Villiers, *Sons of Sindbad* (London: Hodder & Stoughton, 1940), p. 3.
xv Villiers, *Set of the Sails*, p. 231.
xvi Dedication by A. J. Villiers in W. Facey's personal copy of *Sons of Sindbad,* New York, 1969.
xvii Villiers, *Set of the Sails*, p. 233.
xviii Villiers, *Monsoon Seas: the Story of the Indian Ocean* (New York: McGraw-Hill, 1952), p. vi.
xix Born respectively in Scotland, 1943; Oxford, 1945; and Chipping Norton, 1947.
xx Greenhill had earlier initiated the Society for Nautical Research Photographic Records Committee, of which Villiers was chairman. The photographs gathered were held at the National Maritime Museum and were the basis of the collection formally established there after Greenhill became Director; K. Littlewood and B. Butler, *Of Ships and Stars: Maritime Heritage and the Founding of the National Maritime Museum, Greenwich* (London, 1998), p.186.
xxi Foster, D., *Self Portraits* (Canberra: National Library of Australia, 1993), p. 148.

Books by Alan Villiers

We are grateful to William Facey and Kit Villiers for their assistance in compiling this list. For a full list of Alan Villiers' publications, including articles in journals and magazines, see the 'Seafaring Bibliography' in *Sons of Sindbad* (London: Arabian Publishing, 2006).

Whaling in the Frozen South: Being the Story of the 1923–24 Norwegian Whaling Expedition to the Antarctic (London: Hurst & Blackett, 1925; New York: Robert McBride, 1925; Indianapolis: Bobbs-Merrill, 1925)

The Wind Ship (London: Hurst & Blackett, 1928)

Falmouth for Orders (London: Geoffrey Bles, 1928; New York: Henry Holt, 1929)

By Way of Cape Horn (London: Geoffrey Bles, 1928; New York: Henry Holt, 1929). The *Grace Harwar* voyage, with photographs by Alan Villiers and Ronald Gregory Walker

Vanished Fleets: Ships and Men of Old Van Dieman's Land (New York: Henry Holt, 1931). Published in the UK as *Convict Ships and Sailors* (London: Philip Allan, 1936)

Sea-dogs of Today (New York: Garden City Publishing / Henry Holt, 1931; London: Harrap, 1932). Republished as *Modern Mariners: Sea-dogs of Today* (New York: Garden City Publishing, 1937)

The Sea in Ships: the Story of a Sailing Ship's Voyage Round Cape Horn (London: Routledge, 1932; New York: William Morrow, 1932). A book of 112 photographs of the *Herzogin Cecilie* and *Grace Harwar* voyages.

Voyage of the 'Parma': the Great Grain Race of 1932 (London: Geoffrey Bles, 1933). Published in the USA as *Grain Race* (New York: Scribner's, 1933)

Last of the Wind Ships (London: Routledge, 1934; New York: William Morrow, 1934). A book of more than 200 photographs of the two *Parma* voyages.

Whalers of the Midnight Sun: a Story of Modern Whaling in the Antarctic (New York: Scribner's, 1934)

Stormalong: the Story of a Boy's Voyage Round the World in a Full-rigged Ship (New York: Scribner's, 1937; London: Routledge, 1938)

Cruise of the Conrad (London: Hodder & Stoughton, 1937; New York: Scribner's, 1937). Republished with a foreword by Sir Robin Knox

Johnston and an introduction by William Facey (Rendlesham: Seafarer Books, 2006; New York: Sheridan House, 2006)

The Making of a Sailor: the Photographic Story of Schoolships Under Sail (London: Routledge, 1938; New York: William Morrow, 1938)

Joey Goes to Sea (New York: Scribner's, 1939). For younger readers.

Sons of Sindbad (London: Hodder & Stoughton, 1940). Published in the USA as *Sons of Sinbad* (New York: Scribner's, 1940). Republished with a new introduction by William Facey, Yacoub Al-Hijji and Grace Pundyk (London: Arabian Publishing, 2006)

The Coral Sea (London: Museum Press, 1949; New York: Whittlesey House / McGraw Hill, 1949)

The Set of the Sails: the Story of a Cape Horn Seaman (London: Hodder & Stoughton, 1949). Published in the USA as *The Set of the Sails: the Story of a Life on the Seven Seas* (New York: Scribner's, 1949). Villiers' autobiography.

Quest of the Schooner 'Argus': a Voyage to the Banks and Greenland (London: Hodder & Stoughton, 1951; New York: Scribner's, 1951)

Monsoon Seas: the Story of the Indian Ocean (New York: McGraw Hill, 1952). Published in the UK as *The Indian Ocean* (London: Museum Press, 1952)

The Cutty Sark: Last of a Glorious Era (London: Hodder & Stoughton, 1953)

The Way of a Ship: Being Some Account of the Ultimate Development of the Ocean-going Square-rigged Sailing Vessel, and the Manner of her Handling, her Voyage-making, her Personnel, her Economics, her Performance, and her End (New York: Scribner's, 1953). Published in the UK as *The Way of a Ship: the Story of the Square-rigged Cape Horner* (London: Hodder & Stoughton, 1953)

Pilot Pete (London: Museum Press, 1953; New York: Scribner's, 1953)

And Not To Yield: a Story of the 'Outward Bound' School of Adventure (London: Hodder & Stoughton, 1953; New York: Scribner's, 1953)

The 'Sailing Eagle': the Story of the Coast Guard's Square-rigger (New York: Scribner's, 1955)

Posted Missing: the Story of Ships Lost without Trace in Recent Years (London: Hodder & Stoughton, 1956; New York: Scribner's, 1956)

Pioneers of the Seven Seas (London: Routledge & Kegan Paul, 1956)

The Western Ocean: the Story of the North Atlantic (London: Museum Press, 1957). Published in the USA as *Wild Ocean: the Story of the North Atlantic and the Men who Sailed it* (New York: McGraw Hill, 1957)

The Navigators and the Merchant Navy (Glasgow: the Nautical Society, for Brown, Son & Ferguson, 1957)

Give Me a Ship to Sail (London: Hodder & Stoughton, 1959; New York: Scribner's, 1959)

Louis de Rochemont's 'Windjammer': a Modern Adventure in Cinemiracle (New York: Random House, 1958)

The New 'Mayflower' (New York: Scribner's, 1958)

A Seaman's Selection of Great Sea Stories, selected by Alan Villiers (New York: Dell, 1959)

Of Ships and Men: a Personal Anthology, compiled by Alan Villiers (London: Newnes, 1962)

Men, Ships and the Sea (Wasington DC: National Geographic Society, 1962). A volume in the *Story of Man* series.

Oceans of the World: Man's Conquest of the Sea (London: Museum Press, 1963). Published in the USA as *The Ocean; Man's Conquest of the Sea* (New York: Dutton, 1963)

The Battle of Trafalgar: Lord Nelson Sweeps the Sea (New York: Macmillan, 1965)

Captain Cook, the Seamen's Seaman: a Study of the Great Discoverer (London: Hodder & Stoughton, 1967; New York: Scribner's, 1967)

Nonsuch: Hudson's Bay Company Ship Replica. With Basil Greenhill (London: Alabaster Passmore & Sons, 1969)

The Deep Sea Fishermen (London: Hodder & Stoughton, 1970)

The War with Cape Horn (New York: Scribner's, 1971; London: Hodder & Stoughton, 1971)

My Favourite Sea Stories (London: Lutterworth Press, 1972)

The Bounty Ships of France: the Story of the French Cape Horn Sailing Ships. With Henri Picard (London: Patrick Stephens, 1972; New York: Scribner's, 1972)

Voyaging With The Wind: an Introduction to Sailing Large Square-rigged Ships (London: HMSO / National Maritime Museum, 1975)

The Last of the Wind Ships: Photographs by Alan Villiers. With an introduction by Basil Greenhill (London: Harvill Press, 2000)

PREFACE

IN THE more or less successful accomplishment of the voyage of the *Joseph Conrad* round the world I had much friendly help, and I should like very briefly to express something of my gratitude to some of these good folk here. In Copenhagen the advice of Captain J. B. Junker and Styrmand Jens Svendsen was of inestimable value, seeing that these good mariners had been handling the *Georg Stage* for twenty years. In England Mr. A. P. Herbert, M.P.; Captain Gardner, the Assistant Harbourmaster of Ipswich; Captain Learmont, the Superintendent of Pilots at Harwich; and Sir Bunnell Burton, of Ipswich, were all of them good friends to the vessel. In New York my friends were many, but on this occasion I was especially grateful to Mr. Amos Carver, of Baker, Carver, and Morrell; Mr. Arthur Sullivan, of F. P. Hall, Inc., the marine insurance adjustors; Captain Walter Davis, of the Merritt-Chapman salvage company; Mr. Wilfred O. White, of Boston; Lambert Knight, of Vineyard Haven; Mr. Compton, of the London Salvage Association; Professor William Lyon Phelps, of New Haven; Captain Thomas W. Sheridan, of the New York Athletic Club — always a tower of strength where a square-rigger is concerned — Ben Robertson, Jr., of the Associated Press (one of the few newspapermen on earth who gets ship stories right); and Miss Elsie Jansen, of Tramp Trips, Inc., in Beaver Street. In Cape Town Mr. Oscar Thesen was a good friend, and I was grateful to Admiral Sir Edward R. G. R. Evans for his kindly interest. In Singapore the good pilots Captains McAllister and Abbey turned what had been something of a dull port into one of the most pleasant of the civilized places on our list; and the Marine Superintendent of the Straits Steamships Line gave me excellent advice on the navigation of the Sulu Sea. At Bongao in Tawi Tawi I found the Commandant a man after my own heart, but unfortunately I do not know his name. Here in Tawi Tawi Mr. Wilson of Lapid Lapid gave us good sport on his plantation and was a friend in other ways; the Panglima Sarawi of Malasa who piloted us to Balimbing was another stalwart. I should like to call on these again. At Nissan in the Mandated Territory Mr. Tichenor, the planter of Tongolan, gave us ducks, goats, pawpaw, and all manner of good things, nor do I recall that we were able to give him much save a few newspapers. In the Trobriands I met good friends in Monsieur Brudo and his family; here again I find it embarrassingly difficult to recall having done anything to deserve the generosity and the kindnesses heaped upon us all by these good people. At Makambo in the Solomons, Mr. Scott of Burns Philp was a cheery welcomer and a good friend; at Berande on Guadalcanal Captain Campbell and Mr. Strange, for some reason I was never able to fathom, went out of their way for three days to give the whole of my hungry and sometimes boisterous horde of youthful mariners the time of their young lives. They did indeed treat us royally. I wish I could think of something I had done for them. At Owa Raha the indefatigable Henry Kuper was a source of joy and a friend to us all, nor shall I forget his good wife, the Queen of the island, and his ancient henchman the good Mr. Richardson. In Sydney there were so many! From the Governor-General and the Prime Minister to the smallest newsboy, all were our friends and all were interested — the excellent pilots; the good yachtsmen; Captain Stringer the Harbourmaster; the gentlemen of the Ellerman Bucknall office who helped me so much with my papers and the innumerable customs forms; the newspapermen, the old friends many of them, of whom the greatest was Mr. Dunbabin, the Editor of the *Sun*. In Melbourne the Chairman of the Harbour Trust, Mr. Kermode; Sir Walter Leitch; Captain J. K. Davis, the Commonwealth Director of Navigation; Doctor Bell Ferguson; the pleasant young women of the English Speaking Union; Major-General Sir

Julius Bruche; the yachtsmen of St. Kilda, Brighton, Hobson's Bay, Williamstown; Mr. Gough of the Melbourne Steamships Company; Sir Keith Murdoch and Clive Turnbull of the Melbourne *Herald*; again the excellent pilots — these were loyal and stalwart friends. The Kirbys of Lord Howe who made our brief stay at that grand island so pleasant; Mr. Samuel Russell of Papeete, Tahiti, the best agent of the whole voyage; the manager of the Eastman Kodak store in Rio; Mr. Maas of the K. P. M. at Bali; the Harbourmaster of Auckland in New Zealand; Knut Bäcklund of Tahiti; the ceerful Pilot Baille of Papeete; the master of the British steamer *Port Nicholson* who went out of his way in the Coral Sea to check our chronometer; Captain Watson of the Melbourne tug *James Patterson*; the masters of the Italian steamer *Valdirosa* and the British steamers *Tregenna*, *Napierstar*, and *Merkur*, all of whom cheered us on our way; the second mate of the *Malaita* who said he was Bill the Bastard but did not act like that — these, too, helped to make the voyage pleasant for us all.

There remain the great stalwarts, Fritz Egerton and Bruce Rogers: it is Fritz who ought really to be blamed for all this voyage, for if that cheerful fountain-head of eternal youth had not said to me at a certain rather blind stage in my footling career, Here, young man, what about going to Mergui and the Mentawi Islands? (and divers other places I never reached) — why, I should not have gone anywhere. I really believe I would not. And having set out, the noble Fritz, who was my English representative, my guardian, my mentor, and my guide, continued to believe in the worthwhileness of the curious enterprise until the very last. And in B. R. we both of us had a good supporter.

I think I ought to express my thanks, too, to the mariners who came with me, and stayed; to Messrs. Burmeister and Wain, of Copenhagen, for having produced so excellent a ship; and the Committee for the Memory of Herr Georg Stage for having looked after her so splendidly;

and to the old philanthropist Frederik Stage, too, who brought the ship into being and never foresaw, very probably, that at the age of fifty-two, when she had trained 4,000 boys for his native Denmark, the old ship would wander out round the world to sail for the first time the far waters those boys had served with the loyalty, skill, and devotion the same old ship had first bred in them.

And I really ought most heartily to thank God; and indeed I do. I don't know. I don't think much of myself as a sailor: looking back over all this it scarcely seems believable. Full-rigger round the world! It must be easy ... But I know that whatever credit there may be belongs to God — to God and the ship.

ALAN VILLIERS
Ship *Joseph Conrad*,
New York,
October 30, 1936

I

The Little Ship

TO LEEWARD the Dover cliffs pale in the autumnal sun showed me the last of England, and overhead the longshore gulls wheeled and cried for the last time. In the rigging the soft nor'easter quietly murmured into the sails with scarce weight enough to hold them from the masts; aft the soft stream of the wake was almost imperceptible, as the ship, upright and graceful, moved gently through the water. The pilot had left now and the ship was mine, and I looked along the decks and at the masts in mild alarm. What was this I was about to do? What had led me here? Almost in spite of myself, setting out in a full-rigged ship in the year of grace 1934 to make a circumnavigation of the globe, taking this tiny sailing-ship out to sea where she had never been, leading this heterogeneous collection of mariners and schoolboys, sailors and landsmen of eight nationalities, who, taking their last look at England, filled my decks — I in command and leading them, who never had commanded anything anywhere or led anyone to anything. I now Master, who had been Able Seaman and naught else, save understudy to De Cloux, to sail this last of all the English ships, to write *Finis* to a centuries-long line of great traditions, to propel with her sails this last frigate round the world. I found myself filled with a great humility and almost reeled a little, at first, with a knowledge of my own shortcomings. And yet — and yet, I was there. No one else had come forward. I had set out; I had to go on. I had a ship and thirty lives in my hands and I would trust them in no other's now; quickly the work of the voyage and the sailing of the ship so filled my mind that I had no further time for alarms and bewilderment.

We sailed on. Gales blew. We beat, doggedly. We shortened down, clinging to a little canvas with grim determination against the autumn gales. The sea rose; the visibility worsened; the gales increased. It was late October, 1934, and the ship *Joseph Conrad*, 212 tons, was bound down-channel — down-channel, across the North Atlantic, and round the world.

And there stood I to take her. I thought of numerous persons better qualified. But there had been so much talk and no one had done anything. After all, I had found this lovely ship and saved her from the break-up yards, and I had at least been reared in sail, and stuck to it. I was aware of the ocean's endless enmity; aware of the month-long, voyage-long need for ceaseless vigilance, of a good ship's need for the care of all her detail. I had a fair idea of what I was about to try and how it might be accomplished, and I had sailed for years under Ruben de Cloux, stout Finlander, greatest of the surviving windship masters in the world. I had been in the Cape Horn grain-ships six voyages, had served in the Tasman Sea barques, in whaling vessels. It was a good school. I had at least come early to a realization of all that could be learned, all I didn't know — would never know. I had been so long accustomed to the ordinary working of a sailing-ship with square sails that now the management of a ship under sail came naturally to me, though I never before had managed one; and if I had little experience as a navigator — why, I was about to have a lot. I could learn.

So I kept my misgivings to myself, and showed to others only my determination to go on, and held to the reefed tops'ls and beat and beat down that gale-filled sea road that leads from England, and fought against three gales in four days: and when a deputation of my passengers came to me asking that I should run for shelter from the storm I smiled at them and refused. We had the Channel beaten then: what, give in? Go back? No, no, go on! My little ship had shown herself strong and sweet and wholesome in the sea, stoutly rigged and buoyant and faithful: steadfastly she fought against the sea's onrush and the weight of wind, and I only hoped before my God that I would never let her down.

We went on.

My ship was the last surviving frigate in the world. A single-tops'l full-rigged ship crossing three royals, she was 100 feet on the waterline, 25 feet beam, drew 12 feet, grossed 212 tons. She had been, when I found her, for fifty-two years a schoolship for the Danes. She was built by Burmeister and Wain in Copenhagen in 1882, of Swedish iron; her name was then *Georg Stage,* after the shipowner who financed her building, and she had been training 80 young Danes annually. Built for safety, she was exceptionally strong and as able and seaworthy as a good ship could be made. She was fitted with five transverse bulkheads, of steel, dividing her into strong compartments any three of which, undamaged, would keep her afloat. (I was to test this, later on.) Her decks were of teak, her rigging strong iron wire, her masts of iron and pitchpine, her sails good hand-sewn hemp. She carried a big sail plan and could set 10,000 square feet of canvas: she had deep single tops'ls, triple reefed; topgallantsails, and royals on all three masts; she was equipped to carry studding-sails and her long jib-boom set three big headsails. She had the lines of a frigate of a hundred years ago, the strength of a sperm whale in the ocean, and the grace of a swan.

I found her quite by chance as I walked the waterfront of Copenhagen one June day. I had gone there looking for a ship, some kind of an oaken schooner, not too large — strong-built, copper-fastened, that could be changed a little without too great expense and made fit to wander tropic seas. I was rather vague about this ship. She had to be cheap, since I was not wealthy; she had to be small, able, handy, strong. Ships were selling cheaply in those days. Schooners without engines were no longer wanted anywhere; shipping throughout the world was suffering severely from the great depression that had begun in 1929, and vessels of many kinds could be bought for a song. (We had bought the big fourmaster *Parma* from Germany in 1931 and did not have to sing very loudly; she had done well, in the grain trade from Australia.) I was temporarily in possession of some funds from the successful voyaging of the *Parma* and the quiet success of a book or two, principally in America — not much, but enough to buy a ship in those days when ships were cheap.

But I found that I had come to Copenhagen too late. The good engine-less schooners were all gone. True, there were some still for sale, but they did not appeal to me. They were not what I wanted. I had already searched in many places, and had looked at ships in San Francisco Bay and Newport News, in Boston, the china-clay ports of Cornwall, Sydney, the South Seas. In San Francisco a year before there had been a pretty little schooner named *Coquette*, teak-built in China somewhere. I had almost bought her. In Boston I saw a tall two-master that had sunk at her berth in the dock. But she was a frail and doll-like thing, long in the overhangs and high in the masts — too high; and fitted luxuriously below. I had neither use nor funds for luxury, and I soon discovered that the ideas of the Americans when valuing their schooner-yachts were too optimistic for me. Nor did I want a yacht, as such; I wanted a vessel with a deck to walk on and a hull unfilled with tiny cabins, lavishly furnished, and showers and refrigerators and stainless steel — not that I scorned the comforts of modernity, but it was the *ship* that mattered: the ship first, second, last, and all the time. It seemed to me these pampered, bright-work dolls were good for Long Island Sound. At Par in Cornwall was a tops'l schooner, pretty good; I thought of her awhile but did not purchase, though I might have done so. Somehow, I sensed that the ship for me was not yet come: there was something almost providential at last in her discovery.

Disconsolate from the failure of my long search, and wondering if, after all, the ship I wanted had any real existence, I chanced to walk the Copenhagen waterfront down by Langelinie, not with the hope of seeing anything (though powered schooners were often anchored there) but just because — just because my feet had taken me there as they so often had before to all the waterfronts of the world. And there to my surprise I saw a full-rigged ship. She was no ordinary ship; no vessel of that rig is ordinary now. She was of the real old frigate type, gloriously proportioned hull, with a seat in the water like a sea bird; tall, symmetrical masts and tapering yards, all painted a light golden colour, and a long jib-boom projecting far beyond the sweet grace of her cutwater and the bronze figurehead. And she had stuns'l booms and bowlines and hammock nettings and sails that clewed to the bunt, and all those long-forgotten things that belonged to great ships last century: and lanyard rigging and stout channels and many boats. And how her brasswork and her teak shone in the sun! She was small — about 200 tons I thought (much the size of Bligh's *Bounty*) — but what a picture of grace and sea-beauty!

I stopped and watched, and as I looked I saw a crowd of boys ascend her rigging — two to each royal and each topgallant, four to the tops'ls and six to each course – while others manned the capstan on the small fo'c'sle head and began to tramp up the anchor. Whistles blew and, as one sail, the white canvas fell loosed from her yards: down on deck again (with a boy to each top to overhaul the gear) they backed the head yards, braced up the main and mizzen. Now the capstan pawls clanked merrily and the cable came in over the windlass. Whistle again: up and down! Set sail it was then; what a sight! The three tops'ls at once, then the topgallants and the royals, up with a swing right in the crowded anchorage. A few more turns around the capstan and the anchor was broken out, while the little beauty gathered sternway and began to swing as her main and mizzen filled, the backed head yards putting her round in the restricted space on her heel. Let go and haul! Round with the head yards then; and it was a delight to watch her as she stood a moment in her stride, still swinging, halted with the sternway off and just gaining headway as the sails all filled; then moving off, with stately grace, upon her course through the moving and anchored shipping of the harbour. There goes a sailor with a ship, by God! I thought, and read upon the stern *Georg Stage*. I did not know what ship it was, and looked up from my reverie to hear a man saying it was a pity she was to be broken up. What, broken up? *That* ship? It could not be: but I heard the man say she was too old and the new ship to replace her would soon be ready. And nobody wanted the old.

I leapt into a taxi, then and there, and rushed off to the office of my broker, who had painstakingly been offering me vessels of all kinds — drydocks, tugs, trawlers, steamers — for the past two weeks; and burst in upon him and shouted: "Is that ship for sale?" "What ship?" he asked, with some astonishment. "Why, the full-rigged ship," I said, "the old schoolship." "Of course," he said; "they've been trying to get rid of her for some time."

They tried no more. I bought the lovely little ship that afternoon after the most cursory examination (for was she not a schoolship, built and kept up by the Danes? no weakness and no faults would be tolerated there), and did not know until afterwards that she had an engine. Indeed I found this discovery disappointing at first; but it was a very weak and old engine and had hardly ever been used. The master of the vessel for the Danes had not used it: it had to be there, he explained apologetically, for the safety of the boys, if ever for an accident it should be necessary to reach port quickly in a calm. But he had not used it, except once when an epidemic of scarlet fever had forced him to make hurriedly for land. The ship had no need of it, he said; but it was good ballast, and the small screw was feathering and did not affect the sailing qualities. And it was all secured and battened down so that there was no smell.

I was disappointed, for all that. I need not have been alarmed. In the first year of my voyage, that engine worked, I think, two days; in the second year the fuel tanks were empty; it was in pieces, and worked not at all.

The ship was in commission when I inspected her, and I was to take her over when the summer's cruise was done, in the early fall. I had two months, then, in which to decide what I was to do with her — what, and how. I had first to pay for her, and this I could just do. I could pay for her and bring her to England. I thought I would like to make her a schoolship for boys, not necessarily only for boys who intended to follow the sea professionally (for these are now well trained in steam); but for the right kind of young fellow from anywhere. For years there had been much talk in England of the need for such a ship. Well, here she was, if she was wanted. I quickly discovered that she was not. There were cheers, but few applications. It looked for a while as if I should get no boys at all. My mail included letters from retired naval chaplains, retired admirals, and kindhearted and public-spirited old ladies and gentlemen who applauded my move; but in a month there was not a single application from any boy. There were thirty-seven applications from old sailors, mostly long left the sea, who wished to come either as master or as officers; and there were many letters from young girls from so far afield as Austria and Australia. But boys? In six weeks I had one. And I had been prepared to do so much. I would have handed the ship over to a properly constituted committee, had there been one; I would have made no stipulations about myself, for I knew very well that my poor qualifications would wilt before any real survey. But there was no committee and there was neither demand nor place for a real sailing schoolship for England.

I fortunately had been prepared for this. I could still follow my own ideas. I could man the ship with a nucleus of grain-ship sailors, some of whom were English, and I would get some boys. But what should I do with such a vessel? How could I support her running, pay the bills? This was a problem.

I thought and thought, and decided in the end that since I had a ship I might as well embark upon the unimaginative enterprise of a circumnavigation. True, this is overdone in our day, when, upon any morning of the week, at least twelve small yachts are somewhere battling round the world and anyone may make a circumnavigation who pushes the fare across an office table; when cruising liners set out in long procession upon much-advertised excursions to the ends of the earth and back again, all in four months, with surprising cheapness; when aeroplanes span all the continents and most of the seas. But there was still room in the ocean for a full-rigged ship; and if I began to make a long passage anywhere, I might as well continue round the world. I knew well enough, too, that I might be able only to make the one voyage — if that. Then let it be a grand gesture, a long wandering! I thought that, having now almost the same kind of ship in which all the great navigators had sailed — Cook, Wallis, Bougainville, Carteret, Bligh, le Maire, and all those other blazers of the Pacific trail — I might try to make such a voyage as they had made, not as a planned stunt, not as a programmed, advertised excursion, but quietly as they had gone — quietly against the sea, without benefit of canals or of engines.

It was a biggish thing to try. But the more I thought of it the more I liked it. I was steadfastly opposed to all the shams and stupidities with which many voyages in these days have been unduly concerned. I would make no films, advertise nothing, perform no stunts, engage in no radio programmes. I was no scientist and I would not pretend to be one. There was nothing to discover — no lands or islands — and I knew it. I had been round the world nine times already and there was no novelty in that. But I could keep a form of art alive upon an earth which had grown, it thought, beyond the need of it; and I could sail for the sailing's sake, for the sake of the health and the life and the clean wind and all the joy of being there. I could find some boys to share it all, and train them and make men of them; and together we could look upon what man had made of the far islands his wandering forefathers, in just such ships, had found for him. I had some ideals and some beliefs. I had already grown to love that ship — so beautiful! In all her half-century of life she had not been beyond the Baltic and North Sea; she deserved a voyage. Freed from her schooling work at last she could go off to far places and disport herself in the great ocean she was made for.

And one day we went.

I took the ship over from the Danes in the Navy Yard at Copenhagen towards the end of August, 1934, and Captain Junker, master of the vessel twenty years, brought his two small sons to haul down the Danish flag for the last time. He walked down the gangway to the dock unhurried and stalwart between his boys and with some tears, and did not come near to or look upon the ship again. He was to have the new ship; but he had grown up in the old. Now the Red Duster was hoisted and the new name painted at bow and stern — *Joseph Conrad*. I had to change the name, for that was a stipulation of the sale; the new ship would also be *Georg Stage*. I chose the Polish author's name as fitting for the ship and for her voyage, and as giving, too, myself and all her people something to live up to; for Conrad was a noble and high-minded man with great ideals and determination, who had overcome almost impossible difficulties and risen to great heights. The ship was fit to bear his name, and for such a ship there could be no better.

Manning had been an almost insuperable difficulty, though I had long been marking down, in my mind's eye, mariners for just such an enterprise — Horst and Karl and the second mate and the steward from the *Parma*; Hilgard, who had served a voyage there and was now back at school; my brother Frank, who was years in the *Hougomont* and now was off in an oil-tanker somewhere; good Jim, from the *Olivebank* and *Grace Harwar*, and the Frenchman Pierre Berthoud from the *Garthpool*; Jim Johnson of Sydney, from the *E.R. Sterling*; and tall Tom Germein, from the barque *Rothesay Bay* where we had been cadets together years before, if I could find him; and those other able young fellows from Captain Suffern's old merchant service school on Albert Park Lake in Melbourne. But where had they gone? Married, left the sea, or fighting upwards slowly towards the top in great liner companies — I could not find them. If I found them they could not go. I could not find anywhere a suitable young British officer trained in sail, who would go. I did not want an officer older than myself. In a small ship on a long voyage, that is apt to breed difficulty. I was then just thirty: most of the British sailing-ship officers had seen their last service at least ten years before — few of them, indeed, could have been much under fifty. Several who wrote said they would not again face Cape Horn; most of them wanted to be master. But it was to be just that, to make the voyage and to sail the ship myself, that I most wanted: so in the end I found myself compelled to take a young mate from the barque *Penang*, one of the Erikson grain-ships, who was 26 and had been in deep-water sail nine years. He stepped from the decks of a square-rigged ship on to mine; he had little to learn in the way of a ship, few readjustments to make. He spoke good English, and had been in an Australian schooner.

My second mate was a Swede, aged 24, from the

Swedish naval schoolships *Af Chapman* and *Najaden*. I got
the steward from the *Parma* but could not get the second
mate; I brought Horst and Karl from Germany; I took
over two Danes with the ship (they knew her, and there
was much about her strange to me); I tried to track down
every British boy I knew who had been apprentice in the
Erikson fleet, but all save one had been only one voyage
and would not repeat the experience. I cabled Hilgard in
America, not thinking that his parents would let him come;
had my brother pay off his tanker in Brisbane and hurry
home; found the carpenter from the barque *Alastor* serving
temporarily in a steamer, and rescued him from there;
found the cook of the oil-schooner *Navajo* in the Ipswich
docks and signed him on. But it was difficult; my crew
mounted slowly, and I was anxious to be gone. I had first,
of course, to get the ship to England — to Ipswich,
Suffolk's county town, which was to be her new port of
registration. To do this I took an old friend of mine who
had been a shipmate in the four-masted barque *Bellands* and
was now an extra master — Godfrey Wicksteed. He
assumed command and sailed the ship to England; I was
not fool enough to take chances in the North Sea. The
remainder of the crew was composed of divers gentlemen
who had written asking for the chance to sail a little in the
vessel — a clergyman, a physician, a lawyer, some boys,
some yachtsmen — and when they had it, did not all seem
to appreciate it very much. We had not gone far before a
few of them borrowed the motor-boat and cruised round
to trawlers asking to be put ashore. I let them go; the
trawlers would not take them. It was as well we had no bad
weather in the North Sea, but my curious crew was not
without its good points. There were some famous
humorists of whom the chief was the young son of a
British general — an estimable and exceedingly good-
natured lad whose only disadvantage was an infinite
capacity for doing the wrong thing; but he did the wrong

things so cheerfully and was always so irrepressibly merry and bright that I was sorry when he left at Ipswich. He was a good lad; he would have made a fine cadet, but he was entered for a university. The parson was the best sailor; he had real feeling for the sea in him. The lawyer was not a great success as a seaman. He had, he said, intended to sail with the ship on her trans-Atlantic crossing; but he left at Harwich and I was not depressed. But I must say that those among these pseudo-mariners of mine who really were yachtsmen, who really had sailed in small craft, did quite well. The yachtsmen who *sail* are always good, but those whose marine enthusiasm finds best expression in their speech are sometimes not assets in a vessel. I had both kinds, and I began to have grave doubts about the kind of maritime material I should get in England. Of skilled young sailors there were none: how could there be when there were no ships? But a boy or two began to come forward, and in a month at Ipswich I shipped as many as I wanted in the main 'tween-decks — likely young fellows most of whom seemed the right material.

It was a long month in Ipswich. Many problems arose, some of which I had not foreseen. I had some troubles. I had to make some alterations in the ship, to fit her for deep-water voyaging — not much. I added a chart-house, built skids and took the boats inboard, put cabins in the after 'tween-decks for my friends and suitable people who wanted to come (for I was compelled to take the right kind of person, as he showed up, to help to pay the expenses of the voyage), and increased the water supply.

I had some difficulties over registration. I made no secret of what I intended to do — to carry cadets who would be required to pay if they could afford it; and to carry a few other older men so far as they might want to go, to share in the expenses. Was my vessel legally a yacht or not a yacht? She was not a trading vessel. I should never carry cargo. She was not designed for that. Neither was she an official schoolship, having nobody's approval but my own. Then she had to be a yacht. In truth she was no yacht — never was — if by that term one understands a vessel bought as a plaything for the wealthy or for sport; and I was no yachtsman. I never had been. I have never sailed a yacht. I know nothing of fore-and-aft rig, have always followed the sea professionally. But if an amateur is one who does things for love and for love alone, then I was absolutely an amateur. All the earnings I had got from the sea or from anywhere were in this ship: there was and could be no commercial aim about her voyaging. I had bought her with my own savings (and did not advertise the fact that they were then almost exhausted) and was determined to set out on this voyage, and by the grace of God to accomplish it. But profit by it? That never entered my head: that was impossible. I am fortunately one who regards any money that comes my way as a necessity to be used; whatever money I have spent I have always looked upon as automatically lost. I cannot get into my head the idea of investment, of money making money. Never having had any, I had not learned of that; I had been most surprised when the *Parma* turned out so profitably. But it was a little difficult, understandably, to get these ideas into other heads. At times I found myself looked upon as an adventurer, almost a dangerous one, concerning whom there was some suspicion that he was using the ship and the promise of the voyage to beguile cash from the unwary and the young. Well, people had done that: altruistic motives have always to be demonstrated rather thoroughly to be believed.

The problem of my registration was not finally solved until I was about to leave. There were other difficulties — many of them. I was worried by financial problems, by human woes, by red tape and by formalities, until I lived only for the day when I could leave England, get out with my ship, and stay away. I found indeed that I had a good sailing-ship crew; but I was without lieutenants. Where should I find one? My friends could not come. The voyage, they said, would be too long; I was going too far. It would soon be winter. There would be a lot of winter, with Good Hope and the West Winds and Cape Horn. I very much needed then and throughout the voyage some good second-in-command who was not a sailor, necessarily; someone to help in looking after the boys, someone for companionship at sea and to share the responsibilities in ports, where usually things go wrong. I never found one. After all, there are not many persons who can tear up their roots and embark on such an enterprise freely and with open hearts, merely because one asks them to. The number who would *like* to go is legion; but my accompanying friends were — none. I sailed alone. And I found, too, that I had to be careful in the selection of the boys and young men who offered to come so that I did not get some neurasthenic or pale problem wished on me. I turned some down, and began almost at once to hear nasty rumours.

While the ship lay at Ipswich there came almost nightly a procession of pale youths, the most of them obviously maladjusted in some manner common enough with the complexities of our living, to analyse at great length their desire for the sea and then never to be seen near the vessel again. I became more or less accustomed to this; one has to be something of a judge of human beings. It is a queer and depressing business, mustering a collection of young gentlemen for the sea, when the regrettable matter of finance must enter into it. I wished to God then and I wished even more fervently afterwards that I could cheerfully go ahead and take ten or twelve boys without any funds whatever — but I could not, for it would have been foolish to set out without reasonable prospect of continuing. I took several without finance — as many as I could possibly afford. Some strange young men made application to ship for the voyage; one or two came. None stayed.

I should wrong my friends indeed if I did not give them full credit for *wanting* to come on the voyage: but it is an unfortunate fact, somehow, that the more one fits into the scheme of things on the land — the more one does, is worth, contributes — the less chance there is of going off on a long sea voyage. It would be easy enough to assemble a shipload of drones. And it seemed to me that women might be had by the liner-load: but in them I was not interested. There are some problems better left ashore.

But at last I was almost ready and I sailed down the Orwell with a heart that would have been much lighter had I not to anchor again at Harwich for a few days. The little boys Goodchild and Fuller, Ipswichian dinghy sailors, stood on the fo'c'sle head grinning from ear to ear and helped me con the ship, for the weak tug could not hold us in the wind and I'd had to sail — without pilot, chart, or engine. These two little chaps were just the kind of boys I wanted — alert, keen, good-mannered, intelligent, interested in the sea. But how difficult such lads were to find! These found themselves: they came aboard, asking timidly for jobs, and I signed them then and there.

At Harwich there came a surveyor hotfoot from the Board of Trade in London to whom a letter had come alleging that my vessel was a hell-ship. Good Lord! So he had come down in haste to look for blood in the scuppers; and found none, of course, and talked with the boys and all the crew and left well pleased. He was a very pleasant surveyor, but he made a thorough examination, and looked to see that I had a good crew to sail the ship and train the boys. He saw the officers' certificates: fortunately he did not ask for mine.

I had none. I was possessed of no official qualification whatever. But what of that? I had stayed in Finnish ships, when the British sailors were all gone, and no British certificate would help me there. I had not foreseen that I ever might acquire a ship for Britain myself. Nor could I get a Finnish certificate when I was not a Finn. But I was merely following in the best traditions of the sea and sailing-ships, for most of the great trade routes of the world were opened up and sailed for centuries by men who held no kind of certificate. You held command then because you were able to; if I were not able, I should not get very far. But I was rather glad the subject never came up.

When that surveyor was gone, I decided to leave England, regardless of the fact that my preparations were not as complete as I should have wished. What unnecessary problem would next beset me, if I stayed even one more day, I did not know, and despite the fact that it was dull and wet and gloomy and the forecast was for Channel gales, I hove up my anchor early on the morning of October 22, 1934, and departed from Harwich under sail. When the pilot cutter off the Sunk came over to me I was alarmed and wondered: what is she bringing out now to stop me and take me back? But she had come over only to wish us good cheer upon the voyage, and with deep gratitude and a sigh of relief I sailed on.

I had eight cadets and eight others to carry to America: we were thirty-two souls all told. There was £100 in the ship's safe; and the gale blew.

II

Transatlantic

We crossed the English Channel twenty-one times, wearing and tacking, and saw the Casquests and Portland Bill so often that I began to think them the beginning and the end of the world. In the early mornings and the night watches we had often to use flares to scare off steamers that weren't looking where they were going. In any sailing-ship navigation in these days, powered vessels are one of the major dangers; they and their officers have so long become used to an ocean in which the absence of masthead lights suggests that there are no vessels about, that they never look for the coloured sidelights of sailing-ships — the only lights which, by international regulations, ships which use only sail for motive power are allowed. So one has to keep wary lookout for them and have some good flares handy in the chart-house to burn. There is nothing like a sudden flare beneath his nose to scare a blundering tramp out of the way. He thinks it is the land. We narrowly escaped from beneath the bows of four of them going down the Channel, and the weather was not at all thick. We had had the same experience in the *Parma*, the *Herzogin Cecilie* — in all ships. It is the same in the Rio Lane on the Line: look out there! The big meat liners and the mail ships, tearing up from the Plate, give little thought to the possibility of full-rigged ships and four-masted barques working through the doldrums. Fortunately for the square-rigged ship, she makes most of her voyaging far from steamer lanes. It is safer that way.

We saw a four-masted barque outward bound in ballast to Australia beating off Dungeness, and passed her there.

This surprised me, for I could see she was one of the crack Germans — *Priwall* or *Padua*: but we were able to make better boards and stand in towards the smoothness near the land to go round, tacking and gaining. She kept a good offing and wore round; but given one touch of fair wind she would be past us like a liner. I discovered later that we beat this big ship out of the Channel by three days, but she was ahead of us five days at Madeira. In the narrow waters I took what chances I considered safe in order to gain the open sea more quickly; I looked upon the ship as very small, and almost as handy (so far as getting out of places went) as a schooner. I learned better later on. Handy she certainly was, and weatherly; but I learned gradually to look upon her as a big ship so far as her handling went. It was curious how the grain ship sailors had come aboard and, running in the rigging, laughed to reach the royal yards by standing on the topgallants, and grinned with delight at the smallness of everything — toylike, almost, after such giants as the 3,000-ton *Parma* and the big barque *Penang*. ("What bottle did you get her out of?" yelled young Hilgard when he had come over from Plandome. Not he, but one or two of the others who had been only in grain ships, were frankly a little scared at the idea of so small a vessel setting out on a circumnavigation.)

For many days we tossed and fumed around, and the motion of the ship in the short sea was turbulent and violent. It was cold, and the 'tween-decks where the boys lived were a wet hell, housing a sodden and saddened collection of bewildered youthful humanity facing up to its first experience of the realities of life, facing up very well. My boys were all right; though most of them were green with seasickness and wet and cold, and we were long out of the Channel before they had finally got it clear in their minds to which watches they belonged. We had passed the Ushant before some of them knew there were any watches; but they always showed up for their turns.

I began at once the normal sea routine of the ship, knowing that a week of bad weather at the start will teach youngsters far more than they might learn in a year of trade wind Sundays afterwards. They came for their schooling at the wheel and in the rigging, green as they were, and there was no hanging back. I had then, and for a long time afterwards (until we were at last on the road to Cape Horn from Tahiti, almost two years later) a difficult problem in that many of the boys, particularly the older ones, did not want to be sailors. A few had come from mistaken ideas of romance and adventure, expecting these to be served up to them with the ship or with the meals, not knowing that they must be dug with difficulty deep down from themselves — if the digging is sufficiently laborious and never discouraged, and the soil is good enough. One or two had discovered their desire for adventure, I suspected, from motives that were scarcely creditable to themselves. It soon became obvious that, while never serious, human problems would be my most worrying ones: they were, it turned out, on that passage and throughout the voyage. Selecting the personnel for such a voyage even if done by the Archangel Gabriel would still be a gamble, and the devil himself could scarcely pick an entirely harmonious crew from the colossal amount of material at his disposal. I had had, very largely, to take what offered. But I had done very well. True, I harboured then and twice again later, one or two despicable characters; but these quickly departed, and what they had to do and to say did not matter very much. My crew was a good crew, and my boys were all right.

Two days after leaving, I heard on my small wireless set in the saloon of two men who had flown from Mildenhall to Melbourne in an aeroplane in three days; we had left at the week-end of the England-to-Melbourne centenary air race. This, doubtless, was great progress: but there was much more satisfaction in our leisurely wandering along, antiquated, primitive, and a hundred years behind the times as we were. I do not see that so much of what we are taught to regard as progress matters in our daily lives; we should have had more comfort if the ship had been fitted with a heating system, and better meals if she had carried an electric refrigerating plant. But we did without those things, and never missed them. There are many things in life to-day which, so far as I can see, add only to our worries and speed the grave. The spurious softening of living and the abolition of labour can be achieved largely only by some species of dope — radio, to dull our minds; canned food, to dull our stomachs; fast transport, to carry us quickly from offices where the raucous telephone rings all day and all kinds of trivialities pass as toil, to our heated homes where we take laxatives or whatever else may seem helpful at the moment. But I had a ship to sail; I was and am no philosopher. I could leave these things behind. A pot had fallen on the cook's head in the galley, and I had to sew the cut. This I did without anaesthetics and such things, and he did not mind. The spray was in his face and the sea air filled his lungs; he went on with his work.

After the Channel, Biscay was kind, though it was November when we reached those parts and their name is bad. But we stormed from Ushant almost to Finisterre at ten knots, which was good speed for the little vessel; the sea was not great and the wind blew a fresh whole-sail breeze that gave us our best sailing conditions. I headed towards the south for I meant to go westwards by the southern route which is kinder to ship and to crew. There is nothing gained by punching into the westerly gales of the North Atlantic in midwinter; the passage to New York under sail is better made by going southwards to the trades, and then running westwards with a fair wind. Columbus had gone west that way, though he had had the further advantage of starting in mild latitudes; all our early sailing commerce went that way, the first deep water sailing route commonly used by Europeans. Yachts and small vessels (whose crossings are more frequent than the landsman would suppose) also use this route; the early voyagings of small and somewhat ill-found vessels become more easily understood when one has followed in their tracks. The distance is doubled, of course; but the time may be halved. While we crossed the Atlantic in the outskirts of the trade wind zone, fierce gales raged on the steamer lanes, and four large steamers foundered there that winter. We had bad weather only at the beginning and the end — enough of it then, to be sure, but there was more than a month of mildness in between.

Off Finisterre in an electric squall the long jib-boom carried away at the cap. The squall was quickly past and we saved the wreckage of the boom, scarfed it, and rigged it out again. It had been too long for deep water; the shortening of the boom, though unexpected, was no disadvantage but really a strengthening. I noticed that the ship tacked better with the shorter boom. The evening before this squall a Danish steamer named the *Lily*, waddling northwards from somewhere in Spain with a high cargo of esparto grass, came over to us and a big man shouted from her bridge, "Is that the old *Georg Stage?*" as if he were amazed to see the old schoolship there and could scarce believe his eyes. I told him we were, and he blew a greeting on his siren and departed. There must be 4,000 Danes somewhere who were trained in this ship. On the bridge of all steamers under that red and white ensign there probably walks at least one mariner who first heard the curses of a mate round these decks and turned out to the shrill scream of the bos'n's pipe at five-thirty in the mornings. So long as we were in the steamer lanes I saw the Danish motor-ships and steamers pause in their stride as they sighted us, and edge over nearer to see their old familiar Baltic friend driving through the Atlantic in her fifty-third year. Good old ship! they hailed, and with their shouted blessings hurried on, smoke-wrack and floundering screws, and their black bulks dipping and rolling. At Madeira a Dane in a small tug passing by hailed us and shouted, "Is that the old *Georg Stage*?" and a diver working in Nassau harbour, later, looked up startled from his breathing spell as we came in and yelled in Danish "I'll go to hell! The old *Georg Stage*?" and sat in his little work boat a long time staring; and at Bay Ridge, when we were on the rocks, three hundred elderly Danes came down to gaze upon their old vessel, and more than half of them came aboard. At Rio and the Cape it was the same; all round the world old Danes came to gaze in quiet salute at the little ship which for so long had been well loved in their far waters. There was no mistaking her, of course; for no other vessel frigate-rigged has sailed the deep seas in fifty years.

When I left England, I had no intention of calling at Madeira, looking upon all deviations and unnecessary calls at ports as breaking the sea routine and lengthening the voyage. The time to stop at islands was in the Pacific, not the North Atlantic; and I was of the opinion that, so brief a way on our journey, some of the young gentlemen would not be sufficiently settled down to wish to continue the voyage. If they stayed for the trade-wind run I knew their hearts would be conquered, and I could count on them to the end. In a ship calling for such skilful handling and competence of man-power, I did not wish to be changing either my cadets or my crew. It was hard enough to train boys, willing as they were; when they were trained I wished to keep them. But a fine old gentleman who had come from America to sample square-rig with us had quickly discovered that the motion was too much for him, and at his own desire I went into Madeira to land him. I need not have worried about the boys. I gave them shore leave and they came back well satisfied with themselves, converted in two weeks into extremely youthful ancient mariners gazing with scorn upon the anchored steamers in the Funchal Roads, and I had no applications to leave.

Madeira was my first landfall; I was glad to make it. There is a quiet joy in seeing land where one hoped it was, after days of sailing: this was the first time I had conducted a ship across great waters. The days before the landfall were thick with rain, and there were few glimpses of the obscured and watery sun; yet I got what data I could from the unwilling heavens, and stood on, and there upon the nineteenth morning rose the heights of Madeira pleasantly before us. I looked upon the place with great delight, put my sextant in its case that morning with a new regard, and looked affectionately at the chronometer ticking in its stand on the saloon table. I sailed towards Funchal Roads between the Dezertas and Madeira and hoped that some officials would come out so that I could land my passenger without anchoring and further delay; but no one came. The morning was quiet, with little wind: the sea off Madeira is deep for anchoring. I did not want to go too close in as I had to get under way again as quickly as possible, and I did not want to hire any tugs. (The ancient semi-Diesel engine was in its almost permanent state of hopeless breakdown.) As no one came out though I flew signals, I stood into the Roads and let go the anchor near the hulk of the four-masted barque *Gullmarn*, and some hours afterwards two gentlemen came out who were officials of sorts and brought with them an agency fee and a bill for pilotage. Pilotage? Where was the pilot, or the need for him? They explained apologetically that there was only the bill; it was an old custom of the port, apparently. In such circumstances you pay and try to like it; there is nothing else to do. Afterwards came ship-chandlers, a wine merchant, bumboats. We bought bananas and all kinds of tropic fruit; I took in some fresh food, and after the afternoon's leave we sailed in the evening, going out very quietly with a gentle land breeze. The next morning Madeira was still in full sight; we wandered very slowly on our way.

Soon enough we had the north-east trade and stood westwards in the wake of Columbus towards Watling Island in the Bahamas, more than 3,000 miles away. The wind was quiet for the most part and often flukey, but the days passed pleasantly and all hands settled down properly to the routine of the voyage. The sun shone and the flying fish skimmed away before our bows, and the boys slung their hammocks on deck. She rolled heavily at times with the wind almost aft, but this was great square-rig sailing and we averaged over 150 miles a day under every stitch of canvas. I bent all the old sails now, and the sailmaking gang worked steadily sewing new sails for the bad weather of the far south. We cut and sewed all our own canvas, and did all our own work. I had a carpenter who was also a blacksmith and tinsmith; we had a forge, and made a proper workshop in the 'tween-decks. I had taken rope and paint and canvas for two years, and a good supply of all the tools that we might need, and some baulks of timber for spare spars. We were as far as possible self-contained. Except for fresh water (of which we could carry easily sufficient for 35 persons for three months) we were stored to keep the sea without touching land for six months, if necessary. The food was plain, and of the old-fashioned sea-going variety. I had bought all the different kinds of preserved and tinned foods I thought might be palatable and useful, but our mainstay was the old salt junk — beef and pork. This did not always appeal to the more fastidious and to those who had not learned that in some ways old manners are best. The modern tinned foods, if used continuously over too long a period, are insufficient; meat for long voyages is better preserved in saltpetre and brine. We had casks of salt beef and pork, bales of dried fish, potatoes in quantity; we baked fresh bread each day. I had a steward and a cook, and they were always busy. Various kinds of preserved meats and fish and other foods, judiciously assorted with the boiled salt meats and strong pea soup and boiled dried fish, made up the most of the meals; the food was ample if plain, and if there were no luxuries there was at least a three-course meal for every body in the middle of the day.

The galley stove never heated any pot that was not shared by all hands: there were no petty distinctions. I had long had some ideas of my own for the improved running of British ships, and here I had a chance to try them. I abolished all wretched discrimination between "crew" and "cabin" stores, which, in the lime-juice ships I had sailed in as a boy, was carried to ridiculous lengths. We lived alike in the *Joseph Conrad* fore and aft. The kids for 'tween-decks and mess were filled from the same pot. There had to be rations of a few things, such as sugar and milk and jam; the provision room too small to hold all the jam that twenty healthy boys could eat in six months. I had long held a theory that the few miserable pounds saved on food in most ships was well rated among the most stupid economies on earth; but how much of this went to the shipowners and how much was due to the skulduggery of stewards I could not say. If this comparatively small sum were spent instead of saved, the benefits in the way of better conditions for seafarers and better health and more contentment and better *work* all round would be almost incalculable. I spent it. I never tried to save a penny on the food. I never cut down anything. Though many times on that long voyage I did not see how I could beat the bailiff out of the next port, I never stinted the food or the ship's stores in any manner. There was sufficient at all times: perhaps the boys, on apple-pie days and the like scarcely agreed with this; but even his own mother cannot satisfy a boy with apple-pie if he happens to like it. We had apple-pie once weekly, and pancakes with jam twice for sweets; there were bacon and eggs on Sunday mornings, and nourishing soups were served up daily — tomato, vegetable, meat extract. The bully beef was warmed up and prepared in such a variety of ways that a meal of plain cold corned beef with pickles and tomato sauce on Sunday evenings came to be looked on almost as a luxury, so great a change was it. Tinned fish I used sparingly, not caring for the stuff; there is nothing of which the palate palls so quickly and so heartily. I found tinned vegetables nourishing and good, and carried a lot of tinned beetroot. Bacon and beans, curry and rice, porridge with tinned liver and bacon — these were good breakfasts. There was always all the toast that any one wanted, so long as they made it themselves. The midday meal was most substantial; in the evenings we had hash, or fishcakes, or some kind of tinned stuff such as stewed steak (put up in Melbourne and very good) or boiled rabbit with tomato, or fishballs from Stavanger, or salmon made into a savoury stew. Now and again there were rock buns, made by the cook, to round out an evening meal of salt beef and boiled peas; and every afternoon at three-thirty there was a half-hour for coffee in the cold weather, and tea in the tropics. What, afternoon tea? I see ten thousand ancient mariners turn contemptuously in their shrouds. But why not? Are sailors not human? This slight fact appears to me to have been overlooked for some centuries.

There was a reason for our afternoon coffee. One of my innovations in this ship was the scrapping of the eternal four-on, four-off watch system. I should have liked to use the three-watch style, dividing the crew into three sections, each of which would work four hours and then rest eight; but I had not enough to do this and it is not practical in a square-rigged ship. So I divided the day in a manner of my own, based largely upon my experience in the grain ships from Australia. We had two watches, port (the mate's) and starboard (the second mate's); from midnight to midnight the day was divided into only five watches — midnight to 4 a.m.; 4 a.m. to 8 a.m.; 8 a.m. to 1 p.m.; 1 p.m. to 7 p.m.; and 7 p.m. to midnight. In this manner one watch had ten hours on deck one day, and fourteen the next, alternating; the watch with the long afternoon on deck were given the half-hour for coffee to break the watch. So there was no hardship, even in the worst weather, and this system of watches worked very well. I also sent all hands to the wheel, from the youngest boy to the oldest A.B., and gave them hour turns each instead of the more usual two hours. Two hours is too long for a young boy, sleepy and cold in the middle of the night; it is often necessary in steamers where the watches frequently consist only of two helmsmen, relieving one another. But in a sailing-ship there are plenty of hands for the wheel.

I saw that the quarters fore and aft were kept as well as they could possibly be. She was an old ship, built for the Baltic, and when she was launched there was not much concern about ventilation. This was a drawback which nothing but considerable structural alteration could improve, and for this I had neither time nor money; we compromised by sleeping and living in the open air as much as possible. The boys, at first, slept in hammocks; as soon as possible I built them proper bunks. A hammock is an impersonal sort of thing which, when stowed away, leaves one with a vague feeling of having no home in the ship, no little nook of one's own; a bunk is yours, inviolate. There you may put up your photographs from home, of other ships and a girl friend, may be; and cunningly contrive little shelves and holdalls and things, and rig up a curtain for your privacy. You may lie in state, a moment or two before taking the well-earned rest of your watch below, and pridefully survey the rack that holds your fids and your spike and your sail needles, and the little shelf of much-thumbed books, casting an eye briefly upon the picture of your last ship. At least, this is what deep-sea sailors in sailing-ships have always done; some of my college boys, later on, so filled their bunks with junk that there was no room for themselves, and they slept on deck or sprawled over a couple of wooden chests. But for the Atlantic crossing there were no college boys.

The boys looked after their own quarters, taking weekly turns. They were not waited on; some of them, before they came, had only just managed to wash themselves. Many of them knew nothing of life without home comforts. But they learned — learned, indeed, very well. There were some who moaned in the process, loud and long; but to grumble has always been the seafarer's privilege. By and large, the ship settled down very well. I knew I had tried a pretty big thing, taking this ship of youth round the world; I knew that if I could not hold them together, nothing and nobody could help me. Most of the cadets had paid. I took the view that, if they did not wish to be seamen and came in my ship for the benefits of the voyage, it was fair enough that they should contribute something towards the expenses of the voyage. I made this amount low, considering that I had to train them, that their work was of little or no value to the vessel or the enterprise, and I had to keep them for two years, all round the world. I deliberately made the payment low in order that there could be no suggestion of a co-operative enterprise about the voyage. This was a ship, bound seriously upon a voyage — useless or not. We were not a band of idle wanderers each contributing his fair share towards the cost of the voyage, all members of a kind of debating committee deciding what should be done. Ships that set out in this manner (and some do) do not usually proceed very far. If there was one thing I knew thoroughly before all else, it was just this — that ships and the sea are not to be fooled with lest they kill you. There was no debating committee.

I should very much have preferred to have taken all poor boys, or at any rate to have chosen my boys regardless of the question of funds; but I did take as many of these as I could well afford, and my philanthropy, as it was, landed me in financial difficulties more than once. I had no spare penny that whole voyage and could never hope at any time to do anything other than barely square the ledger after years of writing and hard work; and I could have asked for greater sums and secured them easily enough. But this I was stubbornly against. There must be no slightest suggestion of profit-making, of gain; even of making the cadetships pay. This, indeed (as a moment's reflection or the slightest knowledge of ships' costs will show), would have been quite impossible, unless I had taken twenty boys and charged them £200 a year. And the more boys one has, the more trouble: they are expert in the avoidance of work and the destruction of the ship's gear. But I like them, for all that: and I knew I had hit upon the best possible use for the ship when I threw her open to cadets. My idea originally had been to make the rich cadets support the poor ones (without the knowledge of either, naturally) and to some extent this worked. But before very long I was supporting both of them, so far as the upkeep of the ship was concerned.

We had school every day, but it was a different school from any ashore. There were lessons in splicing, in knots and bends and all kinds of plaiting work, in sail-sewing and cringle-making, in making eyes in wire, and turning in the seam of a ditty-bag, in seizings and rackings and marryings of all kinds — all up in the sunshine of the open fo'c'sle head with the long jib-boom reaching over the Atlantic waves, and the sea-foam turned from the old cutwater scintillating in the warm air. There were lessons in reefing, in the loosing and stowing of sails; in sending up and down masts and yards; in the general, and difficult, art of ship-handling: but ship-construction and cargo work were not in our curriculum. As far as possible, the work was practical. The cadets, in their watches, joined in the whole of the ship's work; there was an hour for lessons in each deck watch, and for the rest of the four or six hours they turned to on whatever was going. They chipped and scraped and painted; they scrubbed down and tarred and they greased; they took their lookouts and their "police" and their wheels. When it was calm enough they swam, or we swung out the life-boats and went rowing; for swimming there was always a masthead lookout to watch for sharks.

In such manner the days passed. Sometimes the trade wind was fresh and sometimes it was poor. More often it was poor. One week we made only 400 miles. Sometimes there were rain-squalls and calms. When it rained we caught fresh water and all hands washed. We had one full week of glorious sailing when the ship ran 1,300 miles — 1,060 in five days. She ran along bravely under a full press of sail with the sea big and the sky overcast and a great wake of foam trailing off astern; she set, with her trade wind suit, some 10,000 feet of canvas, which was a lot for a ship 100 feet long, but she stood up to it very well. She was beautifully proportioned and rolled with an easy grace; she had 100 tons of inside ballast, and a deep keel that was not weighted. She had a hull driven easily through the water; in light winds she readily made five knots and, with any freshening, came quickly up to seven and eight. She had to be driven a little to get over ten; but on one of these five days she ran 260 miles. This was the first day of the strong trade, when the sea had not had time to rise. It was pretty fine then to walk the decks and watch the run of her and listen to the driving spray and look aloft at the pyramids of masts carrying their spread of graceful canvas swollen in the sky, and to watch the long roll of her golden trucks beneath the stars. The youthful helmsmen at the wheel found her easy and hummed softly to themselves as she ran, and the lookouts sang, and the grain ship sailors opened their eyes a little and said to one another, God! This is sailing! This is almost as good as the *Parma*, or the *Penang*, or the *Olivebank*, or whatever other ship happened to be their favourite; previously one or two of them had been rather scornful of the sailing qualities of the little vessel. Well, they saw. They saw a lot before that voyage was over, for the *Joseph Conrad* made all her long ocean runs, in times

at least as good as the average grain ships could make —
not the crack big fourmasters, of course; but the barques
Killoran and *Winterhude* and the ship *Grace Harwar* and the
barquentine *Mozart*, all of which were at least ten times her
size.

So we came at last, thirty days out of Madeira, almost to
Watling Island where it is generally agreed that Columbus
made his first landfall. Near here the north-east trade
departed and did not come back again; the conditions
became baffling with sudden mildish storms alternating
with brief periods of calm, and the sea confused with the
swell from all directions, and the ship lolling about and
falling this way and that. Watling Island (or San Salvador,
which also appears to be its name) is lit now and is an
important signpost on the cargo-ships' track from Panama
Canal to the eastern sea-board of America. It is a low,
dullish place, seen from the sea, and after looking at it for
some days with baffling conditions and almost no progress,
I did not care about it half as much as Columbus had done.
It is rather difficult in these days to recapture the spirit of
these old navigators when the wearied Atlantic air is filled
nightly with the raucous shouts of gentlemen glibly retailing
the world's "news" (poor tidings, mainly calamitous,
according to them) and divers persons with insinuating
silver tongues advising American children aged four to
purchase portable typewriters, or reading out the letters of
a mother within the Arctic Circle extolling the effects of a
laxative on her child. The air is full of noise and nothing is
said; the human voice has conquered space to shout of
body odour and its own incompetence. Of course I could
turn the radio off; but sometimes there is good music, and
if one listens long enough with sufficient grim
determination, there are sometimes time signals and
weather reports. A Mitsui motor-ship, very smart and
modern with her name along her side in white letters two
fathoms high, and two tramps and an oil-tanker waddled

by; we saw the lighthouse and the breakers and all the cays, and the wreck of what appeared to be a barque close inshore.

We remained in sight of Watling Island for three days.

At last we came past, after much beating, and stood onwards towards Cat Island and Eleuthera and the Great Abaco, meaning to pass between this last-named and Egg Island towards New Providence, where Nassau is. I had no reason for going into Nassau other than to break the passage and give some diversion to those who were with us only for the Atlantic run; the ship was short of nothing and could as easily have gone on to New York. But I had promised to go there, and so went. We were 35 days out from Madeira before the Fincastle light at last showed up; it was night, and no pilot came (for these gentlemen are nowadays ordered by wireless and at the smaller ports little lookout is kept for visual signals). I stood on gingerly towards the outer anchorage, not daring to go in. This was my first tropic island, my first reef. How ominous was the sound of the breakers as we approached! I was not used to this; our port-makings had not been of this kind in the grain ships. At midnight of the 16th of December the sights of Nassau seemed mighty close; I stood on and on and the breakers roared more and more loudly in my ears; and I sounded and sounded and found no bottom. It was an anxious anchorage — sounding, sounding: no bottom, no bottom, with the deep-sea lead at 100 fathoms out once every five minutes, and the ship going quietly on under easy sail, and the Sailing Directions (*West Indies Pilot* Vol. III) in every paragraph on every page exhorting the mariner to "caution" and speaking of danger: and the breakers roaring on the white sand that now looked so perilously close. "Vessels should proceed under easy sail and be ready to anchor at any instant," says the *Pilot*; and under easy sail we drifted to leeward away from the anchorage with the tide setting us down: the *Pilot* said nothing about that. "Rocky uneven ground," said the chart: no bottom said the lead: caution said the *Pilot*! Inside the harbour was a narrow dredged channel leading to the only good anchorage in there. It was senseless to go inside without a local pilot, and none came. I did the only wise thing I could (for the weather was good) — headed onwards for the breakers, and found an anchorage at last; there we rolled quietly in safety through the night.

In the morning I saw the beach a few hundred yards away and the wreck of a steamer close; the pilot came, and we went in and anchored in the Hurricane Hole; and the coloured minstrels came, playing their guitars, and there was a tourist liner at the wharf. Nassau is a tourist place these days, with expensive hotels and glass-bottomed boats and guides and all that stuff, and when we came in there was a big golf tournament in progress to attract visitors from Florida. American air-liners come down daily with cargoes of millionaires seeking a change of scene, and the great steamships from New York disgorge tourists by the thousand whenever they can find them. I did not see much to keep me in such a place, for it was not interesting and it was the most expensive, as far as the ship was concerned, of the whole voyage — more expensive by far even than Tulagi and Samarai in the Pacific, where there was some excuse for high food prices. In the great hotel overlooking the harbour I saw a tableau showing a pirate putting away some gold; somehow this struck me, in those surroundings, as a little too frankly apt. Nassau was the headquarters of piracy once; it seemed to me it still is. I prefer the older kind myself. I might have joined them.

The boys had leave, each watch a day, and enjoyed themselves well enough; I went alongside and took in water, and departed after three days. The cook was run over by a horse (he said) in Nassau's main street and held the ship up half an hour while he was patched in a chemist's shop; but I found out afterwards he had been racing along the sands on some thoroughbred with young Tilbury and had come a cropper. He was a queer cuss, the cook; I don't know where they got the thoroughbreds and did not stop to inquire. We sailed, and our departing passengers followed us to sea in a motor-boat, taking photographs. Most of them left at Nassau. We were bound now to New York in the depths of winter, and soon it would be icy cold.

It was. The first week or so was warm enough, but once we had crossed the Gulf Stream the weather became bitter at once. We had Christmas in a blow off Hatteras with the mess-room decorated with a tree made of painted wood and canvas and hung with the seven flags of our seven nationalities; and there was tinned plum pudding with brandy sauce and the cook had made mince pies — pretty good; and with full bellies all hands were happy enough.

We had bad weather from Hatteras to New York — strong north-west gales, and bitter cold. The ship was iced up and work on deck was purgatory. The fo'c'sle head was iced so badly the lookout could not stay there; there was ice in the foot-ropes and all the blocks, and reefing was no fun. It blew at gale strength frequently, but we beat along. We saw steamers daily now, iced up as we were, and envied them their fires; and then one day a piece of some Long Island beach — I never discovered which it was, for I had been going by dead reckoning for days — showed up before the bows with a motor-car rushing up and down, honking. There was good time to go round and stand clear of that danger; the same evening we were in the New York liner lane with the Saturday afternoon line of steamships coming out, one behind the other in a long row, and the Ambrose Light blinked a cold welcome. It still blew heavily from the nor'-west but I held to a press of sail for fear of being blown out into the Atlantic again. The fearful cold robbed us of the pleasure of seeing the light, and the night was misery.

In the morning the pilot steamer came and the pilot was on board — a cheerful cove named Kiernan — and we beat in though the wind was still strong from ahead; and anchored on the 30th of December, 1934, on the flats in Sandy Hook Bay. We were 70 days from Harwich of which 67 had been spent at sea, and we had sailed 7,014 miles.

The voyage had had its anxieties; but the Atlantic was behind us now. The Lord had been kind to us and I was feeling rather pleased.

III

Safe in the Harbour

"THE SCHOOLSHIP'S on the rocks and full of water and all the boys have been taken to hospital frozen to death," said the man with the red face on the Bay Ridge ferry. What! That was *my* ship! No wonder I had not been able to see her anywhere in the harbour that bitter morning, with all the liners coming in ice-covered from the sea, and the lighters and the laid-up steamers at the anchorage. On the rocks, by God! Fortunately for what peace of mind I still could muster, I did not believe the remark about the boys: my experiences ashore had taught me to accept the first tidings of calamity always with reserve. But the ship on the rocks! That must be true: no wonder I couldn't see her! The ancient ferry crawled laboriously across the harbour, and I waited in alarm and perturbation for my first glance of the ship ashore.

I had been ashore the previous night, the first night in port after our Atlantic crossing. I had not meant to stay ashore. It was New Year's Day, and two-thirds of the crew had leave; most of them were ashore. I had gone in the ship's motor-boat late in the afternoon, leaving my brother temporarily in charge of the ship; I had a few friends to call on, as is the old custom on that day. I had seen them, and about eleven in the evening had set out for Staten Island to take a boat to the ship where she was anchored on the Bay Ridge Flats. It was mighty cold, crossing from Whitehall to St. George on the ferry; it blew a little from the north-west. I stood outside and noted the little ship's anchor lights burning brightly. It was a clear night. She was all right.

I looked everywhere for a boatman at St. George but there was none there. I called at the police box at the end of the ferry approach and asked the officer there if he knew where I could get a boat, but he said it was impossible. What, on New Year's Day? That was a holiday. There was nothing I could do about it. It was of no use to hail the ship. She was too far out. I had not arranged for any of her boats to meet me, not foreseeing any trouble in hiring a shore boat. There were usually five available on Staten Island. So with some misgivings but no alarm, I found a small hotel, about one o'clock in the morning, and put up there for the night. My misgivings were only those I always felt when absent from the ship; I never cared to be away from her, in any harbour.

It blew through the night, and I did not sleep much.

Then in the early morning I came down again to find a boat. Still there were none, and I boarded the ferry to Bay Ridge to try my fortune there or to hail the ship on the way across. And the first words I heard — not spoken to me but passed carelessly to someone else as the tidings of the day — were that awful news about the ship. How the ferry crawled!

It was some time before I saw the ship, and then the real seriousness of the accident was not at once apparent. She looked as if she had gone alongside the Shore Road sea Wall from choice. She stood there upright with a gangplank to the shore and her hull not fifteen feet out from the parkway. The ferry berthed and I ran. She was on the rocks beyond any shadow of doubt, pounding on them very gently midships, where the harbour waters rose and fell inside her with the tide: but no one was in the hospital, thank God. I had not believed that there was, but the relief at being assured of this was so great that the accident itself almost seemed unimportant.

The situation of the vessel was not fatal but it was bad enough. I gleaned hurriedly what news I could of the accident. She had parted from her chain in a high squall about three o'clock in the morning, and the first thing the watchman saw was that she was *driving* — not dragging — towards the shore lights. Rapidly they loomed up in front of him; he had time only to rouse out the sleeping hands before she struck. She came in broadside on the sea wall off 68th Street, Bay Ridge, on the Brooklyn shore, and brought up with her starboard bilge upon a pile of rocks that some contractor had thrown into the harbour there to strengthen the wall. She was badly holed midships and the after hold was half full. There was a lot of water in the provision room and the provisions were spoiled. Her motor-boat, which had been lying at the boom, had gone and there was sundry other damage. The boys' belongings were all beneath the harbour; she had filled in their compartment so rapidly that there had been little time to save anything. She was full there to the deck.

It must have happened very quickly. From her anchorage she had only to drive across the Bay Ridge Channel and she was ashore. That strong north-west wind — it still blew, and sent the harbour spray driving over the snow-covered ground to freeze there in long white furrows, serrated like the surface of the Great Ice Barrier after a storm — had a long, open drive to gather force over the Jersey flats and down the Kill van Kull: and the little ship with her big rigging offered a great deal of windage. But I could not understand why she had parted from her chain; it was strong, certified, and in perfect order.

There she was, a "wreck" on the Brooklyn rocks; there in the safety of port with the wild Atlantic all behind her. It was ironic, in a way. I suppose I deserved it, but I could not for the life of me see why. But this was no time for reflections; the tide began to fall, and she began to heel over outwards towards the harbour. I had to get her out of there mighty quick.

First I got the boys out of the way. Several of them had

relatives not far away and went to them; an American took an English cadet to his Massachusetts home; three of the smallest chaps went to some friends of mine in Mackay-place, with the ship's cat; some of the older boys took care of themselves ashore without waiting to be told. One or two of them, indeed, went and did not come back. An elderly gentleman in an Olsen tug standing by the 69th Street pier gave all the boys coffee and temporary refuge in his warm mess-room; this was the one kind thing that any stranger did that day. Most just stared.

The tide still fell and the ship began very slowly to capsize. We tried to hold her up by carrying out wires and stout lines to whatever would support them. But as this was a sea wall there were not bitts or bollards, or anything else to which to secure a line except an iron fence and, across the Shore Road, some trees. We took wires to the fence and an attendant came running shouting, "You can't do that! You'll pull down the fence." So we took them to the trees and the police came yelling, "Youse kain't do dat! You'll hold the traffic up." Damn the traffic and the fence! What about the ship? Well, they said, get her outer there. I took the lines to the fence and to the trees, for all that: and still the ship went over with the tide. I accepted the nearest dry-dock's offer of aid (being very careful at the same time to take them on the basis of day work and not salvage; for I had always been brought up to act as if uninsured) and had them fit grappling-irons with shackles and snatch-blocks to the face of the sea wall through which we could lead wires to strops secured to our tops. The tide now began to rise again but the ship did not rise with it. She lay over sluggishly, on her port bilge, with her pierced starboard side exposed to the multitude. Slowly the water crept up her outer side, icing everything as it came; it mounted the bulwarks, crept across the decks, lapped at the skylights' sides — if it got down there an already bad stranding would be tenfold worse.

There was no time to waste. We rove off the wires, and led the inshore ends to three strong motor lorries, to heave away as tugs to right the vessel and get her on an even keel. With the port side of the deck opening up and the after 'tween-decks almost as great a mess as the main, and the whole poor ship seeming now a fearful wreck, the wires at last were clear to heave. Heave away, lorries! Their wheels slipped on the icy ground. The dead ashes of the galley fire were scattered beneath the wheels: heave away again! The wheels turned, this time: the lorries gained. Ah, there she comes! With a lurch she straightened; the mob cheered. I don't know why. The ship was upright again, and that was something. I held her so with strong lines to the grappling irons, and at high water had two of old Olsen's tugs try to shift her, meaning to go straight into dry dock.

It still blew. The tugs could do little. She was fairly hard aground. They could not get in very close. They moved her, and would perhaps have dragged her off but I felt the bottom grind again over the damned contractor's rocks and feared that she would suffer further damage, and sink if she did come off. So I ordered the tugs to 'vast towing and sent them away. It was obvious that this would have to be a proper salvage job, harbour or no harbour.

The night had long fallen then, and I put up the hands at The Owl's Head, a hostelry in Bay Ridge — the only one I could find. Here the older of the grain-ship sailors promptly proceeded to get drunk. For this indulgence I scarcely blamed them. It was damnably cold. There were not beds enough at the Owl's Head that night for all hands and there was still the ship to look after. So they took watch and watch as at sea, half sleeping four hours and then turning out, shivering, to relieve the other half in their vigil by the Shore Road, where they tramped up and down four hours in the snow while their shipmates slept. All through the night the good-natured patrolling policemen came in their motorcars, dropping in to say hello and offer us coffee. Until that night I had always looked upon the New York police as among the coldest human fish alive; they are not. They are a pretty grand lot of fine, upstanding fellows — shot at frequently; sometimes shooting back. I'd spent the night wretchedly in the galley, most of the time, trying to get the fire to draw to keep the frostbite away. New York in January is cold! It is worse by far than the Antarctic in summer, though nobody sends down heroes in great freight-ships to make expeditions and write books about it. There are heroes enough, though, getting on with their work.

The morning was calm, but I went at once to the city and got to work on the business side. In a very short time I had signed a "No-cure-no-pay " salvage contract, with the great Merritt-Chapman-Scott Company, had engaged an average adjustor and enlisted the aid of the worthy Scot who represents the London underwriters — good men, both, and good friends to the ship. I came back with a Merritt-Chapman diver who soon, in spite of the cold, had a temporary patch of mattresses and the like over the worst of the hole midships. He had to be careful lest the ship nip his hand on the rocks with her motion; he had my sympathy, working barehanded in that cold. He also had some rum which was more useful. But he could not get a good patch on until the ship was hauled a little from the rocks. So we waited for high tide again, which was the early evening.

Then a large float came, full of big tanks and a crane (she had been taking fuel oil from the *Morro Castle*), a salvage steamer, and Captain Davis, a strong-faced, strong-voiced mariner who at once took charge of everything in sight in the manner of the old sailing-ship captains. Salvage pumps were rigged, to get the water from the after-hold and the provision room; a tremendous power-pump was lowered from the float on board to cope with the water in the main 'tween-decks, when the diver had that compartment better patched. The salvage steamer anchored ahead to heave us out towards herself as we were lightened. She could not get in close for the shallowness of the water and the restricted room; and she could not anchor in the best place, in the wind's eye, for three old wooden derelicts were grounded there. Close by to the leeward of us was the 69th Street pier. It began to blow again, freshening quickly from the north-west.

Within an hour we were off the rocks, and the crowd, now some thousands strong, cheered again. In the meantime the diver was working feverishly, against the quickly rising wind, to plug the hole midships more securely. It was dark, and he could not see to work; but he continued steadily at his task. The ship was still aground in the mud, and the salvage steamer was anchored fairly far out to a short scope of cable. As she began to heave us out again, the diver's plug at last being as good as he could make it, she began to drag. The wind was blowing a fresh gale then, setting us directly down upon the 69th Street pier, and the ebb tide running down the Bay Ridge Channel was also setting us strongly in that direction. We were a dead weight before we floated, and not much better when we did. The big float with its weight of tanks and crane was lashed to our quarter, adding greatly to the difficulty of manoeuvering us in those narrow waters and further increasing the dead weight against the tug. It had been the salvage master's intention to leave the float in safety beside the 69th Street pier, since he could not leave it aground in the mud or by the sea wall; we had only to get out of there and it would be dropped. Then we should be rushed to the dry dock, not two miles away, with all the big power-pumps gushing water.

But within three minutes of our being properly afloat, the gale howled down a vicious squall, the salvage tug lost control, and all three of us, steamer, float, and ship went crashing into the 69th Street Pier. This was an even worse accident than getting on the rocks had been and damaged

us much more, before we were clear of the pier. The sea
had got up until it was running small combers that broke
along the weather side of the pier; we began to pound
heavily, taking damage badly. The steamer axed her lines
and got away, and so did the float, after the arm of its great
derrick had passed down our mizzen yards like a giant bow
crossing the strings of some protesting violin — twing,
twang, twa-a-a-ng: I looked to see the yards go, but nothing
went. The blundering float moved off astern somewhere
into the night and — I heard afterwards — crushed two
motor-boats lying alongside.

We were beginning to break up forward. What could we
do? It was obvious that if I was to have anything of a ship
in the morning, we had to get quickly out of here. But
how? We were on the weather side; we could not get out
by ourselves. The salvage tug was in trouble enough of her
own, ranging about the end of the pier while her men tried
to get in her towline to make another effort. In the
meantime she had wirelessed to the all-night Manhattan
stations for another tug to be sent immediately. (Tugs
stand by at the Battery with steam up all night for just such
emergency calls.) I suppose that the second tug came with
all possible speed — I am sure it did — but it seemed a
long time, waiting. In the meantime a lot of our rail on the
port side had been stove in, the bulwarks for'ard smashed,
the chainplates of the port fore rigging all torn out, and
every lanyard and deadeye along the whole port side ripped
out and broken. The channels themselves were buckled,
the davits were wrenched out of position, dragging much
of the top-gallant rail and the hammock netting with them;
and it began to look as if our now largely unsupported
rigging would come down at any moment. The diver's
leakmat had worked adrift, and the powerpumps, which
had been able to keep the water in check by idling until
then, ceased working. They could not be persuaded to start
again. We settled down visibly in the water. Lord! were we

to founder here, beside a Brooklyn pier? Poor ship! But she did not founder.

The new tug came. In the meantime the salvage steamer had cleared her towline, and went ahead again. We were full midships to the deckhead again and the afterhold was already half-full with the water there gaining rapidly. We floated only on our watertight bulkheads, without which we must surely have gone down. But as we made rapid preparations for getting away from the pier, I thought that we should not float across the harbour. There was no longer any thought of making for dry dock. It was long after midnight, and the gale blew. Our only chance was to be towed quickly to the lee of Staten Island and lie out the night in the shelter of the big unused piers in there, going far in that we might take the ground with our deck above water, instead of under it.

We set off. The salvage tug went ahead so quickly, without giving us any warning, that I could not get in the wires I had thrown up on the pier to hold us there. One carrying away struck an able seaman brutally across the leg so that he fell on the focs'l head, groaning. I feared his leg was broken, and here were we going out sinking. I had just time to throw him up on the wharf with another seaman to look after him, shouting instructions to a bystander with a car to rush him to the Norwegian Hospital. I don't know why I said the Norwegian Hospital. It was the only one which came into my mind just then. I knew it was somewhere in Bay Ridge. I didn't want any one who couldn't swim in the ship for that harbour ride. Then we went, and tore down some of the pier with our wild ranging in the going; fortunately it was wooden and old, and rotten enough in places. We came out with half a pile hanging to the main channels and the fore topgallant mast cocked alee threatening to come down at any moment.

The salvage tug now went at full speed towards Staten Island across the harbour; and we flew along settling ever deeply and more deeply in the water. The cold harbour rushed in through the hawsepipes and gurgled in every scupper-hole. Our main deck was awash, and I did not see how the ship could float any longer. She had a hundred tons of inside ballast, and here she was more than three parts full of water. The spray, driving over, touched everything to ice; the second tug stood by hurrying aft with her searchlight upon us, not daring to pass a line for fear of being caught when we went down, watching us with her light to pick us out of the water when the time came, I had the sailors who were left aboard (these included the youthful English cadet-captain, stout fellow to the backbone, and a young yachtsman who had refused to go ashore) stand-by clear of all the rigging aft, where they would not be caught in the gear as she went down. I planned that as she lurched under we would jump; we'd have a fair enough chance then, if we did not freeze to death. There would be no further warning. I had my coat unbuttoned. So had the others. The fellow at the wheel had a lifebelt close by. Loose ice-floes from the upper reaches of the Hudson drifted by; by Manhattan's man-made heights I could see the lights in the downtown skyscrapers where the office-cleaners and the night-clerks were at work. And here we were, staging a sea tragedy beneath their very lights, trying desperately to salvage a foundering ship right in the "safety" of a harbour.

We reached Staten Island. She did not sink. We went right in to the corner of an old pier, tying up there in sixteen feet of water where we could not sink, and a feeble-minded watchman came out wielding a waddy and crying in a cracked voice, You can't tie up there! This is a recreation pier. But we tied up, and offered him no answer; perhaps we needed recreation. The salvage tug went back for the float and brought it over later; the salvage master shouting to it to tie up astern of the "wreck" (meaning us) sounded pretty bad.

We looked wreck enough in the morning. But a total

loss we were not. The diver had built in a strong patch of baulks of wood by midday and we had temporarily secured the rigging; before nightfall we had been towed up to the Gowanus Creek and were safely in the Todd dry dock. But my worries were by no means over. We had saved the ship: what then? Looking back on all the accident I felt tired but curiously undismayed. I don't know; I expected to be more worried than I was. The ship was not far from being a constructive total loss: I had no spare funds to cope with so serious an accident. It is the long expectation of greater calamity coming on top of what has already occurred that wears the nerves; but at length there comes the feared calamity — in natural sequence with the others — that doesn't happen and the relief at that is so great that all the others fade into insignificance. The ship is ashore, half full of water. She begins to capsize. We straighten her up. We get her off. She hits a pier. She begins to break up; the leakmats work adrift and the water gains. She is going to sink! Sink, sink, sink, by God! Go under! Who will be drowned? I must answer for them. I brought them here. I hold their lives. But she does not sink; and the relief from that — the joy of that — is immense and endless, so that all the accident which did come to pass is relegated at once to the back of the mind. It is not to be worried over, but mended. It might have been much worse. There is still a great deal to be thankful for.

But I had to pay. I was not a rich man — never shall be: and some of the young fellows who had come for "adventure" now found that they did not like it much, and wanted to leave. Neither then nor at any time throughout the later voyage did I stand in their way; any one who desired to leave could do so, whenever he wished. Four of them went, in all, not including two young men of the best type who had time only for the Atlantic crossing and were already overdue at their desks in London. These would gladly have stayed for the whole voyage.

I found it was not a good thing to have any one as cadet who was over twenty; and I had shipped some who, for their small contribution to the ship's expenses, seemed to think they were conducting a circumnavigation in a yacht of their own. I don't see why they didn't; several of them could have afforded to do so much more easily than I — not in a full-rigged ship, of course. But they could have bought yachts. A staunch vessel good enough for a world voyage (if the greater part of that voyage is made between 30° North and 30° South) may be purchased for £500; all that is necessary to take her round is the ability, the spirit, and the funds. My young gentlemen had at least the funds. They also had the time, or they would not have been with me.

However, they departed, and I wished them well. Who deserts an enterprise at its first reverse is never missed.

We were a week in dry dock and another two weeks alongside in the yard. The structural damage under water was not so bad, but the damage caused by being flung against the pier was widespread and expensive. The main 'tween-decks were gutted; the provisions were all gone; the canvas, the rope — everything — had been beneath the harbour. The best boat was gone; an anchor and chain were lost, and a kedge anchor from the fore channels had been wrenched away by the 69th Street pier.

The first week in the yard was fog-filled and clammy and then a blizzard blew, and it was miserable. It was, indeed, a wretched period for the ship and everybody; as quickly as I could, I made some of the ship liveable, maintaining the crew ashore in the interval, and she soon began to take some shape. The dock-yard people wasted no time; and once the shock of the thing was over I was anxious to be gone. True, the accident was a serious blow to the whole enterprise. I wondered at first whether I should be able to go on; and if I could, whether I might not be compelled to curtail the voyage. A full-rigged ship cannot go through experiences of that kind without the bills against her mounting alarmingly; before I was clear of New York I had lost £2,000. Insurance? I don't know; I am not a business man. Only the actual salvage award — for the successful carrying out of the no-cure-no-pay contract — was paid by the underwriters. But I was left with almost everything else. I paid the bills first and hoped for the best afterwards. Long afterwards, about the best thing I could think of was that at least I was not in debt — at any rate, not then. I paid my way. After New York, the underwriters who, hard businessmen as they were, had a soft spot in their hearts for the little ship, generously extended the policy to give me full cover for any further accidents. But these I hoped most sincerely there would not be.

We lay in Tebo's Basin in a mouldy section of that bewildering welter of humanity, overhead railways, and streets that goes by the name of Brooklyn. Beside us, on the one beam, was Mr. Morgan's sleek *Corsair*; in the next dock lay the white *Nourmahal* being polished for a Presidential fishing party. Beyond her shapely decks rose the high masts of Mr. Lambert's fleet three-master *Atlantic*; all round us lay the miniature — not so miniature, some of them — ocean liners of the very rich with captains and engineers and stewards about, all well paid and robust and very hearty; but never the sight of any owner. The different craft round us there must have represented an outlay of at least six million pounds; the company was a little too aristocratic for my liking, and the battered full-rigger was out of place. When we towed up Gowanus Creek, some fastidious deckhands in the sleek *Corsair* held fenders along her sides that we might not mark them if we took a sheer, and a delivery boy in the *Nourmahal* smiled at the sight of us. Well, he could smile: but we were not so great a wreck when we towed out again, a seaworthy ship, fit to go anywhere. The *Atlantic* settled while we were there, and a

day or two later we read in the newspapers that she'd met a
blow of sorts and lost a sail, and had ordered a new one by
radio to be sent to the next port — Florida, or the West
Indies, or some place. "Cripes!" said the sailmaker. "That's
the way to do it." We went out afterwards and met a blow
of sorts and lost some sails and sprung a mast, but we had
no radio to send in orders and no one to take them
anyway; no such seafaring entered the scheme of our
existence. Between the big expensive yachts by which we
were surrounded and our forlorn and lonely selves, there
was no comparison whatever; they were the goods and
chattels of the rich as country houses are — no more and
no less. And we? God knows what we were; but I felt that
we were at least a ship. I frequently read in the newspapers
of the "millionaire" who was making a cruise of the world,
meaning myself: millionaire! They must be cheap in print. I
was an able seaman.

The New York days were full of distraction. My visitors
were legion, my mail prodigious, and unanswered; I had
some trouble with my officers, and missed a real lieutenant
very much. The carpenter and Hilgard were in motor
accidents, which did not make things easier. I could read
my letters only in the subway going to the city, and attend
to them only after midnight. I had got my boys together
again, and all hands worked with a will to get the ship ready
for sea with the least possible delay. I did not look for
anyone to replace those who left, but they came, inquiring.
I took six likely young fellows — a bit older, most of them,
than I liked, but I found a curious disposition in America
to prolong the boyhood period and to look upon a stalwart
of seventeen as boyishly young. The average young city
American of twenty is not nearly as old, in many ways, as
most European lads of sixteen. Most of my applicants were
over twenty-one.

Fifteen is the right age to begin at sea in square-rigged
ships, but so much of what passes for seafaring to-day can

be learned at academies ashore that it is by no means rare to find oldsters of twenty-three just beginning to acquire practical sea experience. I could find no square-rig sailors. I shipped what offered, signing them as cadets — three college boys, all hefty chaps, deep-chested; two young bankers who had decide they had had enough of the counting house (and good chaps they were); and a quiet boy from St. Louis who looked and was the right material. He was just seventeen; this was to be his college training. He was the only one from inland. The others were all New Englanders. Two of the college boys came, they said, in the hope that the depression might pass while we were circumnavigating. So long as it lasted, they could get no jobs and were becoming depressed themselves. It was better to get away and see something of the world while they waited for a chance to fit into its slightly ill-adjusted machinery. With this philosophy I could find no fault, the more particularly as their contributions to the voyage funds were then most welcome.

While we lay at Tebo's, Bruce Rogers fitted at the beak of our cutwater a magnificent head of Conrad which he had carved out of old wood. This was the quietest and the best thing of all the visit to New York. Leaving the proofs of some masterpiece of printing with which he ought to have been engaged, B. R. came out daily in the snow and worked barehanded at our prow. When it was all ready we shifted over to the Battery, where there was speech-making — not much: it was too cold — and the British Consul-General unveiled the figure-head before a small crowd of shivering literati and mariners, and afterwards there was hot grog in the galley. There was ice at the berth that afternoon, and the pale sun gave weak illumination but no warmth.

I was proud of that figure-head. At least we were the better for that for our visit to New York; and the ship had made good friends. What pleased me most was that, in our predicament — and a ship in trouble is often "pickings" for all hands — no firm or individual tried unduly to profit out of us. I was given good work, good service, good stores at a proper charge; and the ordinary expenses of the ship were very reasonable. Ship-chandlers (Mr. Amos Carver of Pearl Street and old Maine is the grandest ship-chandler in the whole world), salvage companies, tug people, average adjusters, surveyors, insurance representatives, purveyors of fresh food — these treated the ship and me pretty well. Exactly how much of some of this was due to the London underwriters' canny Scot I could not say: but the New York business men were fine. And New York itself? I saw little of it on this occasion but had been there often enough before. I lived two winters at Bay Ridge. New York is a mad and monstrous place I rather like, as cities go: and it was good to get out of it on this occasion with no bad taste in my mouth after all that had happened. I thanked God to be going, but I looked back upon the corrugated skyline with its weirdly contorted concrete cliffs and the narrow canyons of its crowded streets with no cinders in my eyes — even with regrets.

We had come to the 31st of January, 1935, when, with twenty-seven souls all told, I sailed at three o'clock in the afternoon for Rio de Janeiro, with the ship cleared outwards for Sydney, New South Wales. There was a light fair wind. I had a tug pull us away from the berth out of the worst ice, and set sail under the Statue of Liberty. The sails were frozen and hard to set, and we sailed through ice in the Narrows.

IV

Down to Rio

I WAS so eager to be gone from New York that I did not bother about the weather forecast, but went the moment I was ready. I did not wait for a propitious breeze, being determined to go no matter what the conditions. I had been trained to go to sea when ready, and indeed this is almost invariably the best thing to do. If one waits for the "right conditions" one may wait a long time, and then carry the good wind scarce out of the harbour. Ports are bad places for ships and men; to get out of them with the least possible delay was always my ambition. So we had sailed; and the men taking the pilot off somewhere near the Ambrose light shouted from their cutter that a gale was expected. Well, it would be from the north-west; that would be good. It was a fair wind.

The gale blew, soon enough, and we hurried on. I gave her good sail and let her blow off the land, standing out to the eastward without bothering about going to the south, and let the warmth of the Gulf Stream melt the ice from her and all the frozen snow that dynamite could not shift from the scuppers. I took my departure from Fire Island; the first week we ran well over a thousand miles and the sun shone. I had to stand well out to the eastwards to find the north-east trades and to cross the Line with the south-east trade — otherwise a dead head wind — usable so it would not jamb me on Cape St. Roque. The square-rigged ship setting out on an ocean voyage follows no straight line between two points; usable winds matter to her far more than mere distance, and she must seek always to follow such a route as ought normally to give her the best winds. This was what I was now setting out to do. I would go eastwards first, gradually inclining a little to the south; and then when I was sufficiently to the eastwards to head due south and amply weather Fernando Noronha with the south-east trade — why, then I would go boldly on my way. If I could, of course, if I could. The sailing-ship runs to no schedule and finds no winds made ready for her; she has to make her voyages largely under God.

At any rate, it was sense to stand east first where the good winds blew, instead of at once trying to get southing, against the Gulf Stream, and into the region of variables known as the Horse Latitudes. So I stood east a goodly distance, and then the wind came from the south so I could not go that way: well, so it is. There are always reverses. One has to do the best with what conditions the ocean brings, and it is no use to rant and fume about them. We had come almost within sight of Madeira again before we were able to head to the south.

In the meantime I had almost lost the ship. It happened in a Gulf Stream squall about a week after we left New York. I was just congratulating myself on the absence of storms when we were caught aback in a sudden north-east gale, in the middle of a black, rain-filled night, and came almighty near to being blown over. She put her rail right under with sternway and the wind shrieking, and aloft the rags of blown-out sails thundering like the booming of cannon that the storm had loosed on us. The conditions had been worrying and unsettled earlier in the night, with the glass falling slightly and lightning all round. I did not know quite what to make of it, for there is no forecasting the Gulf Stream weather, but at any rate I expected some sort of a change and prepared for it. I stowed all the kites and shortened her down. I was being cautious — or thought I was. As it turned out I was not cautious enough. Then the wind changed lightly to the south'ard and I wore round, to stand east, thinking that this was perhaps the change that had been indicated: but we were scarcely round before the wind, with one mighty, terrifying blast, came with hell force out of the north-east again, solid and dreadful. Flat aback! It was all hands then, with a vengeance. I did not see how the rigging could stand it. The fore and main topgallants and some other sail unidentifiable at the moment blew to pieces at once (which was as well): the rain poured: the wind screamed. Both binnacle lights blew out: she would not pay off.

Under these conditions I had at once to get the ship before the wind again, since it was now directly blowing upon the masts and yards from *ahead* of them, and they were not stayed to take any such strain. They were carefully put up and secured and stayed to take the wind upon their after surfaces; and it was my job to keep it there. I got the spanker off her with all possible speed, but it came in hard; and squared the mizzen yards, leaving the fore and main aback. I tried to get the yards down, but they would not come; I did not use the helm for fear of the rudder being crushed from its pintles by the weight of the sea; for it, like the sails, was designed to run and work with the elements, and not against them. With the afteryards squared and the fore aback she canted herself without the helm, though the sprays broke high over the poop and heavily over her. I had to cant her round until the afteryards filled (backing her into the wind), and then I could regain control. It seemed to take a long, long time: but she came. Good ship! she came. She seemed to know what was expected of her (and maybe thought: What in God's name is that fool doing with me now?): everything stood, once a few sails had gone. She yielded nothing. She canted round and filled her after sails and, still turning, shivered the canvas of the fore and main; so she hung a moment, and began to gather headway. I could use the helm then and the brief battle was won. I shortened down with a vengeance and ran before the wind, and with very little sail ran at ten knots through the night.

She'd blown the fore and main t'gallants'ls to ribbons and the fore course was badly split; a headsail was gone, too. But the masts stood, and there was no damage to the rigging. Taking in the main tops'l — I ran under the reefed fore — the chain sheets took charge and carried away some of the fife-rail; but we had escaped lightly, all things considered. One of the boys had hurt his arm. I fixed him afterwards in the 'tween-decks, when the ship was safe, and looked around at the merry boys chaffing one another and laughing, fresh down from the yards, and little Stormalong in his hammock asleep again already, and young Hilgard tearing round looking for a piece of cheese; and I got to thinking how easily the lot of them might have been at the bottom of the sea; and afterwards, when I could sleep briefly for a while, had a nightmare about a fellow who took a ship out on a voyage without sufficient funds, and lots of troubles, and woke up in a sweat to realize that that fellow was myself. Those rocks ground hard, I suppose — hard and deep. I went on deck again for I could not sleep.

In the morning we saw that the fore topgallant mast was sprung, though not badly. But we had to send the fore royal yard down and unbend the flying jib. We changed the blown-out sails, saving whatever could be saved of them, and wandered on; and there was no more bad weather between that night and Rio de Janeiro. We found the trade wind in due course; and again the flying-fish skimmed away wide-eyed before our bow; and sometimes there were holes in the trade wind where it was calm. Then we swam, with the shark look-outs aloft; or if it was calm enough, swung out the boats and rowed. I saw that the Narrows ice had scraped much of the paint from our waterline, and here the moss was already beginning to grow.

The fourth week out we made a miserable 250 miles, but after that the trade was kinder. We were on the Line in

36 days; and saw there a four-engined flying-boat roaring out of the day-break from Natal in Brazil towards Africa. It had left Brazil probably the previous evening and would reach Africa that night. But what then? It would only turn round and go back again. It was a big and noisy thing, and though its silver sides shone in the first rays of the sun, it was not beautiful as it flew so low. It seemed to me a man-made contemptuous thing, a noisy challenge to the elements. It had no place in the sky, as a bird has; and no place in the sea, as a ship has. It was a roaring mechanical incongruity able to fly. It was full of letters about business, I suppose — doubtless all very important. We rolled along into the South Atlantic morning and, in the quiet night after the full day, rolled along still. One becomes accustomed quickly to the grace of a sailing-ship's gentle motion, but there are times when a full sense of the beauty of it — and the adventure too — strikes one afresh; that night, for instance, with the black sky all gold-studded and the black shapes of the wind-filled sails all rolling, and at the bows the sound of the sea-spray swept aside protesting softly, and lulling, when it sees the sails, into a murmur; and aft the soft light of the straight clean wake as if it were something we were bringing with us, this slender ribbon of bubbling light of the sea trodden down; a luminous bearing from the distant land thousands of miles behind. Land? Is there such a place? Out here the quiet pulse of the ocean beats gentle and dormant, as if there were all sea and no land; as if time did not exist and space were still a confusion to be assembled. It seemed as if we, in our small creation of iron and wood and cordage, had drifted there out of some other world — alone there, alone and to stay alone, and there was no beginning and there would be no end. A burst of accordeon music and of laughter from the 'tween-decks breaks the illusion; and always the morning comes.

We were lucky on the Line. The Doldrums were not bad. We scarcely lost steerage way and were a bare four days from trade to trade, north-east to south-east. Meanwhile, there was plenty of rain, and all hands washed. Neptune came aboard, and baptized the new hands with due ceremony. The south-east trade at first was hesitant and fitful; but we seemed to have lost what few querulous elements we had had, and the ship was happy, too happy to be upset by a few days of poor wind.

A shoal of flying-fish, misguided creatures, flew on board and into the cook's frying-pan; in the tropic evenings the ship was a scene of great content with singing and with music, and late into the night the deck watch yarned on the spare spar beneath the skids — of ships and storms and things and England and of school-days and of great hair-raising adventures that probably never happened. The young Americans had fitted in well, and the English boys had long become old mariners. The Hard Case, with hair on his youthful chest, waited anxiously for his voice to break, so that curses on the toughness of the beef might roll from his tongue a little more as if he meant them; nothing had wiped the grin from Stormalong's happy face since we left England. Nothing ever did.

The south-east trade never did become much good. It was indeed rotten. We barely weathered Fernando Noronha though we crossed the Line well to wind'ard of the St. Paul rocks, and we soon found ourselves carried by the current with the poor southerly wind and jambed on the Brazilian coast. Well, this perhaps lengthened the voyage, but it added to its interest. I did not go round and stand out to sea again, as the big ships do when they see the land; we drew only twelve feet and ghosted down. We saw the bottom sometimes, and the Brazilian beaches were within five miles. But we got along. What wind there was was flukey and variable, but the current was in our favour. By Itamarca we came upon the fishing rafts, queer craft that are nothing but a few logs lightly lashed together in the rough shape of a boat, supporting a willowy mast whose gossamer-sail is trimmed by shifting the mast in a plank cut with five steps. They carry two men and are steered by an oar; they have a roughly fashioned centre-board and sail quite well.

We were becalmed that morning with little prospect of a breeze; I hoped some of the fishermen would come close that I might buy some fish from them for a meal. We could catch none ourselves. But the fishermen paid no attention to us, not being accustomed to trade fish to passing sailing-vessels as their brethren are in the North Sea and the Baltic. I determined to swing out the dinghy and go to them. The ship would stay where she was at least for the morning. We swung out the dinghy and, with two of the *Parma* sailors, set off towards the nearest fisherman. He must have thought we meant no good. He promptly made off, and it was some time before we came up with one of them. They were primitive, like their rafts; but we got some fish — not many. The catch was not very good that day. By the time we had been round to a few fishermen and collected a tolerably good cargo of fresh fish, we found ourselves near the land. It was still calm. There was some surf running, but I thought I saw at least one good passage through to the beach. The palm-fringed beach looked very attractive that sunny morning; there might be some fruit there, I thought. There certainly should have been. We went in, riding the surf easily, and soon had the dinghy pulled up on the sand. We found ourselves by a small village whose squalid huts stood facing the South Atlantic in an unkempt row, with the inhabitants sleeping in the shade in front of them. Nobody as much as looked up as we came in; I don't believe anybody even wakened. Our surreptitious landing on the Brazilian coast was accomplished entirely without opposition, and we looked hungrily round for fruit.

There was no fruit. There was nothing in the place. The few citizens who eventually awoke, for brief periods, did not appear even to be aware of the village's name: at any rate I never discovered it. A man rode a tiny pony by the water's edge, laden heavily with sacks of something, and whanged the poor beast unmercifully with a stick; this was the only inhabitant to show any signs of activity. There was a small local store, not looking very prosperous; into this I now made my way with some doubts, though I thought that at least there might be some fresh vegetables there, or eggs. But there was nothing. The place was a poor copy of our own provision room without its variety — sacks of flour and rice, some biscuits in ancient, rusted tins; some wines; dried, salted, and tinned fish; huge chunks of dried beef that looked like the bark of trees, except that numerous maggots worked happily in them; and fireworks (lots of these) and a bunch of children's sand buckets hanging on a string.

The Indian in charge took our visit most phlegmatically; outside, a Robinson Crusoe figure, huddled in rags, sat asleep on the tumble-down porch. Later, this somnolent and incredibly dirty one arose, shuffled in, crossed himself several times most fervently, and borrowed a match. There was nothing to be bought in the shop or from the village, except a few coco-nuts we gained permission to climb for. With these in the dinghy we launched and departed, a few urchins having assembled by this time to see us off. The adult inhabitants still slept the sleep of the righteous, undisturbed. In the inside passage between the reef and the beach, a flotilla of native trading vessels passed under sail, bound to Olinda or Pernambuco. There was no sound here save the gentle murmur of the sea along the reef; the softness of its caress on the yellow beach was without noise, and the trading vessels passed in utter silence, and it seemed to me there was a national conspiracy between nature and the inhabitants here to foster sleep. Perhaps this was right enough for a tropic beach; but these surely were queer humans who lolled upon the beach of a vastly rich country where they might so easily have tilled and grown so many benefits for themselves. Instead they lay sleeping before hovels with their faces to the sea.

We were five hours from the ship. The fish tasted fine but the coco-nuts were rotten.

Later a breeze came, and in the evening we were off Pernambuco — called Recife now, I believe, to add to geographical confusion — watching the shipping going out and in, and gazing at the town and the big steamers of Europe coming out laden to their marks with the produce of Brazil. Twenty miles away the villagers, in all probability, still slept.

We dribbled down the coast towards Rio with never a day of decent sailing. But it was warm and pleasant enough, and there was usually something to see. Big steamers, now and then, came over to shout hallo — the Britishers *Tregenna* and *Vikingstar* and the Italian *Valdirosa* among others. The *Vikingstar* crossed our bows so close we must have sailed over her log; on the high bridge the officers stared down, all clad nicely in white uniforms. I stood barefooted on our poop, and there was not a shirt on deck except the steward's drying on a line. It blew one day, and it was sad to see the land birds driven out, fighting to stay above the sea but always going down — and once down, never coming up again.

At last we had Cape Frio in sight and were near to Rio, sailing along that day with baffling conditions and gradually picking up the bizarre landmarks of the Brazilian capital — the Sugar-loaf, Corcovado, Tijuca peak and, later, the island of Redondo. It was night by the time we had closed with the approaches to the harbour. It was my first visit in those waters and I did not go in; a quiet land breeze blew in the shrouds and I hove-to under easy canvas, heading south, to await the sea breeze of the morning. I might have gone in, for the breeze at first would have led us in; but I could not distinguish the buoys for the advertising lights round the waterfront and on the hills. The chart was not very helpful. "No reliance can be placed on the buoys," was its contribution: I would not go in by night. The way in was clear enough. It is finding the anchorage in a strange place by night that is difficult. I was being cautious.

In the morning I saw that I could very well have gone. The harbour was open, safe, and commodious. Such dangers as there were were large and obvious. And now there was no breeze; I would have hired a tug had any come out to us. None came. Steamers went by, in and out; we lay becalmed off the grandiose entrance of Rio Bay with the Sugar-loaf and the Christ-surmounted Corcovado now high above us in the clear morning air. The big liners *Augustus* and *Cap Arcona* went in and out again while we waited for wind. Rio is beautiful enough to spend a morning looking at from the outside before going in, though at first glance — so familiar does one become from childhood with pictures of the Sugar-loaf — it looked more like a stage setting come to life than any real harbour. The steamers hurried in and hurried out and the passengers with them; we had the time to look, and the place meant something to us after fifty-seven ocean days.

The sea breeze was late that day, and it was afternoon before we came bowling into the harbour; but the wind when it did come was fresh and fair, and we ran splendidly at a great clip, turning the bay waves to white along our sides and carrying a full press of canvas right to the anchorage. This was the way to do it! (I forgot that I should have been willing to hire a tug.) We dip to the forts, heel a little to the freshening breeze; I straighten up for the anchorage. I see the big Brazilian schoolship alongside in there — the *Almirante Saldanha*. They will be watching us. We are close up now off the navy yard; the port officials' launch comes out, following us, wondering perhaps what we are going to do. What, run right through the harbour? But the boys have been well schooled. A whistle blows; in come the royals and the t'gall'nts immediately after them: then the courses are hauled up in a brace of shakes, and the fore and mizzen tops'ls follow them. Down helm! Spanker to windward! Haul down the headsails! She flies into the wind: back the mainyard! With the main tops'l full aback she comes to a stop within a moment; let go! The anchor is down and the backed tops'l pulls out the chain. With sternway enough on her, that also is clewed up; then it is up and furl everything, with a harbour stow. The officials are alongside and come on board complaining that we have a rope ladder instead of a gangway, and where is the certificate of deratization? Somehow or other, according to them, I appear to have brought the wrong papers from New York. I cleared the ship properly at the Customs House and took all the papers they gave me, going carefully to the Brazilian Consulate afterwards for their visas. But the ship master who carried with him all the documents that all officials want must have his own printing house. It was Saturday afternoon, and we could not get our mail. A ship-chandler was our only welcomer.

We were ashore that night. I went for a spin on the harbour with some of the boys and came across the rusted hull of a barque tied in a corner near the Pan-American airways base. *Mello Franco*, I read on the rusted counter and the bows, from which the figurehead, sadly weather-beaten now, still rises in flowing grace: *Mello Franco*. There is the romance of the Mediterranean in that mellow name; I see old mariners on her decks, earringed and fierce-moustachioed, with bandana kerchiefs about their swarthy heads — long, long ago. Now she is nothing but a pitiful heap of rust left standing there, yet she still has grace. She looks as if the slightest movement would cause her utter disintegration; she seems to have lain where she is for years, neglected in the sun. But there is a quiet sea-kindliness about her still; by the blockless bumpkins and the rusted rail one may sense some dim echo from her seafaring past. I wonder what she has been, in what ports? Probably for years some plodding Limejuice barque, carrying prosaic cargoes round Good Hope and the Horn: the nitrate ports would know her — the Cape, Australia, the Pacific Slope. She has beaten the ocean over many hundred thousand miles and seen much, and here at last she lies in the sun abandoned by the Brazilians. But had I sailed all this way to gaze upon the poor hulk of a worn-out barque? I must see something of the city, too. Cities are so much the same; only their natural settings (in some instances) are different. Rio is as full of streets and people as any other place, all absorbed in their own affairs, dodging traffic and so on, taking an interest in politics, and going to the cinema. I noticed the foul odour of excrement by the landing steps, and was jostled in the ferry throng, and got to thinking about the open sea and that barque.

I stayed a week in Rio, setting up the standing rigging for the West Winds passage to the Cape and beyond to the East Indies, and cleaning up the ship overside — scraping off barnacles, taking in sea stores; and between times watching the wily ship-chandler that he did not get too far to wind'ard of me. There is a type of ship-chandler in a foreign port who is apt to regard stray ships as blown in for his benefit, and he seeks at once to extract as much profit as he can out of their visits. If the vessel is officially described as a yacht, look out! It is far better then to do your own buying. But at that, too, you will be shamelessly exploited; you cannot speak the languages of all the ports you visit. Sooner or later you will have to engage some chandler or go-between. There are gentlemen of that calling of the highest moral standards, who doubtless make fine husbands and good fathers and possibly, here and there, pillars of the Church. But watch them, mariners! They will have no mercy on you. From the moment your anchor is down until you are ready to depart, watch what they send on board, check what they give you, keep an eagle eye on their bills. A "yacht," be she what she may, is to them the best of prey; in yachts they have been taught to

find, all too often, either an owner who can be easily
fleeced or a paid employee who can be got to connive at
felony. It is an ancient practice of most ports, affecting not
only yachts. The whole business of providing and storing
ships is too often riddled with graft and sharp practice —
not always, of course. I make no sweeping assertion of
ugliness against the chandlery firms of the big ports, most
of which carry on well-established business on sound
enough lines, and from which the same degree of good
faith may be expected as exists in the rest of the business
world (rather more, indeed). But my case against a certain
type of so-called ship-chandler is that his only purpose is to
profit as much as possible from his inefficient services as
buying-agent for the ship. Carrying little or no stock
himself (and therefore little risk) his sole "service" is to buy
what the ship orders as cheaply as possible, and sell it as
dearly.

My Rio chandler was the worst of the whole voyage. A
melancholy ghoul of sad and cadaverous aspect with a
dried death's head — cold-eyed, thin-lipped — atop a
scrawny neck, he seemed to me to have one foot deep in
the grave. I was going ashore; would I care to go in his
boat? If I did, I'd have the bill for the trip out as well as his
trip in, and my own. There were few formalities to be
observed for such a vessel — a few forms to fill to get a
clearance. These he would look after, in consideration of
having the ship's business — it was no bother. But I saw
an item on his bill, presented on the eve of sailing, that
read "Agency charge, £10." I well knew this to be a greater
sum than the gentleman would ordinarily earn in a
fortnight, but the ink with which he scrawled that item on
my bill was a total loss to him. Maybe he had read in the
newspapers about the "millionaire."

This buying the needs of ships in ports is indeed a
difficult and often a nasty business. The requirements of a
ship are so particular and diverse, and she has usually so

little time in which to meet them, that there has been in all maritime history much chicanery and plain thieving on the financial side of her visits to strange places. Compared with the narrow, grasping mind of a ship-chandler of the poorer type, a storm at sea is the breath of heaven: in two years of sailing, no ocean, no reef, no calm, no storm ever bothered me half so much as one visit to a civilized port. It takes a clever housewife twenty years to learn to buy properly the requirements of a house in one place: how then can ships possibly cope with the problem in all ports? Great lines may, by building up their own organizations; but the wandering casual ship, the tramp, the coaster being delivered somewhere, the long-voyage yacht — these cannot. Buying is not an art, not by any means. It is a cold and miserable business of the handicapped pitting of the purchaser's wits against the seller's, with the odds mostly on the seller's side; a thankless and laborious accumulation of what is needed from the vast mass of the indifferent, the paltry, and the bad offered — a horrible haggling affair with nothing whatever to recommend it save its necessity to our mode of life. One of the grandest things about our sea life was the entire absence of the profit-motive, and my first act upon leaving all ports was to fling in the sea whatever of their paltry coinage remained in my pockets — usually about threepence, or five cents.

I see I have wasted a lot of space about nothing; but that Rio ship-chandler made me angry. It is hard to keep some faith in human beings.

I saw little of Rio. There is a lot to do in looking after a ship and twenty-six human beings; the boys had leave — each watch a day — and managed to see something. I did not get to the Sugar-loaf or the Corcovado or anywhere; one suburban tram trip was the extent of my peregrinations. It had early been obvious that I was to see little of the big ports on that voyage; well, I proposed going to as few of them as possible. They can be reached in any vessel. I missed again (and was to miss even more during the rest of the voyage) the presence of any real second-in-command. My mate was a good sailor at sea. I had no one to take the boys on shore excursions, trips in the lifeboat and so on, which could very well have been arranged and would have been beneficial. I had no time to spare for such diversions and no one else to send, and some of the college boys were a little old for such pastimes, or thought they were. They preferred to find their own amusements and in port were sometimes hard to hold.

The *Almirante Saldanha*, a high-sided queer kind of an auxiliary bastard-schooner lying by the quay, once dried her sails. On Saturday the sixth of April, I sailed from the anchorage early in the morning, dribbling out with the slight tide and almost no wind. We drifted pretty close to the Navy Yard church and the mooring buoys before she would turn round, but once round she was controllable though we passed within a few yards of the rocks at the forts in the entrance. The Sugar-loaf towered over us at closer hand than I would have chosen, but we were clear of the harbour-mouth before the morning sea breeze came and were able, then, to use it to speed us on our way. The curious contortions of Rio's sudden hills made a background of loveliness as we sailed. I was sorry I saw so little of the place, but it could not be helped.

I was now bound eastwards towards the Cape, having decided, after the New York accident, to make an eastbound rounding instead of westward. The season was far advanced then, off the Horn; and Magellan, without an engine, was no road for us into the Pacific. We might have got through, but we might not. At any rate, it would have taken a long time; and I had a number of boys. The eastwards way gave fair winds towards Good Hope and the East Indies, but it would make our tropic sailing rather hard and the whole circumnavigation much more difficult.

It is better, on any sail-driven circumnavigation, to reach the Pacific by Panama, and go on westwards round the world with the Pacific trades and the Indian monsoons, all fair winds. This is the route usually chosen; but it has become something of a beaten track. I had a full-rigged ship, stouter-hulled than any the great navigators had sailed, and I wished to sail as they had sailed, taking the world and the seas as we found them, without using canals which, to my antiquated way of thinking, were — at least for this voyage — bypaths of softness. I had a good ship: let hers be a real voyage.

In Rio we had sent down the royal yards and bent the three-cornered mainsail in readiness for the west winds of the Forties; but we were a long time finding them. We could have carried studding sails the first two weeks, if there had been any wind to fill them. I made what southing I could, for Rio is at the tropics' edge, and I now wished to get the latitude in before going eastwards with the west winds. But it was so warm and mild, and there was so little wind even on 38°, that the boys were swimming over the side. The albatrosses were with us now, and I fed them some alleged pork we had on board, in three barrels of which the steward could find not the slightest evidence of the flesh of pig. Seventeen of them sat round and waited for the pork, night and morning, growing plump and preening themselves and now and then gargling a little sea water pleasantly to wash down their pork, and making queer noises.

On Good Friday our run was six miles, and the boys swam among the albatrosses. We put the starboard lifeboat over for some exercise and pulled among the birds, feeding them, and in a little while they consented to be fed by hand — even the great albatross — and we lifted one up and placed it in the boat, being mighty quick about it, for the bird objected violently to this unexpected treatment. Poor bird, it had reason enough for it was not in the boat a moment before it threw up all its pork and was most disgustingly seasick. We let it go again; we had meant it no harm. I like the albatross. There is always a friendly, benevolent look in his eye (not like the harsh-countenanced mollyhawk) and he glides so beautifully. I never tired of watching them in high wind or in calm — how they take off and come down like aeroplanes, landing at low speed and skidding on their feet thrust out like a lowered undercarriage; and reach flying speed for the take-off by a laborious and ungainly run on the surface of the water in which their sterns wobble gracelessly from side to side and their great webbed feet hit the water plop-plop-plop. They seem to hold committee meetings together sometimes in the calms, seated all together and discussing some weighty matter most learnedly. And they make noises at each other sometimes, too, and fight (though seemingly only about food, and then briefly); and scratch each other's heads with their strong, curved beaks; and in their graceful flight skim the water often so closely that their wingtips touch. But this does not incommode them; and every part of their body presents a controllable surface in their flying, needed (applied violently, sometimes) at almost every bank and turn. How little control have aeroplanes in comparison! No wonder these sometimes still break mysteriously in the sky. I often saw the albatross, meeting an eddy, suddenly work all his controls so swiftly and so greatly that any aeroplane venturing to use its manoeuvring surfaces with a fifth of the effort would rip off its wings; and I wondered, if this master flier, with his thousands of years of development, finds equilibrium in the air sometimes so difficult, where is proud man? I have seen mollyhawks crash in the eddies from our sails, and they are the next best fliers to the albatross. But I never saw an albatross make a landing he did not intend.

We had been six months on the voyage from England and were nineteen days out from Rio before we came to

Tristan da Cunha, the first of the out-of-the-way islands on our route. The day was so thick with cloud and haze we almost passed by without seeing the island, for the high land was covered with cloud. We were quite close before we saw the land, low down on the sea. I had hoped to touch there, but it was late in the day, with the glass falling and the weather threatening. So I stood as close as I dared, with the wind turning slowly into an onshore breeze and, with the last of the daylight, wore round to stand out to sea. While we were actually in the act of wearing ship I saw two boats coming out, tossing in the steep seas, quite close to us. They were the Islanders. I did not think they would try it, so late in the day and with the sea so lively. I backed the mainyard and waited for them. There were twenty-three men in an old ship's lifeboat, painted brown, and a canvas whaleboat. They had difficulty in getting alongside and nosed into the mizzen channels only long enough to put on board a parson in skirts and a skullcap, and a dark-visaged individual who said he was the Chief and began at once to beg for cigarettes and tobacco and whatever else was going. Then he was violently seasick in the scuppers; but he still asked for tobacco. The parson said there were 166 people on the island and the 167th was expected later that night: we were the fourth ship to visit them in six months, which, so far as he knew, was a "record," though he had not been there long. The four-masted barque *Ponape*, outward bound to Australia, the cruising liner *Empress of Australia*, and a Dutch submarine had been there before us, the cruising liner only a few weeks earlier. They had, I gathered, been well supplied from the liner, but they still wanted whatever was going. This was natural enough, for they did not know when the next ship might visit them.

I gave them sacks of flour, a bale of blankets, an old gramophone, books and papers, and cigarettes and tobacco: the boys also gave the people in the ship's boat what cigarettes they had, and spare clothes. I had read in the

Pilot earlier that day: "Fowls, geese, sheep, pigs, feathers, hens' and seabirds' eggs, milk, moccasins, sheepskins and polished horns of cattle are kept ready for bartering with passing vessels." A sheep would have gone down pretty well with us. We had no fresh food. But their boats were empty, and when they had taken what we gave, they departed with three cheers.

It was dark then, with the wind increasing: I stood out to sea. In the middle watch we saw the island again still shrouded in heavy cloud, standing like a black rain squall squat and sullen in the sea. Miserable and forlorn rock, I wonder that any human beings remain there.

A week of strong west wind at last sent us foaming along, but we were a month out of Rio before the reflection of the Cape Town lights showed feebly in the eastern sky.

V

West Winds Passage

IT IS curious how the land comes up from the sea after a passage of many days across the open water, a passage the progress of which is measured until then only upon a chart with pencilled lines calculated from much observation of the sun and other heavenly bodies, and the working of involved trigonometrical formulae simplified by tables. Slowly the lines across the chart head towards the darkened land-mass in one corner, and for a long time there is nothing but the lengthening lines and water, water, water, which might always be the same, in the same place, only behaving differently, varying its deceits and its moods. Then one day from the whited chart and from the water the land stands up. It *was* there. It has not only its existence in dark outlines on a chart; it is a different land from that we left. It is the land to which we have been bound.

There is no mistaking the landfall at the Cape, the rough outline of the Cape Peninsula — Table Mountain, and Good Hope afar off and, nearer the Table, the Lion's Head, the Devil's Peak, the Apostles, and all those lesser hills, the whole forming a great clod of massive and sterile rock looking as if it had been flung there in exasperation by the gods, at the crossroads of the stormy oceans, with an oath and a wild shout to the sea: Here, see what you can do against *this*! And the sea from that day to this has not been able to do very much — not even to carve out a good harbour.

But my reflections are cut short by the arrival of a boatload of immigration inspectors with, as always, an insatiable demand for crew lists and the like, and the tidings that all the cadets and the crew are "prohibited." That is to say, I bring them at my risk and I must take them away again, or send them away if they leave, or suffer heavy fines. And up on deck there is another fellow in the wilderness without, crying: Where is the deratization certificate? Deratization! I feel like telling him he can deratize himself; and if he can find a rat aboard the vessel or the slightest evidence that one has ever been there — why, I'll eat all the forms his launch can carry out. And there are customs chaps, and so forth, sealing up the ship's stores. In such manner are wandering vessels now received at all civilized ports. But they are nice fellows, these inspectors at the Cape, and indeed if I had not been on my feet thirty-six hours I should have been quite glad to see them. We tie up in the dock beneath a coal gantry, where there is a pack of chandlers' runners yelping to come on board.

"I'll give you one per cent., Captain!" one clamours, and another raises him to one-and-a-half — two — three. Where are their price lists? I ask. But they haven't anything so prosaic; and I gather, between whiles, that this percentage they are offering me is a "kickback" on the ship's bills for my own pocket, a sort of inducement to do business for my profit as master but not as owner. They did not know I was the owner. Graft, indeed; but damitall, I am the owner, and it seems to me a mighty strange "inducement" to offer, that I should accept a commission from my own funds in order to connive at what pretty much amounts to felony against me. Queer world! The profit-motive again, I suppose. I never could get this ship-chandlery business properly puzzled out. Maybe most business is like that and it is quite customary: I don't know.

The people at the Cape are kind, and I stayed a week, engaged for the most part in meeting the multifarious needs of the ship — a spar from which to shape a new fore topgallant mast, and tools to work with; food of all kinds, from marmalade to baking powder, from salt pork to hops for making yeast; spare glasses for the skylights in case the high seas stove in some (they did); marline, cup grease, ratline stuff, sail needles, caustic soda; herrings in tomato sauce, seaming twine; copper tacks, lamp chimneys, round iron, disinfectant; burlap, permanganate of potash — and the list is not yet begun. It is extraordinary how a ship can proceed at sea, living on her stores sufficient unto herself, in need of nothing; yet if she comes into any port her needs are endless.

I found that South Africa is a poor place wherein to buy South African produce, the best being shipped abroad and the inhabitants paying dearly for what is left. I had bought better African stuff in London at lower prices than I could get at Cape Town; however, so it is. I gathered that in many instances the producers collected subsidies for sending their stuff away. In order that the growers could sell their produce at a profit on the world markets, the citizens were penalized to provide the subsidies. At least, so it seemed to me; doubtless it was all in order and had been conceived and established as a way of life by great economists. I am no economist. I merely thought it strange that people, in a country where good food was grown, taxed themselves to have it sent away and then lived expensively upon what remained.

I saw little of the Cape. It was the week of King George V's jubilee, and the city was bedecked with flags and filled with a strange multitude. There was a regatta at which the hardy oarsmen rowed in half a south-east gale that set up a nasty slop on the open water. There was to be, I heard, a whalers' or lifeboats' race for the British ships in port, but though there were some five or six tramp steamers in, it chanced that we alone had a white crew. We were invited to send a crew in a whalers' race against a crowd from some stationary local training-ship, and the naval reserve. I sent a crew with misgivings, as only one of them, a former navy boy, had ever pulled in a whaler before. However, they had pulled a good deal in the open sea, and were in the best of condition. As it turned out, the bad weather suited them, and they won by some seventeen lengths; the ship was presented with a silver cup and everyone was pleased. The Town Clerk and some gentlemen came down the morning of the day we sailed and handed over the handsome cup with speech-making and with smiles, and we left the Cape well pleased. I had met some good friends there, in spite of hurry, and we were all very well received. I found a new cadet, a clean-cut young fellow named Carmichael; paid my bills — there seems no alternative — cleared the ship, secured a Dutch bill of health for the East Indies, and departed.

I swung the ship in Table Bay and had a shore expert adjust the compass which had been giving trouble; he was gone in an hour or so, and we slipped quietly out to sea under all sail past Sea Point bound first to Ampenan or Boeleleng, 6,500 miles away. The compass adjuster's charge was £5:5s., but we had not got very far before I saw that his estimate of the value of his genius was grossly exaggerated. I must add, however, in all fairness to him, that he had not left the compass much worse than he had found it.

It blew freshly at south-east when we left and continued to do so for some days. I stood to the southward on the port tack, planning to get across the Agulhas Bank and out of the short sea and the adverse current as quickly as possible. In comparison with these preliminary aims, getting to the eastward did not matter. That would be easy enough when the time came. So I stood down towards Forty South, and the wind was flukey and variable again. It was early winter then; where were the gales? We wanted the strong west winds to drive us eastwards almost to the Leeuwin before turning north towards the Indies; this was the only feasible way for the square-rigged ship to go. Had I tried to go direct (a course I could not even consider) I should have had the south-east trade a head wind and might have been a year.

It was May 14 when we left Cape Town, but it was the seventeenth before we were round Good Hope. The wind — what there was of it — still hung in the east, and this seemed to bring the Agulhas current farther south, so that, though we had made considerable latitude, we still had the drift against us. We made little over 500 miles the first week out. Then it was calm. We rolled along very quietly, again watching our friends the albatrosses. There was one of these — a big royal with a queer reddish mark across one side of his face — that had followed us to the Cape from before Tristan; we called him Fred, and there was always a piece of pork for him. Now here he was again, and he stayed with us to the Leeuwin. We took rather a fancy to old Fred: he used to watch the stern light-bracket all day, for this was where his pork was placed. Sometimes in the gales he was missing for a while, but he always came back again.

We were twelve days at sea before we had the first westerly gale; but once the gales found us they stayed. Good gales! None was so strong we could not use it, and we ran and roared along with the spume flying. They always began in the same way, in the north with rain and falling glass and growing wind; then they blew hard for a while at north-west, perhaps increasing in that quarter to a hard gale that lasted twelve hours, or twenty-four, or even longer. And then, with a slight upward flick of the glass the wind would jump at once to south-west or south, blowing violently at first from there, then quickly settling down to a moderate gale and blowing the sky clear. That would pass, and we would wait for the next cyclonic movement to overtake us. They passed by at a great speed, one behind the other like trains on the underground. Maybe they go like that right round the world, for there is no land down there to incommode them — not from Good Hope eastwards to the Horn — and while we ran our easting down, the same storm perhaps travelled round the world and caught us up again. Well, we could use them all. Storms of this character cause no alarm to well-found vessels, though sometimes they blow so hard that even a running ship must temporarily heave-to. Strong winds which follow a clearly defined course of conduct, and stick to it, are not worrying. If a ship could run fast enough, of course, she could stay with the one storm and make it take her round the world; some of the great clippers of the early Australian days, with their great length and their tremendous power, made magnificent runs almost exactly in this manner, though they would rarely carry the same movement for more than a week or ten days. And that, indeed, was time enough to hurl them from Good Hope to the Bight. Even the grain-racers of to-day have frequently run down this stormy stretch in fifteen days, averaging 300 miles a day.

It was mighty exhilarating, sailing down there, for all the gloominess of the north-wind days and the rain and sleet, and the cold and the high seas. The sea runs so long that its height does not matter; the ship is so short she is always only in one sea, and behaves beautifully. She is the ideal size for ocean voyaging, though she might be ten feet longer with advantage to her speed. She has beam enough to carry the greater length, and it would increase her speed. It was difficult to get her over ten knots, though sometimes she touched twelve. But she did so much tobogganing — so much climbing up the sides of the great seas, and rolling down their farther inclines with the height of water behind taking the wind from the lower sails. And she was hard to steer — would have been in any event, but with the "adjusted" compass it was guesswork in the gales. I ran before whatever came, when it blew mightily, keeping the jib-boom headed always somewhere east and holding a good press of sail as long as possible. She was a small ship, amply canvased; but I knew that the more we drove before these gales the more quickly should we be gone from those wintry seas and reach again the milder latitudes of the trades. I had only two years or so for this circumnavigation, and now half of the first year was gone with the ship not yet come anywhere. Two years, I decided, is not long enough.

So they came down, gale after gale, and we ran 1,200 miles a week. It was cold and boisterous with rain and sleet: but how she ran! The first of June found the ship storming through the raging sea somewhere below Forty South, half-way between the Cape and Australia, with the strong wind roaring in the rigging and the tops'ls reefed down and Jan, the son of Captain Junker, laughing at the wheel in the rain. I asked him, in a brief lull, why he smiled so happily. At the beauty of the little ship in the great sea, he said, and how bravely she ran — brave and buoyant and almost dry. This would confound the woebegones in Denmark who had said she was afraid to go beyond the North Sea. Afraid! Good Lord! and here she was 10,000 miles from Denmark, running down her easting in the winter's wild west winds. Jan's father had been master of the ship for twenty years and loved her, but he had never had her in a great ocean wind or a long, true sea: now Jan could write and tell him how well she behaved, and the boy smiled at the thought of his father's pleasure.

We raced on in the heavy wind with the sleet-squalls marching one behind the other, overtaking us all day, roaring down upon us from the murk astern, drenching the already thrice-drenched sails and passing on. The hail stings and the wind roars and the gale grows steadily into a real storm — tumult of wind and sea. The sea is very high and the squalls are savage: at midday the main topgallant, that has been carried long over the single-reefed main tops'l, must come in, and nightfall finds her reefed close down. She was beginning to stagger a bit with the weight of sail: that is no use. There is no sense in over-driving, which is merely a strain on ship, gear, and men. Now the squalls grow in number and in strength until the sea smokes in anger and the spray is gathered up and hurled from every smallest ruffle on its tormented surface: the spray flies and the foam streaks and the great seas tower over us higher often than the mainyard. Their crests fall viciously aboard more often than enough, but only their crests: she dodges the weight of water and always eludes the heaviest seas. It is as well she does.

At night it is wild, black, and hailing. As the nights come down here with these yellow slender masts quickly engulfed in the blackening gloom, I feel a tenseness I have not known at sea before: it is the sudden shifts of wind at night that might be dangerous. Yet shall I heave to, or shorten down unnecessarily? No, no! run on: for the masts stand up strong and superb from the reeling decks as if they had grown there and no man had made them; the strong pattern of the cordage and the yards is staunch as the boughs of giant trees. Let her go! And go it is.

I had hoped to look in at St. Paul Island, on our way; according to the *South Indian Ocean Pilot*, it must be an interesting place. I stand towards the island as well as the swinging compass will allow me; and then, when by dead reckoning we are within a few score miles, the wind comes down heavier than ever and the sea mounts and the visibility is impossible, and I run on now fallen off from the course and hoping to God that we shan't see the island. It is full gale now — savage and determined. For the first time I look aloft with apprehension at the gear that has been assaulted and battered and blown upon so much, and see the wooden lower yards waving like willow wands in the great wind, and the foreyard working with the strain of the tops'l sheets like a huge yew bow. The sea is a tortured murk of fiendish water smoking and snarling round us. Now the foamy wake rears high above the stern as if we were suspended from it, only in a moment to fall far below as if it were a writhing cable we were dragging through the sea. Now the long jib-boom points downwards towards the bowels of the earth and, holding to a backstay by the helmsman aft, I catch my breath a second, wondering whether any ship ever dived so deep that she made no recovery. We don't know. If any has, no one has told about it. Some fine ships have gone missing along this road.

I watch the sea foam in its ceaseless anger and feel the driven spume sting my face: day-long and night-long I stand upon the grating now, for there is nowhere to walk, until my sou'wester chafes the skin from my forehead, and my beard grows (grey, by thunder!) and the sea boots on my feet are heavy as a diver's. Day-long I watch the sea and the ship and night-long stand looking, not seeing much, but ready for shift of wind or the sudden swing of indifferent helmsmanship, ready for the sea and, I hope, for any emergency that may come. We are down now to the close-reefed fore and main tops'ls with the mizzen all fast, and a rag or two of the best storm stays'ls: the gale increases and increases.

So the greyness of the morning comes, for which I thank the Lord, and still the wind increases. Shall I bring her up now, heave to? If I do not now, very soon I shall not be able to. I have almost decided to lie to, a little before noon, when the glass gives a half-millimetre jump and the wind jumps with it to the south-south-west. Now the angry and tormented sea is so tossed and torn in all directions that there can be no safety in heaving to. We *must* run! She staggers, lurches, and rolls the sea on board while her three gold trucks heave agonized protesting circles towards the grey sky. But she cannot help it. This cross and insane sea would break upon a whale, and in this wind the albatross is hove to. She avoids the worst weight of the water: quickly now the strong sou'-wester flattens down the sea with driving rain that is soon gone. The sky clears, and the great sea, in a few hours, rolls at us and by again in steady tremendous furrows from the sou'-west — true, now, and she knows what to do in it. Bravely she picks up her stride, and still runs with the foam boiling and the wash-ports clanging and the sea gushing from every scupper-hole and the spray driving over the t'gallant yards. We run on. Day-long I watch again, and in the night, not seeing much but ready: and I watch while the storm blows. The gear holds, thank God. She yields nothing. There are no accidents, nothing carried away, nobody overboard, nobody hurt. These are the great things to be thankful for. There had been much work aloft and on deck; a little slip, a moment's forgetfulness, and someone might have gone.

All hands have worked splendidly as they always did in any real storm or stern emergency — the boys and the grain-ship men, those great citizens of the sea. Wet through, cold, hail-lashed in the storm, they climbed out upon the yards with cheerfulness and zest through day and night and always quickly did what was ordered — quickly and well. Aye, great fellows all: and in the following morning, with the gale survived, there comes aft a deputation from the port watch to growl about the food. Aye, aye — great chaps, real human beings. The pea soup was burned and rather watery too, if the truth be told, but the cook had done splendidly to have anything warm at all. There would have been no growl if the galley had been washed out and they had been given nothing.

It blew up again more than once along that stormy road, but the little ship ran bravely and suffered no harm. We did not carry away a rope-yarn between Cape Town and the Strait of Bali, and no one had even a boil.

I began gradually to incline the ship's head towards the northwards, and there was some pale sun; we were come almost to the longitude of Cape Leeuwin. I turned due north then, making slow progress at first in a high head sea with a light wind, in which the ship bucked and floundered. She did not take kindly to a steep short sea and little wind, and hobby-horsed about miserably that whole long day, throwing the food from the messroom table and tossing the boys out of their bunks. But the mood passed, as all the sea's moods always do. The sea took off and there came fair wind. So I stood to the north somewhere off the west coast of Australia with the land just out of sight, and by 30° South the weather was fine. The royal yards were crossed again and the sun shone. We had broken no records and made no famous runs, but we had sailed over 5,000 miles in a month and we were feeling pleased.

I began to read in the *Pilots* about Ampenan and Boeleleng.

We never did get to Ampenan, which is the undistinguished port of Lombok Island; we were unable to make Lombok Straits, and for a while it looked as if we could not make Bali Strait either. The south-east trade was more east than south-east, and the monsoon was east-by-north. It was fresh, and brought with it a drift of twenty to thirty miles dead to the west'ard. It was this factor which interfered with our course. I pointed up as well as I could though not too high, keeping the yards a little off the backstays to get better headway out of her. Our head was towards Sumbawa, but the drift set the ship steadily to the west. I had hoped to get through to the Java Sea either by the Strait of Alas or Lombok Strait. Bali Strait I definitely ruled out as being a good place for strong-powered vessels but just an unnecessary risk to me. The south-east monsoon, if it ever did blow from south-east, was of course fair wind through there; but the place was a thirty-mile funnel, a narrow gorge between the Javanese and the Balinese hills, a reef-fringed canyon through which the monsoon was apt to whistle at the force of half a gale, and the tides ran at six knots with rips and whirlpools and eddies. It was well lit; but that would not help us if we got in a tiderip or a whirlpool and were thrown at six knots against a reef. No, Bali Strait was out.

I was very glad to go through there, afterwards. That is the way a voyage in sail turns out; you cannot very well plan ahead or arrange your route. You have to make up your mind to which place you are going and get there somehow. Lombok I could give up, since I had to; but I wanted to go to Bali.

The wind, which had been fresh enough to blow the Australian sand on our decks though we were sixty miles from the land a week earlier, was now light, and the set to the west was as strong as ever. In the end we made our land-fall on Balambangan Peninsula, the south-eastern end of Java, and could barely see the Tafelhoek of Bali in the haze. I had to jamb her up and beat to clear Tanjong Bantenan, but once we had managed that, at least we had Bali Strait clear before us. The strait is twenty-eight miles wide at its southern end, and there are no dangers there; it is easy enough to begin its navigation. But the northern end is only one mile wide and on both sides great mountains rise, so huge that now they were hidden in the haze and nothing could be seen. But it is not the narrowness that matters; it is the funnelling of the tides. There is no part even of the open sea that is entirely foolproof, but the difficulties of navigation are always intensified when there is land. A narrow strait such as this, lined with reefs and full of rips and eddies, is as nasty a piece of sailing as a full-rigged ship can face. It had, however, a few points in its favour in that, before coming to the Narrows there was anchorage here and there, where a ship might await favourable tide; and it certainly was well lit. "Sailing ships should navigate this strait only by day," says the *Pilot* very properly, and I noted the advice. I had not the slightest intention of flying in its face.

Once we were past Balambangan we were out of the set and were able to head a better course. I steered towards the middle of Bali Strait, meaning to keep as far from the land as I could. The wind at last was true from south-east and, though it was hazy, the conditions were excellent. But we could not see much of the land and we saw little or no sign of habitation. This was the first of the Isles of Adventure, so to speak, of our voyage; and all we saw that first morning was a giant air liner flying the mails from England to Australia high up in the sky. According to that somewhat antiquated authority, the *East Indies Pilot*, a million people live on Bali, which is a small place, and 35,000,000 on Java, but we did not see so much as a new-born babe out fishing. The land on both sides of the strait appeared arid and not much cultivated; later we saw a native *prau*, about twenty-eight feet long, carrying a cargo of hogs made up in cane baskets, and seventeen people. They bobbed up from all directions as we passed, and grinned a welcome.

Our prospects of heeding the *Pilot's* advice and passing the Narrows by day steadily diminished. Throughout the afternoon we were held almost in the same place by a strong south-going stream, and, though the wind was a fine whole-sail breeze in our favour, we made almost no progress. The early evening found us off Banjoewangi: what should I do? Anchor, and await the daylight, or use the flood and get through by night? The ebb had been running so long and so strongly to the south that I thought the flood (sometimes missing at that time of the year, to add to the difficulties) was about due. Why waste it? The place was well lit. I had only to get on the Tanjong Bansering range lights, and stay on them: the flood, if it did come, would soon rush me through — or I might find myself with the ship suddenly flung by some tiderip across the wind, aback and uncontrollable, setting rapidly upon a reef. This is the danger in such places and, with the Java shore only a mile from the Balinese, there would be little chance if this kind of thing *did* happen. But if one is always to be overawed by the circumstances which may rise against one — why, full-rigged ships would never have been built. I stood on, carefully and slowly — slowly, whether I wished it so or not: but if I ever tried to pilot with great care it was that night.

From Banjoewangi to the Narrows is about eight miles. It has cleared, and the great peaks of Java and of Bali both tower over us. The wind is freshening as we slowly approach the entrance to the Narrows, but it is a clear and peaceful night with the black sea flat, though I hear it clearly breaking on the reefs of both sides. We have the range lights in line — fixed white and flashing red: we begin to gather speed. It must be the brief slack water: soon we shall rush. The wind is strong and strengthening every moment; without the aid of the tide we are running in that flat sea a good ten knots. Now comes the tide: the rush begins! With a greater speed than we have ever made before, we rush on towards the canyon of the Narrows, and the helmsman — it is Hilgard — needs his nerve and all his skill to keep that fixed white and flashing red in line. Sometimes she yaws: quick with the helm there! He is quick; she responds. She is a good-steering ship. Onward she runs. We are in the Narrows now. Port a little! Steady! Steady-as-she-goes! Sta-a-rboard! I con from the fo'c'sle head on the Bansering range, for the visibility is poor from the wheel. The lights are in line. Now they swing. We run through a breaking burst of white-caps of some rip, but she holds her way. The crickets are chirping in the Java forest; the noise of the sea swirling on the Bali reefs rises and rises. We run on. She handles well. The foam boils at the old prow. The wake races phosphorescent astern. Now Tanjong Pasir's light and Duiven's break clear. We run towards Pasir; we sheer towards Java. God! Watch the helm! I hear a monkey chatter in a Balinese tree. But the Lord is kind. We make it.

We came through in about fifteen minutes: the conditions were ideal, and the strait is well lit. I bore off to the eastward round Bali's northern shore, and I looked back over the decks of the little ship at the black sails and all the old tired grace of her, gently heeling to the breeze now as she ran through the night in the Java Sea, for the first time in her half-century of existence. I looked back over her a long time, and I felt rather fond of the little vessel.

Before midday we were anchored off Boeleleng, close up on the reef near the light structure. We had been forty-nine days from Table Bay, and had sailed six and a half thousand miles.

VI

Balinese Visit

IT IS an indifferent anchorage at Boeleleng. The great heights of Bali rise almost sheer from the deep ocean bed; there is a narrow coastal plain on the land, and on the sea a very much narrower reef. Immediately off the reef the sea is hundreds of fathoms deep; you have almost to go right up to the reef to find anchorage and, having found it, take good care that the stern of your vessel does not swing into water which at low tide will not float her. Beneath the light structure, close to the local slaughter-house, the anchorage is fair enough in the south-east monsoon; in the other season it would be untenable. But the weather there could not ever be very bad, or the row of flimsy little houses that advanced almost to the water's edge would never have been placed there. They were so small and so fragile that any high wind would knock them down, and one advancing sea would sweep them all into the water. But there they were, and I took encouragement from them. I saw later that the steamers of the K.P.M. that came in always approached the roads with caution, though they came regularly week after week, dragging an anchor on sixty fathoms of chain very slowly and fetching up sharp as soon as it touched. This it never did until they were close in. Some of the bigger steamers did not anchor at all.

Having now arrived, I wondered what manner of reception the vessel would have. I had not previously been in any Dutch East Indies port and had no special permissions or introductions of any sort. I had none of these things the whole voyage, and indeed never missed them. I knew that, not so very long ago, Holland's East Indian ports had been among the most churlish welcomers of strange vessels. I had some vague idea — or hope, rather — that Bali was still to some extent a preserve from odd wanderers and tourists and the like. If it were, I would most certainly respect the restriction, for I wished that voyage to take no part in the spoliation of the few unspoiled native races or islands which might still remain. But I soon found my fears and my hopes alike groundless. After due interval, an out-board motor-boat arrived bearing the honourable clerk to the harbour-master, and with him a document two yards square to be filled in duplicate with details of the ship in centimetres and metric tons, and all the firearms on board (and would I be responsible for them?), and all the ports the ship had visited with details of the sicknesses thereat, and this and that and all the rest of the laborious detail for which ships are now held tribute in all ports. When, after two hours, I had had time to fill in these things, the harbour-master himself arrived, a pleasant Eurasian with a demand for 100 guilders from the ship for coming to the anchorage. With him there came a man from the tourist bureau, distributing maps labelled "Tourist Routes in Bali," and wanting to book passengers for round trips of the island by motor-car. Lord! I thought; they *want* tourists — and I had thought this the last unspoiled island.

"We 'ave two sousand a mont'," exclaims the man from the bureau with great pride; and asks how many of my boys will come on the round trip of the island. It would be — it would be ... He figured briefly in a little black book and mentioned a sum that, even in gold guilders, was most reasonable. The dancing would be 10 guilders extra. We had heard of the Balinese dancing, no? It was very good. Yes, I had heard of the Balinese dancing and indeed it is exquisite. He went on joyously, mopping his brow, about the delights of a visit to the Forest of Sacred Nutmegs and the Elephant Cave and the Second Largest Banyan Tree in all the World. He was a nice young man; he had been a sailor. But my heart sank at his recital and I found myself, after he had departed, looking sadly upon the tourist maps and things. It is, I suppose, the cruising liners that have done it. There is scarcely a round-the-world cruise these days that does not include a stop at Bali. Ashore in the evening, I saw that Boeleleng was a Chinese town — Chinese, Arabic, Indian: a place of asphalt streets and shops and temples and motor-cars, the clean streets packed densely with Chinese general stores, on the floors of which Celestial babies crawled solemnly. Here and there were a row of Hindu haberdashers, or an open establishment sporting an ancient dentist's chair and a chart of decayed molars, coloured and very horrible. One lands in a barbed-wire enclosure leading by a gravel path between hotel advertisements to the customs station; beyond this sanded welcoming place wait the taxi-drivers, very quiet and courteous. And I hear, when I get back on board, that two female runners have been out from a local harlotry, seeking custom. The connoisseurs report that the place is not so bad.

But Boeleleng is a port; it is not Bali or Balinese. Sooner or later all ports become much the same, offering the same "attractions."

I stayed ten days at Bali, cleaning the ship over side and taking in water from a nearby lagoon, not drinking water (for we were not short of that) but fresh water good enough for other purposes. The boys swam and climbed coco-nut palms and went for day trips in the life-boats, rigged for sailing, to Temukhus and Koeboetambahan, looking in at the Sangsit temple on the way. There were visits to the Balinese theatre at Singaradja, where an interminable performance rambles on in a large tin-roofed shed surrounded by a native bazaar, and the lavishly dressed actors and actresses (except when they caterwaul) are attractive and good. In the bazaar one may find all kinds of refreshment, from little fried rice cakes to Balinese beer. The rice cakes are not bad, but the beer is like the stuff the natives turn out in the Rarotonga speakeasies at the Cook Islands. All the stalls are covered with old issues of American daily newspapers which the inhabitants fortunately cannot read. "POLICE QUIZ DOPI THE WOP IN LOVENEST SLAYING" shrieks the loud headline beneath a bunch of innocent bananas. Flanking the rice cakes is a half-torn page of the same newspaper from which the countenance of a horse-faced man, somewhat bilious, glares beside the sentiment "TO HELL WITH EUROPE." In such fashion, as we survey this animated and pleasant scene, are we reminded of the infinitely superior manner of our own living.

I made the round-the-island tour, though I had not set out on this voyage to make conducted tours by motor-car round tourist islands. There didn't seem any other way to see anything. I could not leave the ship for long; I could not, when we arrived anywhere, hand over control to a lieutenant and go ashore. I discovered very early that my ship was a grand one for making ocean voyages, but, run as I ran her, she was no vessel in which to visit civilized ports. I went on the bureau's conducted tour to Den Pasar in the south of the island, the royal tombs, the nutmeg forest, and all that — six of us in an open car going by way of Temukhus, Poepoean, and Tabanan, returning through Bangli and Kintamani. The route lay along good Dutch roads, past labelled villages and tired dogs: we went at speed, for it was a long way, and watched the inoffensive Balinese, walking gracefully along the dirt and grass by the road-side, scurry frightened out of the car's way. If I were a Balinese, I should be angry at that; some of them looked sullen, most indifferent, and many scared. This is their home — their beautiful and lovely home, wherein they have followed their quiet and cultured lives peacefully through many generations. They need neither the motor-cars nor the roads, and the gaping sightseers who cavort past bring them no benefit. They stand in need of little we whites can bring; they know how to live, and this is more than we do.

The motor-car hurries on. How the Balinese work! Tilling the rice fields, harvesting, sowing, planting, reaping: wherever there was place for a blade of crop to grow, it grew, and where it grew some Balinese toiled. Along the road they passed — men, women, and children — in endless procession, carrying, carrying, everything on their heads. Here and there among them, nearer the towns, Chinese coolies ambled heavy-laden, with that queer shuffling trot that must wear severely on their hearts; but the Balinese do most of the work in the country. In the village compounds some weave; some beat out silverware; some store rice; some are stonemasons in the temples; some repair the homes; some tend fighting-cocks that stand in their cages on the best grass of every hamlet. There are, as far as I can see, no drones. Once we saw a troup of children being dressed in their finery and prepared for a ceremonial dance in some temple: later we saw some of this dancing.

At length, with the mountains behind us, we arrived at the town of Den Pasar, full of Chinese stores, and came to a very good Dutch hotel, along the open corridors of which stood divers Balinese curios — cloth, carved wooden figures, dance masks, sarongs, *kris* — with no one exhorting us to buy them. Bali is still a long way from being wholly spoiled. For this the credit is partly Holland's, but must largely be attributed to the innate courtesy and gentleness of the Balinese. There are as yet few beggars and no "rackets." True, they have learned to levy small tribute for temple visitings and the like; it costs ten cents to see the royal tombs, ten cents for the sacred forest, and so on, which is fair enough. If you do not wish to see these things no one bothers you: but if you are buying native cloth it is as well to be sure it was not made in Germany. There are astute merchants who consider the European product superior to their own and will sell it to you as Balinese with no compunction. I left the gentle Balinese their cloth, for they need it more than we do; the indiscriminate and unintelligent scramble for "souvenirs" is a poor way to foster local arts. If there is sufficient demand for inferior products, they become more inferior. It has been so in Bali.

We arrived at the hotel and ate heartily; but I could not help still thinking of the incongruity of that asphalt road and the motor-cars while I gazed round me at the usual assemblage of globe-trotting Europeans one sees at such places, picking over their food — a stout woman sent something back, though it seemed grand fare to me — looking blasé, indolent, bored. Why do so many of these round-the-world wanderers wear discontent so heavily upon their features? Is it that what they see in the modes of others' living impresses them with the inadequacy of their own? I fear not. It seemed to me then, and the thought became conviction as the voyage progressed, that the sophisticated perambulating white, dissatisfied with himself but not knowing why, possessed of every advantage money can bring him, and only dimly aware there is much money will never buy, can be a more harmful and more dangerous influence among native races than the roar of guns. In Bali, as elsewhere, one hears faint whispers of some of these ambassadors of our culture — the homosexuals, the queer, the near-insane, the blatant and the foolish, though the worst of them do not come as tourists, but usually with the intention of staying. I tried, so far as I could, to make my ship an ambassador of intelligent friendship, but in this I found myself more or less alone — alone with the ship, and in the ship, too. My college boys had not been educated along these lines. I had with me certain young gentlemen who had come only to seek escape; who, soon finding that escape was not so easy as they had thought, became troublesome to me. The manner of their living, their rearing, and their education had so hedged them about and surrounded them with the armour of false standards and narrow ideas that they looked upon native life and everything else dimly, afar off, as it were through frosted glass. What benefit the voyage was to one or two of them I never could discover. They came with great expectation, but prepared to give nothing.

In the evening, after the big meal, there was a dance — a grand orchestra; a man who expressed grace and rhythm superbly with his hands; little girls sedate and lovely with their supple grace and quiet beauty, and two men in masks who harangued each other at great length but utterly beyond my comprehension. The performance was given on a concrete stage before the hotel, lit by a solitary electric light. In the best places in front of the stage were ranged the seats of the whites. They sat there, staring. Beyond a wired enclosure were the Balinese — hundreds of them, permitted to be there by the grace of the management. Interested and animated they watched, while the heaven-sent sat scowl-faced and overfed, and afterwards discussed the rhythm and meaning of it all. I strolled over to a native bazaar and drank some Balinese beer.

In the morning there was a dance in a temple courtyard close to Den Pasar. Here again the tourists sat and the Balinese stood. The curiously assorted crowd included now a score of Japanese students, photographing furiously with German cameras manufactured in their own country, and making copious notes in little books. They were dressed queerly in some kind of European fashion, and were led by a paunchy gentleman of their own race with a cheap cigar drooping from his gross mouth. Behind them stood the Balinese — not many, for most of them were at work. Here stood two gnarled and ancient road-workers with battered coolie hats, the veins in their legs swollen and their feet stunted and misshapen from all the years of plodding and of toil. Side-bearded, stalwart, grey, they stood watching the exquisite performance, oblivious of the whites who crowded them from their own temple yard, regardless of the motor-cars passing on the road.

Along the road, between the cars, the Balinese women walked, carrying, carrying, upright and graceful: in a corner of the temple yard, beneath a tree, a group of little children stood in awe near some of my cadets, watching the dancing with folded arms. A Chinaman went round and round, collecting tribute from the onlookers — seventy-five cents from those who sat, twenty-five cents from those who were standing. The Balinese, I was glad to see, were not called on to pay.

The beautiful music of the *gamelan* gong orchestra began again and I watched the dance — little girls, performing superbly in the temple's dust, barefoot and with wondrous grace. Gold-ornamented, richly clad, entranced by the deep symbolism of the music, they danced the age-old interpretations of the ancient legends of their race. There was beauty in their garments and lithesome grace in their every posture, every movement; their beauty and their grace belonged as much to nature as the clouds banked by the south monsoon on the mountains above them, as the swelling trees that rose from the warmth of their mother earth. They blended harmoniously with the temple scene: everything they did, every wave of delicate arm, tread of soft brown foot, posture of graceful body, was fraught with meaning. Much of it was lost on me, for I was not conversant with their legends, but I knew that here was the purest form of art. Here were art and beauty hand in hand with life.

Beside the road telephone wires hummed, and going back, the little girls marching home were covered with the motors' dust and did not seem to mind. Poor Bali! I still saw the expression on the road-workers' rapt faces as they stood there watching with their *machetes*, mud-stained, protruding from their rough belts — they and all the Balinese, and the blasé whites looking upon a scene of life and legend which was nothing to them but another change of scene upon the shallow round of a conducted world excursion. Poor Bali! Not spoiled yet but soon to be, as every other fair spot upon God's earth has been. Bali, having so much to lose, will suffer more greatly — more greatly even than Hawaii, Samoa, and Tahiti. I wish the Hollanders, a shrewd and intelligent race, would close Bali to all sightseeing and neurotic whites.

We went on to the Forest of the Sacred Nutmeg Trees and the Holy Monkeys — the man from the tourist bureau had said there were 2,000; I counted 20 — and saw the mildewed temple deep in the shade; and afterwards, the second largest banyan tree in all the earth. Who measures these banyan trees? This one in Bali covered a large field. Here were some Balinese exercising their fighting-cocks which the tourists induced them to fight, with kris-like spurs three inches long. In a few seconds, a white cock lay in the dust, heavily bleeding, and a black cock crowed weakly, also wounded. We did not see much of the tree. Then to other scenes, through villages with their names hung across the road for the tourists to read, every village full of temples and of life, and all the roads filled with the burden-bearers, bare-breasted women walking erect and graceful. These women often turned away as the car passed, tired a little, maybe, of arrogant white eyes.

At Boeleleng and Den Pasar the road-side merchants hopefully offered large selections of photographs of their women-folk half-naked and unashamed. Into a little café at Den Pasar came a guide of sorts, speaking some English, inquiring whether we were interested in "nice girls 'ores"?

We crossed the mountains in the rain, and ate ravenously in the rest-house at Kintamani, returning to

Boeleleng in the evening — a good trip. I did not look at the Elephants' Cave and did not find the Royal Tombs trip very enthralling; but, as such things go, the trip had been a splendid one and it was rich in experience. I brought back with me abiding impressions of Bali's intense fertility; of stone figures and temple gates and grassed wayside shrines; of terraced fields and the loveliness of scene into which the grace of the Balinese fits so well; and villages, villages, villages, with grand vistas of mountains and valleys and the sea. Here is a lovely island inhabited by a lovely, quiet, and cultured people. I wish I had had the time to stay a while and learn from them. But I had to sail. I had to go on. I had too many people with me, too large a ship, to think of staying anywhere before the completion of the voyage. The man from the tourist bureau, learning that I was going, came out to express his great regret that I could not stay in port until the twelfth, when there was to be a very fine cremation. So does the tourist business warp our minds, until we think every pious act and ritual of a conquered folk a poppy show to assuage our insatiable lust for entertainment.

I sailed. I had no one to be cremated. On the morning of the 10th of July, 1935, I weighed anchor and, with the breeze very quiet off the land, canted her round and stood out to sea under a full suit of sail. It was clear, for once: the Java hills were exposed and the dim outlines of Lombok's great crater could be seen: the sky was cloudless, and we had to wait until the escaping monsoon rushed out from Bali Strait to have a breeze. I then stood slowly towards Sapudi Island and the strait that divides that place from Madura; and a trio of the older boys came aft, who now found that they had brought with them a souvenir from Bali they did not want.

I liked Bali. I was glad I went there. It is worth visiting even though it is well upon the road towards becoming a kind of Dutch Hawaii. I came almost to like Boeleleng, in the end — Boeleleng the port where sometimes four steamers called in a day, all loading pigs made up in cane baskets, and discharging oil and general cargoes for the coolies to carry out of the barges and across the beach. The coolies toil almost savagely to land their burdens, wading out waist-deep and ashore again, carrying petrol in five-gallon cans, two at a time, and huge crates of merchandise. In the background, beneath a wide verandah, sit the little Balinese wives, working, working, shaking the big baskets of coffee-beans, sorting them by hand day-long, week-long, month-long, for they have no Sundays; erect graceful little figures in quietly coloured coats and loose sarongs. They are a merry gang who work here, though the pay is small, and as they pad softly home in the evenings, they laugh joyously together — in the evenings, with the Arabs fishing from the town's small pier, and the bearded merchants from Bombay emerging from meditation at their mosques. Then all the tiny native stalls are open, with the girls seated by their wares beneath the glare of an oil lamp, always turned up too high; and the happy Balinese, their day's work done, wash in the streams. Once I saw a woman washing a new-born babe, a tiny mite come to a pleasant world, that put out its little hands to grasp the water.

In the mornings, very early, the outriggers come from the sea, sailing swiftly in with their fish; at the market the villagers meet to bargain and to discourse. Here food is good and not expensive, and native tobacco tied up in palm leaves may be bought very cheaply. Fruits are plentiful and the produce of the land is diverse and excellent. Here a million people live and there is food for all. Beyond the town of Singaradja, the high mountains rise, the good mountains that stop the monsoon's clouds and bring down rain for the fields. Bali was well organized by Nature and the Balinese long, long before it was taken by the soldiers of the Dutch — soldiers who were driven fiercely off more than once before they were finally successful. The island is quiet now and needs no patrolling.

The Dutch rule, based as it is, as far as possible, upon non-interference with native life and customs, works very well: they have brought hospitals, and some schools — not too many schools, for the Dutch with their solid sense saw long ago that book learning is of little use to natives. They have brought roads, motor-buses: they have brought the white man and they have brought tourists. If they take their profit from the island, they also contribute; in any comparison of the white-controlled islands the Dutch will stand up very well.

I leave with the stirring strains of the Gamelan Gong in my ears, and see again the infinite grace of the small girls dancing. I hope to God no fool is ever permitted to take them away for a season in Hollywood or on Broadway.

I sailed through Sapudi Strait by night on my way to Singapore to store and to clean the ship's bottom for the passage to Australia. From Sapudi I went on across the Java Sea past Bawean towards Carimata Strait between the south of Borneo and Billiton Island, and from there stood directly from the Serutu light towards the Strait of Singapore. I should have liked to go to the Kangean Islands and the Tambelans, but there was not time.

The run from Bali to Singapore was the quietest and most enjoyable piece of sailing of the whole voyage. Day after day the south-east monsoon blew us quietly along, with beautiful dawns and the whole long days tranquil and superb. It was hazy and it was hot, but these things did not matter. We rigged up awnings fore and aft and set the full suit of studding sails on the fore to aid her speed. The little ship sailed beautifully in light winds; day after day she wandered on upright and graceful as a Balinese woman walking, with the tiny flying-fish flitting before us and porpoises leaping at the bow. One day I put out a boat to look at her, the monsoon being more than ordinarily quiet. She was picturesque and beautiful under her big white sails, with the studding sails making her seem an apparition from the remote past, wandering in this sea, first opened by her ancestors hundreds of years before. For all we saw, we might ourselves be living in those days, for day after day showed no ships, no fishing boats, no junks. Sometimes the steamers came, altering their courses to pass close by and dip their ensigns. It is a long time since a full-rigged ship wandered there with single tops'ls and stuns'ls set — wandered there, or anywhere.

We sailed nine days and crossed the Line again, and then picked up the Horsburgh and stood onwards through Singapore Strait towards Singapore. But in the night between the Horsburgh and the Lima Islands, with the monsoon light, the rushing tide came down suddenly, setting us swiftly towards the reefs of the Lima Islands. There was barely time to get an anchor over, fetching up all standing, while the muddy water, racing past, held us steadily at our anchor under all sail. When the day came, I saw that we were almost surrounded by islands, but the tide changed, and it was easy enough then to weigh anchor and get out. We stood on towards the Singapore Roads, and arrived there that afternoon, coming to anchor in the examination area beside a Blue Funnel liner. A coloured gentleman came out from the office of the harbour-master to clear us and tell us to go to another anchorage, but he did not bring our mail. This had been addressed, as in all British ports, in the harbour-master's care: at all other ports I was gladly shown this courtesy. But in Singapore there is no harbour-master, the title of the all-highest occupying this exalted post being the Master Attendant S.S., and the Master Attendant S.S. had had our mail returned to the post office. I had previously associated the title of Attendant with public works even more necessary to our well being than are harbours; what a Master Attendant was I did not know. At any rate, he did not consider himself a mere harbour-master.

I shifted the ship to the berth the dark one pointed out,

in among a number of laid-up steamers off the mole, and hurried to the post office, fearing that five months' mail might have been returned to the senders. It had not been, fortunately, but it was about to be. Letters are important when one has been out of touch so long, and there were some hundreds of them for the vessel.

I dry-docked at Keppel Harbour and stayed at Singapore ten days, during which I took in six months' stores. These proved to be the best stores bought during the voyage. I had them from a native firm which treated me fairly. At least as far as this firm was concerned, I found Singapore free of the usual ship-chandlery sharp practices. I gave out lists of my requirements to the firms which sent representatives on board and chose the one giving me the best prices, and I never had cause to regret this. I had tried to do this in other ports, but it had not got me very far, mainly because the chandlers' runners, or the chandlers themselves, worked together. I also spent a considerable sum on the engine for, though we had made our ocean voyages very well, I knew we were about to embark on a totally different kind of sailing, a kind of which I knew little or nothing, but in which the assistance of the engine was almost essential. I was setting out from Singapore to sail north-about to Sydney in the wrong monsoon, and this was going to be difficult.

And Singapore? It is a great port, and an interesting commercial centre. It is a Far Eastern cross-roads of which much has been written. I found its streets in the business section well filled with English people either very pale or very red, most of whom looked as if they usually lived in Golder's Green; the streets in the native sections were full of God knows what. There were hotels, tram-cars, business houses, and a very good hospital; you could buy a good Chinese meal for a few cents, cooked while you waited in the street. The ship and I made some splendid friends at the Pilots' Association and the Merchant Service Guild. I had the compass readjusted; shipped two young people to come with us to Sydney (and they fitted in very well), and departed from Singapore Roads a little before midnight on the last day of July, to be out of touch with civilization until we reached Sydney.

▲ The ship that became the *Joseph Conrad* – the Danish training ship *Georg Stage* in Copenhagen c.1900, with cadets aboard. Note the leadsmen standing in the chains.

◄ The author, Master of the *Joseph Conrad*.

▶ The view forward from the poop. Hands to the halliards.

◀ *Haul!*

▶ Sailmaker Karl Sperling (lower left) at work.

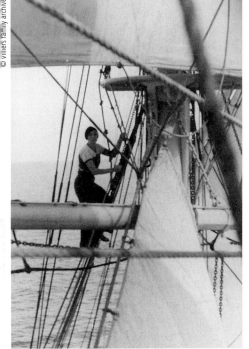

▲ Standing, left to right, Second Mate Hans Pedersen, Boatswain Horst de Wolff, and Sailmaker Karl Sperling. Seated, Fritz Egerton, to whom Alan Villiers dedicated the original edition of this book, and who, with his wife Kay, was aboard for the passage from Copenhagen.

◄ Kay Egerton aloft.

► Studding sail set to make the most of a following wind.

▲ Getting a view from the mizzen shrouds.

▲
The mainsail with the clews hauled up.

▶
The author's friend, Master Mariner Godfrey Wicksteed (in the centre of the boat in nautical cap), leaves the *Joseph Conrad* after completing the North Sea passage and handing over command. Captain Wicksteed was highly regarded as an expert on tall ships and a rigging advisor for the *Cutty Sark*. He died in 1997 at the age of 98. Nearest the bow of the boat, also wearing a cap, is Bruce Rogers, who carved the *Conrad*'s figurehead.

VII

Through the Sulu Sea

I DID not sail from Singapore by night from choice but because the tide served then; I had to obtain special permission endorsed on my clearance to move from the anchorage after nightfall. The tide was good and the wind better, and we were past the Horsburgh long before sunrise. Taking my departure from there I headed across the China Sea with a fresh monsoon, steering towards the coast of Borneo by way of Subi Kechil, passing north of the light and continuing then toward Sirik and Miri, Borneo oil-tank port, and so passing in a general north-easterly direction up the coast of Borneo outside the coastal banks, making my landfall on the light at Balabac Island. My friends the pilots in Singapore had sent me to the Superintendent of the Straits Steamships Line there for advice on the best manner of accomplishing this section of the voyage, and the passage of the Sulu Sea. I found this gentleman and his captains most helpful, and indeed should have been at a loss to know how best to put these difficult seas behind me had I been without their excellent advice. The volume of Admiralty Sailing Directions known as *Ocean Passages for the World*, a large and concise work containing complete directions for all kinds of vessels going from anywhere to everywhere else, which had hitherto been my stand-by in planning the voyage, was not of much use on this occasion, bluntly offering the opinion that the only way for a square-rigged ship to sail from Singapore to Sydney in the south-east monsoon was to get away from those waters entirely and then go south-about round Australia, making her longitude in the west winds.

This, too, was the sensible way to go, but I did not wish to go to Sydney except to refresh the crew and take in stores. I wanted to see some islands, and the only way to do that was to go north-about. Perusal of the excellent wind and weather charts published by the United States Hydrographic Office gave me scant encouragement; it looked as if the whole long way from the Sea of Celebes to beyond the Solomons was one endless stretch of doldrums — "thirty-five per cent. of calm," I read dubiously in the weather roses over most of this part of the Pacific Ocean. Continued calm is about the worst enemy a sailing-ship can face; but I hoped that I might somehow negotiate the Sulu Sea (where the monsoon would be ahead) and find, perhaps, the wind more southerly than south-west in the Sea of Celebes. This would be fair; I could then make my way towards the Pacific, south of Mindanao, and find the east-going counter-equatorial — if I could, of course.

I was well aware that the route I chose presented many difficulties; I knew very well that Abel Tasman showed good sense when he sailed southwards to reach the unknown east on his great voyage centuries before, the voyage that led to his discovery of Tasmania and New Zealand. These being no spice islands, did not make him popular. As far as I knew, no circumnavigator had ever gone the way I now intended; they had without exception come from the east to the west across the whole Pacific or, if they had gone eastwards, had passed to the south of Australia. But I had the engine now. At least, I hoped I had the engine. The thing had been overhauled as well as possible at Singapore. It did work. Engineless vessels are fine for the open sea, but for such waters as those of the Eastern Archipelago and the South Seas, to be without power — ample power — is to be severely handicapped. With much of the way lying through belts of calm and doldrum conditions, through reef-infested waters filled with incalculable sets, tides, drifts and currents where the lead is no guide and the surveys are too often incomplete and somewhat vague, where a ship may one minute be bowling along with a good breeze, and the next find herself pounding upon a coral rock suddenly thrust up in the sea without any warning, and where, even now, small islands may still be discovered — in such waters as these, even the full-powered vessel must navigate with caution though she has control of her progress at all times. How then, would it be with me? If the engine worked splendidly — which I gravely doubted — I had fuel enough for four days; the passage, like as not, would take four months. More than that, indeed, if I stayed at many islands.

Well, there I was, and I had further to remember that I should have the west-setting equatorial current strongly against me, its influence spreading over an area of the North Pacific, hundreds of mile wide on both sides of its counter-current. It had been my invariable experience, not only in this ship, that it is always much easier to find adverse currents than those in your favour, and I looked forward with no pleasure to the prospect of some long acquaintance with the Pacific equatorial. But it had always been my policy not to be unduly dismayed by an array of circumstances against me: what of these natural difficulties? I had a good ship, a good crew. She had been dry-docked in Singapore and was thoroughly clean. Indeed I had been more worried in Singapore than I should ever be by the sea and the difficulty of ocean voyages; it had been expensive there without the unforeseen charges of the college boy's hospital and his fare home. I had also found it necessary to discharge one of the officers, for the safety of the ship; him also I had to repatriate, and one does not send human beings from Singapore to New York and Europe for eighteen-pence. What with the renewal of insurance and so forth my expenses there amounted to almost £1,000. I had left the place with barely £100 and that was all I had. The ship was all there was on earth to my name — the ship and a few books. Well, we were stored for six months: I should not miss civilization, and I did not mind a hunt a month long for the elusive counter-equatorial; to work out through the Sulu Sea would cost me nothing save anxiety. Such problems as I now faced were under God and no man would bill me for them. The storms and the navigational difficulties of that ocean voyage, though I came near to losing the ship more than once, never brought me any depression of spirit or undue mental stress. It was the man-made haggard problems of the land that worried me and gave me nightmares.

But now the sun shone, and we sailed onwards in the China Sea. The monsoon, for the time being, blew steadily in the high sails; and the daily routine of the ship at sea was peacefully re-established. At first we made good speed, but then the wind fell light and we sailed along upright and silent through the China Sea with the coast of Borneo unseen but close. The greenish-blue water was littered with tree trunks and logs and forest jetsam of every description. We saw sea-snakes; oil-tankers bound to and from Miri passed us by; we did not see Borneo. I noticed on the chart one day a place called Niah, said by the *Pilot* to be the headquarters of the edible birds' nest industry. It was a pity to pass this by when we were so close; I had always wanted to eat a bird's nest, but those I had seen until then seemed scarcely suitable for the purpose. Here we were, a few miles from a town of the right kind, and we had to pass by. I shall have to go back round the world again, I fear, to look in at all the good places I learned of this voyage — learned of, but did not see.

We saw rain squalls and waterspouts, which I gave a wide berth, and then it was calm. A little swallow flew from the shore into the saloon, and drank ravenously. I put the dinghy out and pulled round to look at all the trees and things floating in the water, many of them big enough to inconvenience a ship. I found them to be mainly crabinfested logs probably swept by the rain down the Borneo rivers. We caught some crabs and saw many tropic fish flitting round the sunken roots. These, however, we could not catch. We were ten days from Singapore to within sight of Balabac Island. I had not used the engine, thinking to conserve the fuel; I did not want to use it except as a last extremity or for going into small harbours in reef-surrounded islands. It was calm when we saw the land, and we lolled round all day with the pitch bubbling in the seams beneath the sun in spite of the awnings. A Swedish motor-ship, bound probably from Zamboanga, came over to ask us, by flags, if we needed anything, and being assured that we did not, circled once round us, and dipped her flag. Her name, I read, was *Peiping*. The Finnish carpenter was very excited and shouted across in Swedish.

We had had a curious-looking steamer in sight all day; I was convinced she was a derelict though at first glance she appeared to be in commission. She remained in the same place; she was low in the water — too low; she made no smoke and I saw, as a gentle evening breeze brought us closer, that she was gutted and that the afterdeck was awash. Late in the evening, with the clouds banked low over Borneo and all the western sky a flare of brilliant colouring, I dropped a kedge on a reef not far from the Balabac light quite close to the derelict, which I now perceived to be aground. We could not get any farther with that breeze, and I had always wanted to board a derelict. It was the night of the full moon for the month of August. I put out the dinghy at once and rowed over, with Hilgard, and saw that the derelict was the gutted hull of the Japanese tramp-steamer K—— *Maru*, a long old vessel, narrow and deep, with all her holds full of water and the after well-deck all slime where every rising tide had washed. Giant crabs ran at our approach as if they had been long accustomed to being undisturbed. We boarded her, using care, and passed the dinghy on its painter under the rusted stern. Even in the moonlight one could see the reef below the surface upon which the deep-loaded tramp, almost upright, stood: for'ard her two anchors hastily let go, with the chain up-and-down and still slack, told of flurried seamanship after she took the ground. She needed no anchoring; she was there to stay. She had been there two years or more, by the look of her. Here and there her steel decks were rotted through and the ironwork of the deck-houses crumbled to the touch. In the moonlight the shapes of fishes were dimly to be seen in the holds. She was full of queer, sad noises, like a lonely beach with a quiet sea breaking: the crabs ran and the slime squelched and the sea broke over her gently aft as if the very water were sorry for her fate, sad to see a big steamship piled up here where the beams of the lighthouse shone on her bridge. Everything of value was long since gone. She was gutted fore and aft; first by some skilled salvage gang — you could see that — and then, I suppose, by the first passer-by. But I had not come on a marauding excursion; I was interested in the ship and not her fittings. I paused a while on the crazy remnants of the once-proud bridge and stood there, ruminating upon the futility of ships without water under them and the finality of getting on a Sulu reef and I looked across at the riding lights of my little vessel lying silent and still beneath the Borneo sky, and hoped I should never leave her in a like predicament. Who knows? We do our best. I very nearly left her worse off than that, one day. But that was a long time afterwards, and it was not in the Sulu Sea.

In the morning, still calm, some of the boys pulled over to the derelict to catch fish (or try to) and to swim in the holds. The forehold was the best. The salvage people had got most of her coal cargo out of there; you could dive into the lower hold from the 'tween-decks and have a good time. It made an excellent sharkproof enclosure.

Later a faint air came, and I hove up the kedge and went on. We had left the yards hoisted and the sails clewed up to them and not fast, that they might be set quickly; and under all sail I steered now to pass into the Sulu Sea by the south of Balabac Island, meaning to go onwards through the Nasubata Channel as the opportunity came. I had to be very careful round those parts; I was following the advice of my friends in Singapore, and found it good.

I had not got very far before the breeze died and the daylight ended, and it was impossible to proceed further or to look for the Nasubata Channel. So I nosed in cautiously towards Dalawan Bay, on Balabac, to get the anchor down and wait for better conditions: Dalawan Bay offered the best anchorage in that neighbourhood. It was small and protected by two horns of reef that contracted the narrow entrance; it was night then and I could not see. I anchored as soon as I had soundings, somewhere off the mouth of the Bay, and put the dinghy over to pull round, sounding and examining the anchorage as was my custom. This done (I could have gone a bit closer in, but the darkness is deceptive for conning ships even in well lit waters), we pulled into the bay and landed on a beach. The moon broke through now: the beach, so far as we could see, was untrodden. Round the curving head of the bay reached a shelf of sand holding back the nearby jungle in the moonlight; here and there the jungle, thicker than elsewhere, came almost to the water's edge. Giant trees, festooned with creepers that hung from them like ropes, stood within twenty feet of the water. All the jungle hummed with sound so that the very earth there seemed to be alive. Queer creatures moved with a sinister rustle of protesting leaves — they were probably cows — and we held our breath. The night air stirred quietly, and the sea coming there to wash the sand lapped at the beach silently as if it were afraid — afraid of the darkness and the dank tangle of the woods. The jungle was so thick we could not penetrate it. We did not try much there by night; it was a weird place. There were certainly snakes about, if nothing else, though

135

they would have been more afraid of us than we of them.

In the morning it was still calm; we could not go on. The sets are said to be strong in the Nasubata Channel and I did not want to take unnecessary risks. I gave the boys leave to explore the shores of the bay, to stretch their legs and sail in the life-boat a little, to wash in the fresh water streams and get some exercise. At the head of the bay (which the daylight showed to be a very good one) we found a small stream with water enough to take the dinghy a good distance inland; we went up this with the matted trees of the jungle meeting over our heads most of the way. Here and there in the back-waters the dinghy grounded; we did not get very far. One of the boys shot a snake, a nasty looking thing that was lying in a tree. It writhed a little and fell into the water. Later on by the side of the stream, when we could get no farther by water — we had come perhaps two miles — we found a jungle trail that led to a small clearing where some natives had made a garden, and there was a small house, a primitive place standing on stilts in the middle of the clearing. There were no people here. At the stream's entrance we saw three natives working on the cane floor of a new hut. One of them spoke a little English which he said he had been taught at the American school in the town of Balabac; the others had a few Spanish words. They looked rather fierce and somewhat afraid, as if they thought us tax collectors come to levy tribute. They were dressed in cotton pants and singlets bought in the Chinese store at Balabac.

On the other side of the bay we found an extensive clearing where a Manila man, who felled timber there for a company in New York, had his home, his cattle, his hogs, and his coco-nut grove. He had been in the American Navy at one time and spoke fluent English. Round the walls of his small home I saw large notices in Spanish exhorting all and sundry to vote for Somebody as President of the Philippines. (It was then approaching the time for independence.) He chatted pleasantly and seemed pleased to see us, but he warned us to be careful on the beach, and swimming. A few days earlier, one of his timber-cutters had been seen sitting on the beach, and when they came back he was not there — only his hat and a piece of one leg. They saw a huge alligator slinking away beneath the water. Life was, he said, quiet enough round those parts, though he brought out his *bolo*, a heavy, brutal knife beaten from the native steel, to show us. It was no plaything. Sometimes the Japanese came poaching, he said; they seemed to think they could do what they liked. They came ashore and cut down some of his coco-nut trees. If he had been there it would have been different, but he had been away. He picked up his *bolo* and his eyes glared. Some of the armed constabulary from Balabac had later apprehended the Japanese, but they continued merrily on their way with the constables, putting them ashore at some place on Palawan, and keeping their arms. And there were, he went on, mighty bad people at Kagayan and in the Sulu Archipelago. Were we going there?

In the midst of this pleasant and instructive day a small and undistinguished coasting vessel arrived to load timber for Manila. Once a year she came, and she had to choose this day. She came almost alongside us and a stout greasy individual shouted to ask if we were in distress? We were not, we said, and noticed his disappointment. Then, had we permission to visit these Philippines? Were we cleared inwards from a port of entry, with pratique and rubber stamps, and all that kind of thing? We were not. We were but lately come from Singapore and were bound through the Sulu Sea towards the North Pacific and Australia: we were not visiting the Philippines. That had been no part of my intentions. We were anchored off Dalawan Bay awaiting a fair wind; the Sailing Directions advise just such a course under the conditions then prevailing.

The greasy one seemed not to realize we were a sailing-ship: we were inside the territorial limits (it would be hard to go through the Sulu Sea and stay outside them; and there is no anchorage at Dalawan off the Balabac shelf), and were therefore a highly suspicious vessel, probably piratical and, at the very least, smuggling. He was desolated, of course, at the thought of causing trouble to a gentleman of his own good calling, but he felt it was his unpleasant duty to summon a gunboat from Manila. He had tried already to rouse the constabulary at Balabac. Unfortunately the day appeared to be a public holiday and there was no one there. Well, well, well. I knew, of course, that Dalawan Bay was scarcely a port of entry. I did not expect to find anybody there, or any commerce. If sailing-ships, before making such contacts with the unwanted land as the nature of their voyagings forces upon them, must always first seek the fool permits of some port of entry, then the making of such a passage as I then had before me would be impossible. The nearest port of entry was Holo in Sulu, several hundred miles away. If I could have gone there I would not have anchored. And to be taken for a smuggler! It was humorous. What was I smuggling? I asked this strange bird, since I had not the vaguest idea what might be smuggled into that lonely island. Dry goods, he said — dry goods and bad people. Dry goods! There was poor market for haberdashery round there, as far as I could see. Whence came the bad people? From Banguey, he said, Banguey and North Borneo. Bad braves from these ignoble territories were being smuggled into Palawan and Balabac; his government had told him to be on the lookout for them. They were knifers, butchers, who slew the inoffensive residents and took their fields. I made a mental note to try to go to Banguey some day. Probably, he went on, I had some hundreds on board. Well, he could come and look. But, instead, he began calling with his wireless, getting busy to Manila first, urgently imploring the authorities there, I gathered, to despatch a gunboat or two to apprehend this highly suspicious and dangerous vessel on their coasts.

I laughed at him, but he was serious enough, though before the day was out he was convinced that, after all, we were nothing but a peaceful sailing-ship bound harmlessly round the world, anchored there for lack of a better place to await a wind. I gave him a note explaining my presence on the coast for the Chief of the Constabulary at Balabac, and with his timber on board he departed. But I think he was a very disappointed man, and he still expected that a gunboat would be sent to apprehend me.

Dalawan Bay was a very fine place, apart from the meeting with the suspicious one; but I saw there little outlet for the dry-goods business and less attraction for bad people. About all they would get, if they ever came, would be some coco-nuts and a few cows. We were within 200 miles of Dalawan Bay for the next ten days but saw never as much as the smoke of a gunboat — not a gunboat, not a traveller in haberdashery, not a cut-throat from Banguey, or anything else in the least exciting or unusual.

The Sulu Sea is an interesting stretch of water where the wind blows two ways at once and more debris floats than comes down before a Mississippi flood; where the tides turn corners and swing round curves without either order or reason. It is bounded in the north and north-east by the southern Philippine Islands — Mindoro, Panay, Negros, Mindanao; in the west by Palawan and Balabac; in the south by Borneo; and in the east by the Sulu Archipelago. It is indeed hemmed in by land, and being itself a headstrong and petulant place, this appears to annoy it. At any rate, it does its best to get out through all the channels open to it, and its tides, its sets, its currents, and its streams are diverse, unsteady, and incalculable. Round all its edges it abounds with reefs, and the way out is a maze. It is lit, but not very well. The sun glares savagely upon it all the year round; the great Borneo rivers give it their rain. No ships which can help it go there; but it is used by shipping quite considerably. Sandakan, Zamboanga, Ilo Ilo, and Cebu are best reached that way, and the main route from the south to Manila is through the Sulu Sea. A good deal of it has not been properly surveyed and the mariner is advised to proceed with the utmost caution. "Navigation in all these waters ... requires caution," says the *Pilot*, referring to the East Indies in general, "on account of irregular and uncertain currents and the prevalence of coral formations which may have escaped detection even in recent detailed surveys, and of which the lead very often can give no warning." Typhoons sometimes sweep across the Sulu Sea's northern edge.

In this pleasant neighbourhood we spent ten days making 200 miles. I would have used the engine on many occasions in that exasperating period, if I could: but it would not work. We began well enough, getting through the Nasubata Channel without much difficulty, though here we witnessed the peculiar phenomenon of two different winds meeting and blowing, for a while, side by side. We were in both of them, at different times, and also in the calm patch between. In each we could see the sea running before the other, in exactly the opposite direction; here it would have been possible to witness the extraordinary sight of two vessels passing each other, bound in opposite directions, each with her yards squared to a fair wind. I had often heard of this but had been disinclined to believe in it. In the Sulu Sea it would have been quite possible.

The reefs were thick at that end of the Sea, and I navigated cautiously towards Kagayan Sulu, using bearings from Balabac and Banguey Peaks so long as the visibility permitted (remembering to view the result with caution as the day advanced, for mirage plays queer tricks here. Each hour I used Marque St. Hilaire position lines and soundings to check the bearings). As night came down, I wondered whether to stand on, the wind being good then, or to lie until daylight to the kedge. I stood on, but it was an anxious night. There is no light on Kagayan Sulu and I must have come close that night to numerous reefs. If any of them had touched my ship — why, I should have stayed there, with the K—— Maru. I was glad to see Kagayan Sulu right where it ought to be, in the morning.

It was hot then, and flukey and calm, and we had that place in sight three days. But I did not mind that over-much, for once safely there, the worst of the reefs were behind me. We saw the islets Kinapusan, Pomelikan, Mandah, and Muligi, but I did not head towards any of these though Muligi looked attractive. Kagayan has no port of entry, and I had no need to go there. So I beat and drifted about to catspaw doldrum airs, tacking when the ship had headway enough and wearing when she had not, not getting anywhere much for all my pains, dribbling and drifting day after day through tide rips and light overfalls, with long lines of floating logs and trees and old coco-nuts and all the jungle debris floating by, and once half of a native fence on a small piece of tangled earth that must have come down before the flood of some mighty stream. We drifted within three miles of a tiny islet marked on the chart as Mambahenauhan. It was calm, and I put out the dinghy and pulled over to discover, if I could, why so small a place had so long a name. I found the place a small piece of brown rock, almost sheer, steep-to, with a narrow ledge-like shelf on which it was possible to land.

Tiny tropic fish swam in pools between the rocks, and crabs ran, and overhead the disturbed sea birds wheeled and cried. The top of the rock was accessible in one place but thick with vegetation and thorns. I saw a fireplace of stones where the natives had been cooking. While we were there, with the evening coming down, a small boat from Kagayan came up to the islet. It was a prau from Kagayan to Holo with copra, thirty feet long and carrying eleven hands all told, an uncertain number of whom were passengers. The vessel, I noticed, carried several well-kept fowls which had been trained to perch with their after parts outboard — a very useful accomplishment for sea-going poultry in any small craft; but I hope they went 'bout ship when they laid their eggs. This they doubtless had been trained to do, and they would not drop their eggs in the sea. Some stalwart young fellows landed from the prau, with fish-spears, and soon had a string of fish and several crabs for their supper. One of them was chewing gum, and they both had a little English. I went back to the ship, and we dribbled on.

Chart of the Sulu Sea, showing the track of the *Joseph Conrad*.

We came one night within sight of a light off the coast of Borneo — Taganak, outside Sandakan — and I went round to keep away from the coral patches in that neighbourhood. We beat there day after day, though in truth not beating half as much as just putting the ship about to changing airs; there was scant progress in such sailing. But what could be done? The wind, if there was a wind, kept its general direction from the south-west. (It was the south-west monsoon.) If it had been strong we could have beat out. But it was just loafing. The days were hot and enervating. Once, after a particularly trying twenty-four hours, the noon position showed that we had drifted back some fifteen miles. But I was not unduly worried over that. There was no point in being worried; it was dispiriting, of course, but the only thing to do was to keep on. I had been studying the *Pilots* and the charts for those parts and had come across a place called Balimbing in Tawi Tawi, in the Sulu Archipelago, labelled on the Admiralty chart in warning letters, "Pirates." What, pirates? I had to go in there. "The little isles that surround Tawi Tawi are sparsely inhabited and have generally been regarded as refuges for pirates," says the *Eastern Archipelago Pilot*, Volume 1. It sounded good. I was not going to pass by a place like that, gunboats or no gunboats. I saw there was a constabulary station at Bongao, the chief town of Tawi Tawi; I would pay my respects to the Chief there and explain to him my business — or rather, my lack of business. It has invariably been my experience that people in real charge of anything are seldom infected by the fool airs and the stupid ideas of their underlings or their unofficial assistants. I would go to Tawi Tawi: though an attractive place named Ompapui, where wild pigs abound, also sounded, rather well. We could have done with a few pigs, and I should have liked to see Ompapui.

It was all very well my reading of the pirates (probably long dead) and deciding to go to this place and to that: we could go nowhere without wind. It was calm now and stayed so, and more hot and humid than ever. It rained every day; when it was not raining the sun burned fiercely. There were nights when the calms were more still than any I had previously known, even on the Pacific Line, with all the sky so dead that the very twinkle had gone from the stars, and the sea was flatter than Bricett pond, and all the ship was still — motionless, not even gently lifting with that slow movement so seldom absent from the sea: all quietened, with the sails blackened shapes hanging dead from the yards, and not a block creaking. It was a calm unnatural, foreboding, almost frightening. The helmsmen softly spoke the unsteered course to their somnolent reliefs: the lookout on the focs'l head stood in silence in the same spot, not moving. The red and green sidelights threw long reflections in the dull water to stay where they were thrown, not rippling, not shimmering. The second mate on watch hung over the rail aft as if he had been built there with the ship, and was as incapable of movement without wind as she was. Calms such as this, when all the tiniest ripplings of the sea have gone, and with them even the quiet gurglings at cutwater and stern, are unusual outside a tropic lagoon.

In the course of time we made some progress. Eight days after leaving Dalawan Bay, the north-eastern end of Borneo was in sight at daybreak; the setting sun showed us exactly the same sky-line. Tree trunks, coco-nuts, jellyfish, and tide rips drifted by, and it was as hot as Hades. The navigation lesson in the afternoon was much interrupted by my looking for the Pearl Bank, and several times mistaking mirages for it, for a line of floating coco-nuts can look astonishingly like a reef when your eye is near the water-level.

But we passed all the banks and all the reefs and, a week out from Kagayan Sulu, had come at last within sight of Tawi Tawi. Now, for once, the second mate was able to induce the machinery to work — it was calm — and I went into the anchorage of Chongos Bay between Papabag Island and Sanga Sanga.

It was evening when we came to anchor behind an island of coco-nut groves with a native village on stilts close by, and Bongao Peak, bluff and wooded and worn, holding up the rain-clouds of the south-west monsoon. I looked about me for the pirates of Balimbing but saw none, no gunboats, or port officials, or visitors of any kind. I was mighty tired from that trying passage of the Sulu Sea, and turned in for a night's good rest, leaving a double watch on deck just as a precaution.

VIII

The Pirates of Balimbing

IN THE morning no officials came near the vessel, nor anyone else, save a native selling fish (I bought enough for two feeds for all hands for an old pyjama coat), and a pompous-jowled native in blue silk pants trying to sell jewelled *kris*. In the afternoon, I went in myself to report the ship's arrival to the commandant at Bongao. We were anchored close to Bongao though out of sight; there was a clear channel through between Papabag and Sanga Sanga. Bongao itself I found to be a pleasant sleepy place of palms and beaches and a rickety wharf, the township fortified by an old stone stockade and inhabited mainly by uniformed members of the native constabulary. I walked past the white stone church and, in its burial ground, noticed the headstones of some white men's graves. Farther along the wide, sandy roadway was a wooden jail from which some dark citizens peered forth, quiet and bewildered. Above them, immediately overhead, was the guard-house where a stout sergeant sat cleaning his accoutrements. There was a barracks, outside which, in the shade, some recruits were drilling; above a well-kept lawn brusquely labelled "Off the grass!" the flags of the United States and of the Philippines were flying. On the right side of the roadway, looking towards Bongao Peak, were the residences of the officers, and farther on a few shops, and beyond again, the post office and wireless station. Along the beach on the southern side was the water-village of the Moros, built out on stilts above the sea. On the foreshore was the market-place, and near here were some shops. I saw some children playing in the shade. There were no Europeans.

I found the Commandant, a pleasant-faced rotund Filipino, seated on the verandah of his home dressed in shorts and a pyjama coat of rich blue silk.

"Good afternoon," I said, "I've come to report the arrival of my ship."

I'd brought the papers — the certificate of British registry, the bills of health, clearance from Singapore, visaed crew-lists, and all those things. He welcomed me cheerfully and was not over-interested in the papers. Fortunately a customs inspector had just come in by launch from Holo: what slight formalities there were this gentleman attended to. I had to have some reason for being there; I was in, I said, with engine breakdown and to refresh the crew — true enough, for the engine had broken down, and we should have little opportunity after Bongao to get any vegetables or fresh food before we reached the South Pacific. That, according to all the directions, I feared would take some time.

For once I was not displeased when the customs man, entering the ship in his notebook as arrived with engine breakdown, described her as a schooner. A schooner with engine trouble is not so bad, but a full-rigged ship would be disgraceful. I described her as a full-rigged ship, of course; but he had heard only of schooners. The Commandant, I discovered, had seen us sail by the previous evening but he thought we had anchored overnight and gone. He said there were no further formalities — no dues, no charges, no worries; not even a form to fill up. I wish some of the greater ports would take a lesson from Bongao. The Commandant left the conduct of my ship and her people to me; she was an English yacht, and that seemed to satisfy him.

I yarned with this pleasant man a while, about Tawi Tawi and its history, and the history of his constabulary post. It is a quiet place now, he says. Trouble? There is not much:

not much thieving. Sometimes there is a murder, of course: sometimes a Moro runs amok and kills a Christian. The Moros, I gather, are the Sulus, the original inhabitants — Moslems, said to have come from somewhere in the Malay Peninsula. They are not Filipinos. Their stronghold is the Sulu archipelago, of which Tawi Tawi is the southernmost island, and part of North Borneo. They are the subjects of the Sultan of Sulu and have never come entirely under either American or Spanish influence. They and the Bajaos, the gypsies of Borneo and the Sulu islands who spend their lives in small boats, had formerly been left much to their own devices. The Bajaos were quiet enough, a peaceful and inoffensive folk: it was the Moros who caused whatever trouble arose. Usually, when they ran amok, they carved up a school teacher — not from any distaste for his honourable calling, but because the teachers were mainly Filipino Christians. It behoved one of the faithful to destroy a Christian, if he could, and the teachers were the only Christians about. Two of them were disembowelled a few weeks before our arrival, at a place called Parangan, near Balimbing, some six miles away. He lost three soldiers in the battle which followed. It had been humanly impossible to prevent their loss, he went on, as if accounting to me for this military calamity that had upset the routine of his post: they were buried in the cemetery, up there beyond the school. The white men? They were traders, Wolfe and Cornell, murdered some years ago. The place is safe enough for white men now, quiet most of the time.

And pirates? I asked, reminded of these gentlemen by his reference to Balimbing. They were out of business, too. The American control had put a stop to that. The Spaniards had never really controlled Tawi Tawi; after some skirmishes they hadn't bothered much, as far as he could see. The people of Balimbing were a pretty bad lot. He believed that even now they would be pirates if they saw the chance: they had always been inclined that way. They were a warlike bunch, too: he'd grant them that. They used to make raids in Celebes and northern Borneo, taking slaves for the market at Sarangani, but they made their last raid into the Celebes in 1912.

The people of Malasa, the village in Chongos Bay off which we were anchored, had come originally from Balimbing, breaking away from the main village in a tribal feud. They would bear watching, but it was safe enough with the armed guard so close. He had had very little trouble; most of the old village jealousies had simmered down, and the Moros had learned that — at least while the constabulary was there — piracy and slave-raiding and such pursuits were not really worth while. Balimbing had been destroyed once by the Spaniards, who tired of the natives' ungentle ways; but the town was rebuilt as soon as the Spanish squadron left. The people had taken to the bush for the duration of the bombardment and returned when it was over. Then they built the town again, and carried on. Large numbers of their fast boats had been destroyed, but they built more. They were still the best boat-builders of the Eastern Archipelago, though they mainly built boats for sale now, and to carry on the traffic with Borneo. Borneo was British, and Tawi Tawi, for the time being, was American; but the traffic between the places had gone on from time immemorial. The people had intermingled and come and gone freely, and no flying of a flag with crosses on it over Borneo and a striped flag over the Archipelago would now stop them, or any manner of law or regulation, short of keeping a fleet of destroyers on the spot. They probably smuggled a bit, too; it was impossible to prevent them. They carried on much as they always had, no matter what distant country claimed their islands.

I walked back thoughtfully to the rickety wharf in the hot sun, and along the sandy way saw the little children playing school games on traced patterns in the shade. Pirates? Not here, anyway. There were five stores, I counted, four Chinese and one Japanese, outside each of which appeared signs beaten out of metal exhorting the citizens to buy a brand of American cigarettes that satisfy. I went back to the ship, and in the evening welcomed on board the Chief of Malasa, Panglima Sarawi, who arrived on board armed with a large revolver, and attended by a numerous bodyguard. He came, he said, to welcome the vessel and to inspect her, if he might; he had with him as interpreter a school teacher in a collar and tie. I thought the teacher eyed the revolver and the *kris* of the bodyguard a little nervously. I showed them round; the gang of them would scarce fit in the saloon. They departed with smiles, after several hours, and invited all of us to visit their village.

Tawi Tawi, showing Balimbing, previously headquarters of the Moro pirates. The *Joseph Conrad* anchored in Chongos Bay.

I stayed at Chongos Bay a pleasant week, for the place was interesting. The wide waters of Bongao Bay, from Bongao itself northwards to Balimbing and Bilatan and out to Sanguisiapo and Laa, were ideal for sailing trips in the life-boats. We went to Balimbing, Parangan, Batu Batu, and through a tortuous channel between Sanga Sanga and Tawi

Tawi itself to a place called Lapid Lapid, where there was a small basin for Bajao boats, and a white man had made himself a plantation. I went up here with a load of magazines and such small things as I thought a white man in those parts might care for, and found there the former superintendent of Sulu schools, a tall, elderly American, pensioned now from his good work, and settled there, pioneering. He had a Moro wife — a remote cousin, I heard, of the Sultan of Sulu — and his wife had some merry children: he might, I suppose, be considered by the uninformed and the stay-at-homes as having "gone native." It is customary to associate this idea with deterioration and a life of ease and beachcombing in lotus-eating lands; but there were no lotus trees in Tawi Tawi. This was a pioneer of the real school, working hard on the large plantation he himself had hewn from the boulder-strewn hills and the wild forest. He worked very hard indeed, and he was lean and tanned and alert and lithe, and his strong brown hands were hardened with toil. "Come on in, strangers!" he called as we came to his clearing, after miles of the moist, heat-belching paths past gardens where peanuts grew, and all manner of tropic fruits, and coco-nut groves. Some well-groomed Moro children scurried out of sight, dragging a tame monkey with them. I put down the magazines and the other things. He thanked me for them, but I had not needed to bring anything there to be assured of a welcome.

We stayed to yarn. He had been in the Archipelago many years — since 1907. Oh yes, he'd been home once or twice in the interval; you grow away from home. Gradually, if you give yourself to your work, you find, he said, that so many of your interests grow and your life is so centred there that, when at last the time comes to go away — why, you stay. At home all things have changed and everyone has forgotten; you have been cut off from that and cannot re-enter. The home you remember is there no more and, if you return, it is as a ghost of the long past to wander idly a few years, lost in unshared reminiscence, and then to die. No; he had stayed.

"I'm kind of caught out here," he said, in answer to the rather foolish question from somebody whether he liked it. No, he didn't so much *like* it: it had grown round him. So here he was, with a large plantation from which he was trying to produce all manner of things. On it many native families had settled, and in the little port, with the rocks and the fish stakes and the clear water, Bajao boats found refuge. They called him in Bongao the Father of the Island — generous and kind. It was a native who told us of him: that was the place, he said, to get refreshments. Anything on his plantation he would share. Gone native! I wish a like disease would take us all.

He had no comforts. He had made no attempt to set up a Dutch home. His house was plain and very simple. He was no exploiter of the people. He had taught them and trained them over many years, and now in his declining days was turned pioneer among them. The Moros do little pioneering themselves. They are satisfied, seemingly, to stay in their stilted villages over the water, finding their livelihood mainly in the sea; nursing their grievances, harbouring their ill-feelings and their jealousies, armed one against the other. From this white man they had a noble example of another way of life — this teacher who plodded barefoot in the steamy fields he had cut out from the bush, and tilled the soil. *He* was the pioneer and he was doing the pioneering, fighting the over-abundant forest in that hell-heat, stemming the all-powerful efforts of those great producers the Rain and the Sun, and sinking all his pension (which would have made a pleasant retirement in America more than possible) to keep things going. Much of Tawi Tawi, good soil as it is, is pig-ridden and infested with mosquitos: the market for its products — copra, peanuts, bananas and such things — is greatly depressed. The pioneer in these days works hard for scant reward.

He was rather behind on things, he said; he was out of the world. We were the first whites he had seen for a long, long time — indeed the greatest number of whites who had ever been to Lapid Lapid. (We were five.) He had formerly subscribed to a few good periodicals, but things were bad; his subscriptions had run out and now nothing came to him. He had his news from such pages of old copies of *The San Francisco Journal* as the Chinese storekeeper in Bongao wrapped round his few purchases: by this means he had heard recently of the default of the European nations on their American debts. What had come over them? he asked. Did they want the money to prepare for another war? He walked back with us, in the late afternoon, towards our boat: we talked a lot. The heat belched from the hot earth as if a fire-door had been flung open in the stokehold of a giant liner, and the crust of the earth had hardened, though it was raining slightly when we came. He walked with us and talked of nations and of peoples. "All is greed," he said in the end. "I am better here."

We went back again to Lapid Lapid, to the Teacher's, and went with him to hunt pig. The wily boar was absent then, but we brought down a buffalo, a rather domesticated animal, I regret to say. But we needed meat; it would all be eaten before it spoiled. It was steaming hot, as usual: in the open paths, one's clothing, though it was only shorts and a light shirt, stuck to one's back, and the heat was almost insufferable. We marched for miles through the plantation and along jungle tracks and came here and there on small clearings in the valleys where the Moros were grinding rice; but there were few of them inland. At one place a small girl, about twelve years old, was skilfully wielding a piece of polished wood with which she banged at a great bowl of unhusked rice, lying on the ground — thump, thump, thump: and it looked so easy and she was so young that some of the cadets offered to relieve her. But they could not husk that rice. She smiled;

they did their best. That piece of wood was heavy and the job was mighty hard. She took back the wood and went on with the job.

It was nearly dark when we got the buffalo; in pitch blackness we began the march back to the boat. The way was by bogs and jungle and marshes and a precipitous stream; carrying the animal (though it was a young one) was a prodigious task, a grim matter of setting one plodding foot before the other, slipping sometimes, unseeing, prodded by branches and torn by thorns. The carcass was slung on a long pole and carried by four men, but the way was so difficult two could not walk abreast, and the dead beast collided with so many trees that after a mile we had to give up the idea of bringing it back whole, and quartered it, the more stalwart of the fellows now each taking a quarter — weighty enough, under those conditions. The smaller fellows brought up the rear with the skin and the heart, and the guns. We slipped in streams and slid down banks, and wandered slowly on, and at last, when the meat was delivered safely and portioned out, swore we would never again undertake such a journey — not even for beef steaks.

The Teacher had the children looking their best that day to have their photographs taken, an experience they had not suffered before. He himself had put on a pair of shoes, but I saw that he took them off to walk the bush. He paid us a visit on board, on the Sunday, bringing his little girl who danced and sang, and a bag of peanuts and a great deal of fruit and things — very good of him and very welcome. I liked that man; I hope for him that he may long continue to live out his days pioneering in the Sulu bush, for I saw that he was profoundly happy there, happy without any of the things usually thought necessary; happy with his living and all his kindnesses, his ideals, and his work.

The Panglima Sarawi, a pleasant-countenanced man of middle age whose usual attire consisted of a fez, a shirt, a sarong, and a large revolver (this he had a permit to carry, as a head man; mere *Datus* and such could have the *kris*, many of which were old and very beautiful; and all had *bolos*), put on an exhibition of Moro dancing for us at his home in Malasa. His home was a spacious, airy, and not unbeautiful dwelling of rough wood situated in the best strategic position of the village which stood on piles in the sea. Beyond it were reefs which would worry a stranger; the shore nearby was rough and overgrown with jungle. One crazy, dangerous "bridge," constructed largely of the rotten bottoms of long defunct canoes, connected the village with the beach; over this you proceeded at your peril. Nearby on the beach the people of Malasa built their boats; a little distance inland was a clearing where they grew things, though in truth not much. They are excellent boat-builders at Malasa, building quite large vessels. We saw some of these beneath the trees where they were being finished. They were high in the ends like the old vikings' craft, and beamy, with great sheer and great flare; the Sulus have been building this kind of boat for centuries. They are seaworthy, able, and fast vessels, and many of them are beautifully decorated and carved.

An even crazier bridge than that to the shore connects the row of houses; naked brown children scamp about and chatter and stare, and two little boys bale out a waterlogged fishing canoe by the foreshore. Some of the elders have a dirty look, piratical enough to outward appearance; but they say nothing and do nothing except to crowd in at the dance. Inside the great room of the Panglima's home, two half-naked stalwarts bang on an immense drum and on instruments made of metal looking like inverted cooking pots of the type generally chosen by comic artists to portray the boiling of missionaries. A woman plays monotonously on a row of brass gongs which hint, now and then, that they could be tuneful if only she would let them be. But she never does. We sit in chairs and on the

155

wooden floor with the water beneath us, and the little girls dance — a weird shuffle, mostly, with jerky movements of the arms. It is not very beautiful, after Bali. The little girls are richly clad in velvets, gold-ornamented, and in silks: one of them is the Panglima's daughter, aged perhaps twelve. After the girls come little boys, stamping dexterously to the drums, little fellows about four. They jump and posture with their hands. There are other little boys who will not dance despite all the exhortations and threats of the schoolmaster, but run away and howl. There are little girls who look on enviously and would be only too pleased to exhibit what dancing talent they possess, but they are not permitted. The dancing lasts some time and it grows dark in the Panglima's house: an oil lamp is lit, throwing strange half-lights into the big corners and upon the performers and their pirate parents. The big brass vases and the ornaments by the walls are distorted to queerly human shape. The dancing goes on.

It was all very interesting, and it was very good of our friend the Panglima to put it on. But it was not — well, it was not very good. But perhaps we should not first have been to Bali.

The Panglima, who spoke no word of any language that we knew but was nevertheless our very good friend, offered to be our pilot to Balimbing, whither I sailed in the starboard life-boat. I saw that the Chief had his colt fully loaded that day, and he brought with him some little parcels of roasted rice to eat, and for us. We had given him something too. We sailed in rain squalls through the wide bay, with Bongao Peak and the islands for our landmarks: past Batu Batu (where a colony of Christian Filipinos is established) and other villages to a place called Parangan where we put in to visit the Panglima's son and to inspect the school. The school was new, just completed, erected to replace the structure in which the two teachers were murdered and the three soldiers died. After this atrocity the authorities thought Parangan would be better with Moro teachers, since there would be considerably less chance of losing them. The Panglima's son was one of these new teachers. The school, I noticed, was very American, even to the mottoes and the legends on the walls: Move Your Bowils Twice Daily: Eat More Fruit; I Must Brush My Teeth, and so forth. The Panglima's son was a bit of a pessimist about it. The children, he said, learn little and remember less. If there is harvesting to be done they do not bother about school, and it is impossible to induce the parents to allow the girls to go. Somehow schools did not seem to fit so prominently upon the Tawi Tawi scene as they had been intended to do, and an education scheme such as that must be expensive. I wondered how long it would continue after independence.

The people of Parangan kept out of our way, mistaking us perhaps for another group from Manila come to avenge the dead Christians; such as we saw looked no more homicidal than any subway crowd in America — not half so alarming.

But Balimbing was the place I came to see. We arrived there late in the afternoon; it is the biggest village on Tawi Tawi — a big place, on piles, placed in a strategic spot with a mountain behind it effectively cutting off attack from the land, and a tortuous passage through the reefs to reach it by water. The inhabitants seem less clad even than their relatives of Malasa, and fiercer visaged; not long ago they were the scourge of the seas. Many a recruit went out from here to join the great pirate chiefs of North Borneo in the days when daring raids were made as far away as Papua and Batavia, when Raga the Bloodthirsty pillaged and slew. They sent out their own raiding proas, too, some of which were surprisingly large; they did not scruple in those days to cut out whatever luckless European vessel might come in their path. To Europeans they showed no mercy, torturing and murdering them in fiendish glee; they thought all whites were Spaniards and took their revenge for the iniquities and the tortures the Spanish heaped upon them. The Spaniards had some curious ideas about colonization in those times. Raga himself, and more than one of his chief underlings, had hidden at Balimbing and on the small islands that form a maze from here to the northern end of Tawi Tawi. Such waters were ideal for the hiding of villainy and of loot in the days before steam power and long-range guns. But those days are now all gone, at least for the time being; at Balimbing we were met by a school-teacher still in possession of his bowels (I hope he also was a Moro) and I saw the children playing hop-scotch on the sand.

"Hallo" said the teacher. "Well, here they are — the Pagans of the Sea." He said it as if he were conducting an excursion, though no tourist liners go through those parts nor do yachts ordinarily visit Tawi Tawi; but I was surprised. I offered, an unclad pirate with a bloodthirsty face some English cigarettes but he courteously declined them, saying he smoked only a certain kind of American cigarette which, he said, was "toasted." Pirates! It seems to me high time the Admiralty removed the libel from their charts. But — I don't know. It was perhaps only habit that made the Panglima so careful always to be armed.

I saw a mosque, but the teacher said the villagers do not use it much. While I spoke with him, a group of the natives came, some of them with prayer-mats, beautifully hand-made, and others with silver-handled *bolos* which they were willing to exchange. We were shown the school, the kindergarten (both it and the school better than some in the lesser English villages), and the boats building on the community wharves — mighty good boats they were. Two particularly piratical specimens leapt into our boat soon after we arrived and I thought at first they might try to take it, but quickly saw that their interest was only to examine it. They were the master-craftsmen of the Balimbing boat-builders and they had not seen a ship's life-boat before. They felt the sails, which were tanned with some green preparation to preserve them, went through the equipment, handled the oars (and did not appear to think highly of them) and the masts and everything, throwing out the anchor and delightedly trying out everything they could, most of the time with huge grins and animated conversation. In the end, so the teacher translated, they said she was a very fine boat indeed; they looked as if they would like to keep her.

I left there in the evening, not staying very long, with the rain clouds piled on the Balimbing hills and the boat in a tide rip, jumping violently. Back on board, at the anchorage, I heard that the operator from the wireless station had come out with grave news of impending war in Europe, between Italy and England. Italy and England? It was too mad to be believable; but it might be true, none the less. And I had thought there were pirates at Balimbing.

If there was going to be a war, I thought I might as well push on from there and continue the voyage to Sydney. But first, next morning, I went in to the market place at Bongao, it being then the market day, and found it a big day with a gathering of the undergraduate schoolma'ams and the masters and a civil-service examination of some kind for the Filipinos. The Moros took no part in this, and I could not discover what it was about except that it was, apparently, the day for the periodic tally of the school teachers.

All the purchasers from Simunul and Laa and Sanga Sanga and Manuk Manka were there, and the Bajao men from their boats, big and long-haired and unkempt with placid faces that were curiously meek and savage at the same time; and the tails and the fins of newly caught sharks stank to the heavens in the Chinese shops. In the market were bananas to be bought for a song, raw or ripe or cooked, and honey and sugar cane and coco-nuts and eggs — hens' eggs (few of these) and larger seabirds' eggs, each wrapped carefully in its own fresh leaf. The strange mob milled around — Moros, a tall Bajao spending the proceeds of a successful shark-hunt, here and there a *Datu* or a *Hadji*, though these were few. The market is an open pavilion in that part of the bay by the village on stilts where the Moros live. In a corner a woman fried banana fritters with coco-nut oil, and little children, on the outskirts of the crowd, scampered on the crazy boards, laughing and playing. The inhabitants were strangely attired, but European garments of a kind were much in evidence. Datu Amiral — he of the blue silk pants and the jewelled *kris* who was on board the first morning — was in town for a council meeting. He was, I gathered, a councillor for Malasa and those parts. *Datu* is a title meaning prince of sorts: but there seem to be many titles here — many titles, and not much respect for any of them. He was attired in raiment that would have put him instantly on any Hollywood payroll, white silks, flowing and gold-studded, with a jewelled *kris* across his back, very grand. He posed for his photograph looking quite satisfied. I gathered my purchases, sending them back on board (I'd bought as many bananas as possible; we also could try our hands at those fritters, which tasted fine), and set off for the Commandant's house to clear the ship outwards, thank him, and say my farewells. But there was no clearing of the ship to be done — no dues, no papers, no clearance. "You've all been quiet and well-behaved, and everybody's been pleased to see you," he said. "Why, when you're ready, just go." That was a good Commandant.

It was evening when I got back to the ship; all hands turned in, except the watchmen, to get a good night's rest before the long passage to the South Pacific. I meant to sail at daylight in the morning.

But late that night we had as queer an adventure as occurred throughout the voyage. I scarcely gave it credence when I heard of it first; but it was perfectly true. Anyone acquainted with the outlook and the habits of the Sulu Moros and the casual manner in which they contract matrimony will well understand it. The long and the short of it was that, while we slept in the night, the Panglima of Malasa came on board, complete with his revolver and his retinue, and what he sought was my youthful cadet Stormalong as prince consort for his daughter. I thought that kind of thing ceased happening fifty years ago. They came, mysteriously, the watchmen reported, in several boats, one of which was the Chief's large boat in which there was an orchestra. There was an interpreter — not the teacher — who asked for Stormalong, not by name, of course, since they did not know his name, but as the small boy who saw the dance. The watchmen said the boy was asleep. They came aboard. All the boys were sleeping on deck, in hammocks or rolled in blankets; the Panglima went carefully over them all, looking for Stormalong with a flashlight. The Hardcase they found — Dennis, Dave, Harry, John, Twynam; but no Stormalong. At last they discovered him, sleeping on the focs'l head. The Panglima awakened him and asked him at once, would he like to stay at Malasa? He wanted a white son, the interpreter said; would Stormalong stay? He could be married to the little girl, if he liked (they seemed to take it for granted that he *would* like). The Panglima grinned encouragement. Stormalong, rudely awakened (and never at his best when he has just been called), astonished, disbelieving, and somewhat dreamy, blinked. Was he dreaming? What was all this about? It gradually penetrated to him that it was no dream; the little girl in silks and gold was now on board and it looked, to Stormalong, infernally serious. He gathered up his blanket and ran for the hold, where he hid until the morning. It was only with the utmost difficulty that the watchmen with some assistance and after pretending many times to search the ship, could prevail upon the Panglima and his delegation to return disappointed to Malasa.

"I reckon it's an insult!" shouted the small boy in the morning, as if the hand of no dark maiden could ever be good enough for a man of Suffolk. He had feared it might be a decoy to eat him. The Hardcase, however, had no such qualms. What a career to cast aside! Prince Stormalong, white chief of Malasa! The Hardcase wondered ruefully why the little girl had not chosen him. He could have had a good time for years, fishing and sailing on the bay. And the little girl was quite good-looking.

I sailed, and the Panglima's orchestra came out to play farewell, a rather sad one. The little girl was not there and we did not see her again. We passed out into the Sibutu Passage, going close under the Bongao Peak, the famous peak where the fabled Tree of Life is said to grow, to eat of the leaves of which will bring unending life. The inhabitants, being sensible people, do not try to reach it. It is inaccessible, in any case, which is as well if it possesses that dreadful power. To live for ever unchanged on earth! The ghastliness of such a fate is maddening to contemplate. It was on Bongao Peak, too, that the four giants lived — Bassi, Tainga, Pat, and Anjutal, famed in local legend. These are the gentlemen, the legends say, who once, when a Spanish legion was laying waste Tawi Tawi, descended from their home among the clouds of the peak and, bending in a row with their sterns towards the legion, let loose their wind in a great gush that burned the Spaniards to instant death. Those were giants! The people who thought of them and treasured the legend could have had little regard for Spain.

So I sailed, standing down Sibutu Passage, beating against the monsoon until I could fetch the Sea of Celebes by way of the narrow strait between Simunul and Manuk Manka. We came through this strait and stood on, but the wind dropped and we made very little progress. We made very little progress, indeed, for the next several days. Five days after leaving Tawi Tawi we could still see the island,

and wrath was hot against the uncrowned Prince Stormalong for keeping us there by bringing the "vengeance" of the little princess upon us. Stormalong, wise young man, kept out of the way.

IX

Nissan Lagoon

I BEGAN to be worried in the Sea of Celebes. Our rate of "progress" at first was no better than in the Sulu Sea, yet as far as I was able to discover, this should have been the best section of the voyage. The worst was still to come; the really difficult part would begin when we were clear of the Sea of Celebes and were trying to make easting through the Southern Carolines. I could not, then, solace myself with the usual reflection that the poor progress of one section of the voyage would be made up for by good in another; I was in the only sea from which I had any reasonable expectation of tolerable conditions. It began seriously to look as if the northern passage would be impossible, and I ruefully considered trying, instead, to work to the southward through the Strait of Macassar, if I could, and so out into the Indian Ocean by one of the central passages and then southwards to Australia.

Five days after sailing from Chongos Bay it was still calm — calm of that depressing, hot, and stifling order that only those seas can breed, calm so deep it becomes impossible to remember that there ever has been wind, or to conceive again a picture of the sea in which the wind blows. It was so dead that the clouds were mirrored perfectly in the sea by day and the stars by night, and the sails hung down so lifelessly that half their shade was gone. The helmsmen, bare-backed, sweltered in their sweat at the open wheel; the pitch bubbled, and spilled out over the clean decks; the drinking water had become insufferably hot; and always overside, where we might have swum, huge sharks were waiting. The galley refuse of three days still lay alongside, not moving; some empty tins thrown overboard two days out from Bongao were still there on the fifth day, for there had never been slop enough on the sea to overbalance them and fill them. They glinted at us in the mornings and lay beside us all day; they caught the rays of the morning sun on the one side and the rays of the evening on the other, and we looked at those tins until the sight of them became so unendurable a reminder of our stagnation that I put the dinghy over and pushed them down. Calm, calm! The refuse still stayed; I could not make that sink. I did not care to use the engine though it had been repaired again (as well as the second mate could do it) at Chongos Bay. If the Celebes Sea, where the monsoon ought to blow, was so bad, we should need more than four days' fuel to get to Australia. I hung on, waiting for a faint air of some description that we might use; and an adverse current set us in towards Holo.

The youthful Stormalong still kept out of sight as much as he was able. Beginning as a joke, the boys' anger in the course of the hot days became real enough. If the calm had continued any longer they would actually have thought that Stormalong's rejection of the Malasa princess was responsible for it. As it was, there were many threats to send him back in a boat, and I swore one day that I would start the engine and go back and hand him over. Even in these days, man against the elements finds it easy — natural, almost — to revert to his old superstitions. It would not have been so great a step from our condition then to implicit belief in the ability of the princess to hold us in that calm. We haven't altered.

But at last a breeze came, a faint doldrum air with rain. We moved on a little and had the Sulu Islands out of sight, and saw instead the heights of Mindanao, and Sarangani, that former headquarters of the trade in slaves. At length there came a sunny morning, early in September, when we reached the Pacific at last, sailing grandly into that vast ocean with a bone in our old ship's mouth that had not been there for weeks. We entered the Pacific through the narrow gateway between Kawio and Marore, north of the Sangi group, outermost of the Dutch Celebes. The wind was fresh and fair, and Kawio with its beaches and its hills and its coco-nut groves, seemed one of the prettiest islands we had seen. I should have liked to anchor there, to pay a visit; but there was no port of entry and I had to hurry on. We sailed through tide rips off the north-west end and saw a large village on Marore, and all the praus out fishing sailed swiftly from our path wondering, perhaps, what was this apparition come among them. A full-rigged ship had not passed that way for thirty years.

Here we left the East Indies behind us, and I regretted I had seen so little of them that voyage: we had been only to Boeleleng, Singapore, Balabac, Bongao. We'd seen a little more than the bare list might indicate, of course; we had sailed through Bali Strait, and Sapudi Strait, and had seen the fast boats of Madura with their funnelled sails; and by Bawean, and Carimata Strait; and by Seraia and Subi Kechil. We'd seen Borneo at its northern end, and Kagayan Sulu and Mambahenauhan — little enough, indeed. We should have stayed two months at Chongos Bay, and gone to Ompapui and Sandakan, and made a boat trip up the Segama River; and gone in to see the bad folk of Banguey, probably as harmless and as libelled as the boatmen of Balimbing. It was strange how in each place it was the people somewhere else who were "bad."

I had only two years; I could not stay out longer than that. Two years is too short a time in which to sail a hundred-foot square-rigger round the earth; and I had to cross the Atlantic three times and sail its whole length twice. That was, indeed, the error of my journey. There was too much Atlantic.

So we came to the Pacific and, with the aid of the Lord,

found the east-setting counter-equatorial, and sailed on —
on and on and on, a long hot hard road. It rained every day
and sometimes blew, though often we had days of doldrum
conditions. The current was strong and we progressed
steadily to the eastward; through the Western Carolines,
past Sonsorol and Pulo Anna, and Merir and all those
other low islands of the Japanese mandate. We saw the
blue streak of Sonsorol early one morning but I did not go
in there — neither there, nor into any other of the
Japanese islands. The Japanese are doubtless making good
use of their mandated islands; but I have gathered that they
wish to be undisturbed and I did not take it on myself to
disturb them. All I had against them was a lamentable
tendency to look upon unheralded strangers as spies. I was
not a spy and did not wish to be taken for one. So I sailed
by, well out, my principal object at that stage of the voyage
being to avoid islands rather than to call at them.

At length we progressed until we had sufficient
longitude run down to head southwards towards the strait
between Bougainville and New Ireland. I turned south
then, crossing the Line (for the third time since leaving
England) on the forty-ninth day out from Singapore. So far
our progress had not been so bad, all things considered;
but it soon worsened. We found the doldrums again,
stifling hot and calm, with the glassy sea sometimes ruffled
fleetingly by faint whiffs of wind that went before the yards
could be braced to them, and always seemed to take the
ship aback, robbing her in sternway of far more than they
would have sent her ahead. There was a long, uneasy swell,
as if the great volume of the unfeeling sea itself, hot and
broiling, felt the intense unending heat of the overhead sun
and panted in protest. But that it does not; it heaves and
rises and falls slowly, in great content, as if nothing would
please it more than that we should stay there for ever,
gently heaving, rising and rolling too, while barnacles and
tempers grow, and we roast and stew and sweat and swear

here until Doomsday. But these are passing moods: it rains, and the air is cleared; it blows, and the tempers are cooled. Somehow life seems better again, and the sea, though still a worried mirror of the dead sky, not utterly so heartless and bitter and cynical and depressing.

Sometimes we found things to interest us, even in the calms. A bird flew aboard one evening, very tired — a land bird, by the look of him, from some lagoon in the Carolines. He rested on the mainyard but could not balance there with the rolling. He fell on to the life-boat cover and we took him, expecting him to die. Some were for eating him, but I gave him water and he rested, and next day was lively enough, busily examining the decks for food. He was a young bird of the curlew family; we named him Oscar and he soon made himself at home, though at first it was difficult to find something he would eat. We found some suckers on the log rotator and these he ate with relish; we caught some sharks, and he gobbled up the suckers from them. Before long, he was not at all particular, eating whatever was going, as every one else did. He got to know his name, and ran to the galley when the cook called him. He had a bath of sea water in the scuppers, and spent hours each day happily bathing. He was a nice bird, Oscar, though he could never get over an undue interest in fresh paint. Once another bird came, of a different type, a wild little bird something like a brown magpie, with webbed feet, though he was not an ocean bird. Wild and intractable, the newcomer refused to be friendly or to eat or drink or do anything. Oscar did not like him, and he soon died.

We often caught sharks. The boys cut out their backbones for walking sticks, but we never tried eating them. Once, after a small shark had been lying in the scuppers nearly half an hour, disembowelled, with a capstan-bar rammed down its throat, it was thrown overboard and promptly swam away. We had thought it long dead.

Another shark, much larger, attracted by the blood, rushed at it and ate it in a wild flurry of blood and foam, a grucsome and awful sight. The shark is a mean, low fish, and the sailors' intense and brutal hatred of him is understandable. To sharks we showed no mercy, ever; but they were always with us, always ready, in the calms, to take the line. If there was a breeze at all they were too lazy to keep up with us; they lolled aft in the sunny surface waters while their little striped pilots swam here and there, examining the garbage and the bait. Several times we saw large sharks leap violently out of the water and thwack themselves down again in what seemed to us an effort to rid themselves of an undue accumulation of suckers. We would see the suckers swim away, only to be back again in a few moments. They were probably laughing.

One day, in a flat calm, a school of blackfish came round the ship, and, more with the idea of doing something to break the monotony of the calm than anything else, I put the dinghy in the water after them, taking the carpenter as harpooner and the second mate with a gun. We had no lance. We could not get among the whales, try as we might, for they were timorous and easily scared. A long shark followed us persistently in spite of cracks on the head with the boat-hook and the harpoon. It attacked the oars and went for the bottom of the boat, until we became tired of it and let it have the gun. It was quieter then, and swam away; but in a little while it was back. There were bonita and large flying-fish also about, but we caught nothing. The day passed pleasantly enough though we caught no fish; the sunset was most beautiful, and some rain in the early evening cleared the air.

Throughout this period, which passed much more pleasantly than I had ever expected — we sailed 2,200 miles in the first three weeks from Bongao in spite of the very poor beginning — I had considerably more medical work to do than I had ever had before. Almost all the boys had some kind of tropic sores, mostly on the shins and feet. It was a rule of the ship that sand shoes had to be worn ashore on all tropic islands, where it is stupid to go barefoot; but in spite of this, some of them had infected feet. One or two had really nasty ulcers on the shins which proved most recalcitrant. The ordinary healing methods were of little use against these things, and I was busy for two hours a day, cleaning and dressing. But I missed a medical man. I had several times tried to get one. I thought there must somewhere be a medical practitioner — young or old — who might have benefited by the voyage. If such there was, I never found him. I had to cope by myself with any medical problems which came up; and I used, as far as I was able, the cure of Nature. That is to say, I kept the wounds clean and left Nature to heal them. Nature is a good doctor. Those tropical ulcers, however, worried me. It was very hard even to keep them clean, and to get any response out of them seemed impossible. I had two of the patients under treatment for five months, and found, generally, that the treatment by bandaging them with antiseptic adhesive tape and leaving it on for several days, was best in the long run.

By this time the vessel was becoming rather foul on the waterline and the next strake below, and I began to think of putting into some convenient lagoon to careen her and clean the bottom. Where was there such a lagoon? The islands round those waters are principally volcanic, with few anchorages and no harbours. I did not want to stand down among the Admiralty or Bismarck groups for fear of my inability to get out of them. I should have, then, the southeast trade a dead head wind and should be in a bad position. I read carefully through the sailing directions (*Pacific Islands Pilot*, Vol. I) and studied the charts. The only likely place seemed a lagoon marked variously on my charts as Nissan, Sir Charles Hardy Island, and Green Island, and shown with as many different shapes as it had names. The Nuguria group might have done but, at least on most of the charts, Nissan looked better. It was in a good position, well to windward of New Ireland. I changed my course a little to head that way: it was more or less directly in my path.

I should have gone first to Rabaul to enter the ship, since Rabaul in New Britain is the port of entry for those parts. Nissan is one of the many islands in the Mandated Territory of New Guinea, those former German colonies which are now controlled, more or less, by Australia. But I could not get to Rabaul. If I went there with a fair wind, how should I get away again? I should have an endless and dispiriting beat through St. George's Channel; I should subject my vessel to unnecessary danger, or at least to navigational difficulties which might prove her undoing: I should further lengthen a voyage which was already long enough. I made no attempt to go, then, towards Rabaul. This port of entry fetish, necessary though it may be, adds immensely to the difficulties of navigating a square-rigged ship about the world in these days. If one finds, for any reason, that one wishes or requires or needs to put in at any island for any purpose, one is unable to do so (short of being in actual distress) without first going to a port of entry and securing the appropriate rubber stamps. It is all very well for powered vessels, and they should be made to do it, but there is little consideration for the sailing wanderer in these days. A schooner would not be so badly off, for she can work so much better than the square-rigged ship against the wind: windward work in a foul iron ship is purgatory in those waters. It is right enough, since all the islands have been long since portioned among the peoples of the northern hemisphere, that each should control its own and, I suppose, cast the usual barriers round them. There are tariff laws and shipping restrictions, and so forth; odd vessels cannot be permitted to wander here and there at their will doing what they like. They might cause trouble among the natives, unlawfully carry people away or leave some behind; bring disease. But if I had any communicable disease on board, I would not try to go to Nissan; I had nothing to land, nothing to sell. For the continued prosecution of my voyage and in the interests of the health of all hands I had to go to Nissan and I could not go to Rabaul. So I went to Nissan, and left there with the trader a letter stating the facts for the Administrator at Rabaul.

At least, I went into Nissan when I could. It proved rather difficult. I stood down past the Kapingamarangi Islands, which consist principally (so far as the chart is aware) of a large low atoll reported — I quote the latest Admiralty chart — to lie about nine miles eastward of its charted position; felt my way past the Lyra Reef (position doubtful); was driven one day past the Nugurias where I did not investigate the chart's allegations, here and there, of "good passage," "safe passage," and so on; and came eventually in sight of the heights of New Ireland. Later we saw the islands Feni, Tanga, and Lihir. The wind was fresh then from the south-east and I had to beat, standing in close towards the New Ireland shore (represented on the chart by a dotted line at that locality), but not anchoring anywhere. I kept masthead lookout the whole time, and was careful in those waters. There are no lights, and night sailing is difficult. Bearings, when almost every island is out of position, give poor guidance. We saw little of New Ireland beyond some plantations very well kept. Once, two steamers, a Japanese and a Greek, wandered by, deep-loaded with wheat from Australia. We must have been upon the Sydney-Kobe lane.

The wind was still ahead. I beat on, carrying as much sail as the ship would stand. We were fifty-six days out from Singapore before the low atoll of Nissan was at last in sight. In the evening we were close by, but the place is little known and the Directions are not even sure where the entrance is. (It is "apparently" between Nissan and the small island of Barahun, and all the charts are different.) It is foolish to attempt to enter such a place in bad light, without proper precautions: I shortened down and stood off and on until the morning. In the night it blew up half a gale, and we were blown away.

Two days later, after being blown away from Nissan, we were back again in a wind so fresh that the little ship staggered under the t'gall'nts. It rained, and the weather was dull and gloomy and threatening: I got close to the entrance but again could not go in. I would not go in there without an examination first; I wanted to send in a boat to sound. My disagreeing charts agreed that there were fourteen feet of water in the "apparent" entrance; but coral grows, and I wanted to know, before I took the ship that way, that what was described as apparent was also real. A ship's keel is no thing to sound with, in the entrance of a coral lagoon. No, I must send in a boat. But how? The weather was too bad.

I stood away again, this time in some dejection. It did not seem possible that we should ever come to Nissan. But the weather fined in the later morning and the wind decreased; so I stood back again, as close to the entrance as I could safely get, and sent in the dinghy with the carpenter and two of the best men, Jan and Hilgard. Their instructions were to sound thoroughly in the entrance (which they had first to find) and then, if there was water enough there to float us in in safety, to hoist a French flag on an oar so that I might know it was safe to bring the ship in. The French flag shows up well against the water.

They went in, and we stood off and on. Then the wind freshened again — freshened and freshened, until it was blowing more than a strong breeze. The sea rose. It began to rain. The sea increased so much that I did not think the dinghy could come out; what could I do? Wait outside until the weather cleared? Or perhaps they were lost! I searched the seas anxiously — no dinghy. Wind and sea still increased — still no dinghy. We had been getting farther from the island; I wore ship again, being under short canvas, and stood in on the dangerous tack towards Barahun. The island was now a lee shore, but I had to find the dinghy. Many sharp eyes kept lookout aloft. I did not think that the dinghy would dare come out; probably they lay in the entrance, showing the French flag — or maybe not. But there was nothing in the entrance.

I stood towards the islands, on and on. It was ticklish work. I did not want to stand so close on that lee shore that I could not get away again, but I must find the dinghy. Now I steered towards the entrance, the break between Nissan and Barahun, conning from the fore crosstrees; I had decided then that the dinghy must be waiting there. I would take a chance on the French flag. But there they were! They had come out! In that frail pine dinghy — but they are sailors, real sailors. The sea was so high now that I could not see the dinghy until we were close upon it, and then the first thing I saw was the French flag, flung high on a crest. I ran down upon them, picked them up quickly as we rolled past, and left the dinghy on a long line astern.

There is an entrance, they say; it is between Nissan (at Pokonien Point) and Barahun. The least depth they had was sixteen feet. (We draw a fraction over twelve.) Inside the lagoon they had twelve to twenty fathoms — water enough in there. It is only the entrance that is dangerous. Well, we are pretty close now. I square up and stand in, under easy canvas. The wind has increased to a moderate gale. From aloft I can see no entrance, though now we are pretty close: the sea breaks furiously on a reef which seems to extend right across. But, as we come in, I see a break, quite close to Barahun. How narrow! And there the bottom is clearly to be seen. Sixteen feet? I hope so! We are on it now: from the crosstrees I see the rocks beside us, and hear the surf's roar, and see the coco-nut palms of Pokonien so close; and there ahead the water seems to shallow again, ominously. We have good way. She makes eight knots under only the fore and main tops'ls, the fores'l, and a few stays'ls: with good men at wheel, anchor, windlass, and all four leadlines, she rushes in.

I hold my breath as she comes on. There is little sea here now; thank God for that! We straighten in the coral gateway to choose the streak of heaviest green from the confusing array of surface colours ahead, colours that vary sharply, indicating the shoals and the depth of water. I have not much time to choose. Quickly, quickly! Starboard a little! Ah, she comes — steady now! It is the place of darkest green in a poor selection: there seems to be a shallowing inner bar right across. Sixteen feet? I *hope* so! But there is. She comes across. The fish flit frightened in the gloomy depths; the water deepens, and the flattened area of the huge lagoon in now all round us. We are across the bar and I have now only to choose an anchorage. I get away from the entrance, and let go. Within ten minutes the native canoes are out to us, wanting tobacco, selling pigs.

Nissan lagoon, and Pinipir, showing the track of the *Joseph Conrad*, and where she was hove down by the beach.

Nissan was first seen by Captain Carteret in His Majesty's sloop *Swallow* in the year 1767, on a voyage round the world. Behind that brief statement of historic fact there lies the story of one of the most remarkable and courageous voyages ever made, a voyage not much written of, not very rich in discovery, but rich in courage, determination, and human endurance beyond praise. Captain Philip Carteret, R.N., stands out even in the brave company of his fellow navigators — Byron, Wallis (with both of whom he sailed), Cook, Bligh. This "neglected and gallant officer," not long returned from his voyage under commodore Byron in H.M.S. *Dolphin*, was appointed to the command of the *Swallow*, sloop, to be tender to the *Dolphin* on a second circumnavigation. Wallis was to have the *Dolphin*. Carteret, being informed of this, at first felt pleased, since his first voyage had given him a taste for South Seas wandering, and the hardships which, in those days, usually included a more than even chance of death by disease, not to speak of other risks and hazards, in no way frightened him. But one look at the *Swallow* made him somewhat doubtful. She was old — thirty years old — and she never had been much good. She was obviously unhandy, the sort of clumsy vessel that makes a sailor's heart go down within him, a craft in which no mariner on earth could take much pride. Why she had been chosen for the important service she was about to perform, Carteret did not know, and he began to think she was intended to accompany the *Dolphin* only as far as the Falklands, there to be relieved by a more suitable vessel — if she reached the Falklands. As he watched his new charge being fitted out, the conviction grew on him that she could not possibly be intended for a voyage round the world. While the *Dolphin* was well supplied with everything she could want, including a considerable quantity of iron for gifts to the natives and a forge for working it, and trinkets and toys of all descriptions, the *Swallow* received nothing beyond bare necessities, and scant allowance of them.

Several times Captain Carteret petitioned the Lords of the Admiralty for some better provision for his vessel, which he perceived was not even to be properly supplied with rope or with junk for making it. His petitions went unheeded; in answer to his queries he was told that the *Dolphin* held enough. But, as all long voyages of vessels in company had shown, there was grave danger of the ships being parted: the *Swallow* should have been properly equipped on her own account. She was not. She was not even given proper sheathing against the ravages of the tropic worm, though it was usual, when sending vessels on tropical employments, to provide them with well-fastened extra planking as a defence against the destructive toredo. There was nothing on board to trade with natives, either to secure their goodwill or for profit. The vessel was overcrowded, and even at her berth before the beginning of the voyage she was leaky.

In this poor old tub, Captain Carteret, with Captain Wallis in the *Dolphin*, set out from Plymouth Sound on Friday, August 22, 1766, bound on a voyage of exploration and discovery to the South Seas and round the world. The object of this voyage was more particularly to discover the southern continent, the probable existence of which had been discussed by geographers and scientists for many years. With this in view, the ships were to double the Horn, or work through the Straits of Magellan into the South Seas, and proceed westwards in a high latitude looking for what they might find. This no ship had ever done. They were to be no exception to the rule. Such a voyage should certainly have been attempted the other way, but the recommendations of Lieutenant Maury for making eastwards passages in high latitudes were not then known. Long before Maury, however, Cook was to make this passage from the west to the east; Bligh followed him, on the first commercial voyage to Tahiti.

At sea it was quickly found that the *Swallow* would neither tack nor steer, nor could she, under all sail, keep up with the *Dolphin* under reefed tops'ls. This was galling to Wallis and Carteret alike; but they went on, putting in at Madeira as their last civilized port. Here occurred an incident which ought to have been brought to the attention of William Bligh, later commander of His Majesty's transport *Bounty*. Nine of the *Swallow*'s seamen, having some money but no leave, swam ashore naked from the anchorage with their money in kerchiefs tied round their heads, but finding the surf too great to land, had to swim out again. They were hauled before Carteret, expecting to be flogged. They were nine of his best seamen, and Carteret well knew that they did not intend to desert. They explained that they sought nothing but a last "skinful of liquor" before the ship finally departed from civilization, and both by looks and words expressed their contrition and their willingness to undergo any punishment that might be given them. Carteret, saying that he hoped they would risk their lives only on more important occasions in future, observed that if he required good swimmers for any enterprise he knew now where to apply for them, and told the men to "put on some cloaths and turn in." A murmur of satisfaction, we are told, ran instantly through the whole ship's company at an act of kindness which was extraordinary in those days. Henceforth, Carteret, who had already shown himself a fearless and resourceful commander, had every man in that ship thoroughly behind him.

In the course of time, the poor *Swallow* arrived at the Straits of Magellan, and passed through. Carteret now asked Wallis what he should do: the sloop was obviously nothing but a nuisance to the larger vessel. He himself thought it best to scrap the *Swallow*, or send her home with the sick: he would stay, he offered, as First Lieutenant of the *Dolphin*, under Wallis, feeling that he could be of more use there. If he remained in the ill-found *Swallow* he could be nothing but a hindrance to the expedition. But Captain Wallis had his orders, and stuck to them; these stated that the *Swallow* was to accompany the expedition. However, the Straits were no sooner successfully passed than the *Dolphin* sailed out of sight, and was not again seen by those in the *Swallow*. Nor would Wallis consent to put proper stores aboard his less fortunate consort, feeling, perhaps, that he might need all he had for himself.

After vicissitudes which would have dismayed any weak man and a good many strong men, Carteret now found himself in a leaking and ill-found ship which was unfit to make the passage from Spithead to Plymouth under her own sail, without sufficient stores or food, left at the Pacific end of the Straits of Magellan to find the rest of his way round the world. He could have doubled the Horn to the eastward at once, and sailed home that way; but he was made of sterner stuff. The orders were that his vessel should proceed on the journey; very well, she would. She did. She at once encountered a gale which lasted twenty-three days, in the course of which she was several times nearly lost, and extricated from perilous positions only by the most consummate skill in seamanship. During all this time she "experienced an uninterrupted course of dangers, fatigues, and exertions. She worked and sailed very ill, the weather was dark and tempestuous; and the boats, which the exigencies of the ship kept constantly employed, were in continual danger of being lost." She would neither tack nor wear without a boat or a couple of boats to pull her round; these, then, had constantly to be swung out and used, which was difficult work in bad weather. For some days the ship lay to under bare poles "and the water at times was torn up and whirled round in the air, much higher than the masts' heads."

Captain Carteret made for the island of Juan Fernandez to take in wood and water and refresh the crew but he found the place a Spanish fortress, and sailed for Mas-a-fuera "since we could not suppose the Spaniards well disposed to receive English visitants." At Mas-a-fuera he found a high surf. Anchoring with difficulty, he was blown away and was three days beating back again. But he took in some water though no refreshments. He then stood to the westward in accordance with the general orders for the voyage, but it was the winter season in the far south and it was impossible to make much westing without going into the region of the south-east trade. However, he held grimly on, doing his best to carry sail to drive the sluggish ship in order to prevent the possibility of perishing by famine. He discovered Pitcairn's Island, named after a son of Major Pitcairn (who fell at Bunker Hill), who saw it first, but they could not land there. Other similar islands were seen, not one of them offering the slightest refreshment to the now starving and scurvy-stricken crew. The ship, to make a bad position very much worse, now "admitted great quantities of water and was otherwise in a very crazy condition." Her sails were rotten and her rigging, which was, of course, rope, began to go. Nor had they any rope with which to repair it. They were forced to the expedient of cutting a length from the hempen cable and, after reducing this to the original oakum from which it was made, starting afresh to spin yarn and make rope of the size they needed. They had no proper tools for this work and had to make them. More and more men went down to scurvy; they began to die. Carteret himself was seriously ill, so ill that his recovery was despaired of. There was no surgeon. The First Lieutenant was also ill; Carteret and he were the only navigators. Still they fought their way westward against winter gales and fierce adversity, sticking to their orders, working through uncharted seas in their crazy ship.

The *Swallow* was now so foul she would not answer the helm, and they had constantly to use boats to pull her round. Carteret seemed to be dying. At length, having crossed most of the Pacific between the twentieth and thirtieth parallels of south latitude, he decided that he must give up the intention of continuing on that difficult course, and bend all his energies towards getting the ship and the survivors home somehow. He, therefore, stood up towards the trades. Had he had a proper vessel, or had the wretched *Swallow* even possessed one fourth of the equipment she should have had on board, Carteret, in all probability, would have forestalled the famous Cook as the real discoverer of Australia. However, he was not to have the honour of any great discoveries, though his accomplishment was not lessened by that.

He stood up now towards the Santa Cruz Islands and saw them; he anchored off Santa Cruz, hoping to be able to establish friendly relations with the natives and secure at least some coco-nuts. But the excessive stupidity of the master who, sent to find a better anchorage where the ship could be careened, went ashore instead and cut down coco-nut trees, caused almost immediate hostilities; the master himself was killed, and three of the best surviving seamen died of arrow wounds. Seven other seamen were seriously wounded. The *Swallow* was leaking more than ever. Carteret, who could scarcely stand erect on his deck, could see pigs and coco-nuts and fruit ashore, but he had nothing with which to placate the natives and he did not want to open fire on them. He went on. Before leaving, he had been forced to fire on some of the natives, in order to land a watering party. They took in water, but of fresh food they had none.

He determined to stand on towards the place called by Dampier, New Britain, where there might be sustenance of some kind. It was on the way here that he discovered the Carteret Islands, and Nissan. "We called this flat, green isle Sir Charles Hardy's Island," says the account of the voyage. But they did not go in. They had no one to man the boats to pull the bedraggled sloop into Nissan lagoon; and they knew well enough that, if they did go in there, they could expect little help from the Melanesians, a wild, fierce race in those early days. So the *Swallow* sailed by; and when at last she came to an anchor off New Britain, and some fresh food could be found, not the combined strength of all hands could weigh the anchor. They had to wait until they were strong enough, to go on.

Still they sailed westwards with the *Swallow* now sinking. Thirteen men were dead and thirty more dying. The natives of the Admiralty Islands, which Carteret named, attacked them; south of Mindanao a large pirate prau of the Moros opened fire on them, to receive a raking broadside that sent her, doubtless mightily astonished, at once to the bottom. The north monsoon had set in; they could not go to windward against it, or reach Batavia. Carteret took the stricken ship into the Celebes port of Macassar, and sent a note ashore asking the governor for leave to buy food and to shelter and refresh the crew. The governor replied by ordering him to get out at once and to anchor nowhere on those coasts. They were of the wrong nationality.

"God, sir!" said Carteret to this unbelievably swinish official, "I will run my ship ashore in your town and we will sell our lives there as dear as possible, if you do not grant me this permission!"

He weighed his anchor, with great difficulty, and stood towards the town. He was then given the leave he sought, but many of the crew died. The deplorable condition of the ship was repaired as well as it might be, but, since she should have been condemned, she was still far from seaworthy even after her overhaul. In the East Indies more of the crew died; but Carteret himself lived to bring his indifferent charge homewards round Good Hope, by way of Table Bay, St. Helena, and Ascension (speaking M. de Bougainville's *Bourdeuse* on the way.) He anchored at Spithead on March 20, 1769, after a voyage of two years and seven months.

Such a man, then, was the discoverer of Nissan. I thought of him and his poor *Swallow* as I looked round me at the anchorage.

In the evening I landed at Pokonien to watch the primitive natives broiling their evening meal of fish taken straight from the lagoon; and walk a while through the white man's abandoned plantation on the point. Here the great depression has sent the buildings derelict, and the coco-nuts lie strewn heavily on the sodden ground. Now the sun is out and its setting over the broad lagoon is beautiful. The quietened wind sings softly in the high palms and the blue waters lap lazily on the golden inner beach while the surf of the wild Pacific roars outside. It is all peaceful and romantic and vaguely adventurous, as a South Seas island ought to be. But in the lagoon the long shapes of hungry sharks are often to be seen and the fierce stingray abounds; the golden beach soon gives way to a jagged coral strand, poisonous to the bare feet. Behind the plantation clearing, the jungle is dank, mouldy swamp; and through the high palms it soon rains. Then it seems that this is not at all what a South Seas island ought to be.

The people I saw were Melanesian, and I fear, not now very interesting. They might have been once; but now the remnant of them is gloomy, scabby, sad. A wholesome, upstanding, clean-skinned specimen is rare; perhaps the recruiters have taken all of those away and only the rejects remain. But in all truth they are not very attractive; and the men are more handsome than the women. They are quiet; speak pidgin-English volubly; wear loin cloths, and (if at all possible) felt hats; live in grass houses, in small, compact villages; dislike work, but like bargaining and tobacco, especially tobacco. For this they brought out fish, coco-nuts, fruit, limes, pigs, bows and arrows — everything they had; but it had to be the right kind of tobacco, a strong, black twist of American manufacture, used as currency among the remoter South Seas islands for years. Besides this they always demanded a supply of paper, newspaper for preference, though a few pieces of toilet paper would do. With this they rolled themselves stout cigarettes, one whiff from which would send many a European under the table. They were also mildly interested in highly perfumed soap (though I think it was the perfume that attracted), in gaily coloured lap-laps (loin cloths), and in peroxide. They used this to bleach their hair, a fashion that has been current among them for years, although formerly they used lime. With a head of thick peroxided hair surmounted by a brilliant red flower, a Nissan brave feels good enough for anyone.

I had no peroxide to spare. What I had I used for medicinal purposes, and this the natives regarded as a great waste. They were nice fellows; they hung about in their canoes all day, and looked on in wonder while we worked.

There was work enough to do. I had gone in there to heave down the ship, if I could, to clean at least the upper strakes beneath the waterline. To do this I first roughly surveyed the lagoon, choosing a place where I could bring the ship in almost to the beach which rose steeply and was lined with trees. I brought her there and anchored her, bow and stern, mooring her in line with the beach at a place where she would just take the ground at low water. Then I carried out lines to the trees to hold her fast, and rigged tackles from the fore and main crosstrees to the largest of them. When everything was ready, all hands hove away on the tackles at low water, heaving the ship over. She came fairly easily at first but then stubbornly, so that it took all hands a hard morning's hauling to get her sufficiently over. It was interesting work. No one in the ship (including myself) had ever seen it done before; it was prehistoric, almost, like the single tops'l ship. But we enjoyed it; we cleaned the ship and learned a lot.

We stayed in under the trees until the cleaning was complete and then warped out to a safe anchorage. It blew fresh every day, and every day it rained — rained and rained and rained, though this was not supposed to be the rainy season. The rain poured into the gloomy lagoon, fringed heavily with its monotonous circle of wet trees. The water was not blue on days like those, but black; the sun shone seldom and, outside, the Pacific surf pounded ceaselessly on the coral. The island is all coral. Coral crops out everywhere: crabs scurry, huge bloated things, and lean pigs grunt in the marshes. Through the water, fish flit, multicoloured, at tremendous speed: the waving frond-like arms of the starfish and the octopus stretch for their prey from every sea-wet rock. In the forest the smell is of a dead land, rank, black, almost putrid — repellent and awful. This was no tropic paradise! Not Nissan's gloomy, huge lagoon.

Yet when the sun shines it is attractive enough, even beautiful in a sombre way: and there are fair coves on Barahun. But in the lagoon sea-snakes swim, and sharks; by the foreshore you dare not paddle for the poison prongs of the vindictive stonefish, lurking invisibly. Morose Nissan! It all seems brooding, resentful, sad, as if it did not care for the coming of the white man, the sailing gods who brought copra, and weird beliefs that never seemed to bother them very much, and a fierce desire for profit and for trade. No, no, perhaps Nissan does not care for the changes that have come over it since Captain Carteret first sailed by, and the white man, long afterwards, came among the islands.

X

Calling at the Trobriands

NISSAN was a primitive sort of place. If the Great Depression lasts much longer, it will become even more primitive. It could easily revert to its pre-"civilized" days — a scrapping of missionary medallions, a discard of "lap-laps," an end to the head-tax, and Nissan, in ten years, would be about where it began. There is a white trader there, a determined man holding stubbornly to the last of the great plantation from which he tried desperately to wrest something of a living. Much of his hard-done work is now abandoned, for the poor price of copra on world markets does not make its cultivation worth while. Like so many planters in the South Seas in these days (particularly in the British South Seas, where their plight seems to have been overlooked), he was just hanging on. He was a soldier, a fine upstanding man — hard-working, lean, tanned: he had one eye, the other being somewhere in France, and he walked with a slight limp. I liked the trader.

The traditional picture of the gin-soaked South Seas trader may have been true once of a type of man in the less important islands, but it is a gross libel on the traders of to-day. They live no lives of indolent ease, with grass-skirted maids to wait on them, while the palms grow and the coco-nuts fall on the ground and the copra somehow climbs out and dries itself. The grass-skirted maids have scurf on their breasts, and many of them are venereal; the copra, even if it made itself, would yield little profit; and any man whose task it is in life to control Melanesian labour in an island under League of Nations mandate had better forget there

ever was a lotus tree, for he will never eat of its fruit —
neither its fruit nor any other that he has not tenfold earned.

From daylight until dark the Nissan trader worked —
worked, worked, worked, superintending the gathering of
the fallen coco-nuts and the drying of the copra, the upkeep
of the property, the health and the work of his forty "boys"
(every male native who can walk is a "boy" until he dies),
getting their food for them from his stock and from the
lagoon. Twice a year the District Officer put in on his tour
of inspection to see that the labour was properly treated and
that no one had been spanked. The trader had not once
been off the island in sixteen years; in all that time we were
the second strangers to put in. He was alone, and preferred
to remain so rather than to be one of a small white
community into whose joint interests, pastimes, shams,
bridge parties and quarrels he would be forced. It is better
to rely on oneself for company than upon the inevitably
doubtful qualities of a mixed mob. How long would he stay
there? He did not know when he could get away, if ever;
the plantation now was all he had, after those many years,
and he had to hold on to that.

The civilized policy that played so great a part in "opening
up" the South Seas, of getting the producer in the
middleman's debt, keeping him there, and profiting by his
product, has grown so well that, though intended originally
for the natives, it now embraces most of the whites. The
producers of copra, if there is ever again any profit in their
commodity, are for the most part so deep in debt that they
will produce for years only to satisfy their creditors. Many
of them, realizing this, have long since given up the hopeless
struggle. On island after island I have seen the plantations
abandoned and going back quickly to the original bush. To
the stolid native, who always could find what he needed in
his islands, the ways of the white have indeed been
incomprehensible.

All the natives at Nissan are Catholics, as medallions

strung about their dirty necks testify. There was but one dissenter, a Methodist named Karakee Joe, house-boy to the trader; Karakee was from New Ireland. The natives had but a vague idea of the essential differences between the manners in which they were supposed to worship God, and there was peace in the land. There was no theological argument and there was not very much worship, either. They looked forward to the visits of the missionaries because the missionaries were nice fellows who gave them things, and, so far as I could see, this was about as deeply as their religion went. They took life as it came, and were not bothered much with any conception of the hereafter. Their ideas of heaven as a place high up in the sky had recently suffered a rude shock, since one of their number had been recruited to work at the Bulolo fields in New Guinea. He was taken there by aeroplane and kept a sharp lookout during his journey through the sky. In utter disgust he reported on his return that the white fellow had been telling lies. Heaven? There wasn't any heaven up there! Only sky — he had seen.

If some missionary did not put in an appearance soon after my departure to reply to the logic of this Man-Who-Had-Been-There, the natives of Nissan, by now, are probably digging into their coral in a vain search for hell: and, if they do not find that, their conception of Christianity will vanish entirely. What? no hell, no heaven? They cannot conceive of these ideas in the abstract; the notion of a heaven-bound soul has slight appeal to them. Whatever good comes to them, they want their bodies to be there with them to enjoy it; and they like the idea of the living bodies of their enemies and of the socially inferior frizzling in hell, prodded by the forks of the demons. Religion without hell, I fear, would lose much of its attraction to them. Well, we told them about it.

They are a quiet lot, the dwellers of Nissan in these dull days, though a mild old man who came aboard was pointed to with pride as a murderer. He sat on his haunches in a dugout canoe which two children paddled; he had a very old felt hat and an older clay pipe, of both of which he made the utmost use. He did not look to me very much like a murderer. He had killed a trader in the old days, they said — a German trader. It was a queer yarn. The trouble on Nissan has usually been concerned with women, of whom there are not enough to go round. (They just don't get born, the trader said.) Competition for the hands of the fair, then, is hard; the young bloods in former days often indulged in "daring" competitions, doing fool things to show their manhood, and the one who dared the most, or did the biggest fool thing, won the girl. The sure way to oust a rival was to think of some "daring" act which he could not imitate or surpass. This noble old fellow, being above the usual intelligence, hit on the idea of murdering the trader. There was, he reasoned, only one white trader. If he hit him with an axe and exhibited the remains — why, the day was his. The nearest trader was on Bougainville. So he killed the trader, and thus won his bride, and was happily married, I hope, and lived peacefully ever after. His kinsfolk, however, did not live so happily, for in the course of time the Germans heard of the murder and sent a punitive expedition to impress upon the natives the impropriety of such behaviour. They did this in the usual manner, by burning a few villages and "reducing the population," but they missed the murderer. This was years ago, before the war; now he came often and sat about happily in the sun, and no one seemed to bear him any grudge. His record in daring, I gathered, stands unrivalled to this day.

I saw some elephantiasis, loathsome disease: skin complaints were common — scabby legs, scurfy skin, ulcerated shoulders. Each village had its medicine boy, who, so far as I could gather, had at some time been appointed by the government and given a brief rough training. At the time of my visit, the District Officer was

189

long overdue and no medicines were left. In the picturesque words of the medicine-boy of Pokonien: "all fella messin finish: catchem more gubment bimeby."[1] I hope he did. There was need of it.

I went out from Nissan early one morning, under power in a flat calm; I should have been a long time trying to sail or to kedge out through that entrance. On the lagoon, as we departed, a tall native with elephantine feet and a flower in his limed hair chanted a weird dirge; a huge stingray, touched by our keel, darted angrily out of the way. A dog barked on the foreshore, and the bird Oscar, which I had set free here, stood watching us go. There had been no keeping Oscar on board once he heard the other birds and smelled the land. I took him ashore and let him go, hoping that his wings, which we had lightly cut to save him from flying overboard at sea and being drowned, would quickly grow. Poor Oscar had become so accustomed to a life without danger that he paid no attention even to dogs. I feared he would quickly reach some native's pot, and this he probably did as soon as we were out of sight. But he was still there when we left; we could recognize him by the white paint he had smeared from the bulwarks on his tail.

I left Nissan bound towards Tulagi, in the Solomons, port of entry in those parts. We were getting short of water and also needed a few stores. We had done quite well for fresh provisions at the lagoon and left with five pigs, two goats, four ducks, twelve fowls, and a good supply of lemons, oranges, coco-nuts, pawpaw, bananas, limes, nuts, yams, and taro; at the anchorage we were plentifully supplied with fruits and fish and crabs. The limes, lemons, and oranges were of very good quality and had, I think, been introduced by the Germans who also had brought the ducks. Nissan was uncommonly well stocked with pigs.

---

[1] All the medicine was finished: he would get some more from the Government by and by.

For the first four days after leaving Nissan it was calm, and there was a current setting us to the west. I shut off the power as soon as we were clear of the lagoon, reserving it for difficult channels of that kind. We were set steadily towards New Ireland; on clear days we could see land all round us — Feni, Tanga, New Ireland, Buka, and Bougainville, all of which are included in the Mandated Territory. They were interesting, and I wish we could have visited all of them; but we were now almost three months out from Singapore, and I pressed on. Or, I should say, I tried to press on. Then the south-east trade came, fresh, with a considerable sea, and the set against us was stronger than ever. At that time of the year, the transition period between the two seasons — the south-east and the north-west — we should have had a reasonable proportion of usable winds. If the southeast trade had blown from the south, I could have gone to the east, on the starboard tack; if it came from the east, I could have stood south on the port tack. Any wind from west or north was fair, but it never once blew from those directions. My course, to reach Tulagi, was roughly towards the south-east — and from there the wind came. It blew a moderate gale twice. I had my trade wind sails aloft, which had then been subjected to the hard wear of many tropic days and hot sun and rain. They began to go. I could not hold sail; my royals split, and then the topgallants. The headsails went; the courses were good and they stood, but shortly the fore and main tops'ls, the most important sails in the ship, also began to show bad signs of wear. Whenever possible, we clewed the sails up aloft and sewed them as they were bent: when this was not possible we sent them down, repaired them, and bent them again. I had a full Cape Horn suit in the sail locker, but I did not want to bring this out. It would suffer unnecessary wear in those regions and would be spoiled for the stormy west winds, where it would be needed. So I did what I could with the old sails, and kept on.

It became dispiriting after a while. The delights of tropic sailing are all very well in an amply powered schooner running before a fair wind: to go westwards over the Pacific before the trade can be enjoyable. But to try to beat a full-rigged ship eastwards against the trade is no joy at all. All one's ideas of the idyllic tropics — if one still has any; mine had vanished almost with my boyhood — must be scrapped; getting to wind'ard becomes a desperate, long-continued fight with the odds heavily against one. Even had I wished to use the engine (and I could not get over my curious idea that this was a kind of sacrilege), it was of little benefit. The thing had generated fifty horse-power when it was built in 1916. Many of those horses were now dead, but if they had all lived and had a hundred more with them, they could not have pushed the ship, with her big rigging, against wind and sea. Nor was it much use to beat with sails and engine, for she would not point higher than six points, in a sea; and the yards, hauled sharp on the backstays, caused so much chafe that the sails and the rigging would quickly go to pieces. No, we had to sail: well, that was what we were there for.

The current now pushed me far to the westward of the Trobriand Islands, near which we then were, and over amongst the uninhabited Lusancays. I determined to put in here, if I could, and get the anchor down while we thoroughly overhauled the sails. We could not spare the tops'ls from the yards while we tried to beat, without losing hopelessly. If we were driven much further down to leeward we should be in an awkward situation, and might have to wait for the coming of the north-west season to free ourselves. There was no fault in the ship, which was as good as ever; and for a full-rigged ship she worked to wind'ard very well. But the conditions were too much for her short length; in the troubled calms that the strong trade left, she bucked and rolled and flung her broad bows into the swell, and went bodily to leeward and backward. It was my fault for being there; I ought to have stayed in the counter-equatorial current of the North Pacific until I was to wind'ard of all the Solomons, before standing down across the Line. However, there I was, and something had to be done about it. It freshened up, and I stood towards the Lusancays on the port tack, making about SSW with the drift and the leeway. The Lusancays are poorly charted and, as far as I could see, little would be gained by surveying them, for ships are well advised to stay away. We stood several times almost to the edge of the great reef that surrounds them. They are a group of cays on a shallow coral bank of considerable extent off the north-east coast of New Guinea. Beyond them there is nothing but reefs and the D'Entrecasteaux Islands to New Guinea. I could see no anchorage; I could find no entrance into this vast lagoon and, if I had found one, would have been most careful about using it. It did not look the kind of place in which a full-rigged ship would be safe, and the weather was such that I dared not send out a boat to investigate. Our dinghy was suffering from seventeen broken ribs from its battering in the sea at Nissan; beside that I had only a Norwegian pram and the ship's life-boats. The pram was very small, and I could not spare a crew for a life-boat.

The sails became worse, in spite of all our efforts to take care of them. The wind was no better. I beat and beat, and mostly lost: after beating for two days and covering, by the log, more than 400 miles, we found we had lost five. We came in on the Lusancays to leeward of the place where we had been two days before. Nowhere was there anchorage. I computed, from a series of accurate observations, that the set towards the NW — directly against me — was at the rate of from forty to sixty miles a day. This was serious.

I decided to go into Kiriwina in the Trobriands, if I could. Here there was anchorage, and here I could procure refreshments, too, though I was not in need of these. I still had fresh water sufficient to take me to Tulagi. But how was I to get to the Trobriands? I was within sight of

Kiriwina then, to leeward of it. I beat on. I did not have to regain much of the lost ground in order to enter the channel between Kiriwina and the smaller island of Kaileuna, which with Kitava, form the Trobriand Island group. There was, I read in the Directions, an assistant resident magistrate at Losuia, on Kiriwina. That was good; I could go and see him, as I had seen the commandant at Bongao. It was scarcely probable that Losuia would be a port of entry but, at any rate, there was someone to report the ship to. Round northern Australasian waters, there have been in recent years many scares of strange vessels, usually said to be of the sampan type, which raid trochus beds and bêche-de-mer on the local reefs. I did not wish to be confused with these marauders; I wanted no trochus or bêche-de-mer, and though my vessel was decidedly no sampan, she was certainly a strange craft to be in those seas. I did not wish to be mistaken again for a mysterious vessel probably engaged in nefarious practices. I suppose the charge would have been either that I was blackbirding, or bound with a cargo of coolies to work for the Italians in Northern Queensland. I was nothing but an honest citizen with a ship making a difficult voyage, and I did not want there to be any mistakes about it. So I headed, when I could, towards the passage between Kiriwina and Kaileuna, to Losuia. It proved rather difficult to get there.

In the end, I had to come in by night, after beating for ten days. I did not care for this night piloting, since there are no lights in those waters, and they are very poorly charted, but I knew I should either go in then, when I had the chance, or not at all. By that time we had a regular routine for such difficult work, and every man had his post. There were six leadsmen, one in the fore chains on each side, another aft, and three at the patent deep-sea apparatus which sounded to 300 metres but had to be worked by hand. The carpenter was at the windlass, the mate with his maul on the fo'c'sle head by the starboard anchor, the second mate aft, and there was a picked helmsman. Everything was ready to fetch the ship up at a minute's notice. I would have sent a boat ahead to sound if I had had one. It has to be like that when you are wandering through coral reefs. They rise up quickly: there is scant warning. I knew from the chart that the wide bay on the western side of Kiriwina, where Losuia is situated, was full of reefs, though the channel between the islands was shown to be tolerably clear. But how is one to preserve a bearing in a dangerous channel when it is dark and there is nothing on which to get a bearing? There are fast tides, swift streams, which, more often than not, set *across* the channels instead of directly through them; almost anywhere a sudden outcrop of coral may grate on the keel. Coral is hard.

I usually conned from the fore cross-trees, by day, with the sun behind me, since I could better gauge the depth of the water by its changing colours from there and see the dangers; but at night ill water is the same unless it breaks. I went, then, out to the jib-boom end, about thirty feet before the vessel, fairly high.

In this manner we at last approached the channel into Losuia, early on the evening of October 13, 1935, when the ship was almost a year out from England. I held my breath. The wind, for once, was fair, barely fair. We could just hold the course. The moon should have risen early; it did, but it was so cloudy that its rising made hardly any difference. I could not see. I went on in, groping, groping. The channel was narrow. The land was close. I could hear the wind in the trees, hear the natives, talking and laughing: I saw a village fire. I had only the fore and main tops'ls set, the stays'ls and the spanker. No bottom, no bottom! chant the leadsmen — no bottom! The chart (long since committed to memory) gives nothing but confusing "depths" of no bottom at eight and twenty fathoms, here and there; we sounded continually with the deep-sea lead to sixty, eighty and 100 metres and came right through the channel with no bottom.

(The for'ard leadsmen swung hand leads on twenty-five fathoms.) No bottom, no bottom! The chant is worrying as we stand on. I hear the water lapping on the reefs; a dog barks. Shall we come through and into that reef-filled bay, without finding anchorage? I want to get the anchor down now as soon as there are soundings I will take no more chances. But we get no bottom. No bottom, no bottom! I cannot drop the anchor in the sea. I clew up the fore tops'l; take the main from her: her way seems prodigious on this quiet night. There *must* be anchorage! I am worried, very worried, for I know how precipitately these reefs rise. When you are in soundings you are aground. When we have almost reached Boli Point, the deep-sea lead suddenly has a reading — forty metres: up and down it goes in its gear aft: thirty-seven metres: twelve metres. The hand leads have bottom at seven. Hard-a-starboard! Into the wind with her: let go! Let go it is; the cable roars in the quiet night; she brings up nicely. The torn sails are furled at last, and the yards are trimmed. The riding lights go up, and we have arrived.

Chart of the Trobriand Islands,
showing the anchorage of the *Joseph Conrad*.

I put out the dinghy, as was my practice, and sounded round. The moon was clear then, almost full; we had to pull a very little way from the ship to get on a reef. But there was room enough: she was all right. Leaving a watchman on deck, all hands turned in for a good night's sleep.

In the morning, examining the place from the masthead, I saw that we had chanced on the best anchorage, so I stayed there. Ahead of us, the wide bay between the horns of Bwoioa and the wooded southern end of Kiriwina seemed full of reef of that same nasty pale green tint which had distinguished the Lusancays; it was a locality best left alone. Perhaps there was a channel through to the south; I could not see one, and did not look any closer. We could go out the way we came in. We were rather close to the fringing reef of Bwoioa; half a cable from the ship there were two fathoms.

I liked the appearance of the island. It is coral surrounded by fringing reef; the tops of the trees seem to be about 300 feet above sea level. The land, such as I could see of it, appeared fertile and well planted. There were numerous villages of dome-like grass houses, some of them along the shore and others inland, all of them appearing, from the masthead, very orderly, neat, and well laid out. I could see many gardens, and the whole appearance of the island was such as I had not expected to see anywhere in the Pacific in these days. It seemed to be almost unspoiled. I could not see the government station from there.

Several native canoes came out to us, with yams, coconuts, fowls, and sweet potatoes. They also brought grass skirts to exchange for tobacco, but I was unfortunately without a supply of the stick tobacco they demanded. They brought paddles too, and one man had a model of a pearling canoe for which he asked "fibe chillun."[2] They knew some English here, though the horrid abortion of

---

[2] Five shillings

Pidgin was not in general use. The natives were upstanding fellows, light-skinned, clean, well-built; they looked more Polynesian than Melanesian, and there was an entire absence of the morose scabbiness of Nissan. They were animated, cheerful, and welcoming. I did not allow them to come on board, but let them stand in the channels and sit along the hammock netting, from which vantage-posts they stared in wonder at our clean decks, and the cannon, and the maze of lines. We began at once to unbend the torn sails, and to set about repairing them: almost the entire suit urgently needed overhauling. The natives looked on and chattered among themselves. I made no attempt to land; I wished only to use this refuge to repair the sails.

The quiet peace of this gentle morning was rudely interrupted by the arrival of the official launch from Losuia, to set on board a fellow in white shorts with a close-clipped moustache, a sharp jaw, and cold blue eyes. From this gentleman there was no welcome. He was, I gathered, the assistant resident magistrate. Had we been to Samarai? he asked. Samarai? Where was that? I had a vague idea the place was up some creek somewhere in the East Indies. No, I had not been to Samarai, and had no intention of going there. If we had not been to Samarai, he said, we could not remain at the anchorage. It appeared that this was the port of entry for Papuan territory. It was the same old problem: if I could have gone to Samarai, wherever it was, I would most certainly not have gone to Losuia. I pointed out to the magistrate that I had brought my ship into the waters of his domain only to find anchorage and repair the blown-out sails, and for no other purpose. I did not care especially about the Trobriand islands and desired no contact with the land. The anchorage we were in was the only one in those parts; I was there and I was going to stay there until my ship was fit to take the seas again. He seemed to imagine that we could repair the sails in five minutes, and be gone again. I told him it was three days' hard work, at the very least. We would get it done as quickly as possible and then be gone.

The magistrate was only endeavouring to carry out the law. The Trobriands are Papuan territory for which the ports of entry are Port Moresby and Samarai. Samarai lay some hundred miles away to the south, beyond a maze of reefs which were not navigable by my vessel. But surely, a sailing vessel, properly accredited and with her papers all in order, with a clean bill of health and making a harmless voyage, might, if she can, find such haven as she needs. Often on that voyage, I felt envious of Captain Cook and Wallis and Byron and all those pioneers (though never of Carteret), for, when they put into islands, they were met only by spears and stones, never by tax-gatherers, immigration inspectors, and assistant magistrates. Spears and stones may be placated by exhibitions of firm friendliness — the great Cook excelled at such things — or met with their kind. But magistrates — they hold a mean advantage over us all. They are the Law. They can make long reports about us and charge us with every kind of misdemeanour, and bind us laboriously with red tape.

The conduct of this Governor-General of the Trobriands, though he was within his rights, contrasted strangely with the quiet common sense of the Filipino commandant at Bongao, a man with a really turbulent people to rule, and now and then a taste of warfare. He sent the islanders smartly about their business, and I saw that they seemed afraid of him, as well they might be of one who could jail them with a word: but he softened, once in a while. The personal side of him, when it showed through, was quite the reverse of the official: I grew to like him as a man, before we were gone, but as an official, as the ruling representative of the Great White at the Trobriands — why, I frankly thought the whole place would be much the better for his absence. The fact that he received us churlishly did not greatly affect my opinion. I was anchored, and I was going to repair my sails. But I saw, in the very short time I was there, that this Kiriwina, last of the happy islands of the South Sea, deserves a man of lofty ideals and experienced, far-seeing judgment, a paragon of administrative and formative excellence, a man grown old in the scientific survey of the Pacific and its peoples, an administrator, in short, capable of preserving this last vestige of Paradise for the world. This little man had set out, I heard, to *improve* it — he and the missionaries.

As soon as his back was turned I saw another launch; it was a trader, very drunk, with a bottle of gin. He said he was the Bishop of Melanesia, though he looked to me like the Earl of Footscray, and he invited all hands ashore to his inn. He really had an inn, I discovered; he drank so much that he had to take out a licence as a hotel to get his own supplies.

I wish I had seen a great deal of the Trobriands. I liked immensely all I saw. I went ashore, with the magistrate's permission. He wrote me frequent official epistles telling me to get out; but ashore he was all right. I discovered that something of his hostile reception was due to the fact that, in former days, Kiriwina had been the haunt of boozing young bloods from Samarai in quest of sex. These gentlemen, and others, had brought venereal disease. The Trobriand Islanders, as the magistrate pointed out, have moral standards different from our own and the maidens attach no special importance to the sex act beyond considering it, rightly enough, as a necessary natural function. In this they are encouraged by their age-old belief that copulation and conception have nothing to do with one another, children being the spirits of their ancestors who creep into the bodies of the women, unknown to them, while they bathe. A husband recruited to work on a distant plantation (though the Trobriand Islanders do not often go away and are not much recruited) might return, after two years, and look upon his spouse's newborn babe without the slightest trace of jealousy. She had bathed a little carelessly, perhaps. A married life based upon such ideas as this has many advantages, more particularly in an island where nothing is known either of the need for, or the practice of, birth control; but such beliefs make the natives easy victims to venereal disease. For years Kiriwina was a blot even in the Pacific through this dreadful scourge; nothing but many years of determined medical effort and strict control could check the evil. Things are better now; but the evil is not entirely eradicated and probably never will be.

I fully sympathized with the desire of the magistrate to keep the misery of venereal disease from the people as much as he could. No one was allowed ashore from my ship after dark, and no one from the island came to the vessel. By the permission of the magistrate, the boys in two parties were enabled to see a little of the coastal village by Losuia. Each party was ashore for a few hours only, and they saw no more of the Trobriands. Some of them told me afterwards that they were approached by old men who asked them if they would like to buy their daughters? Pretty girls, too, and quite willing; but I had scared the young gentlemen thoroughly about disease, and had given them to understand that this was still a hot-bed of it.

Losuia itself, though I did not care for the sight of the prisoners toiling by the government paths — their wrongdoing seemed trifling — was a pleasant place surrounded by well populated villages of happy brown people who played cricket on the mission field and met us smiling on the little wharf. The boys and the men were dressed simply in pieces of twisted fibre covering something of the crotch, made fast fore-and-aft on a string of twine, or sometimes, with the pearl divers, on an ancient army belt bought from a trader. They all had large mops of fuzzy hair in which red flowers had been thrust, and, here and there, a feather. Into the lobes of their ears they had spliced small rings; a few had them also in their noses. The girls and women, many of whom were pleasant to look upon, wore abbreviated grass skirts which, as they walked, swung seductively on their rounded forms. Some of the men and women had their hair shaved and their bodies blackened with soot; these were in mourning. All of them were clean, muscular, well-built, and most attractive in appearance and behaviour. To walk along the lagoon paths was entrancing, though the magistrate took care to send an armed policeman with us when we went. The blue-robed dark-visaged constable, trailing his gun, seemed curiously out of place there, though the constabulary I met were good fellows. They did not seem to take their duties with regard to us very seriously, whatever may have been their instructions, and we found them cheerful guides. The way was through clean, pleasant villages — in a few of which I saw the horrible rusted sheet-iron which has become so common in the islands — past well-kept gardens, swimming pools, pigs, very fat and very contented; coco-nuts, bananas, pineapples; and frequently groups of sturdy natives carrying the produce of their fields, like the Balinese. In each village the people came out to welcome us as we passed, eager to make friends. They offered us pawpaw, coco-nuts, limesticks, gourds, and such things, and they appeared more eager to give than to sell. But I had nothing with me to give in exchange, and therefore did not accept their presents.

Often on the broad lagoon we saw the fast canoes of the islanders sailing, coming and going from the nearer islands. The Trobrianders have always been great sailors; the manner in which they handled their big canoes was grand to see, and we cheered them as they passed. They were as interested in our "big canoe" as we were in theirs, and they always sailed close by. Some of the cadets tried once, not to sail, but to paddle a short distance in a canoe from a village near the southern end of the lagoon, but they could not master even the art of balancing the vessel and were quickly thrown into the water. In the Trobriand canoes the outrigger is so short a distance from the hull that its balancing effect seems minimized; but the natives can handle their craft beautifully. Indeed, these Argonauts of the Western Pacific, as Professor Malinowski has well called them, are among the most skilled of native sailors. Until more recent years they were accustomed to make long trading voyages in their larger canoes, covering many hundreds of miles; they still sometimes venture towards the nearer of their neighbouring islands on trading voyages, though in these days such trading as is done is more often carried on in the white men's efficient but unlovely powered luggers.

As we came out to sea under sail from the lagoon a large native canoe came with us, and I sailed from Kiriwina with an abiding impression of the grace of this able native craft and its lithesome cheery crew, naked and happy, smiling in the sun.[3]

---

[3] The reader interested in the Trobrianders is referred to the works of Professor Bronislaw Malinowski: *The Sexual Life of Savages* (London, George Routledge: New York, Harcourt, Brace and Co.), *Argonauts of the Western Pacific* (London, George Routledge: New York, E. P. Dutton & Co.), and *Coral Gardens.*

XI

The Solomon Islands

I SAILED out from Kiriwina as soon as the sails were ready. I wasted no time. I had gone in only to repair my sails and with that done, departed. I secured from a friendly trader a supply of sweet potatoes (the Trobriand islanders are expert gardeners, producing yams and sweet potatoes for export to the surrounding islands), and fresh fruit; and so I passed down the passage into the Pacific again and saw, as I sailed, that, coming in, we must have passed very close to the fringing reef. Outside, I put her on the starboard tack, and began the dour beat again towards Tulagi. What a stubborn passage that was! We beat, beat, beat, with the current and the wind always against us — out past Woodlark (famed for its gold) and the Laughlans; northwards towards Vella Lavella and Treasury Islands; south towards Rennell, beating, beating, beating, with the wind and the rain. For six weeks we were within 500 miles of Tulagi and never once could head in its direction. Day after day, week after week, I beat. From Nissan to the Trobriands is about 300 miles; we sailed a thousand: from Kiriwina to Tulagi is perhaps 500 miles; we sailed 2,000. The trade wind blew frequently at the force of a moderate gale, and it was not steady either in force or in direction. Try as I might, we seemed always on the wrong tack for whatever shift might come; the wind backed and veered without reason and gave no prior indications of its intention. Sometimes we made ten miles after a day's hard slogging; sometimes we lost. The engine, even if it had worked, would have been no use in the head sea.

At last we came within sight of Rendova and Montgomery Islands of the Solomons, and the conditions worsened. We were then within 200 miles of Tulagi, and the night was miserable beyond words, with endless cold rain and sometimes hard squalls, only to be followed by cat's-paws from all directions. All the time there was a big swell in which the ship jumped so much, heading into it, that it was impossible to stand; and the night was so black that the topsails could not be seen from the deck, or the probable direction of the next cat's-paw or squall even guessed at. At midnight it blew so hard that the mainsail and the topgallants had to come in; next day it blew almost a whole gale. I beat and beat on fruitlessly against so great an array of adverse circumstances that even the ship seemed dejected, and the short road to Tulagi stretched out interminably ahead. At length I reached a position from which a southeast wind would have been fair; I could make a board with it then to Savo and reach Tulagi. The wind then came from the east, and I could do nothing. So it is with all sailing and indeed, all living — difficulty after difficulty, but one must keep on. In the end there is a reward, if it be only sleep.

It fell calm, so calm the sea flattened. The engine, when we tried to start it, broke down. It could only be of use in a calm. We drifted close to Rendova, and saw the abandoned plantations there smothered with overgrowth; no smoke from copra-drying shed rose here. It blew up again and we progressed a little, towards Pavuvu and Guadalcanal. The repaired sails began to go, and in desperation I sent the Cape Horn suit aloft. We got in among the islands. A navigation light or two would have been appreciated; we had seen none since Balabac. On Pavuvu, smoke rose here and there and the plantations seemed in order; this is one of the chief producing islands for the great combine controlled by the Lords of Soap.

The ship was ninety-three days out from Singapore before we came at last to Tulagi; we made most of the last eighty miles with the engine, in a calm. For a while the engine went well enough; from Savo onwards there was a light fair wind. It was as well; the engine was in serious trouble again. I was anxious to make Tulagi harbour before nightfall, as I had no chart. I had prepared as good a plan as I could from the description in the *Pilot*; but in the end I had to go in by night. There are range lights which lead one in; but the place abounds with reefs and small islands, and the set is across the range. The light fair wind hardly gave me steerage way, and it was difficult to keep the range. I breathed a great sigh of relief when the anchor at last was down. Ninety-three days! It had been a long, hard road, beset by navigational difficulties worse than any storm — baffling, trying, depressing. Yet the worst of the passage was over now that I had reached Tulagi, and I had always known that the north-about way would be hard. The mail steamer was in, to go out in the morning to Sydney. I sat up all night writing letters; there would not be another mail for a month. It was peaceful and calm at the anchorage, with the stars mixed in the tall cordage, and all the ocean's roll temporarily departed. And this, thank heaven, was a port of entry. I could secure the official rubber stamps at last.

I stayed a week at Tulagi, and Makambo. Tulagi is a small island off Ngela, interesting chiefly because of its geographic position among the Solomon Islands with which (apart from attempts at tax-gathering) it seems to have little other connection. Makambo is a small island off Tulagi of about the same degree of interest. Tulagi is a place of hills and tin roofs, with a club, golf course, wireless station, Chinatown, gaol, government house, British flag, and all the rest, scantily populated by whites. Prisoners do the rough work — the Public Works Department was disturbed at the moment by the small number of gaolbirds on hand — the whites carry on business and the work of administration.

Prices are high, naturally enough, though they compare more than favourably with Nassau's in the West Indies. The only place to eat is a Chinese restaurant on the water-front, called Sam Doo's, where Australian beer is half-a-dollar a bottle.

The Chinese section is on the low part of the island by the water-front, facing Makambo. Here there are some small wharves where the Chinese ketches discharge their smelly copra and depart with trade goods: now and again a recruiter comes in from Malaita with a picturesque craft and a load of labour. There is an excellent company of constabulary which, while we were there, paraded with due ceremony for the opening of the local parliament or Advisory Council — four very fine elderly men who, with the Bishop of Melanesia (then temporarily absent) and the Resident Commissioner, meet pleasantly together at intervals and discuss recommendations for the consideration of the High Commissioner of the Western Pacific at Suva in the Fijis. What, if anything, ever gets done by this means I was unable to discover; for, seemingly, even the High Commissioner has insufficient powers over the British Solomons Protectorate. The Colonial Office, in London, exercises the real control; the Commissioners are simply civil servants entrusted with the administration. The ceremony of the opening of "parliament" in such a place was curious to behold. It was staged with what pomp and show could be mustered, and the lap-lapped constables, all with fixed bayonets and very smart, lined up beside the weather-board Parliament House for inspection. They seemed to enjoy it all, and the waters of Tulagi and Gavutu harbours sparkled below pleasantly in the sun; but it seemed to me that both the Commissioner and the elderly gentlemen were well aware of the futility of the proceedings.

The British Solomons Protectorate was depressed. The natives dislike work at the best of times; the climate is severe on white men. Meanwhile the Chinese multiply. They seem contented, and open no parliaments.

Tulagi is frankly and plainly a headquarters for white living, a place where laws are — not exactly made, since that apparently has to be done somehow between Downing Street and Suva — but thought over, discussed, and sometimes vaguely suggested; where white meets white, lives with white, thinks white, and plays golf and tennis and cricket and so forth. And works, of course; there is work enough. The administration is not over-staffed. The Solomons comprise a large area with many troubles to be smoothed over, though the district officers usually go out and attend to these. The district officers are not to be found in Tulagi, though now and again their trim craft look in for stores and the handing in of reports.

I made a visit one day to Gavutu, another of the smaller islands off the coast of Ngela which have long been used as white headquarters. Gavutu is a low and pleasant island from which the great soap company controls its copra plantations in the Solomons. It is hot and humid: a white man working there, or anywhere in the Solomons, needs his leave. The soap company owns many large plantations, most of the copra being sent to Sydney for use in the factories there. Malaita boys are used for labour, but the supply is decreasing steadily. These wild young men are by no means the ideal plantation labourers; one heard of a plan for the introduction of more tractable Asiatics, but I hope this is not done. The evening before I visited Gavutu, there had been a fight of some kind. Some boys had been brought in to be paid off, and apparently some enmity flared up. I saw two of them who had been seriously injured, lying in the hospital there — one with a fractured skull and another with half his face bitten off. A Malaita boys' fight is an all-in affair: the white men who walked in and stopped this encounter took their lives in their hands. Now and again a plantation manager is still knocked on the head. While we were there the young manager of one of the outlying stations was badly injured in a sudden attack.

The great group of the Solomons is a most interesting place to visit, if one has a small ship, amply-powered, and the time. But it was no place to stay with a full-rigged ship full of boys. It is too unhealthy; white crews of vessels remaining any length of time in the islands are much bothered by ulcerated sores on the shins and ankles. When once formed, these are most difficult to treat and almost impossible to banish so long as a ship remains in those waters. Some types of malaria contracted there are serious.

We went alongside at Makambo, and were hospitably received and very well treated. The boys played cricket with a Tulagi eleven, though I had to send some baseball experts to complete our side, and a Finn and a Dane who had never seen cricket played in their lives. The boys played tennis, sailed boats, and swam in shark-proof enclosures. They had a thoroughly good time, though the climate is enervating.

Everyone at Tulagi was more than kind to us. Indeed I have not anywhere come across a more pleasant collection of white men and women than is to be found on that small island. The white planter of the Solomons, as I saw him, is a splendid type; he suffers much and puts up with much for little reward; and if in these days he can meet his indebtedness, he considers himself lucky. The problems of depopulation and the handling of labour are beyond his control; he has to use such labour as there is, and do the best he can with it. The Malaita boys, most virile of the Solomon Islanders, are energetic enough; but they require firm, tactful, and intelligent handling. The planter, if he has trouble, knows too often that it is he who stands most chance of being judged in the wrong and punished. The actual use and treatment of the native labourers is perhaps a little too thoroughly regulated, while the root causes of such ills as arise from the system continue very largely to be neglected. There are white men who should never handle labour, white or brown, but the Solomons soon find these out. They are more apt to flourish in the Mandated Territory, where in the good years many persons entered planting by taking over the former German properties, without any very clear idea of what they were about, and with little or no experience. There the policy of the Australian administration, taking its mandate from the League of Nations more seriously than most, has been a bewildering gyration between almost the pampering of the native labour on the one hand, and the creation of unnecessary difficulties for the planter on the other. The Melanesian native is mentally a child, though there are many Papua-Melanesians and pure Melanesians who reach a higher standard of intelligence than some whites: children must be disciplined, and punished, when necessary. Anyone who runs a ship — who controls or manages anything — knows that existence itself is threatened if there is no discipline, even in the handling of one's white equals. To foster in the already perplexed and confused native the modern idea that he can do what he "can get away with" is no contribution towards his progress. It is a question, indeed — a question into the pros and cons of which I shall not enter — whether new countries, whose peoples might find full occupation in working out their own destiny, ought ever to be entrusted with the control of native races. The record of Australia in this respect (disregarding, perhaps, the treatment of her own aborigines) seems to be better than New Zealand's.

When I came to clear the ship — ships pass about the seas these days more labelled and docketed and sealed and rubber-stamped than anything that travels the earth — I asked the pleasant officials, What about this port of entry business? Am I always to be plagued with that? In addition to entering your vessel in when you arrive, in the proper manner, you are also required to enter her outwards in the same way before you leave. That is to say, if you wish to visit the Solomons, you first report at a port of entry

(Tulagi, Gizo, or Faisi); go round and visit the places in which you are interested (and you may be required to carry a customs officer with you to see that you break none of the tariff laws); and finally put in again at a port of entry, and clear. Then you go on to some other territory and repeat the whole performance. This is all very well for commercial vessels, and not particularly inconvenient to well-powered yachts but, if I were required to go twice to Tulagi, I might as well prepare to spend the rest of my life beating round the Solomon Islands. I had been invited to pay visits to plantations on Guadalcanal, at Berande and Marau Sound: if I accepted, must I return somehow to Tulagi to clear, and then beat out *again*?

The officials were good fellows. They said, as the Commandant at Bongao had said, We will trust you. You may go to these places; come back and clear again if you can, or go to the station at Vanikoro, but, if you cannot, it will be all right. We know you will leave no one behind, and no disease; and that your contact with the natives will leave no evil consequences for us. (Odd wanderers might cause serious trouble, round such places as Malaita — one of the few remaining places of some danger in the modern world.) I gave my promise, and kept it. I still hoped to be able to beat as far as Vanikoro, but the season was advancing and I had grave doubts whether I should get there.

So I sailed from Tulagi, going out under power. We had again got the recalcitrant engine to work — or rather, the second mate had: he was a mechanical expert, who was also my best officer on deck, and he had grown almost to like the thing. Once clear of the range, I shut off the engine, because of shortage of fuel and our probable greater need of it later, and we began again to drift and battle and dribble on in the baffling airs in the manner to which we had so long become accustomed. But Berande was not far, just across the Sealark Channel, almost within

211

sight of Tulagi. We were anchored there next morning. A cheerful Scots Australian came out to welcome us with a sweep of his browned arm towards the shore. "Liberty Hall, boys," he said and, being a Scotsman, meant it. We were promptly given a splendid three-day holiday, though what anyone on board had done to deserve so delightful a treat was beyond my comprehension.

Berande was a good place, a large plantation of coco-nuts and rubber where hospitality has been traditional for generations. It was at Berande Jack London stayed (and afterwards wrote a book which residents claim is not completely accurate). Since his time visitors of all kinds have met with kindness there. The boys rode the lively young horses along the beaches and through the wide plantation fields. Three of them fell off, but no one was injured, though quite a few had never ridden before. We saw the copra cut and dried, and the wild Malaita labour practising a stamping dance for the Christmas celebrations. We saw the labour given its ration of stick tobacco, soap, and matches on Saturday afternoon, and the trade store opened for them to make such purchases as they wished — clay pipes, mostly. We visited the villages near by, small and not very interesting, each with its church, and its old men seated under trees. We rode to Tetere, along the coast, to see the monument to eleven Austrians from the warship *Albatross* murdered somewhere near by. It is not so long since the white man had to walk warily here, and life was cheap, both brown and white. But the missions and the government have brought a change, a surface change at any rate, and killing is now rare. We travelled in an eight-cylinder American car — the only one in the Solomons — along a new bush track to what may some day be a gold field greater than New Guinea's Morobe; and maybe not. The track was a winding forest trail that sped past jungle and native gardens, and sometimes left the matted growth unexpectedly for a wild career over a treeless plain which, without any reason whatever, suddenly appeared. There were several of these plains, all large, all uncultivated. Then we came to a mountain stream, and the boring machines, and got out and walked. The country was wild and primitive.

There is gold in the hills behind Berande. Now and again, we heard, the chief there sends in a nugget or two, though no one knows exactly where he gets them. But if the white man gets any, he will earn them. Mining of any kind under such conditions must be expensive and difficult, and is likely to remain so.

I sailed in the early morning from the anchorage off Berande, making down the passage from Guadalcanal and Florida towards the open sea. I had not time now to make Marau Sound. The wind drew ahead again and I beat and beat. The combination of navigational difficulties presented by these islands is such that I wonder the early navigators survived them. The channels are deep troughs, surrounded by reefs and shallows, serrated with rocks and coral growths over which the tidal waters boil and eddy; discoloration from the mountain streams muddies the water so that the coral heads may not be seen; baffling winds, now light, now strong, change so often and so suddenly that one is bewildered even to know on which tack to keep the vessel. Pitch-black nights, and rain; poor anchorages; high mountains, coughing their willywaw winds, spilling their black rains add to the difficulties; and always through these confused waters the general westward set of the trade wind drift sets the eastbound ship back and back. Suddenly reefs loom up ahead; one must go round quickly, to save the ship; yet to make any progress in the head winds one must constantly stand deliberately towards danger. It is better in a powered vessel, which may pick her way; but many even of those have been lost round the Solomons.

I had been anxious to make the Solomons. Now I was eager to get away. I was beating through Indispensable

Strait, between Guadalcanal and Malaita, with the long island of San Cristoval in sight; I stood on towards the eastward trying to make towards Vanikoro and Santa Cruz and down through the New Hebrides to Sydney.

We did not make Santa Cruz, or Vanikoro, or any of those places. A week out from Berande we had made good only one hundred miles; at that rate we should have been another month. I did not have the time to spare — neither the time nor the provisions. A full-rigged ship carrying twenty-eight souls cannot remain cruising indefinitely. There is a limit to her water supplies, to the provisions she can carry, and to the tempers of the crew. The longer she stays round these tropic islands the greater the susceptibility to disease. Fortunately, I had not as yet been troubled with fevers or other serious complaints, but many of the boys had tropic sores which proved stubborn and difficult to heal, and one or two had badly ulcerated legs. Medical work — for I was still the physician and surgeon to the expedition, as well as being master, navigator, chief instructor, guardian of the younger boys, and many things besides — now kept me busy for at least two hours a day. The boys had stood up very well to the long demands of the heat and the rain, the long trial of the baffling conditions, and the hard slog to wind'ard; but there was a limit for them and for every one. It was high time, I decided, that we began to think of more temperate regions. The tropics had begun to pall.

I gave up the idea of standing farther to the eastwards and went about, being to wind'ard now of San Cristoval, to stand towards the south'ard on the other tack. I was now so far to wind'ard that I could easily make the course for Sydney with the Trade a fair wind; I had only to stand on full-and-by on the port tack, and the set would give me my westing. I looked at the charts, and saw that I should pass through the unnamed strait that separates San Cristoval from the two small islands off its south-eastern end, Owa Raha and Owa Riki. I decided that I would try to anchor for a while at Owa Raha, where the chart showed a break in the reef called Port Mary; I could leave a note for the district officer there, explaining that I had been unable to fetch Vanikoro.

It was easy enough to make Owa Raha, though again I came by night. I would not, however, take the risk of trying to pick up the anchorage at Port Mary without daylight. There are no lights and there was no moon. I sailed by, and the breaking of the long Pacific swells on the Cape Surville reefs was an ominous sound in the dark. I lay to when I had an offing, and sailed back in the morning. I was glad then that I had not attempted any night piloting, for the harbour was nothing but a break in a dangerous reef — a break that, safely entered, gave pleasant and secure anchorage in one of the loveliest little bays we had yet visited.

Our first welcomer was a trader who had been a master-mariner and a sailing-ship sailor, Henry Küper, formerly of Germany, who had been in the *Parma*. He had not seen square yards upon a ship for twenty years, and he was very pleased to see us.

XII

The Dance of the Tree Men

I WAS glad indeed that circumstances took me to Owa Raha. It and its sister island, Owa Riki, were two of the most interesting small islands of the whole voyage. The people were clean, friendly, and welcoming; Owa Raha, though long under white influence, still possessed enough of the primitive to be interesting; and Owa Riki, called by Mendana, Santa Catalina, had not changed much since the Spanish navigator first saw it. The small bay of Port Mary (which no one ashore knew by that name), though open to the west and north-west, was secure in all other weather and almost idyllic in its beauty. Fresh water bubbled from springs into the bay, so that it was possible to put one's mouth to the sea itself and drink copiously of delightfully cold and invigorating fresh water; the fruits of the land were plentiful; and fish and crays abounded in the waters. What refreshments could not be secured there could easily be obtained by a boat trip to Star Harbour, at the eastern end of San Cristoval — the trader said this was a good place to heave down a ship — where swine and cattle thrived, and the trader had a large plantation. Owa Raha was more his home, his sphere of influence; he did not try to make a living out of it. Bêche-de-mer from the reefs off San Cristoval, and shell, and the copra of his plantation, gave him that.

Ashore, I saw that the villages were well laid-out, almost as if a town-planner had been at work there. The grass houses were well constructed and thoroughly clean. The islands, being coral, are low; but the interior of Owa Raha reaches a height of 500 feet in one place. The island is really a raised atoll: except where it has been cleared for the natives' gardens, it is well wooded. There are two fresh-water lakes in the interior. A well-kept path leads the two miles across the island to the villages on the other side; the way along this path, though the heat is severe and the coral outcrops hard on the feet, is most beautiful. By the western shore, near Port Mary — the village here is Upuna — one passes through a large village with a church. Just beyond the village clearing, the woods begin and continue the whole rough way to the eastern shore. Here the great Pacific swells roll in on the fringing reef, curling and breaking in austere majesty; the natives fish, and the children play in the warm waters close by the beach. The coco-nuts which grow here are for food and drink; their tall trunks lean westward from the trade wind's blowing; and, high above in the cloudless sky, the frigate bird flies. There are two villages on the eastern shore, one Christian and the other, newly made, to which the heathen have retired. The numbers of the heathen were growing, I heard.

Here were the *tambu*[4] houses where the idols were kept, the carved wooden fish and the replicas of canoes of great antiquity. Here, too, the skulls of long-dead high chiefs are still venerated and worshipped. By Upuna, on the western shore, there is still one of these *tambu* houses, though it is very small: here repose the skulls of three chiefs. Beside the *tambu* house is the place of the canoe-builders, an industry still connected largely with *tambus*. Here we saw the natives leisurely at work on some magnificent small vessels. They had a few European tools which they used very well, but they were building the canoes, which were sea-going vessels, in almost exactly the same way as their distant ancestors had done. They were building them up from

---

[4] The *tabu* of Polynesia.

solid planks, sewn together, and caulked with some resinous gum. The lines of these new canoes were beautiful and seaworthy.

I gathered that the possession of a good canoe had been regarded from time immemorial as a necessary stamp of manhood on Owa Raha — the possession of a canoe and skill in using it; proficiency at the hunt and in fishing; virility and a general standard of decency such as would make one a fit and useful member of the community. These were the old standards: something of them still survived. But a great deal was lost, the trader said: even to Owa Raha the policy of stamping on the native customs, of removing, as far as possible, the natural joy from their lives, had been extended. However, there were no missionaries there at the time of our visit; none were expected, and the natives were slowly reapproaching, largely as the result of this unusual trader's guidance and care, something of their old condition of joyous and natural living. There was a different spirit on Owa Raha and Owa Riki, different from that of any other place I knew in the Solomon islands, or indeed elsewhere in Melanesia. There was almost a holiday spirit — no labour lines, no barracks, no plantations. The natives, too, seemed to be in splendid condition and were a fine, upstanding lot.

Much of this was undoubtedly due to the attitude towards them of the trader who lived with them, and in this he was perhaps helped by the circumstance that he was married to the daughter of the last reigning chief and had so himself become a kind of hereditary chief of the island. He had married the daughter of one Bugga-Bugga, last of the paramount chiefs of Owa Raha, who had left no male descendants. Bugga-Bugga's head reposed in the wooden replica of a fish in the *tambu* house by the beach, and from all that I have heard of him, he must have been an outstanding nobleman. His daughter, though she had a son of twenty, was still comely. At the time of our visit she had at home with her a son of sixteen, a solidly built, intelligent, and most attractive young fellow, and a truly delightful little girl of six, whose countenance was the fairest we had seen in any of the Pacific islands. Their home was a collection of airy bungalows built in the native fashion in a line facing the beach: the trader, being a sailor, had everything ship-shape and Bristol fashion, not only in his family dwellings but throughout the island. He had cows, pigs, and poultry: the fruits of the tropics grew at his doors, and the fish of the Pacific swam in the lagoon waiting to be speared. His cutter was drawn up on the beach by the front door; across the narrow strait he could see the smoke rising from the drying-sheds of his copra plantation on San Cristoval; behind him was the large native village where both his wife and he were held in general veneration. Of white companionship he had none, and he did not miss it; his bêche-de-mer fisherman, the companion of his marine exploits and his right-hand man, was an old, old coloured gentleman named Mr. Richardson, from Philadelphia.

"Ah was one of de first white men in de islands round heah," Mr. Richardson proudly claimed, and he was as black as the ace of spades. He, too, was an old square-rig man, and he had been a master of pearling and trochus luggers. I liked Mr. Richardson, liked him very much. The woolly-headed old reprobate still stood straight, despite his fourscore years; and the muscles of his one good arm bulged and rippled as he walked. He danced a hornpipe as he came over the rail and began at once to sing, in a splendid baritone voice, old forgotten sea chanteys, melodious and immoral. Good Mr. Richardson! When he had sung and danced his fill, which took some time, he sat down on the spare spar by the hatch and began to yarn. He jumped up now and again as he thought of some further verse of a sweet old chantey and, throwing a line from its pin, roared lustily to the boys to trail on while he sang. He hauled at some of the lines until I thought he'd break them, and when he had tired out the boys he enrolled a gang of the islanders to do the trailing and yell the choruses. He'd been in Yankee clippers and Yankee hell-ships: here was a real old-timer. He had been wandering the world since he was twelve, though he had been in the Pacific since an oreladen skys'l-yarder, outward bound from Noumea, opened up and left him to pull ashore some hundreds of miles and land, near dead, somewhere on San Cristoval. That was how he had come to the Solomons; he had rowed there.

When he had really settled down, and began to tell of his maritime history, the old man was extraordinarily interesting. He spoke of hell-ships and of brutal hazing, of being kicked about and belted with belaying pins, of hell roundings of the Horn and starvation; of islands, adventures, and of pearls. When he had nearly done, he began to tell of the very worst ship he had ever sailed in.

"You boys like to heah of de biggest bass'ard of all de ships Ah eber sailed in? Yeah? Waal dat ship, sah, she *was* a bass'ard an' no mistake." And he went on to give copious horrible details in support of his assertion until all hands were thoroughly assured that his name for the ship was almost a term of endearment. He described the captain, the owners, and the mate; he went into long details about blood and belaying pins; he told of the idiosyncrasies of the afterguard and the skulduggery of the agents. That ship and all about her stood up for hour after hour to as savage a beating as any gale had ever given her in her long-gone sea life: and in the end, the old man, his eyes rolling and his voice a little thick at the memories of the abuses he had suffered in this pleasant vessel, swore a great oath, "By Goad, Ah get so much hell from dat ship if Ah ever meets de descendants — yeah, de grandson, of dat bass'ard owner, Ah give him back what Ah got — or somepin' of it. Ah woant live long 'nuff to give it all."

"Geepers," said one of the American cadets, "my grandfather!"

It was. The vessel which had so aroused the coloured mariner's ire had been the full-rigged ship *Panama* of the G——d Line, of New York. The youngest member of that family was a cadet on board.

For a moment Mr. Richardson stared in unbelief: for a second longer he looked as if he would keep his oath; and then he just said, "Waal, Ah'm danged." And "danged" he was. We never had another yarn out of him.

His later deficiency in this regard was, however, made up for in some measure by the trader, whose stock of reminiscence was beginning to open up after we had been listening to him for three days. He told of strange native happenings, of fights single-handed with basking sharks, of killing oxen with a look, of tidal waves and hurricanes and of great storms; of ships and the sea and pearls and savages; of bêche-de-mer and Rennell Island; of the ill effects of introducing Sikiana divers (who are Polynesians) in waters where the sharks had been accustomed only to black native forms; of medicine men, and *tambus*, and the strange methods of catching a shark which had tasted human blood; of the queer workings of the native mind. He told us of the trials of the early traders, and of the death of Frankie, a Pole. Frankie had also been one of the early traders. He gave fish-hooks for copra and trochus and bêche-de-mer which he sold, in his turn, at a handsome profit. But Frankie became tired of the sight of natives, of copra, of fish-hooks, and of trochus. One day the trading vessel brought him his supplies which included, as, usual, a case of square-face gin. He sat down and drank the gin. As he was just finishing this pleasant pastime a native arrived with a sack of copra.

"Frankie," said the native, "me wantum fish-hooks." And he put down the copra.

"I'll give you bloody-fish-hooks!" said the pleasant Frankie, and shot him dead. Some other natives near by thereupon — quite rightly — grappled with Frankie who was firing wildly. In the course of the scuffle, Frankie's head happened to poke through the rough window of his store. A native outside seized the opportunity and speared him to death. It was no loss, I thought, a tragedy of gin. No, said the trader, a tragedy of fish-hooks.

Frankie had been his first partner. He is buried now in the small graveyard of Owa Raha, together with several other whites. Most of the headstones have been knocked down by earthquakes, and the graves are not cared for very well. The inscriptions which are still decipherable show that the sleepers were all very young.

The trader's wife, the last of the line of the pure Bugga-Bugga's, had in her possession all the family heirlooms and the "crown jewels" of the island. These we were permitted to see; a collector's eyes would have shone at the sight. So did ours, for that matter, though we knew well enough we were allowed to see these splendid things only out of kindness and for friendship's sake. They are not for sale. Exquisite shell ornaments of the most delicate workmanship from Sikiana and Owa Riki, armlets, bracelets, necklaces, nose ornaments, togas and headgear of native cloth, mats, weapons, ceremonial staffs and ornaments and objects richly carved and inlaid with mother-of-pearl — what a collection it was! It was contained in three large sea chests and was now not much used, though the trader's wife and little daughter bedecked themselves in the ancient finery for a farewell dance and at the Dance of the Tree Men, later on. These things, the trader said, were the treasure of the people in his wife's keeping; he knew well enough they would be sought for any museum. But their place, he felt, was the island. I hope they remain there always.

The trader himself had a good collection of native weapons, shields, utensils, carvings, and so on; but he had recently lost a good many in the last tidal wave which had destroyed his home. The buildings we saw were only temporary, he said, and he was sorry that his dwelling was not in better order. But it all looked rather fine to me.

Owa Raha and Owa Riki.

We went with our friend the trader to Owa Riki, in his cutter. Owa Riki is a small island surrounded by fringing reef in which there is no real break; there is poor anchorage only at one place, off the native village. Here the reef is broken a little and there is one tortuous passage through to the beach. The negotiation of this, through the rollers, is dangerous even in a cutter; but the trader showed no loss of maritime skill in his handling of his craft in these difficult conditions.

There are only about a hundred people on Owa Riki. Somehow the schools and the teachers and all those great uplifting influences seem to have passed them by, for which, one gathered without difficulty, they are devoutly thankful. A peaceful and industrious folk living a simple life satisfactory to themselves, they ask only to be left alone — a privilege that to-day is rarely granted to their kind. I could not see that they had missed much: they were happy, healthy, and contented. Though they were inclined to eye us suspiciously at first as perhaps a crowd of the government's men come to collect the head-tax, when they knew that we were come merely on a friendly visit they were most hospitable. I saw no sullen looks or morose jowls. The people were unclad (a few of the men had a piece of bark, and some of the older women wore a small fringe-like apron), and their homes were primitive, but they were clean and seemed well suited to the needs of their occupants. This surely ought to be all that is asked of any dwelling. They were cool, shaded, airy, and watertight; in front of most of them were small verandahs where the women sat with the children.

To welcome us, the young women staged a dance of which I am afraid the missionaries would not have approved. The lascivious motions of much South Seas dancing have long been an attraction to elderly males of a certain type; and throughout Polynesia some of the dancing was almost unbelievably full of erotic symbolism. Now it is to be found only in the night clubs: anyone in search of aphrodisiac stimulus will be well advised to stay away from Owa Riki. There are night clubs everywhere, and that kind of thing. There was nothing in the least wanton or improper in the dance of the Owa Riki naked girls. There was the suggestion that the human body is fertile, for the natives have long regarded the fertility of the body as symbolic of the fertility of the soil. The dance of the harvest, though it is concerned with both, is by no means improper.

The maids of Owa Riki danced very well, though somewhat monotonously. They kept up a sort of time by hissing through their teeth while a choir of four old women sang very sadly. When it was over, they walked calmly away, their usual phlegmatic selves, and went on with the housework and such things as they had been doing. Another group of women, more elderly (though not old) danced with shrubs and such greenery as the island possessed, which was a great deal. They were bedecked with palm fronds and leaves and, as they danced, these things fell from them, and they were not at all embarrassed. Why should they be?

There is, for heaven's sake, nothing "improper" in the human body and there were grace and suppleness in these.

When the women had finished their dance, the men began. Their dance was more gymnastic and more elaborate. They also were decked in foliage, and had a choir of five who solemnly chanted dirges with grim monotony. The men had dance-sticks like killy-killies, many of them carved with representations of fish or the frigate bird; they kicked at the earth and danced most energetically, hour after hour, while the choir sang. They were still dancing as the evening came, and we went down to the beach to depart towards Owa Raha and the ship. Their chief, Kio Kio, an unimpressive middle-aged man with a bald head, and a mild case of elephantiasis in one leg, came with us to the beach; I gave him a few presents. The natives had been good to us; they had given us fruit and coco-nuts, and a good show. As far as I could see, the subjects of Kio Kio were a stalwart, healthy lot; I wish for them long continued isolation and contentment.

The natives of Owa Raha also gave us a dance. This, indeed, was something memorable. From probably the earliest occupation of these two small islands, dancing has been traditional with the people. Much of the old dancing has now been lost, for the early missionaries frowned severely on this innocent pastime. Very few of the dances seem to have been wholly concerned with incitement to lust, though at some neighbouring islands the natives used such dances to beguile the blackbirders ashore, where they might be slaughtered and their vessels looted. Most of the dances were interpretations of events in legendary or actual history. By the singing of chants which told of the great deeds, and by the interpretations of the dancers, something of the long-past happenings was preserved. We were privileged to see just such a dance which had been saved — resuscitated, indeed in the very nick of time — by the trader. I should be quite prepared to hear from almost any missionary that this trader was a "bad influence" in the islands; but it seemed to me that whatever his disadvantages or his shortcomings, he was doing splendid service both for the natives and for anyone concerned with research into the manners and customs of the Pacific. He spoke perfectly the dialect used on Owa Raha; it had been his habit for years to talk with the old men and to learn from them as much as possible of their earlier lives. One day, in the farthest village on the eastern shore of the island, he came across an old man who told him of the Dance of the Tree Men. The trader listened. It seemed dull, at first, but he listened patiently. (If one wishes to learn anything from natives, patience is the first requisite.) He came gradually to realize that this dance must be a representation of the whole history of the island. He listened attentively then. Did anyone else know of this dance? The ancient informant was too shaky on his legs to perform it, but they found two other old men who knew of it. Gradually they rebuilt the whole dance — the trader and these two natives — and now they had taught the younger men to do it. This they do with enjoyment and very, very well.

It was the Dance of the Tree Men that we saw.

It was staged on the foreshore by the beach before the trader's home and began in the cool of the afternoon. First came a choir of five old men, chanting: these stood in a row singing the long, long song of the story of the island. After them came the background performers; in this case a chorus of shrub-clad men who pranced and stamped and waved their dance-sticks to the rhythm of the chanting, and jumped on the earth with great energy and considerable grace. Their timing was especially good, and their sense of rhythm was superb. They danced on and on; at first I thought nothing more would happen. Then the Tree Men began to come, clay-covered, grotesque figures, climbing down from the trees of the nearby forest and lurching unsteadily on their feet, staggering about, learning painstakingly to walk. These were the original dwellers on the island, the earliest men of whom the legends make mention. They lurched queerly in time with the chant, now grown stronger, and looked about them at the sea. They were primitive fellows, by the looks of them; they had a few women with them, and some children. The women carried the children on their backs. While these danced the weird shuffle of the tree-dwellers, three canoes filled with black men glided in silently to the beach. The black men, fierce visaged, landed in the guise of friendliness only to fall upon the clay-covered tree men as soon as they were near them. Now the chant swelled; the semblance of the fight was strongly done: tree man and marauder danced and fought. The tree men fought stubbornly, retreating towards the bush; the marauders pressed after them. Some fell on both sides, but it soon became evident that the tree men would be defeated. The few survivors of them were at length routed, and fled, trying to take the bodies of their dead with them.

The dance was now taken up by the black men, joined by a few of the tree-dwellers to show, perhaps, that the tribes had intermingled, as indeed they probably did. They danced on; more marauders came; they faced tidal waves, earthquakes, hurricanes. They made clearings, tilled the fields, caught fish. They seemed at this stage to pass through a considerable period of tranquillity; they became mighty fighters and were able to keep off intruders. Then came the first of the navigators, Mendana. If the legend of the dance had any basis in fact, Mendana had a hot reception here. There is a record that he lost four men at an island which was probably Owa Raha, and was driven off. Mendana was beaten off with terrible fighting in which firearms were used for the first time; the natives trembled — all this was in the dance — but the Spaniards went. There followed more years of tranquillity disturbed only by great storms and such things, taken as a matter of course.

Then the white men began to come: the natives watched this invasion with alarm. The dancing showed the coming of the traders, of missionaries, and of disease. The movements and the pantomime showing the coming of disease were superbly done and terrible. All the leading parts throughout the dance were taken by two men in great bull masks; their work was magnificent. They showed the coming of skin diseases, colds, tuberculosis: their attempts at reproducing the commonplace cough were in themselves ghastly and tragic, for these people did not know how to cough when chest ailments first struck them. Many died from the simplest colds. Some still do. They showed these deaths.

Years passed. The white men stayed. They brought breakdown of customs, of *tambu*; they brought schools; and in a satiric finale the two extraordinarily capable performers did the dance of the queer strangers taking photographs. (The island has been visited twice in late years by photographers.) How those men could dance! Hour after hour they went through the pantomime of their historic performance. It was all unexpected and excellent but, looking back over it, a little too true. The greatest tragedy was the coming of disease. Here the chanting grew low, and the shrub-clad ones stood still a while, a long while. The population of Owa Raha has declined sadly since the coming of the whites: a recent census of the whole Solomons showed the total number of natives to be many thousands below even the government's pessimistic estimate. There has been much of tragedy here — some wilful, some unavoidable and deeply regretted: but the record of the white in all the islands calls for no cheers. The dancing was ended, and we came slowly away. I met the chief performers, and thanked them. They were from the heathen village of the eastern side.

That night, for I meant to sail in the morning, I gave a little party on board for the trader, his family, the dancers and all the natives — a show of fireworks, and some music and singing. We could not do much. The trader's wants were simple; he had not, he said, had a real meal of salt horse and pea soup and such delicacies for thirty years. Could we fix him some? We did. With his trusty henchman the ancient Philadelphian Negro Richardson, he ate heartily of salt horse far into the night. And the natives danced, and danced, and danced, so that it was again they who provided most of the entertainment. How they danced! The trader's wife and little daughter (until she fell asleep on a stays'l lying on the deck) did the traditional women's dances; the men danced and danced and danced — the dance of the frigate birds and the shark (that was good fun), and dances which were incomprehensible to me. Hour after hour they went on, thump-thump-thump on the decks until the beams of the strong hull shook. On and on they danced and sleep paid no heed to them.

In the intervals, the trader and Mr. Richardson sang chanteys, and the boys sang, though they did not know the old chanteys. One of them was fairly good with the accordion, he whose grandparent had owned the *Panama*. For all the excellence of his playing, Mr. Richardson still looked upon him with extreme disfavour. I handed out Burma cheroots and Balinese cigarettes, but not being stick tobacco these found scant favour; we fired some rockets and the guns. Long after midnight with the show over and the party done, the cheering began, round and round. We were soon hoarse, but the islanders went on until the morning; and when the trader could think of no other subject to cheer about, he called vociferously for an infinite number of huzzas for himself. He was a man, I gathered, of few inhibitions. But he was a human being, a white man whose ways could be understood, and who did, in his own way, what seemed to me an infinite amount of good in those islands.

We went out in the morning, and the natives, waving green branches of eternal friendship, followed us for miles in their canoes and the trader's boat. I turned her in the harbour under power, for the anchorage was a restricted one; outside we gave her the sails, sail on sail and glided along quietly and gracefully in the tropic morning. Off Owa Riki, more canoes waited to cheer us on our way; the sun shone, and the whole Pacific world was smiling. I saw, as we went, the looks upon the faces of the trader and his fisherman; their countenances, as they looked for the last time upon square sails gently filling to the trade-wind air, had upon them an expression that was profound and memorable. Long settled in the islands, these ancient mariners had not expected ever again to see a full-rigged ship come floating unheralded into their lives. They gazed up, drinking everything in, for this was the last time they would see such a ship and they knew it.

So we went out to sea, with the haunting melody of the natives' song of farewell in our ears; and for a long, long time looked back pleasantly towards Owa Raha.

I was now bound direct for Sydney, New South Wales. In a day or two the trade wind came fresh, from the east-south-east, but the set to the westward was so strong that we could not sail better than full-and-by. We had now to pass through the Coral Sea which with a fair wind was easy enough. It is a bad place, this Coral Sea, full of sets and reefs and currents, the whole unlit and very poorly charted. I chose the way which avoided the reefs by the widest margin, and we went on. With the trade piping merrily we began to snore along at near two hundred miles a day.

Then the fever broke out on board.

I suppose I had been fortunate that we had not been visited by it earlier. But when it came it was bad enough. It was malaria. I had had that before, in French Somaliland, but this variety was something new to me. We must have got it from Owa Raha. It struck suddenly, and the prostration was extreme. It became plain that we had no attack of ordinary malaria but one of the pernicious types which are sometimes contracted in the Solomons. One after another went down, to stay down; there was no rapid recovery from that prostration, not for many, many months. The carpenter, Jan the able seaman, Dennis the cadet, Ben Sowerby who had been with us from Singapore — these had it. Others began to go. I had it myself, a little. It was nasty. I began to fear that the whole ship might have it, and to wonder how we should ever get through the Coral Sea; but there were, after all, only seven cases. The carpenter, Dennis, and Jan were the worst. The carpenter had never been ill in his life before; a lusty young Finn, broad-shouldered and powerful, used to doing a hard day's work all his life, he took badly to being laid up. Time after time he struggled up on deck, almost in delirium, and had to be carried back to his bunk by the weakened watch. The only cures I had were quinine and various mixtures to induce sweating and reduce temperature. Against this particular brand of malignant intestinal malaria, at least in its initial stages, the common remedies were of little use. The attacks lasted from a week to ten days, at first; afterwards they usually lasted from one to three days, and came irregularly. Nothing seemed to be able to get the germs out of the body, though ten days in the Royal Melbourne Hospital, later on, almost managed this for Dennis. Dennis was fifteen, one of the youngest of the cadets; the after effects of so serious a fever were rather bad for him, and the spell in hospital came in time. However, he strengthened again afterwards, and long before the end of the voyage was one of the strongest and ablest lads on board. Jan and the carpenter, however, suffered a long time. One of the American cadets went home.

It was about 1,700 miles from Owa Raha to Sydney. We made the first 1,500 in twelve days, going down between the Chesterfield and the Kenn reefs, giving all the obstructions of the Coral Sea as wide a berth as possible.

The set was heavily to the westward the whole way, but this at last was in our favour; the sailing, for those who could enjoy it, was very good. I planned to make my landfall on the Australian coast somewhere south of Sandy Cape, where the south-going current has its beginnings; we did this, eventually, but the current was not there. From Sandy Cape to Sydney the way was beset by baffling airs and light winds; We were a week making the last 200 miles, beating and beating wearily, reported by ship after ship and lighthouse after lighthouse, until the good people of Sydney must have wondered what we were doing. A boy fell over-board, and was rescued. He was cleaning the dinghy and slipped into the sea. We backed the mainyard, dropped the dinghy into the sea, and picked him up again. But I had been alarmed about sharks: we had seen several of them about, big ones; and the Australian shark is notoriously an unkind brute.

Before we at last reached Sydney, the fever was more or less under control. In most of the cases, at least, the first acute prostration had passed. I gave a great sigh of relief when the Coral Sea had been safely negotiated, and all that kind of navigation was, I hoped, well finished; for I meant to have a brief look at Australia and then make the best of my way leisurely across the South Pacific, and so home again round the Horn. Going eastward as I was, I planned to make for Mangareva or Rapa through the west winds first and then to take a round turn westwards before the trade, round Tahiti way, and by Borabora, Aitutaki, Samoa, Tonga, and such parts. When it was time to turn for the Horn, I should stand to the south, and then it would be easy to recover the lost longitude and begin the road home.

All these plans, however, were to come to nothing, but I did not know that. I did not know what the future might hold when at last, on a grey morning in mid-December, 1935, the little ship arrived off Sydney Heads and sailed in. We had been 131 days from Singapore, and were a year and two months out from England. Until then, in spite of fever and all kinds of adversities — rocks, storms, reefs, and difficult navigations — and all the problems of the ports, things had gone well. We had discovered nothing and achieved very little; but we were all still there, though a few of us were pale and a little shaken, temporarily, from the fever. I had sailed a very small and a very old full-rigged ship half-way round the world, and kept together a heterogeneous, and by no means unanimous, collection of seagoing human beings over 30,000 miles, and tried to make it all seem worth while.

The welcome of the port was vociferous and sincere. A customs man arrived with voluminous forms covering several square yards, demanding copious details in triplicate of everything on board down to the last roll of toilet paper, the last bar of soap, and the copy of the Regulations he left with me bristled with such welcoming phrases as "Penalty £500." There was a man with him shouting about state taxation, and it rained.

XIII

Local Boy Makes Good

THE SHIP was anchored in Double Bay, Sydney, for ten pleasant days. Many visitors came on board, and the boys and the crew were treated royally. As always in the big ports, I rushed about a great deal, achieving little; keeping appointments; dodging traffic; looking after the ship's buying, and the ship's sick: first, with difficulty, entering the ship in and swearing this and that, and filling up always more and more copious forms until I began to fear there would be a paper shortage in Australia; later, with more difficulty, entering the ship out again. The regulations for the management of ships in Australia are voluminous and apparently unending; supervision is strict and, I suspect, costly; the passion of a new people for government seems combined with an undue emphasis upon the complete satisfaction of their insularity to such an extent as to make the visits even of non-commercial overseas ships a form-ridden burden to those who bring them.

I hesitate to criticize my countrymen, the warmth of whose personal welcome far more than made up for the officiousness of the infinite forms; yet it is a curious fact that, of all countries, Australia is least visited by wandering vessels. May not this overgrowth of regulation have a little to do with it? Sydney, I gathered without difficulty, wants and almost demands tourists, being assured, rightly enough, that there is much in New South Wales and the Commonwealth generally to attract and to interest them — sport (plenty of this), beautiful scenery, a fine climate, and so forth. Tasmania is a beautiful place; the Great Barrier

Reef is unique; there is the koala, and here and there, even an aborigine. The cities are large, prosperous enough, and possessed of most of the usual amenities for the entertainment of visitors. There is perhaps an over-emphasis on the necessity for closing the front doors of bars at six o'clock sharp every evening; and the frigid ferocity of the average waitress, asked to serve something at any other than the few set hours, seems well buttressed by an impregnable wall of regulations. With a few exceptions, it is conceivable that the arrangements — even those affecting our primary needs — of most of the hotels could be improved. In a country possessed of so many advantages, populated by a care-free but resolute people noteworthy for their courage, their hospitality, and their resource, it is a pity that such minor blemishes, which a little common sense could easily remove, should be allowed to continue.

A survey, strict almost to the point of savagery, was made of everything my unfortunate vessel had on board upon her arrival. All the heavily dutiable items were placed under seal (I had little of these), and an accurate inventory made of everything else, so that, when the time came to leave Melbourne, my next port, duties could be paid on all that had been used or consumed — food, paint, ropes, canvas, everything. If I cut a sail while the vessel lay in an Australian port, I should have to pay duty on the canvas; if I painted the ship, I should have to pay duty on the paint; if I bought fresh eggs in Australia and fried them in lard from America, I should have to pay duty on the lard. I had known of all this, from previous experience in the grain ships, and brought very little into Australia. I knew Melbourne was a good place for storing such a ship as mine, in food at any rate, and I meant to take in provisions there for the voyage to New York. In the meantime, we lived on fresh food, bought ashore, as we always did in ports; and did such work about the decks as was possible without the consumption of dutiable goods. An expert in the Customs House, that well-populated temple of parsimonious precepts by Circular Quay, wished to charge the ship with light dues for the Bahama Islands. We had come from New York, had we not? (I had cleared from New York to Sydney.) If we had gone from New York to Rio we must, he argued, have used the Bahama lights. They are on the way. The force of this argument was a little upset by the fact that in order to head towards Rio we had first, being a square-rigged ship, to make easting past the Azores and we had, on that passage (and indeed on most others) used or seen no navigation lights whatever, apart from departures and landfalls. I pointed out, moreover, that, on the passage from England to New York, I had made my landfall on Watling Island and had made good use of several of the Bahama lights. I had then, I went on, gone into Nassau, where, so far as I was aware, no manner of expense to which the ship could be subjected had been overlooked: yet at Nassau there was no mention of this queer subject of the Bahama lights. I must add that I did not pay for them in Sydney, either.

The visit of the little ship to Sydney attracted a great deal more attention than I had bargained for, being accustomed to go into ports and out again almost unnoticed. Sydney people and Australians generally have always been interested in their own history, most of this being recent enough still to be discoverable with some accuracy. Perhaps the similarity of the old frigate to the ship in which Cook had first sighted the coast of New South Wales and sailed past the entrance to Sydney Harbour, and her resemblance to many of the ships in which their forefathers had come to the young colony, appealed to their imaginations. But the good citizens of Sydney have always been intensely ship-minded, apart from history. Naval officers were the first rulers (and military officers, incidentally, the first exploiters); and in the first years, ships brought the very food that saved the settlers from starvation. From then until to-day ships have been the link with the outside world, and now Australian and New Zealand ports are almost alone in the world in the spontaneity and depth of their sincere maritime interest. The waterfronts, apart from much of the unfortunate neighbourhood of the forlorn Yarra, are a pleasant Sunday afternoon walk; visiting warships and unusual vessels of all kinds attract great attention.

I found myself for once a minor newspaper figure; was asked to broadcast; and hobnobbed a little, very briefly, with the great. This was transitory enough to be pleasant; but when the press of citizens eager to visit the ship made it profitable for a ferry service to be begun from Circular Quay, and the populace began to encumber the decks so much that we could do no work, it was really time to call a halt. I had always taken the view that anyone who was sufficiently interested in ships and the sea to come to our gangway should never be sent away. It was a standing rule of the ship, though for legal purposes the usual "no admittance" sign had to be hung out, that no one genuinely interested in the ship should be refused permission to see her. The flow of visitors had, until then, not been immoderate. Indeed, in most ports there were none. But in Sydney they came by the thousands. There were old mariners, veterans of the *Cutty Sark*, the *Romanoff*, the *Thermopylae*, and the *Cimba* — there must be more real old salts in Sydney and Melbourne than anywhere else on earth — young mariners, yachtsmen, naval officers, artists, musicians, editors, pilots, economists, Ministers of State and high officials and hundreds of the citizens all crowding in the ferry. I saw, after a few days of this, that, as it was unfortunately impossible to chain down all the belaying pins, and I rather liked the little ship as she was, the ferry service at least would have to stop. Some enthusiasts were so taken with the ship that they tried to carry away even the réd customs seals from her, prying them and their accompanying red tape from the doors where officialdom had set them. This was too much. There was a penalty of £100 or something for that kind of thing — against the ship, of course, and not against the enthusiasts. I had then reluctantly to exercise some effective manner of control over at least the non-maritime section of the visitors, and name set visiting hours — a thing I should have done at first, but I had had no idea there would be so great a crush. It seemed to me that Sydney, with the vast cruising ground of the whole Pacific so close outside, would have been an excellent home for the little ship upon some future occasion; but I was bound round the world, and could not think of staying anywhere. And I had been born in Melbourne.

The days in Sydney passed pleasantly enough, though I had my worries, worries of a serious kind that I well knew could not be fought off much longer. The boys went sailing, horse riding, and surfing, and the older of them took trips into the country. I tried to ensure that they had the opportunity to see at least something of the real country, not much of which, if the truth be told, penetrates in these days to the great cities. As far as cities go, Sydney might as well be San Francisco except that it is on the other side of the Pacific and has only one harbour bridge. In these days an inhabitant of any white city anywhere, if he were to sleep and suddenly wake up in any other white city where his language was in use, would find little difference in his new environment and would not be incommoded. But the country of Australia — the slow-growing charm of the great bush; the quiet beauty of the vast, sun-filled plains; the wonder of the long, almost untrodden sands, offers much to interest even the jaded world traveller, if he has the eyes to see.

I sailed out of Sydney harbour on the morning of December 18, 1935, bound to Melbourne in Victoria. We beat out from Double Bay, to the wild delight of the two pilots who had come for a holiday, and the disgust of the boys who did some of the work. Aeroplanes flew overhead and launches followed us, taking photographs; there were many people on the cliffs and in the balconies of the houses watching the ship as we passed by. We beat against a fresh nor'easter and flood tide from Double Bay to the Heads; some of the boards were very short. Many steamers came and went as we beat there, blowing on their sirens and dipping their flags, though the usual seamen's strike was keeping most of the Australian vessels at the wharves. The pilots were the stout fellows, Captains Brew and Finlay Murchison, the same Scots Australian who had the barque *Wathara* many years and distinguished himself by saving her threatened rigging with a preventer stay that he took aloft himself, in a bad blow off the Horn; the brother of the good mariner Murdo', who had the *Lobo* and the *James Craig*. It was years since they had had the opportunity to handle a vessel under sail; they took turns at the wheel and would allow no one else to go there, and tacked the ship alternately. When we were out, we spliced the main brace with a flagon of strong rum belonging to an artist who had come aboard in Sydney. That was a morning's beating! It was a grand day of sunshine and fresh wind with the little ship, as if aware she was on show, turning back the foam of the harbour with a sweet grace. Under a full press of sail she beat and beat, thrashing her way right out of the harbour through the ferries and past the steamers — going about now almost beneath the high rocks of a precipitous cliff, with the shouts of the sailors and the booming of the backing sails echoed on the cliff sides; now, a few moments later, swinging on her heel almost on top of the Sow and Pigs shoal — backwards and forwards, every sail drawing to the best advantage, and the ship heeling and picking up more motion and more life as, tack by tack, she approached the Heads.

We were clear at last, and backed the mainyard; the pilots departed, very pleased, and we stood out to sea alone, with the nor'easter a fair wind. I should have been delighted had it blown us to Melbourne, but that, to say the least, was extremely improbable; the nor'easter at that time of the year is a passing wind, apt to bring nothing but a sudden shift of the wind heavily to the south. Melbourne was about 600 miles away, to us; but I knew we should be fortunate to reach it in less than two weeks. The Australian coast is often a difficult one for the square-rigged ship to navigate. My admiration of the great Cook had increased a great deal since first we made our Antipodean landfall.

We were no sooner outside than the cook came to me, aft, to give me a letter from the superintendent of the General Hospital saying that, if he went to sea in the ship, they would not be responsible for his leg. He had a very bad tropic ulcer which had defied treatment for months. The letter gave him instructions to remain in Sydney at least ten days, reporting at the hospital daily for skilled treatment — and he brought me the letter when we were at sea. Well, I should have to save his leg, in spite of him, or cut it off. It was a grim job.

The beat round the Australian coast to Melbourne was the most difficult short passage of the whole voyage. It was midsummer then, but that seemed to make the weather worse. Sudden shifts of wind, violent onslaughts from the west and the south-west, a huge and confused sea — these combined to impede our progress. The good nor'easter did not last six hours, when once we had beat out against it; and we did not have a fair wind again until we were come to Wilson's Promontory. The wind persisted from the south with the pall of the greying sky closing in: the glass dropped steadily, and at night-fall of the second day there was that queer faint moaning in the rigging that tells of a coming gale. It came.

It was then Christmas week, a week ushered in by a hard gale and driven out by a worse one. For the first time, I had to heave the ship to. The weather became too bad to stand on against it. First we had, in the brief space of twenty-four hours, four winds at gale force, each from a different direction, with the sky gloomy, threatening, and the sea ugly and so confused that the bewildered ship, not knowing how to shape her motion in order to maintain her balance, threw the pots from the galley stove and the plates from the table. The increasing gusts grew and grew until at last it was a violent gale from the south-south-west. From this direction it blew at gale force during the next thirty-six hours, with frequent violent gusts so strong that the rigging, with the ship down to a minimum of canvas, was strained severely. I had to heave-to. I goose-winged the close-reefed fore tops'l, and hove her to with that and the small storm fore topmast stays'l and the mizzen stays'l showing to the storm. Under this canvas she lay-to very well, though she rolled heavily. The sea was wild and fiercely turbulent and the wind screamed, but she began in the afternoon, still hove-to, to dry her decks. We lay out the storm in safety this way, being indeed better off than most steamers, for steamers must, as far as possible, continue to pound into whatever comes along; but I found afterwards, when I could get observations, that we had been driven almost 200 miles out into the Tasman Sea.

Christmas Day found us still trying desperately to get this back, and the gale still blew, though moderating. The sea was lumpy, ill-tempered, and confused; it was savage weather, and all hands were out most of that Christmas Day. Sunny Australia? All hands looked at me with some resentment for coming to such a place, for this was the stormiest coast we had been on. It was probably most unusual weather; but it is my sad experience that the most unusual kind of weather is very common indeed, everywhere. We were blown about, on that short run, quite a lot. But we lost only one sail and the ship suffered no damage.

It was the last day of 1935 when the ship arrived in Melbourne and anchored inside the Gellibrand light, in Hobson's Bay. It was exactly a year since we had arrived at New York: again I felt the curious mixture of mild elation at an important stage of the voyage being now behind me, and uneasy alarm amounting almost to a sense of impending disaster. The plain truth of the matter was that the condition of my finances had long been worrying me. The sum of my resources was now £30, and I had a ship and some twenty-eight human beings to get half-way round the world. And I had some fever.

I had known when I began that this question of finances would be a worrying one. I was not wealthy, far from it. But with a generous advance from my American publishers for a book and some magazine articles, and with the earnings of my other books and whatever else I could write and sell (which was not much), I had hoped to get along. I lost heavily in New York, and recovered little from insurance. I had various unforeseen expenses which made a further hole in already small funds. The running of a ship such as mine was an expensive undertaking, though I looked after everything myself and ran her as inexpensively as I could without stinting anything, and seeing that all hands were as contented as possible and, above all, well fed. The ship cost me about £100 a week to run, reckoning wages, insurance, port charges, and all expenses. I paid fifteen hands and, though I gave no handsome salaries, I paid what I could. Most of my sailors were from the grain-ships, and I paid them more than they had been receiving there. I paid myself nothing. As far as possible, I advanced the sailors and the officers and petty officers their wages as they earned them, not wishing to pile up a large account to be met on my return home.

It might well be asked why, since I had not a reserve of funds sufficient for the voyage, I had set out? Did I expect someone to give them to me? I most certainly did not. No one was behind me. No one would give me anything. I had taken especial care to see that there was no suggestion of any manner of sponsoring for this voyage, which I was determined should not be spoiled by any commercial considerations. I was not sailing this ship to exploit anything or any natives or any person. No scientific body, quite properly, had the remotest interest in the vessel. As far as I knew, none ever wished to have, though I should have been pleased to do what I could for science, any science, at no expense. It seemed that the scientists could get where they wished to go faster and more comfortably by other means; the oceanographers required trawlers, and the geographers had more need of theodolites than of vessels. I was entirely a private citizen. And I was, further, cut off from participation in any of the ordinary sources of employment for my ship since she was not registered as a commercial vessel, not that there is much loose employment for odd ships anywhere on the earth these days.

Well, I knew all this when I set out. But I was resolutely determined to complete the voyage; I knew well enough I was buying a great deal of trouble when first I bought the ship. I could have afforded to take a smaller vessel, a ship which needed no professional crew and could have kept the seas, at a tenth of the cost. But I had been — well, almost inspired to buy this ship. So far as I knew, no one else would have saved her from the break-up yards; no one else would have made any sailing-ship available for British youth; no one else would have tried to sail this lovely ship round the world. Anyone could have done so: she had been for sale some time. So I started; and I depended, after the serious setback of the New York disaster, on resource to show the way.

I could have taken, as they came forward, suitable persons to share in the enterprise, to sail in the ship a while and breathe pure air and see strange scenes. I could not and would not seek such people, and very few ever came forward, very few. I sailed most of the way with the guest cabins empty; certainly on all the difficult passages, with the exception of that from Samarai to Tahiti. Any idea of running a ship on a round-the-world voyage purely upon the contributions of such odd citizens as desire to come, and actually do come, is foredoomed to failure. I knew that. There have been many such schemes but few successes. To the best of my knowledge, only one vessel has circumnavigated the globe successfully with paying guests, the American schooner *Yankee*, Irving Johnson master; but that was a carefully organized and painstakingly planned expedition for the purpose and, moreover, a voyage that was planned and executed with no other idea.

I would not run my ship for paying guests. It is possible, by putting up with a great deal, to sail a schooner in that manner; but it would be foolishness in a full-rigged ship. It was indeed the high cost of having all my boys with me which was largely responsible for the serious condition of my finances as I approached Melbourne; without the boys I should have been well off. True, many of them had paid something to be there, but the total sum secured in this way did not come to one-sixth of the costs of the voyage. I had been, I fear, so anxious to avoid any possible taint of profit-making that I had leaned over backwards, and the premium was too low. Indeed, one of the American boys told me afterwards that one of the principal reasons for his coming was that he could not live so cheaply at home as he could with me on this round-the-world voyage.

Well, there I was, near enough to bankruptcy, arriving in my old home town. The outlook was worrying and the recurrent attacks of fever did nothing to relieve it; yet I believed as stoutly as ever in the voyage and I was not unduly dismayed. I had sailed the ship to Melbourne and, by thunder, I would sail her home again. To give up the voyage while the ship floated was unthinkable.

For a while, however, it looked as if I might have to. My £30 went the first night. There had to be advances for the crew, and there must not be the slightest hint of financial insecurity. They had to be fed; the ordinary running expenses of the ship had to be met. I earned a little by writing for some Australian papers, and from photographs; this was a temporary help. The distressing debility and bodily weakness which followed the prostrating attacks of malaria were a further severe handicap, making any kind of effort extremely difficult. It was only by great exertion of will that I was able to go on, and to preserve an unbroken front towards the world. How long I could do this I did not know — for the ship, I thought, a long time. But there was no joy in my visit to Melbourne, and there were no happy reunions, though I was well received. Though not so much as in Sydney, I was still the Local Boy Made Good, the local boy who had gone away vaguely somewhere or other in a ship, and now returned after many years with his own vessel. The maritime enthusiasts and the yachtsmen were good to me, good to all hands. I was asked here and there, to speak, sometimes, though I hated this and the listeners abhorred it far more, even, than I did. All sorts of distinguished citizens were eager to inspect the vessel.

I was at my wits' ends how to get funds. I thought of raising my needs by mortgage, for a sum one-fifth of the value of the vessel would have been sufficient. But I could get nothing — either by mortgage or bottomry bond or respondentia bond or any kind of advance or loan. I was informed that the vessel, not being commercial, was not regarded as a pledgeable property. A commercial vessel in need of funds by bottomry bond has usually three securities — herself, her cargo, and the freight to be earned by delivering the cargo. The money advanced is usually for the purpose of allowing the vessel to proceed with a voyage and collect the freight. The advance is always very well secured. In my case there was no freight; there was nothing but the vessel. True, she was free from encumbrances, but the voyage was worth nothing. She was earning nothing, could not earn anything. Her value, in case of a forced sale in those waters, did not exceed what she might bring for conversion to the Tasmanian timber trade, which was then doing rather well, or into a lighter. Who wanted a full-rigged ship? She was worth no more than she would bring. Her replacement value, the obvious value of the material in her, the sum I had paid for her and for her alterations and improvement — these things did not count.

It did not take many visits to the bankers, the brokers, and the shipping experts to be convinced that they had no money either for my ship or for her voyage. In desperation I even thought of the money lenders, who daily advertised their exceeding benevolence and willingness to advance sums from £5 to £5,000. These gentlemen were unanimous in their disapproval of the whole enterprise. What, advance money on a property that would then sail away? Nothing doing! Bring them in some good bricks and stone, they said — a nice paying hotel, or something like that. Then perhaps they would talk business. I could very well understand the money lenders' reluctance: it might be difficult, in the case of my failure, to force a sale in a distant port, harder still to supervise it. Money lenders, whether bankers or "investors," invariably look upon the worst side with the utmost pessimism they can muster. This is not a little. Things began to look serious. After some days in the city I returned to the ship at Williamstown and looked round me at this worthless property upon which no money could be raised. She did not appear to me to have shrunk in value.

I was now anxious only to raise sufficient funds to get out of Melbourne and sail directly either to New York or to England; but daily my situation became worse. I could name no sailing date. The day was fast coming when no device would suffice to hide the grim fact that I had no further funds. I had no rich relations; there was no one anywhere to whom I could turn — no one indeed, to whom I *would* turn. I had good friends; but this was my mess.

Then, one day, there came on board one Cecil Thrilp (which was not his name), who asked if I would go to an island in the South Seas after some gold. Go after gold! I would have gone after a treasure in post-holes and bilge-water to get out of Melbourne then. And yet ... there was something queer about this gold.

Mr. Thrilp was a swarthy man, lean, with a morose countenance. I could not help wondering why, if this gentleman knew so much about gold, he was not a little happier in his expression. He might, I thought, have had some gold to spend. But Mr. Thrilp, I gathered in due course, was a promoter. He was interested in the promotion of a company for a gold-mining venture on an island in the South Seas. At that time new gold-mining companies were being formed every day. Recent exploitations at the Fijis, at Misima, and in New Guinea, had been successful. Gold, for some obscure reason connected with the incomprehensible workings of our economic system, now that it was more useless than ever, was an even more valuable commodity than it had been before. Almost any ass, it seemed, could bring forward a proposition and someone — the public, I suppose — would finance it. In this instance, so far as I could comprehend the details, some ass knew about some gold on some island and Mr. Thrilp was forming a company to exploit it. In order that no rival concern should discover the whereabouts of this Eldorado it was necessary to transport the company's expedition there in secret. Hence the need for a ship, and there were few odd vessels about in Australian waters. Why not buy a Tasmanian ketch? I asked; but these were all busy in the timber trade and also were scarcely suitable. There were no small steamers available. The company, moreover, had no need of a permanent vessel; they merely wished to land the expedition secretly. Once that was accomplished and the claims pegged, their men could look after themselves.

It all sounded rather interesting. I had, the whole voyage long, been looking for some unusual kind of adventure and none had ever reared a tired head above the horizon. Now here was Mr. Thrilp with his talk about gold. How opportune it was he did not know; but I knew. The severity of my own economic stress did not mislead me into being too greatly off my guard; but I was eager to believe the best of this enterprise, mysterious as it might seem. I did not know, at first, where the island was; it seemed strange indeed that the transportation problem could not be solved more simply. But schooners are scarce and steam chartering is costly, and to buy a ship is usually ruinous to the uninitiated. (It bothered me enough.) There was the minor objection that my vessel, not being a commercial ship, could not be used for money-making purposes; but about this, Mr. Thrilp said with great truth, I need not worry. My ship could not be chartered; but would I accept a directorship of the excellent company? It would then be a mere fortunate circumstance that a director chanced to possess a ship of his own, in which to transport the gold-getters secretly to the island. My acceptance of a directorship would bind me to secrecy; as for the costs — this unfortunately was where I was vitally interested — these would be made up to me partly by means of my director's fee, and partly in vendors' shares of the company. I did not care about the shares, but I was in serious need of funds. Well, I went into the matter then, fairly deeply. I met another of the principals, an elderly gentleman who was obviously sound; I met the company's lawyer, in Collins Street, and after that saw a great deal too much of that handsome but largely useless thoroughfare. I learned where the island was; I met the Man-Who-Had-

Been-There, the famous prospector who knew about the gold. This gentleman, unfortunately, appeared to me to have about the same substance as Mr. Thrilp. However, it seemed that he had satisfied the experts, whoever they were — I never did discover — that the find he claimed to have made was worth investigating. There were moments, however, when I was oppressed by a vague suspicion that these experts were more concerned with the gold to be dug out of a company in Collins Street than from a mine on any island. But I fear that, about this time, I was developing into a cynical, if not a suspicious person.

The long and the short of it was that I agreed to associate myself with the enterprise, at least to the extent of taking the expedition to the island; but I insisted that my resignation from the directorate should take effect automatically on the day of my departure from Melbourne. Somehow, I never did quite believe in all this expedition; it was too opportune and complete a solution of my financial difficulties ever to come true. The island, I discovered, was Sudest, in the Louisiades, where gold had first been discovered some forty years earlier. The main lode or reef had, however, never been discovered. The prospecting member of the expedition, he of the querimonious countenance, claimed (as far as I could make out) to have made this important contribution to auriferous science. Sudest may be a most attractive island — I never saw it — but it suffered one grave disability so far as I was concerned. To get there I had to go again through the accursed Coral Sea, and in the cyclone season. This circumstance did not appear to bother the Collins Street gentlemen very much. Perhaps they were unaware of its significance; but it was a serious thing. A Coral Sea cyclone can show a West Indies hurricane how to be really bad-tempered: to be caught in that reef-filled sea in such a disturbance was apt to be fatal. In undertaking to make a voyage of this kind I well knew that I was adopting desperate measures. Yet what was the alternative? The abandonment of the whole expedition and the stranding of my crew. No, I had to go. There was nothing else for it.

Well, there I was, ready. The prospector was there, with a gentleman to accompany him to cheek his finds and a roustabout[5] to look after the camp and do the cooking. I was anxious now to embark these fellows and be on my way, with my director's fee used to pay my bills. This it would have just done nicely; there never was any thought of profit in the scheme, so far as I was concerned.

Days passed, and nothing happened. I began to read inspired accounts in the newspapers of an expedition for treasure to an unknown island, under sealed orders, and all that kind of thing: and then I made the alarming discovery that the company had neither funds nor existence. It was said to be entirely underwritten. It was not. It was not even registered. I insisted now that these formalities should be rushed through with the greatest haste. But there was still no money. The company made an appeal to the public, through a hastily prepared prospectus, for funds, having previously announced with gusto that no shares would be available. The public, naturally somewhat shy of such an enterprise, produced no funds. The brokers were equally baffled by this queer concern, about which so much had been given out mysteriously to the daily press and yet so little was known. Since this was, at this late hour, the only possible means I had of escaping from Melbourne, I was rather badly caught in the ghastly botch. I had been in Melbourne three weeks. I was all ready to depart, except for paying some bills; I was now hopelessly committed to the ungolden enterprise for good or ill. I could not see that any good would ever come of it; but I had to get out of Melbourne. I was desperate. I was now so short of ready funds that I often went without meals on my many

---

5 Handyman.

exasperating trips to Melbourne; but because of the malaria and my worries this was no hardship. I was not hungry. When I came to Melbourne I still had some money to my credit in London and in New York — accumulated royalties, and so forth. This I had cabled out, and spent, though I had been trying to preserve it for necessary expenses later on. My need of funds would not pass with my departure from Melbourne — if I ever did get away from the place. It began to look as if I should not.

All this dreadful time I was still the local boy made good. No one had the vaguest idea of my real predicament. As in New York, with the ship on the rocks, the telegraph messenger boys had trudged through the slush and the snow to me with messages of congratulation from friends in England on the successful accomplishment of the Atlantic passage, now I was the envy of the juvenile populace, and almost the pride of my former instructors. It is, thank God, difficult to receive the acclaims of the citizens of one's own town and I shall never have them; it would have been worse in Sydney. Yet it was strange to come in there, owner-master of this last frigate, this last world-wandering full-rigged ship. If nobody, not even myself, knew very clearly what the voyage was all about, at least it had the semblance of romantic attraction.

As I fought through the days, striving desperately to get away from Melbourne, and returned to the ship each evening, there came nightly on board something of the grim pageant of all the wasted years. I watched the unrolling again of the past years, the reopening of the half-forgotten chapters of my youth. I had been born in Melbourne, had gone to school there and then to sea; I had spent there fifteen undistinguished years. Some of the years had been unhappy ones and I would have preferred to forget them; yet I could not.

Old school-fellows came, and I saw myself again at

school in Essendon — not liking it: poorly clothed, the son of a poor writer of verse who gave his talents and his life for his ideals, and his strivings for the improvement of the lot of the lower classes, suspected of pacifist tendencies — for this was war time and the school was fiercely "patriotic" — and of ideas for the improvement of the economic system. I worked in glass-bottle works in the holidays to get money to pay sports fees, which were compulsory, and buy books; and in the mornings delivered newspapers to the homes of many of my fellow-students unknown to them (for the round began at half-past-five). Time and again I was hauled before the assembled school and exhibited as a horrible example, because I had lost my school cap and, until the holidays came and I could go back to the bottle works, I had not the money to buy another.

There was no money at home. My father had died then, still young. I was thirteen. These exhibitions to the bitter ridicule of school-fellows bite deep at that age; I found myself still hating the very thought of that school, and I did not wish to see anyone from there save, perhaps, companions in indignity. Yet they came — good teachers (for it was only the head who exhibited the bad examples); classmates; this fellow and that fellow, now chemists, school-teachers, business men, naval officers — happily married, many of them, and doubtless most estimable citizens. I should have been glad to see most of them had I not been so profoundly worried by my parlous financial position and the desperate steps I was taking to get out of it; yet it was ironic, for they envied me — some of them. They envied me, and my stay among them was a nightmare.

From Melbourne, too, I first went to sea. From the ship I could see the wooden wharves where I had first looked at square-rigged ships, and the windows of the glass-bottle factory where one could watch in a brief spell the laden sailers going up the river. How often had I watched from those open windows (there was no glass) and longed to be in one of those ships! I had, on the afternoon given up each week to sport (I was too tired to play and had little interest), escaped from the school and gone to the wharves, there to walk a while slowly and listen to the wind from the bay blowing in the high riggings, to gaze on figureheads and cutwaters and the grace of ships and the ways of strange men, and ruminate upon the attraction of it all. Escape, escape! This had come to be all I dreamed of in this city, years before; and I had escaped, and now was returned with my own ship, a thing of which I had never dreamed: and was more greatly in need of escape than ever.

I was entertained by the Literature Society, though I knew not why; and spoke over the air with a distinguished general; and was hailed by the sea scouts; and read queer things I had not known about myself in newspapers. I walked again the wharves whose planks I had worn, years earlier, looking forlornly for a job in anything that floated, from which I could never find work in a vessel of my own flag: I saw too long again the sunswept busy streets I knew too well.

Into the ship they came, these youthful ghosts from the past — school-fellows, shipmates, fellow-reporters from Tasmania, fellow-cadets from Captain Suffern's school at Albert Park, mariners, labourers, journalists, whalers — old friends, some of them, whom I was glad to see; but most had only been acquaintances. Here was the reporter, good fellow, on whose motor-cycle in Tasmania I had hurried to my first murder, and had botched it because I could not bear to see the scattered scalp of the bloody corpse blown round the walls of his poor hut. I had been a navvy once, in the early Tasmanian days before I could find newspaper employment, striking the dull earth with a duller pick; here came my comrade in that employment who hated it as much as I and was in business now, and hated that. And —

oh God, so many. It hurt. The fever hurt. My mariners and my boys had begun to grow restless. When would we sail? I wished I knew.

The gold company of Mr. Thrilp was an utter failure. It passed out of existence without ever having drawn breath, save in publicity. But at the last moment, when all hope seemed gone, another group interested themselves in whatever proposition there might have been, and took over the prospector and his scheme. They also wished to take over the idea of sending the expedition in the ship; but they reduced my director's fee, which originally had been barely sufficient to cover the expenses of the voyage, to an amount which just covered my indebtedness. I was caught. I could take it or leave it. Well, I took it. The expedition joined the ship, after I had been a month in Melbourne, and I paid my bills and departed. Even the prospect of a cyclone in the Coral Sea did not appal me after a month of Collins Street.

I was bound for Samarai in Papua, port of entry for the Louisiades, by way of Auckland in New Zealand.

XIV

In the Cyclone Season

ON THE morning of Thursday, January 30, 1936, I sailed from Melbourne. It was a grey morning with a fresh south wind, and I had to beat down the bay. I thanked heaven to be gone from Williamstown, which was not a pleasant place to spend a month, and I was mightily relieved when the smug sprawl of Melbourne was out of sight. A destroyer and a small steamer flagged their good wishes as we beat out. There was some slop in the bay, though it is almost inland water, and two of the gold men were seasick. The other two stowed away their considerable armament and a colossal medicine chest in a tin trunk, made to be carried on a native's shoulders but heavy enough for an ox; it was full of catheters and knives and things, and antiseptics and expensive preparations, but there was not a laxative in the outfit or any quinine. It was the gentleman from Sudest who had planned this array; even his leader looked at him dubiously as he examined it. They had a sack of picks and some tents and other gear with them, though not much; they meant to buy their outfit at Samarai. They were established very comfortably in the after 'tween-decks, where they set about making themselves at ease for the voyage.

Exactly why they were setting out in a full-rigged ship to sail to Sudest via Auckland and Samarai when they could have travelled much more easily in a liner was a matter of some mystery to them; it was also a mystery to me. There were occasions when, thinking the thing over, I suspected that the value of the ship to the enterprise was, perhaps, not so doubtful after all. She had attracted a great deal of notice in Australia, and the voyage after gold, being somewhat unusual in these days, had had more than its fair share of publicity. If the expedition discovered anything on Sudest of sufficient value to warrant the flotation of a big public company, the publicity which the ship had attracted to the beginning of the enterprise would make an excellent foundation for the campaign for funds. Whoever stood to lose by this voyage (and I was now losing heavily myself), the brokers of Collins Street, I thought, knew what they were doing. Well, I suppose that is their business; the formation of gold-mining companies is always something of a gamble.

I fear my Collins Street adventures rather sickened me of Melbourne, for which I had had no great esteem before, and the visit was quite spoiled. The ship, however, was treated very well, and the boys were given a good time. The Harbour Trust authorities charged neither dues nor wharfage, and the Pilots' Association, good fellows, took the ship in and out and neglected to send in any bills for the service. It is not easy to take a full-rigged ship into or out of Melbourne, which is scarcely ranked among the best harbours in the world. I bought stores and food to last the ship to New York, I hoped, and spent more than a thousand pounds. I drydocked the ship and cleaned her thoroughly; whatever she needed she must have, no matter what the financial stringency. Advances to the crew, purchase of provisions, meats, rope, canvas, paint, oil, kerosene, charts, and stores took the rest of the money. Again I did my best to have the engine put in working order, for I knew the waters round Samarai to be worse than any we had yet sailed. It would be madness to be there without an engine. I had the engine thoroughly overhauled, and shipped some extra drums of fuel. The ship was in need of a new set of braces, to be cut and made from many coils of expensive rope; the rope I bought in

Melbourne was excellent stuff. I knew I could take no chances with the cyclone season. The gear had to be perfect in every detail; for after the Coral Sea, there would be Cape Horn.

The customs officers of Melbourne, too, were much more human than their brethren in New South Wales. When I came to the customs house with my lengthy and voluminous inventory so painfully compiled at the port of entry — the whole of the contents, except paint and canvas we had not broached, did not exceed fifty pounds in value — they said, Hallo, what's this? That's the inventory, I said, pointing to the large columns and the multifarious entries labelled Beer, bottled (quarts), Geneva and gin (bulk), Tobacco manufactured n.e.i.[6] including the weight of tags, labels, and other attachments (lbs.), Opium (lbs.), Confectionery, including candied and crystallized fruits (lbs.), Fancy Goods (barber's stock) see endorsement on back; Fish fresh smoked or dried (but not salted) or preserved by cold process; Oilmen's stores n.e.i. being Groceries including Culinary and Flavouring Essences (non-spirituous), Soap Dyes, Condition Foods, and other preparations used in the household, including Food for Birds; Toilet Paper — and so on, and so on, over four square feet.

I pointed to the list showing our consumption, which, since we had bought everything ashore, was not much, and suggested that they had better come down and check the stuff. We might, after all, have surreptitiously consumed quite a lot of Soap Dyes, or Food for Birds. I had gathered in Sydney that this would be the crucial point in my fiscal career. Making the inventory, they said, was nothing to checking it. I'd see! Well, I saw, sure enough. I showed the obliging officials my receipts for £1,100, spent in the country on fresh food and sea stores and all manner of

---

[6] N.E.I. is officialese for "not elsewhere included."

things. And that was the end of the interview. Dammitall, they said, you've spent enough in this place; and they wrote upon my outward inventory "Consumption Nil" and charged me no customs duties whatever. Well, that was sense. I'd brought in food that I had to have, worth about £50. I'd used as little of this as possible, and had spent £1,100. But it really was decent of the customs men in Melbourne not to go through the whole wearying rigmarole of checking and rechecking the inventory. It is the petty annoyance of these things, the interference with one's liberty, that hurts far more than the cost, which in my case at least would have been trifling. The laborious detail connected with the preparation and duplication of countless stupid and unnecessary forms is a real trial in bringing a ship to Australia and taking her away again. In Sydney I had had the help of an obliging shipping agent, but I had no such help in Melbourne. However, the officials were kind. I must say that never, at any time or in any port, did I have real trouble with an official connected with the reception of ships, nor did I ever meet one who was wholly unpleasant. They were doing their jobs, and they did not make the laws.

In Melbourne I even found an honest ship-chandler, who ranked at once with the only other two completely straight firms I knew in the whole world, one in London and the other in New York. But I found I had to keep a careful watch on some of the purveyors of provisions.

I had the malaria experts on board to try to combat the miserable scourge. They did very well, though Melbourne is not a centre for tropical medicine: a pleasant Scots medical man, who was also a yachtsman, was a good friend to the ship in this regard. Dennis, the young cadet, was patched up well in hospital, and when he returned on board with his Sister and his doctor, both of whom chanced to be attractive young women, many of the other boys regretted that they had not been cot cases too. Jan and the carpenter, who would hear of no hospitals, continued to be none too well; I received now, however, copious instructions for dealing with their cases — instructions which proved to be most satisfactory. I tried to get a doctor to sail with me, but could not. Some of the boys still had tropic sores, and the cook's leg though saved would require skilled attention for a long, long time. I was returning to New Guinea in the worst season; a doctor would at least have taken the medical worries off my mind. The right doctor, that is; the wrong one would have added to them.

I had to beat out of Bass Strait, for the wind stayed ahead. We saw the Melbourne Heads two days, and the next night saw Tasmania; but in the course of time we passed into the Tasman Sea again, past Deal Island. It was then February, which is a comparatively quiet month in the Tasman Sea, a fact for which I was devoutly thankful. We could then concentrate upon getting the ship in thoroughly first-class condition for the passage of the Coral Sea — the two passages, for we should have to get away again from Sudest to the eastwards, and to beat out of the Coral Sea was the only way. I was going to Auckland to pick up some people who planned to sail with us to Tahiti from there, and the gold men needed a small boat.

Our passage of the Tasman Sea was leisurely. There were no storms. The gold men, only one of whom was under fifty, settled down and seemed to find the sea life to their liking, in the beginning, at any rate. The man from Sudest, who in Collins Street had been represented to me as a master mariner, had been strangely silent on things nautical since he came on board, and he never ventured to hazard any suggestions, except that more ballast in the bottom of the ship would relieve the heavy rolling.[7] The leader of the expedition was a man of different mould; a

[7] This would have made it much worse.

mining engineer well over sixty, he was a man of vast experience. When he chose to draw upon the fund of his activities in Africa, Australia, and Far East, and throughout the Islands, he was instructive and entertaining. I soon realized that he did not think much of this Sudest expedition; it was simply his duty to report on the value of the prospector's find, if any. It was for him to say whether an exploiting company should be formed or not. He seemed to me to be a man too important to be stowed away in a sailing-ship for a two-month voyage that would have taken a steamer from Brisbane two weeks: but there he was. As the weeks passed, it dawned upon him, too, that his time could have been better occupied. He was, I presume, well paid. The other two members of the expedition, which surely must have been one of the strangest gold-seeking parties that ever set out, were an assistant to the engineer (a fine old chap who never did learn to stand up straight on the ship's deck), and a youthful roustabout.

They were all glad when at last we reached Auckland, after an uneventful run of twenty-six days from Williamstown. I was glad, too. At Auckland, a very pleasant place which I had often visited in Tasman Sea barques, there was a mild exodus of the older cadets. Five of them left here. Fever of different kinds had something to do with the departure of one or two of them; the others felt that they had been in the ship long enough, that it was time they got on with the serious business of living. With this attitude I was entirely in agreement, though, unfortunately, I was losing two of my best cadets. These were the cadet-captain, Tony Evershed, who had to get back to England to be in time to enter one of the great universities, and a young American named Ed Lane, a banker. Tony and Ed were as stout fellows as ever walked the decks, and we missed them. Tony had been in the ship a year and a half, and Ed had been fourteen months. The others had been a similar period and, at least, they had had a fair taste of the life. At Auckland, too, the opportunity at last came to ship a British officer, a young man who had some real experience of square sail. He was an Australian who had been in the *Mount Stewart* and the *Richelieu*, and in Tasman Sea barquentines. I shipped him, and paid off the grain-ship mate who had been with me from Copenhagen. I had to send the latter to his home at Helsingfors, which was an expensive business; and I should have to return the Britisher to New Zealand from England or America, at the end of the voyage. This manning question is a difficult one in these days, particularly for me. I had trained five cadets to the point where some of them were stalwarts in the vessel and all were useful, only to have them leave. They were signed on for three years, but I never thought of standing in the way of anyone's liberty. I could, perhaps, have kept them to the agreement they had signed, but I did not wish to do that. To the young men returning either to resume or to begin careers, this might have been unfair. So they went, and I had to look round, hastily, for others to take their places.

It appeared that I had come to the right place. There had been hardly any applications for cadetships while the vessel was in Australia, and indeed there had not been a spare bunk there. I had not foreseen the exodus. The long spell in Melbourne; the difficult passage of the Coral Sea that was ahead of us; our return to the reef-ridden waters of the fever-stricken Melanesian islands; and the fact that we should certainly have to round the Horn in the depths of winter — these things had perhaps something to do with the thinning of our numbers in New Zealand. At first it seemed as if I should get no one in their places, but the New Zealanders are a sea-loving people, and the youth of the land has a thirst for adventure. Though the ship remained at Auckland only a few days, and I did no advertising, I shipped five young New Zealanders. Two of them, it is true, did not stay with us very long; but the other three were first-rate fellows. If they did not entirely make up for such stalwarts as Ed, Tony, and Fred Sturges (who had gone back to work from Melbourne), two of them knew something of yachting, and they all three quickly settled down and became good mariners. They were well-built, solid fellows, quiet, decent, and intelligent, and that was all I wanted. More than that, I was glad to discover, later, that they possessed a moral standard higher than most. They were good representatives of the ship, always.

At Auckland I had good tidings on the worrying financial side. I had had a windfall, I heard, in the sale in America of the radio serialization rights of one of my books; a juvenile there was doing very well; and I was asked for more articles. This was good news. If the fever had not still been so worrying, and I had not had the Coral Sea before me, my mind might have been at ease. I had indeed problems enough, as I well knew, and these were likely to grow rather than to decrease in the next three months. But, for the time being, all was well; my finances were sound again; the gold men had got their boat, and we left Auckland more British in our personnel than ever. It was strange that I had had to go to the Antipodes to bring this about. I had shipped Jim Evans from the *Grace Harwar* at Melbourne. He was a first-rate fellow, and I made him leading seaman.

It was February 27 when we sailed. I hoped to reach Samarai in between twenty and twenty-five days. If there were no cyclonic disturbances, the south-east trade would be a fair wind. Getting to Samarai ought not to be difficult; it was making Sudest afterwards, and then getting away, that might be awkward.

The beginning of the voyage was quiet. I meant to pass close to Norfolk Island, if I could, to have at least a glance at that interesting place; but the wind was adverse. I did not have to make much northing before picking up a southerly wind which soon developed into the Trade, and for a time all went well. The Trade was fresh and we bowled along. Having a fair wind which, with good fortune, might have seen me to Samarai, I could pick my way. Again I chose the path through the Coral Sea which was farthest from the greatest number of reefs, and most free of obstructions. This was the old route up between the Chesterfield and the Kenn Reefs, and then midway between the Mellish and Lihou. The Coral Sea presented little difficulty from this angle. The days were pleasant and we made good progress. A British cargo steamer, probably on a great circle course from Panama towards Brisbane, came out of her way to signal her longitude, a gracious act on the part of her commander. The comparison of longitudes at sea was, in the old days, often the only method by which square-rigged ships on long passages could check their chronometers, the accuracy of which is the keystone of longitude observations. The steamer, having constant wireless time signals, and being able to check and recheck her position by radio bearings, can navigate much more accurately than the sailer. It was a little after noon when the *Port Nicholson* came up to us, and her officers had just reckoned her noon position. It agreed with mine, and for this I was glad. I had no wireless and was now at least assured that the chronometer was keeping its rate.

Once well into the tropics, I watched the weather like a hawk — the sea and the sky, and the barometer. While cyclones by no means blow up every week, February and March are the worst months for them; they grow up when the Trade wind is disturbed, and the hot sun of the southern summer upsets the normal currents of the upper air. A cyclone once started — cyclones, hurricanes, typhoons, are all the same phenomenon — rushes madly through many hundreds of miles, destroying whatever comes in its path. The wind reaches so great a force no sail can stand against it; and a ship without sails is not manageable. As the storm-centre passes, the sea rises so high and is so confused that it alone suffices to engulf many a small vessel. No sea storm is more dreaded than these tropic furies, whether in the Caribbean, the China, or the Coral Sea. They always grow up under the sun, among groups of islands at the west of great oceans — the West Indies, the Philippines, Mauritius and the Indian Ocean groups, the Melanesian islands, and the uninhabited reefs and cays of the Coral Sea. If caught in the path of one the lot of a sailing-ship is desperate; a steamer can often run from the path of the storm. To-day weather stations are dotted over most of the hurricane areas to send out warnings of approaching disturbances which may develop into the dreaded storm; I could not hear these warnings. But the hurricane does not come unheralded. There are many indications, some of them infallible. If one is only able to read the signs and deduce what is coming, action can often be taken to avoid, if not the storm, at least the worst of it — at all costs, its centre. The chief of these signs is in the sky, the ominous threat of which is unmistakable. The sunsets and the surprises immediately preceding a hurricane are usually glorious, and they mean hell. Whiffs of cirrus radiating from an apparently fixed point of the horizon; halos about the sun and moon; a heavy swell, for which no recent or present wind can account; an exceeding sultriness in the weather; an interruption of the barometer's diurnal range — all these are signs. We sailed on, hurrying, for I was anxious to be gone from that sea; and I watched and waited. It seemed for a while as if we should have a good passage through.

Then the weather began to be worrying. On the thirteenth day we rolled along towards Samarai with our broad wake streaming back over the high following sea, with the day grey and wet and overcast, with some squalls and frequent light rain, and the barometer higher than usual. At nightfall the sky was heavier, with some curious tints, and the clouds racing before the moon were cirrus;

the sea was higher than it ought to have been, but it ran true. It is foolish to read the portent of a storm into signs which may mean nothing but rising wind; nor do all conditions which breed hurricanes invariably bring forth these monstrous winds. Some dissipate before they gather their full strength; some die out quickly before they have properly begun. But I watched very closely, and ran on.

On the following day, the wind hauled to the north of east, freshening steadily, rising to the force of a moderate gale; and the diurnal range of the glass was non-existent. Later, the wind remained true at east-by-north and the sea grew out of all proportion to the weight of wind. The dawn was wild with a sickly hue, and all the torn clouds flying: it looked bad. There was a violet hue in the dawning, and a sullen cloud bank grew far out on the windward horizon. It began to look as if we were in for a cyclone. I was in a bad place. If I were caught in the dangerous semicircle of an advancing cyclone — that is to say, if I found myself in a position from which the whirling circular winds of the storm would sweep me into the storm's centre — then I should have no alternative but to heave-to. I could not heave-to and drift for the waiting reefs to leeward of me and on all sides except the north, towards one of which I must invariably be set. If I came anywhere near a reef, the ship was gone and everyone on board; within three days there would not be a piece of rusted iron to show where we had been, or a piece of driftwood larger than a match. The combination of wild reefs and maddened wind can be too much for any vessel, even a full-powered steamer. I might very well be in a tight corner.

I kept my misgivings to myself. It began to be obvious that we were in for it; and there was only one thing to do. Since the steadily rising wind remained in exactly the same quarter, we must be directly in the path of the oncoming storm. How far away was it? That I did not know and could not find out. But I watched closely for any shift which would indicate to me whether I lay in the navigable area, or what was very likely to be the fatal one. Still there was no change, beyond the increasing wildness of the threatening sky and the growth of the wind and sea. Shall I heave-to while there is still a chance? No, no! I cannot do that! I can only run, scud before the path of the storm. There is no room to heave-to: any dallying may be fatal. So run it is, beneath as full a press of sail as the ship will stand, for I know that I must at least get past the worst of the reefs before the real storm breaks, that I may, if it comes to that, have a reasonable hope of lying-to with some sea room. Run, run! She foams along at ten and eleven knots. I know now that the ship is in the freshening gale of an advancing cyclone (which may yet dissipate): I can only run. The barometer falls and keeps falling; the sea rises and keeps rising, and is now confused. The sky is ugly and grows uglier. Run, run! How beautifully she does run! I keep the main t'gallant on her, pinning my faith on the ease with which sail comes in, in this little ship, even in a high wind; and run and run. I run with the wind on the port quarter and keep it so, bound towards the north: rolling, rolling, the ship boils on. The foam creams before her in wild wonder at the onrush of her sail-crowded advance as she treads down the waters: the spume blows above the yards; the sea booms, and the wind roars. Run, little lady!

So I ran, and ran, and ran — 100 miles, 200 miles, 300 miles. Almost imperceptibly the glass began to rise again and the wind eased, though it was squally and unsettled and there was a deluge of rain. I saw the grey clouds in the heavy southern sky gone mad and rushing in circles; but we were gone then, thank God, from that part of the horizon. And I saw that the main topgallant mast was sprung, and that the trestle-trees of the fore topmast had fractured on one side and sunk. This seriously weakened the ship aloft; but the cyclone had gone.

The weather was disturbed for many days afterwards. I had run off to the eastward by keeping the wind on the port quarter, and now found it difficult to get this longitude back; but I still counted on the south-east season having set in towards Samarai so that I should not be bothered with north-west winds and unsteady conditions when I made my landfall. The sets in these waters are always considerable and incalculable, but they are especially dangerous at the changing of the seasons. I did not know, and could by no means discover, whether it would be best to approach Samarai from west of it, reckoning on an east-going set left over from the north-west season, or from the east with the west-setting stream of the Trade. The set had been steadily to the westward almost since leaving Auckland; but these problems in the Pacific are insoluble. I had to guess; I had to take a chance on it. As a matter of fact, I could not even do that, for we had no sooner picked up the first reef of the Papuan waters than the wind came howling out of the north-west at us — a quarter from which officially it should long have ceased to blow — so strongly that I could do nothing but head-reach against it and drive almost bodily to leeward. There was no time even to be sure which reef we saw, for one reef is very like another; but observation showed it to be Uluma, a short forty miles from Samarai.

But the wind blew me away 200 miles, and we were another week. The beat-back in that hot and humid atmosphere against the wind, the set, and the sea, was dogged to the point of desperation. The conditions were peculiarly adverse, combining in themselves such an array of difficulties for the ship to overcome that I sometimes thought of going to Sudest (which was then close by) and throwing the gold men out without bothering to go to Samarai first. I could not, however, do this. I had to go to Samarai because the place was the official port of entry for the Papuan groups and all the Louisiades, and because the gold men had to get their outfit there. I beat on. To the north of me were unlit reefs, a long line of them, stretching from the eastern end of Sudest to New Guinea, with here and there a few narrow passages through; to the south of me were more reefs. I had only the sea room in between them in which to beat, and the set, which hitherto had been to the west, was now running eastwards at fifty to sixty miles a day — dead against me. The engine was useless against adverse conditions in the open sea, and I did not think of it, though I would have used it if I could; we had to overcome these difficulties without power. The weather was so bad and the visibility so poor that I knew I should be lucky to see the reefs before I got on them; and if I got on them, we stayed — we all stayed. I had to be careful. The rain beat down upon the ship in sheets; the wind blew at gale force, and I began to think this must be the outer region of another cyclonic disturbance (we heard later that this it most certainly was); and the ship, under short canvas, lurched and stumbled. The gold men, sprawling in the chart-house, bemoaned their fate, though this did not help anybody.

My weakened rigging was a serious handicap, though we had made a tolerable repair of the fractured trestle-trees with wire lashings, and had fished the sprung main topgallant mast. The three royal yards had had to come down, and the flying-jib was unbent. I could not show a topgallant sail to anything of a breeze. To repair this damage properly was a big job which could not be undertaken at sea. I had to find some quiet atoll somewhere, if I could — a place like Nissan — get the fore topmast down on deck, and make a new main topgallant mast. In the meantime I could do nothing but beat on. The gold men moaned and moaned. The weather continued squally and unpleasant. Several times I saw the reefs again, each time driven farther down to leeward. At last, on a clear day, the ship, close-hauled on the port tack and under a press of sail, approached the line of the Papuan reefs at a place which I thought was near to Bramble Haven. I had decided that, since I could not beat against the set outside, I would adopt the desperate measure of getting in among the reefs and making Samarai by the inside passage. Determined on this as the only possible means of accomplishing the difficult voyage, I stood boldly on. The manner in which the ship was being set to the eastward was sadly apparent as she approached the reefs: I hoped that in the inside passage the sets might sometimes change and not for ever be against me. But it was a dangerous way to go, as I well knew, and examination of the charts was not comforting. "No survey of these waters" covered much of the area through which I had to pass, which meant that nobody knew what was there. You had to look for yourself. "Caution: Little is known of the extent and depths of the shoals in this vicinity"; "Apparently very shoal"; "Breakers reported here"; P. D.[8]; "Conflict Group reported two and three-quarter miles farther to the south-east"; "Reported Clear Passage on this line" — so ran the legends on the Admiralty chart, the latest one available. There are no lights, not even in the Jomard Entrance, which is commonly used by steamers bound to the Far East from Australasian ports. With regard to the sets, and even the tides, the information was more ambiguous. These were almost completely guesswork; and they were all strong. The reefs that were charted came up sheer from the sea, many of them with no warning soundings. There were few anchorages — very few. The sets depicted were invariably across the channels instead of running clearly through them one way or the other. The whole chart indicated as bewildering a set of navigational difficulties as ever a square-rigged ship, I thought, could be called upon to face. "Clear passage along this line" — that was all very well; but how was I to find the line, when the few small cays from which bearings might have been taken were out of

_____

[8] Position doubtful.

position? How keep upon it, when the strong sets were incalculable? This whole area was further complicated and confused by the abundance of tide rips, eddies, and overfalls, many of which cause so severe a disturbance of the surface water that they have every appearance of coral reefs. Where a series of overfalls meets the sea of a fresh breeze, breakers are apt to be reported: breakers usually mean reefs. The multitudinous display of "reefs" of this kind adds further to the already full load of the navigator's perplexities; the whole zone of the reef-studded Melanesian seas is enough to make a master mariner grey. My full sympathy went out to the masters of steamships who habitually (though not from choice) navigate these waters. A steamer, moreover, has to run to schedule, and this was one curse I was spared. If I had the conditions too greatly against me, I could anchor — if I could find anchorage, of course: the steamer must make her port when she is expected. The safe conduct of valuable vessels and passengers and cargo through those New Guinea waters is little assisted by the charts or other aids to navigation; the difficulties, indeed, are more than any master mariner ought to be called upon to face.

However, there I was, standing towards Bramble Haven, determined to reach Samarai by the inside passage, since there was no other way of getting there under the conditions. I cleared the south-western horn of the Bramble Haven reefs, conning the ship from the fore crosstrees with my heart sometimes in my mouth; but it became instantly obvious that we should not be able to get through between the Long Reef and Bramble Haven. There was a further reef to leeward — another of the Haven's surrounding reefs — and this I could not weather. We were being set directly upon it. What then was I to do, in this predicament? There was only one course open to me, and that was to bear away at once and run into Bramble Haven.

This I did. From my vantage-point aloft, I watched the seas breaking on the reefs close by and, as we came into the Haven's entrance, I saw the coral bottom of the huge lagoon suddenly sheer up. God! the sight was nerve-racking after many hours without sleep, and long-continued struggle with adversity. How could I guess the depths? The leadsmen were sounding in stalwart relays; but the trouble with coral is its unevenness. Even from aloft there is scant difference discernible between a depth of two fathoms, which is not safe, and depths of five and six fathoms, which are. Too often one discovers the shallow water only with the ship's keel. Much of the coral here is black, showing the misleading darkness of good depth; coral usually gives quick betrayal of shallows, but this is not invariably the case.

I stood on. The soundings were all right. The entrance was clear; as far as could be seen, the whole great lagoon was clear. But now that I was in it, I could not very well get out. Evening was coming on; it would have been madness to try the inside route to Samarai between Long Reef and the Conflicts by night. I might have run through the break in the north-western reefs of the Haven; but it was too dark now to pilot by eye among coral reefs. There was anchorage in the Haven. I anchored; and thanked God. I put out the dinghy and sounded round; she was all right.

Chart of the *Joseph Conrad*'s beat towards Samaria, showing Bramble Haven and Wari.

I lay there throughout the night at safe anchorage by the Duperré Islands on the northern side of the lagoon; the next day the wind was fresh from the nor'-west, with rain squalls, and I stayed at the anchorage.

Since we were now delayed at Bramble Haven, I thought we might as well examine the place, which was not without interest. It was a large lagoon more than ten miles across diagonally, with five small islands set upon the reefs of the northern side. I landed on four of these islands, all of which were uninhabited. I landed on the three Duperrés, and Punawan. The Duperrés are not of much use except for the driftwood on them, but Punawan, the easternmost, seemed inhabitable. On the others we saw only birds, crabs, and eels swimming in the rock pools; and on one of them the tracks of a four-footed animal which might have been a cat, though how a cat could get there I have no idea. We did not see the creature, but the tracks were fresh that morning.

The islets are silent except for the faint sound of the wind in the foliage; the great lagoon is silent and weird as if it were half formed, an infant of an atoll growing these thousand years to go on growing countless thousands more. Man is unwanted, unnecessary, there. The small waves of the green water turn softly on the golden beaches; in the interiors of the small islands, the mangroves stand impenetrable in the marsh.

Punawan is older — drier, warmer, higher, and more clear. It is inhabitable and occasionally inhabited. It seemed to be used by parties of natives, probably from the Louisiades, who came to fish and take the turtle. I saw a grass hut well made, surrounded by the sign of the *tambu* to keep away marauders; strings of the dried skins of turtle eggs swung from the trees, and there were other curious insignia of the dread *tambu*. Some of the island had been planted for copra once, though the palms had long been

▲ *Joseph Conrad* in a light air.

▼ On the fore topsail yard.

▲ The accident – *Joseph Conrad* driven onto the rocks at Brooklyn after her chain parted in a squall in New York harbour.

▲
Three figures on a winter afternoon in New York.

▶
Working aloft.

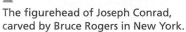

The figurehead of Joseph Conrad, carved by Bruce Rogers in New York.

▲

'Stormalong' (Stanley Goodchild), youngest member of the crew, with ship's cat.

◀ Sailscape.

'Over the top' – climbing the futtock shrouds in the big seas of the Southern Ocean.

uncared for; pawpaw grew there, and, in a shaded clearing, was a primitive arrangement for catching water, and some putrid water in an old iron tank. Here, too, was a dugout canoe, hidden under leaves. The stems of the palms near by bore the hieroglyphs of many strange native names, cut in deeply with European knives; some of them seemed recent. We saw several places where the natives had feasted on turtle and had flung the well-cleaned calabash aside. This and the ashes and the marks of feet were all that remained. By the firm beach we saw the tracks of a lone native, recently made; but there was no one on the island. Pigeons cooed in the thick wood of the northern end; the undergrowth everywhere rustled with the hurried escape of big lizards. In the lagoon, fish abounded. The grass hut seemed livable. It contained sleeping-mats and a rough table made from twigs. There were no utensils of any kind — nothing but a native drum with which the lone occupant had beguiled the evening hours. He was gone now, and it looked as if it was some time since the drum had been used. Punawan was livable enough; it was a pleasant island. But somehow I would not care to stay there. The attraction of wandering on forgotten beaches and primitive life and all that kind of thing is much more appealing when one sits in an armchair, and reads books. That beach was mighty hot, and existence on that lonely island would have been maddening, after a while.

On the beach of the lesser Duperré, the central one, the young cadet Stormalong kicked up a skull from the sand. It was weatherworn and small: it might have been a woman's. Whoever she was, she had at some time suffered a hearty clout on the head. How had the skull come to that lonely place? If natives did not live there, they would scarcely use it as a burial ground; it was too far from the nearest populated group (the Conflicts or the Deboynes) to be burial ground for them. It is not long since strange things happened in these neighbourhoods; the tribes of the remoter Fergussons are said still to be partial to human flesh. Perhaps this was the skull of some victim of a long-past feast. I had no means of telling. Perhaps the youth, if it had been a youth, had slipped on a banana peel on the beach and in falling cleft his skull on a trunk. The discovery of a human skull bleached in the sand of Duperré was good food for fantasy.[9]

The following morning was flat calm, and I went out under power.

---

[9] Stormalong, with some difficulty, succeeded in keeping this skull until we reached New York. There he became scared lest the friends who were giving him hospitality might object to its presence in the house, and he presented it to the Natural History Museum. He was told that it was a very fine specimen of a *child's* skull.

XV

On Wari Reef

I HAD sounded in the north-west entrance as well as I could, but one cannot examine a great lagoon in a day. All the entrances to Bramble Haven seemed to be negotiable, with care. I came out in the dawn, with calm and rain in the offing, conning from the fore topgallant mast-head as usual, and the leadsmen were at their posts. We moved slowly at easy speed; I could see no place free from the bottom's glint. I had grown to like less and less these coral-filled atolls where the hard bottom can rise at any moment and take a bite out of the ship, a bite that may, only too easily, be permanent and fatal. I had taken every precaution I knew. I had the best charts and the latest Directions; I had good helmsmen, good leadsmen, a good crew; the ship steered easily and was most responsive; she handled splendidly both under sail and under power. I was as cautious as I knew how to be. I had made soundings previously, from the dinghy. If I had had a good motor-boat I would have sent it ahead, sounding the way, but we had no motor-boat and could not spare a crew for the life-boat. Sounding in the dinghy was painfully slow. Kedging out, too, was not without drawbacks; the channels are narrow, and an unmanageable ship can easily be caught in a set and swung across them. What then? It does not help her much to have a kedge out somewhere ahead. In the sets and tidal streams which vessels encounter in these waters, the idea of using her own boats to tow a full-rigged ship is scarcely feasible. I tried this later on, and paid for it heavily.

In the meantime we passed in safety from Bramble Haven, and I was greatly relieved when the last of the sea-floor dropped from view. A good breeze came then from the south-east and we were able to shut off the engine and to sail. It was fair wind. The visibility was excellent. I kept double lookout from aloft and stayed there myself; there were no soundings now, but the leadsmen were ready. We passed through tiderips, overfalls, and large masses of driftwood, and saw the Conflict Islands, the Kosmanns, and Long Reef. By bearings from these places, and by a series of observations, I tried to find the line of clear passage and to stay on it; but it seemed to me that the Conflict Islands had been charted by a man who passed by one day, and made but the most cursory of examinations. I could not make the actual appearance of the islands correspond with their representation on the chart; but, as far as could be seen, the water was clear all round, clear of all obstructions. As far as I saw, and I looked very closely, deep-draught vessels need not hesitate to use this approach to Samarai. It is entirely free of dangers; I checked this later with the masters of luggers and schooners at Samarai. They said they had sailed it often and had never seen any new dangers.

Later in the day, with a good fresh wind, I could see the curiously shaped Siga Rock, and later Bell Rock, Rika-Rika, and the islands of the Engineer group. This gave me a better opportunity for fixing the position of my vessel by a series of bearings crossed with position lines, the only way to pilot in those waters. I was hurrying on to reach anchorage, not meaning to stand onwards to Samarai by night — not meaning at all to be caught in those waters after nightfall. But the sun clouded over; the visibility became indifferent, and then bad. I could no longer fix the position of the vessel; I stood on, hoping to find anchorage before it was too late, before the coming of the night.

I had been making towards a place called Hoop-iron

Bay on Moresby Island, intending to anchor there for the night and move on in the morning to Samarai. Then in the late afternoon, when it was too late to make for any other anchorage, a heavy rainstorm came down with a fierce wind which swung violently to the south-west. I had to shorten down in a great hurry and get some tucks in the tops'ls, while the ship, driven from her course, sheered dangerously towards the low islets south of the Engineers. Fortunately the wind quickly swung to the south-east again, so that I could continue to steer the compass course: the compass was now the only guide I had. The rain continued; it rained and rained. Night came down, robbing me of all hope of finding Hoop-iron Bay, or any anchorage. If it had been clear I could have groped in there. I had had good enough fixes before the rainstorm came. But now I was in a hole again. What could be done? What was the best course? There was only one possible safe course open to me, and that was to go on.

Once briefly, through some lighter rain, I saw the heights of Moresby Island and Bell Rock, and again hurriedly secured a poor fix by cross-bearings. All the land shut down again at once, and we did not see it again that night. I *had* to go on. In such a place there could be no thought of heaving-to and waiting for daylight, for the sets would have wrecked me, like as not, long before the morning. Sets are insidious, cancerous things, like calumny, not to be seen or judged or gauged or tracked to their course, but serious enough and apt to be fatal. A ship keeping a compass course knows only that her head points in a certain direction. At the same time her hull may be bodily set to leeward, as an aeroplane is in a high wind; but she does not know it, if there is no bearing to check her course. The compass course will remain the same. The whole ship, with her head perhaps still pointing the right course, is driving sideways into danger. In the approaches to Samarai this was the greatest hazard; yet I had to go on, for that was the less dangerous of the only two courses open to me. The other had been to find anchorage. But the night was so thick with rain that it was quite impossible to see the land; in such a place anchorages are few and far between, and groping towards them in thick weather, one is much more likely to come on the fringing reef.

No, no; I had to give up thought of anchorage. There were no soundings, or I could have dropped a stream anchor where I was, though the wind was fresh and there was some sea. The chart had now lost its whiteness, and bristled with such warnings as "tiderips," "heavy overfalls," and so on, with arrows this way and that, showing streams at from two knots to six, without order and without plan. The tidal information was vague and apologetic: the tides are an insoluble riddle in those seas. It was utterly impossible either to calculate or to observe the way in which the ship was being set. The only certainty was that she would be set — and across the channel.

I was now heading towards the comparatively narrow waters of the passage between Sideia and Seriba on the one hand, and Doini and Rogeia on the other. It was a bad night with quite a sea, and unsafe to put an anchor down in open water. I thought desperately of standing in somehow for the lee of Doini, but I could see nothing; it was too dangerous. I had had my fix and knew my compass course, if I did not know the true course the ship was making. I groped on, praying for a let-up (if only for an instant) in the rain. There was no sky-line. There was no greater density anywhere to indicate the land; yet land towered on both sides of me, dangerously near. No, I should have no further warnings! If I were to see any of these islands, it would be by brushing into them; and then I should, as like as not, see a great deal more than I wished. I posted double lookouts, myself conning from the jib-boom end (though there was nothing to con by), and stood onwards under easy canvas. We had soundings now for the deep-sea lead and this was some help, though not much. Nothing of Samarai could be seen, though we must have been close. There were no navigation lights. The light on the entrance to China Strait did not show in that passage. There was no moon. The rain did not let up; there was no clearing. I stood on, anxiously. I could only keep an accurate compass course from the late afternoon's last fix, and hope to see something before I struck it.

A little before midnight it cleared, for a moment, and I saw a light right ahead — a weak light, as if it were the reflection of a street light on wet coco-nut tree-tops. I saw now some more lights — a few windows, shining dimly. Samarai! It was not more than 300 yards away. I swung up quickly now for anchorage in a sheltered place between Samarai and Seriba: the leadsmen had bottom at twenty-one fathoms: down sail! let go! The cable roared. The night cleared and the air was still. The one shore light — it must have been a street light on the hill — was extinguished. It was midnight. It had been nerve-racking, coming up that channel. I never expected to make Samarai by night. Piloting round there was bad enough by day. But there we were.

In the morning I saw that the fringing reef of Samarai was perhaps a hundred yards away. An official was on board with a bill for light dues; his comrade brought the usual voluminous forms, and I bent once more to the task of compiling an inventory with the origins and values of all things on board. We had made it, all right. Ashore I heard people saying that the captain of the sailing-ship had come in drunk; for how else would he who did not know those waters sail the East Channel to Samarai in a rain-filled night? They did not know I listened. Drunk: good Lord! So calumny begins, I suppose; but it was a new experience for me. Perhaps the good folk of Samarai have not enough to occupy their minds.

I did not care much for Samarai. It is a small island, used

chiefly as a centre for exploitation and administration, and devoid of interest. It is populated by whites living largely upon imported foods from Sydney, doubtless paid for by the proceeds of Papuan exploitation. There are five stores and two hotels, and one can walk round the island in twenty minutes. From the small jetty, interesting craft depart with missionaries and traders and plantation managers for Milne Bay, the Trobriands, the d'Entrecasteaux group, and other surrounding islands; but for the most part, the residents of Samarai seem to regard the best view of Papua as the jetty of their own small island seen from the stern of a Sydney-bound liner. Miners and gold men use the island as a base for operations in Misima and Sudest. I quickly discovered that Sudest had been well combed already, and many claims were already held. No one had so much as heard of our expert who, in Collins Street, had known so much. I had long ago reluctantly come to the opinion that this gentleman was as good a prospector as he was a master mariner; well, he had had a good trip. It appeared that he had had enough of it, and he and the other members of the expedition decided that after all, since it was easy enough to hire a lugger for the trip to Sudest from Samarai, they would go that way. They did. So ended the quest for gold, a quest in which I had never believed very much.[10] I had been sailing two months and was now stuck here far down to leeward in the Coral Sea, to beat out again — and that would be hard. But the gold voyage, ludicrous as it was, had got me out of Melbourne, and that mattered.

I wasted no time at Samarai. I took in water and such things as the ship needed, and departed. I did not attempt to repair the rigging there as this meant at least two weeks' hard work: we had had north-west wind outside and I hoped something of that wind might still be left, to blow

---

[10] The expedition paid only a brief visit to Sudest and found nothing there to justify its enterprise.

me to the eastward. The wind had been mostly from the
north while we were anchored off Samarai, in China Strait.
I did not wish to be caught in that awkward corner when
the south-east season came in strong. I knew that the
passage out of the Coral Sea would be much more difficult
than the run through it. I now planned to make towards
Tahiti, or for Rapa, there to overhaul and repair the rigging
thoroughly for the run home round the Horn. The
carpenter had already begun to shape a new topgallant
mast from a spar I had bought in Melbourne. I bought two
spars there, former derricks from the steamer *Dimboola*;
they were both very handy before the end of the voyage. I
decided, then, to get out from Samarai at the first
opportunity and, since I did not now have to go to Sudest,
to stand out to the eastwards by the inside passage, going
under sail when the wind was fair, and under power when
it was calm. It was mostly calm at that time of the year. By
this means I should get out to wind'ard, past the Conflicts
and Bramble Haven, past the Deboynes, Misima, the
Renards, Sudest itself, and Rossel. Here it was imperative
to have power. It was unsafe to attempt such navigation as
this without an engine. My engine was only fifty horse-
power and was far from reliable, but for the first time on
the voyage we really needed it. I had, on such sailing, to
make anchorage somewhere every night. I was determined
to attempt no more night sailing. It is too bad for the
nerves. It should have been easy enough, with the engine,
to find night anchorage, in good weather — off Wari
Island, off the Kosmanns, in Deboyne Lagoon, perhaps
even at Rabuso Creek in Sudest. (I rather liked the idea of
going there after all, and having a look at the place, though
if there were gold there, it would have to get up from the
beach and bite me.)

I sailed from Samarai before daylight one morning; it
was calm, and I went out under power, down the clear
channel by Rogeia. Punctually at two bells in the morning

watch the engine broke down utterly. What exactly was wrong with it, beyond the fact that it was hopelessly worn out, I do not know, but I believe the main bearings had fallen off, or something equally vital. At any rate, there was now no engine. It looked, indeed, as if there never would be an engine again. Nor was there.

Well, well! It was bad. For the first time the thing was desperately important. We were still a full-rigged ship, of course; but the outlook was not good. The only way that I could possibly get to Tahiti was to stand to the eastward as much as I could and then get out to the Coral Sea, and after that, to run eastwards somewhere between 35° and 40° South, with the first of the autumn's west winds, to gain my longitude (more than 3,000 miles of it) and then to stand up towards Tahiti in what I could find of the south-east Trade on that side of the Pacific. If I could not get away from that awkward corner of the north-west of the Coral Sea where I was then stuck, I should very likely have to beat for a month to get to windward before I could even begin the passage. If only we could have made some easting by the inside way, we should have been able to get through the Coral Sea on one board, without being jammed on the Great Barrier Reef or the coast of Australia. It was still the cyclone season. As well as being the sensible way to make the passage, this was also the most interesting way. If I had to go out into the open sea at once (as I should have to do without power) we should have nothing but a dreadful slog to wind'ard, worse by far than anything we had previously attempted, with, after that, a west-winds run and perhaps forty or fifty days without seeing anything. This was, I thought, a poor way to cross the Pacific. But I could not, dare not, take the inside passage without an engine. We had been more than fortunate, coming in.

It was calm then, and we could not do anything. I put the ship under all sail, and we dribbled on. To make matters worse, the Danish second mate, who was the engineer, and a very good one, had had his right ankle badly infected from a coral scratch at Bramble Haven, and was now laid up in a bad way with blood-poisoning. When he would be in a fit condition, even to examine the engine, I did not know, and no one else could do anything with it. He expressed the view that this breakdown was final and that nothing could be done. It seemed as if the only thing was to make for the open sea. With the calm and the sets, however, I could not make towards anywhere. By nightfall we had drifted close to Bell Rock and I fetched up there for the night, lying to a bower on the Shellard Ridge. This was an open place of no use in a blow; I hoped it *would* blow (but from somewhere nor'ard). Then at least I could go out to sea. We had made thirty miles from Samarai; and there we lay through the night, rolling beneath the stars.

Next morning it was a flat calm, but I saw the set was to the east, and hove up and departed. No wind blew that whole day, and we dribbled along with painful slowness with the stream, passing between Bell Rock (also called Mamara-mama-weino) and the small island of Ika-ika-keino. My object now was to get out to the open sea, since that was the only prudent course. I hoped to get south from Bell Rock, but without wind this was impossible. I had, then, to go round Wari Island and hope sooner or later to pick up an air with which the ship could make at least sufficient southing to get out between the Uluma Reef and the Stuers Islands.

But no wind blew: we drifted so close to Bell Rock, which is steep-to, that I contemplated sending out some hands on the jib-boom end to push us off, but we drifted clear. In the afternoon it became obvious that we could not reach the open sea that day. I had to find another anchorage, for it was not safe to drift by night in those waters without wind and not under control. The nearest anchorage was off Wari Island. I put out the starboard lifeboat, which was a fine boat, with the port watch to pull, and sent them ahead. They made some difference while the set was with us, but we drifted by the place where I had meant to anchor, and could not reach it. This was a shallow bay on the northern side of Wari which looked good enough temporary refuge for the night. With this gone — and once by we could not get back — my only safe course, I considered, was to make for the better anchorage of the other side of Wari Island, between the island and its reef. There was good shelter; according to the chart, the place, though not ideal, was not specially dangerous. The Directions gave it a good name as offering "good anchorage with shelter from every wind," and added the interesting detail that "fish, yams, coco-nuts, fowls, pawpaw, bananas, and mangoes" were procurable by barter. Since I could not anchor outside, I made for the inside anchorage, the boat pulling the ship's head towards the south as we drifted by the island's eastern point. Just as we had reached, after much labour, a point off the break in the reef between a small detached island and the main reef to the south, a faint air came from the south'ard which quickly grew until I could sail with it. I could not get out to sea with this wind, but I sailed into Wari lagoon, conning from the mast-head as always, and with the boat ahead. I did not trust this place, and let go as soon as I was well inside. The Directions might commend the anchorage, but the lagoon looked mighty foul to me. It was full of niggerheads and great banks of mushroom coral. Going into a landing on the beach, the lifeboat had not gone a cable before it grounded and could get no farther. Even the dinghy took a reef a few hundred yards from the ship, and the whole of the lagoon towards the western end was foul beyond description. It could be navigated with difficulty by the natives in their dugout canoes. However, the anchorage was very well sheltered and seemed right enough. We had sailed in without difficulty, but I was already anxious to be gone from such a place. From Wari we had not far to go to the open sea. I sounded round with the dinghy and examined the passage by which we had come; there was not much room, and now that we were in, we should need a fair wind to get out again.

I landed on the island and walked along the volcanic sand of the narrow beach to the villages at the western end. Here oranges were growing, and there were grass houses in some disrepair. The natives, grass-skirted and pleasant, were broiling fish over open fires or making mats and baskets from the fibres of palms and leaves. Model sailing-cutters were lying about — sailing is the natives' sport — and dogs barked. On the raised reed floors of the grass houses were tin pannikins, hurricane lamps, mirrors, and other evidence of the advance of man. Young males were scarce, probably having been recruited. I bought oranges and lemons, and some fowls, in exchange for stick tobacco.

The next day was flat calm, stifling, and I could not get out. Since I could not go to sea, I gave the watches shore leave to visit the island, port watch in the morning and starboard in the afternoon. They went ashore to walk and swim, and to barter old shirts and things for curios. The natives, at my request (since we seemed to be hopeless fishermen ourselves and never caught anything), made a great drive in the lagoon for fish but caught not enough for their own supper. It was an interesting sight to watch them rounding up the fish with the ever-lessening circle of the nets from their canoes. They were pleasant natives. I noticed again the absence of virile young men, though there was a party of Papuans fishing for trochus in white men's boats.

Chart of Wari Island, showing the reef where the *Conrad* touched.

These gentlemen spent most of the day asleep in their boats in the shade of our bows; but they woke up in the evening. Most of the male inhabitants of Wari appeared to be retired commercial gentlemen, grown old in the service of the whites, and come back here to their native place, to end their days. Having returned, they had, doubtless, the choice of the maidens; some of them had large families. Many of the children were attractive to look at and extremely intelligent. There was a native mission teacher, absent at the moment, who had a better grass house than the rest; there was also a native constable to keep order, a benign and elderly gentleman who hastened to put on his shirt of office at our approach. He did not seem overworked. There was a councillor, too, who had served in Government launches in his younger days. To what council he belonged I was unable to discover — possibly that for the Rural Development and Uplift of the Louisiade Islands — but he was a very charming fellow. The natives, I saw, were good gardeners and great fishermen. Each man had his own canoe, and there were also some ancient cutters lying on the beach. There were pigs in palm-trunk styes, and some of them had been blinded. There was a good path between the villages, and the place was clean and tidy.

After sunset there was singing on the beach by the lagoon, where the natives sang melodiously, happily seated in their grass skirts on the sand. Above, the huge coco-nuts quietly fanned their fronds in the faint evening breeze; at the natives' feet the waters of the still lagoon washed gently. The girls and women sang; the men stood watching. After a while, they turned to the simpler kind of missionary hymns which a leader, with a hurricane lamp, read from a book in their language; the singing was good, and the evening quiet and very pleasant. It was agreeable to sit there on the sand and contemplate this gentle scene.

The next morning I came near to losing the ship.

The day was a Friday, but in the early morning there was a chance to go, and I took it. I remembered that Friday was a day traditionally ill-omened for departures; this was not a setting-out, but a continuance. The wind was very light from the north-east, fair; the day was ideal; the sun was behind me for watching the coral heads; and the tide was setting towards the entrance. So I hove short and departed, under sail. I sent the starboard boat ahead again to help keep the ship straight; the leadsmen were fore and aft, sounding; I had Jim Evans at the wheel. I dragged the starboard anchor on three fathoms of chain; I dared not drag more when I knew I had to pass over soundings of less than four fathoms. The third mate was in charge of the towing boat; the mate and the carpenter were for'ard. The second mate being laid up, the bos'n was aft. I conned from aloft, standing on the fore topgallant yard, and from there looked round me at the island and the reefs and was relieved to think that I should soon be gone from all such places. From Wari to the open was less than fifteen miles, once through the entrance.

All went well, at first. The ship was being set a little towards the southern reef but was still well clear of it. I could see the coral bottom plainly enough, but we had sounded there and had three and a half to seven fathoms. The boat was holding her head out. The soundings were decreasing; but so they had done when we came in. We were still, I thought, sufficiently clear from the reef. The dragging bower touched nothing. Ahead of us, the way seemed at least as clear as the path astern through which we had come. As we came to the last few yards from the entrance, she sheered towards the reef. I shouted to the helmsman to keep her up, but he answered that she was not steering; the boat, pulling manfully on the weather bow, had no control over the ship in the strong set. The set outside, I now saw, was *across* the entrance — directly across, at four knots. It was the effect of this, already being felt, that gave the ship a sheer towards the inside of the reef. Only a few yards more to go!

Then the forefoot touched, very lightly, and we slid up on the ground.

Nothing further happened. We stood there so gently that it was difficult to believe we were really aground. Nor were we then in anything like a serious predicament. There was fortunately plenty of room to carry out an anchor; plenty of room to heave the ship off. She had gone on very gently and did not pound or scrape. I sounded round and had over three fathoms everywhere, except under the bow; we drew twelve feet. Forward, where she was held, the soundings showed eleven feet. The tide was going out. I sent two of the boys down with water-goggles such as the natives use, to see how badly she was held. They reported that the forefoot was resting lightly on a coral bed. She had not even scratched the paint. I now worked feverishly with all hands to get an anchor carried out, since it was hopeless to think of backing her off with the sails. If she had been uncontrollable with them when she was afloat, they were useless now that she was aground. I clewed them up, though I left the yards hoisted so that they might be quickly sheeted home again if they could be of use. I carried out the stream anchor, for our bowers were aground; the starboard one I left down for the time being, and the crown of the other was resting on the coral. So I had the stream anchor carried out to clear water ahead, and led the stout wire secured to it to the for'ard capstan — our only power. Here all hands hove away as mightily as they could. The sun blazed down upon them, the sweat poured from them, the capstan groaned — and nothing happened. The ship did not budge. I knew I must work quickly, because the tide was going out. Heave away, there! They hove manfully; and the anchor dragged. We were heaving the anchor home to ourselves. It wouldn't do. We had to get out a bower, somehow. I should have done that at first, but the grounding was so simple I thought the stream anchor would suffice. It got me into greater trouble. As we were working on the bower to get it clear, a slight swell rolled in and the ship, which, despite appearances, must have moved a little to the smaller anchor, lifted her stern and swung right round on her bow. This was still aground, so that in the new position her stern was outside the entrance and in the breakers. Previously, the whole ship had been inside, in the smooth water.

Now she was in a really bad mess, a thoroughly desperate position. The sun still shone; the day was ideal, but the thoughts that came to me, when I had time to think of anything other than immediate measures, were far from pleasant. To lose a splendid ship like that! For I knew these coral reefs: once on them, and in the breakers, very few vessels ever come off again. I could not lose heart. I had to get out of there. She began to pound.

We worked frantically to clear the bowers, the heavy anchors at the bow. The vessel's stem was now resting against a coral outcrop beyond the reef, and her bows were fast aground. The breakers rolled in more and more; quiet enough at first, they seemed to increase every moment and the ship began to pound heavily. The ship was in grave danger of becoming a total loss; she had only to stay on the reef and roll over with the falling tide, and it was the end. If she pounded much more, she would knock holes even in her stout iron hull, and fill with water; the rigging would come down. If she capsized, the glass ports along her sides would soon be broken in. No, no! The possibilities were too terrible to contemplate. I looked aloft and saw the fore and main topgallant masts, both already weakened, swaying ominously with her poundings; if one came down, both would, and God knows what besides.

All hands worked furiously to get the bower unshackled and carried out. It was the only chance. The shackle was recalcitrant but we got it clear — the herculean carpenter and the mate — and the ring lashed to a spar across both lifeboats. But the anchor was aground; we could not lift it, and the boats could not move. There was so little water that the flukes of the anchor touched the coral while the ring was in the boats. What should we do? That is for ever the question in these emergencies. If we could not raise the anchor, we could perhaps cockbill it with a tackle from the grounded fluke up to the boat. This worked. With the end of a new coil of strong wire fast to the ring, and a third of the coil hastily stowed across the boats, the lifeboats were now able very slowly to set off with a crew of stout rowers on each off-side, the anchor cockbilled and fast to its spar between them. How slowly they rowed! But it was heavy work. I had led the wire over the port quarter, since we should have to go off stern first; the boats pulled towards the deep water in the entrance to drop the bower there, and heave the ship out to it — if she would come.

If she would come! It seemed as if her bottom would be hopelessly pounded in before ever they could get the bower down. The wire, paid out from on board, fouled coral outcrops in the lagoon. I kept three boys, who were good swimmers, stripped naked to dive down and clear it each time it jammed. The jagged coral tore their hands, and there were sharks and stingrays in the lagoon; but they cleared the wire. Everyone worked splendidly that grim, hot morning. With the wire cleared, the boats could go ahead a little better; we paid out from on board first and, when this was become too heavy and they could not row, they paid back their wire. The farther they went, the heavier the wire became. They made progress with the greatest difficulty. Still the ship pounded and pounded. But they had to go on. It they dropped the bower too close we were no better off. Row, boys, row! They rowed! Rowed as they had never rowed before — all hands, able seamen, sailmaker, cook, cadet. All the rigging shook now with our pounding. I sent down one of the swimmers aft to see if she were taking much damage there; but he came up in a moment and said her keel was taking the blows and, by thunder, she was *breaking the rock*! Good ship!

But it could not go on. I got to thinking of the immediate problems of food and transport if I lost her there; these would be great. I had twenty-eight human beings in my care. But there was little time for thinking. The boats had gone as far as they could go. The ring of the anchor had been lashed with several turns of strong new manila; one blow of the axe on the manila stops, and the anchor was down. Now they rowed for their lives back to the ship to heave away on the capstan, a forlorn and desperate hope. Yet the swell, though it made us pound, was a blessing to us, for if there came a bigger sea to lift us only a little, while we hove for our lives, she might come. She *might* come — and she might not. If she stayed that tide she stayed for ever. Heave, my hearties! I could scarcely bear to look, as the strain came on the wire and the breakers ran, to see whether she moved or not. If she did not? There was nothing further I could do. There were no tugs to call upon; it was hopeless to bring anything from Samarai. The only way we could get there would be to row, and by the time we returned there would be no ship. Heave, hearties! Oh, strain there! Heave a pawl! They heaved until the sweat made the teak planks slippery beneath their bare feet; the barrel of the capstan groaned until I thought the wire would bite right through it. She pounded still. Heave, *heave*! God! she was *moving*! Keep her going! Keep her going! In rolled a swell a little higher than the rest. Her stern lifted; her bow freed. She came! Off, by God — hove off with a capstan. She slid from the grip of the reef, and, with a grinding rasp, was in deep water.

This was not the end; she was off the reef, but she might have taken fatal damage. Sound all compartments! The carpenter quickly reported that she was not making water anywhere. I thanked the Lord for her splendid

Danish construction, the strong Swedish iron in her, and her big keel. We hove out to the bower, took up the boats and all the gear, recovered the whole of the wire and the anchors, set the sails, and departed towards the open sea. The wind freshened and we made good progress. A small trickle of water was discovered in the after peak, but this soon stopped and never started again. We had been on the reef four hours.

I steered to pass between the Stuers Islands and Uluma Reef, conning from the mast-head again. We passed through heavy tiderips and rollers, and twice the murderous coral of the bottom rose again to glint a malignant eve. It made me worried even to see it there, and I desired nothing so much as the deep blue of the open sea. I was determined, now, to take my chance in the open waters of the Coral Sea, come what might. By the evening we were once more in the ocean.

That coral grounding scarred deep. As I watched the ship in what I knew might very well be her death throes, I was greatly disturbed. I felt not the slightest anxiety about the possible loss of a property I owned, though she was all I had in the world; somehow this ship had never seemed to me like a piece of property. I owned her; I had bought and paid for her. My name was on the certificate of registry as the owner of her sixty-four shares. But she had seemed to me too fine a thing for anyone to own. She was a trust, as a work of art is; for she was a thing of use and grace and infinite beauty, this last expression of man's sailing art of all the centuries. Because I happened to have paid for her, was she mine? What is property, anyway? Nothing is ours completely, save ourselves. But she was my trust, this little ship; as she had been when we set out and as she had seemed always; the longer I sailed with her the more the idea grew. I could not lose her on that callous reef; I could not leave her rusted form to break there and to die. If she must go, it should be at sea, where she belonged.

I had been doing my best to get her clear from that lagoon. I was doing my best, but she went on the reef, and only by the grace of God we saved her.

XVI

To Windward!

THE CORAL SEA is that part of the South Pacific Ocean which lies between New Caledonia on the east, the Great Barrier Reef of Queensland on the west, the south-eastern end of New Guinea and the Solomon Islands in the north, and roughly the parallel of 25° South in the southward. In this whole vast area, which contains some of the most dangerous reefs in the world, there is not one navigation light, or any aid to navigation whatever; much of the sea has never been surveyed, though it is known to abound with reefs and shoals. The abundance of coral reefs gives the Sea its name; they exist here by the thousand. Over the southern section the south-east Trade wind blows fresh the year round; for more than half the year it blows home to the New Guinea coast, being disturbed there only by the fitful north-west season from December to March. In this same season, cyclones blow with devastating violence. These storms may also be encountered in April and May, and other months. Over the whole of the Sea there is a steady set to the west, which is often intensified in the near proximity of the reefs. Many of the reefs cannot be seen until a vessel is almost upon them; they give little or no warning of their closeness. It is of little use to heave-to in the dark hours, as the old navigators did, for there is always a fair chance of being set upon a reef while out of control. Some of the reefs do not break, except in the heaviest weather and cannot be seen at all until a vessel is upon them. To add to the already manifold difficulties, the sets are increased in the neighbourhood of the reefs by tidal streams setting, with the rise and fall of the water, directly on and off these razor-toothed mounds of misfortune. Visibility is by no means always good, and in these waters is much subject to mirage.

For many years, since the usual navigation of these waters has been carried on entirely by steam vessels which keep to set routes, little has been added to our knowledge of them. In former days they were much sailed by whale-ships from American and Australian ports, and by the Queensland blackbirders bound to New Caledonia, the New Hebrides, and the Solomon Islands. It is largely to these indifferent navigators that we owe our knowledge of the reefs, and we know very little; more than half the Coral Sea awaits survey. Many of the dangers that are charted are not shown in their true positions. The steamships, bound with wheat from Geelong or from Sydney to the Far East, can safely keep to a prescribed course which is known, from long usage, to be free of dangers; but the sailing-ship, dependent on the wind, and largely at the mercy of the currents, enjoys no such advantage. She cannot choose her way, unless bound through the Coral Sea with a fair wind, as I had had the good fortune to be on my previous two passages. She has to stand into danger, to pass through uncharted waters, to contend with everything that comes. In April and May the skies are often obscured by rain, so that it is frequently impossible to observe the sun by day or the stars by night; and the most accurate and constant fixing of the vessel's position by astronomical observations will not suffice to keep her out of danger. It is of little use to be aware of the ship's position, if such reefs as are known are out of position, and there are more not known. In such waters the square-rigged ship must proceed with the utmost caution, and navigation is a nightmare.

Here then, down in the farthest leeward corner of this most dangerous sea, with no circumstance in my favour and nothing to aid me; with the set and the wind directly contrary and my way barred by a thousand reefs and shoals; with the rigging seriously weakened, and my ship herself but barely escaped from destruction and perhaps gravely strained (for these things are not at once apparent) — here, then, was I, about to begin the dogged and almost hopeless beat of a thousand miles to windward, with afterwards the whole of the Pacific to sail across towards Cape Horn.

As soon as I got into the open waters of the Coral Sea, after being upon Wari Reef, I perceived at once that the set was against me. Gone entirely were the north-west winds which had so impeded the ship on her passage towards Samarai, and in their stead now blew light easterlies. It is always so. Adversity piles upon adversity; yet one must do one's best. There could be no giving in — not ever: indeed the relief at being free from the dreadful embrace of the reef was at first so great that navigational difficulties seemed of no great importance. Yet I did not belittle the array of circumstances against me. I tried desperately to make towards the east, somehow, in order to get to windward of the Great Barrier Reef, and as many other reefs as possible, before the south-east trade blew home. The endeavour was vain. We began to lose almost at once.

Having regard to the ship's seaworthiness which, after her savage pounding, was questionable, I had determined to continue with the voyage and beat out of the Coral Sea; but at the same time I well knew that any serious defects which might have escaped observation would very quickly be shown up under those conditions. If it were really necessary, I would go into Brisbane or Sydney to dry dock. This, however, I had no need to do. The ship was not damaged. I had had two good swimmers swim along the keel before leaving Wari Island, after coming off the reef. So far as they could see, there was no damage, beyond a scratching of the paint from the keel aft. But the ill effects of serious accidents are apt to show long afterwards, and I watched the behaviour of the ship carefully during the long beat out of the Coral Sea. On that score at least I was spared further worries. She had taken her hammering without a murmur and had yielded nothing even to that iron-bound reef. I was again devoutly thankful, as I had been in New York and at sea in many storms, that she belonged to a day when ships were built with pride of construction and of workmanship, when craftsmanship still counted, and good work for the work's own sake was still believed in. No modern vessel of thin steel plates would ever have come unscathed through that hammering on Wari Reef.

Since we had so narrowly escaped from that danger, I was determined that I would risk no more. I began to beat, day after day, with a wary eye on all reefs, carefully holding the vessel as far as possible on the tacks which kept her at the greatest distance from known dangers. But very soon we were among the reefs again, and remained among them; it could not be avoided. The adverse set was my greatest enemy — the unseen, constant drift of the surface waters towards the west, bearing me back each day as much as, with great labour, I had made, setting me always back, with neither respite nor change, nor hope of change. This was an enemy with whom there could be no parleying, from whom I could expect no mercy. The wind, even in the Trade, sometimes changed; it was never fair, but sometimes, hauling to the east, permitted me to stand to the south'ard on the port tack or, veering to the south, let me make some easting on the starboard tack. The wind gave me chances and was a clean opponent. I could see what it did, judge its force, and be certain of its direction. But the pernicious and perpetual drift of the surface water, silent and invisible, changed only to accelerate towards the points of greatest danger — the thousand reefs: giving no sign, no indication; permitting no calculation of its probable effect until the result had come; defying forecast, analysis, and reason. The extent to which these surface drifts, sets, or currents (whichever they may be called) affect the navigation of vessels in the deep sea is little comprehended by the landsman. Fast steamers are able to alter their course by a slight adjustment; they use the same sea lanes so often that they are fully acquainted with the probable strength of the forces arrayed against them; their actual speed can always be calculated. To them, the menace of ocean sets is not so great. None the less, many are still lost annually through this cause.

The sailing-ship, taking her speed from the wind, very often not able to trace her movements with accuracy by dead reckoning (since both her course and her speeds may vary very much in a brief space of time), continuing for indefinite periods in the open sea without a landfall to check her navigation or the accuracy of her instruments, robbed by gloomy skies of the chance of astronomical observations, and without equipment to receive radio bearings, is at a serious disadvantage. There are few parts of the open ocean entirely devoid of the influence of set; a bottle thrown overboard anywhere will invariably drift to some shore in the course of time. It is only in the eddies of the great currents, in such places as the Sargasso Sea, that the surface of the sea is comparatively still. Even here there is some movement. The main streams of the ocean currents are tolerably well known; but it would be impossible to compile a wholly accurate chart of the sets, of the movements of all those great bodies of water that are put in motion by more or less permanent winds, and the seas bordering the river-like main currents whose movements can definitely be traced. There is still a vast amount of research and investigation to be done before man's knowledge of the surface movements of the sea is complete. I discovered in the ensuing month a great deal about the sets of the Coral Sea, but I never found one in my favour.

Well, the beat was begun. The fight was on. On the one hand, the handicapped ship on which I could no longer carry a topgallant sail in a fresh wind, the beautiful little full-rigged ship whose only advantages were her strength and her superb seaworthiness: on the other hand, the great forces of the mean and callous ocean concentrated and intensified in the dangerous Coral Sea. All April I was beating. Easter came and went; I was still beating. On and on and on, in stifling heat, through rain with the drinking-water gone warm in all the tanks, and the pitch bubbling in the seams; with the Cape Horn sails aloft, suffering heavily, and the gear chafing; and, for the first time, with the open manifestations of a few malcontents on board. As the days passed, the insidious work of calumny and intrigue had begun to have some slight effect: if ever discontent could be expected to spread in a vessel it would be here, under those conditions. So long as we had a clean storm to face or an open sea voyage to make, with its reasonable proportion of good and bad conditions, the spirit of all on board had been good enough; but this day-after-day, seemingly endless battle with adversity showed up the weak, the cowardly, and the mean. We have these always with us; but there were occasions when I thought of the ancient practice of marooning as an enviable and necessary one, a fate more than fit for the spreader of malign evil in a sailing-ship at sea. Desirable as it might have been, fully justified and wholly earned, I could not maroon my few misguided malcontents. In these too-regulated days it is against the Law.

Indeed, though the attitude of one or two of the fellows was worrying at the time, there never was any active trouble. It seemed to me that I had shipped, at various stages, odd young gentlemen who were more expert at living upon the bounty of their parents than in anything else, and if they were so — why, this was partly the parents' own fault. Some of them seemed to have been under the delusion that they had embarked upon a joy-ride; and this the voyage could never be. Life is not like that. There has to be a great difference between disciplined sailing in a properly conducted ship, and joy-riding. It seems to me the well-disciplined fellows in a ship are usually the well-behaved, and the most self-controlled, ashore. The idea that life at sea is a gorgeous holiday is erroneous; the difficulties that come up in ships are much the same as those that come up in any living, but at sea they must be overcome.

Navigating the Coral Sea, we were dependent, in the last resort, on our eyes. For this reason, and because the view from high aloft is very much wider than from on deck, I kept a constant look-out posted on the fore tops'l yard: the boys, in general, kept these turns. I found that some of them were taking books aloft to read. It was impossible to see them from the deck; and a boy who must constantly be watched is of no use in a full-rigged ship, or anywhere else. There has to be some trust, some loyalty — if not to the ship, at least to shipmates on board; there must be some conception of duty. But it was precisely in this important aspect of communal living that a few of the young Americans proved sadly deficient on this voyage. The idea of disciplined living had not been brought home to them; the discipline even of their minds was slipshod and untrained.

At sea now, because we saw no reefs though we beat amongst them — it was my duty to see none, a duty to be performed only by endless effort and unceasing vigilance — they thought there were no reefs. Aw, what the hell! So the look-out read. What in the name of God some of these youths thought they would find at sea, I do not know. It seemed impossible to get into their heads any conception of mutual co-operation for the ship's safety and their own, or any idea of the necessity of doing all things thoroughly and well, both for their own sake and lest they kill you —

the price of neglect and lack of vigilance at sea is desperately high. None of them had been called upon to pay that price as yet; I took good care that they should not make me and their shipmates pay it for them. I had told them, earlier, why a good look-out was so necessary; I tried not to give orders which seemed unnecessary, or the reasons for which were not quite clear. I now called all hands and said, perhaps with some fierceness, that I would strike down the first fool who endangered the ship in this or any other way. Because I always insisted upon immediate and proper obedience to all orders, I had heard in Samarai that I was another Captain Bligh. I was to hear this kind of thing again in Tahiti, but nobody listened there. Captain Bligh! In the safety of saloons ashore my ship was reported as a hell-ship, I heard. Well, if she had been, she would not have got very far; but without proper discipline she would not have got far, either.

The Lihou Reef first barred my way. The Lihou at least has the advantage, from the navigator's point of view, of possessing a few low cays which show above the surface; but one has to be very close to see them. To offset this minor advantage, the chart, which here breaks out in a profuse rash of the dotted lines and hieroglyphs which stand for shoals and reefs, cheerfully records the fact that the "western part is unsurveyed." The same remark applies to the Tregrosse reefs close by; the whole of the way inside the Lihou to the impenetrable wall of the Great Barrier is full of dangers. It was unsafe to stand down into those waters. I went about and headed towards the north-east again, since that was the best I could do. I had to pound out four days on the losing tack before I was far enough to windward of the Lihou to try again to weather it: I went about, and again could not clear this big reef. Approaching all these reefs one must remember that three vital factors are working steadily to set the ship towards destruction.

The reef being to leeward, the very scend of the sea itself — the movement of the waves caused by the wind, as separate and distinct from the whole motion of the surface water which never stops — is as adverse as the wind; then there is the tide, unknown here and incalculable; and, finally, the accelerated current sweeping across the whole sea, which, no matter how the reefs are placed, seems always to set towards them.

No, I could take no risks here. I had to keep from the proximity of reefs at all costs. I beat and beat; past the Lihou at last, the Marion loomed up, a large ambiguous mass on the chart but a camouflaged terror on the sea. "Heavy breakers" — keep out of them! "Apparently foul"; "Reef reported by the ship *Wansfell* 1864, P.D." read the legends on the chart. Nearer in towards the Great Barrier were more reefs reported by the ship *Wansfell* in 1864. Had no one seen them since? I felt inclined to head towards these places, and to investigate at last these navigational dangers so long unseen, but I resisted the temptation. This is work for powered vessels, financed by governments, with every facility of accurate navigation and unlimited funds at their disposal. I kept away from such places, for I could not be sure even of the course I made, and the days now were filled with rain.

I stood away from Marion Reef, though it was said to have anchorage. "The inner portion of Marion Reef has numerous coral heads, but has only been partially examined," says the Sailing Directions (*Australia Pilot*, Volume III), adding that, with the sun in a favourable situation, it might safely be approached from the north-west. But I had no sun. I drove the ship under what sail I could carry in the fresh Trade towards Mellish Reef, to the eastward. A sand cay here, I read, "affords ample space for the encampment of a shipwrecked crew while preparing for a passage to the mainland." This was encouraging. Beyond were the Bampton Reefs and much "dangerous ground not surveyed," and many reports of reefs and shoals and rocks, the positions and even the existence of which the chart admitted to be doubtful. "Reef and sandbank (position approximate)": "Dangerous ground eastward of this line (not surveyed)": "Shoal ground, *Darling*, 1879 (not seen by H.M.S. *Lark* 1882)": "Breakers reported (position approximate)": the *Henry Miller* reef, the *Minerva* shoal, the *Bellona* shoal, the *Nereus* reef — these scattered their destructive fangs over many miles of the unclean waters, and the positions of none of them had been found with certainty. The barque *Henry Miller* had a good idea of the reef to which she gave her name, for she stayed on it; so had other vessels. But there are, in those waters, reefs enough to go round. You may find one for yourself, if you are so minded. By the somewhat abrupt and possibly fatal means of inscribing the name of your vessel upon the chart as the finder of the *So-and-so* reef, position doubtful, you may achieve some permanence in the printed word. The chart round there has been unaltered for fifty years, as far as I could discover, and it is likely to stay that way.

Between these abodes of marine fatality, with the Great Barrier upon the one side and all the maze of the Chesterfields, the Bellonas, the Boobys, the Avons, and the rest on the other; with the vast collection of the Lihous, the Marions, the Wansfells, the Fredericks, the Kenns, and God knows what, in between; with, round and about all this, the waiting multitude of the half-discovered, and everywhere the menace of the unknown — here I beat. For a month I beat. In the first week I sailed 800 miles and made 200; in the second week the ship sailed 950 miles, and at the end of that time was perhaps twenty miles nearer to Tahiti. But I had to go on. Go on, go on! That is all that one can do. Useless to bemoan the circumstances that ill fit a full-rigged ship for windward working (she is good for Cape Horn): unavailing to go back when there is no place to return to but Samarai or Port Moresby. And after that? There was no other route towards Tahiti. This was the only way my ship could take. The second mate, partly recovered from his blood-poisoning, had long since discovered that the breakdown of the engine was complete and final. In a way I was glad even of that, for it always seemed to me a meanness to have so fine a ship and to hide in her hold a noisome engine. But there were not lacking some who shouted: Go into Brisbane, go into Bundaberg. go into Maryborough. He *can't* go on without an engine! He *can't* make it! We'll be short of water and of food! I went into no ports, and did not run back anywhere. I beat on. But there were times when I felt inclined to fling a curse at Collins Street, and I found it difficult to remember charitably the gentleman who had "found" the gold on Sudest. I slogged on.

At last, after many days of strong wind in which we made nothing, and of calm in which we drifted backwards, there came a chance to drive down the passage between the Saumarez and Swain Reefs of the Great Barrier and get out, or almost out, of the Coral Sea that way. I took the chance. "The mariner is cautioned to give the Barrier Reef a wide berth. The recommended track is 200 miles to the east of it," says the cautious *Pilot*; I came within three miles, and we heard the sea breaking. But we got through. It was a black night, moonless, with some rain: it blew fresh from the east. We came down between Saumarez and Swain, and I was glad when it was morning. I was then, at the end of a hard month's beating, clear of the worst of the Coral Sea; but I was jammed on the coast of Australia. I had still to beat, and beat, and beat, back against the wind towards Wreck Reef (where all the islets are strewn with wreckage), for two hard days of fresh wind, and then back again; and I could not clear Sandy Cape. I was being set upon the Breaksea Spit: out again to sea! Would this never end? Sometimes it seemed not. I beat a week off Sandy Cape in fresh and squally weather, with some of the squalls at the force of a moderate gale. I single-reefed the tops'ls and stood on. The sea had grown big, and the little ship, too short to make good headway under those conditions, flung herself into it and at it, leaning heavily and driving hard, bucking and staggering and sending the spray over the tops'l yards. It rained and blew, and our progress was a wretched travesty of sailing. The next day was worse; and still I held her on, not jammed too closely on the wind, for that would not help, treading down the turbulent seas with her broad old bow and flinging the spray all over her. To wind'ard! To wind'ard! It was a long, long cry that stayed with us through many days and many nights. To wind'ard! To wind'ard!

One day it was ended. With a let-up in the wind we cleared Sandy Cape and stood down the coast of Australia, the wind fair for the first time in thirty-one days. We had made a thousand miles to wind'ard in a month, and had beat out of the Coral Sea. I took a fresh departure from Cape Byron and, having been in the Pacific Ocean for six months, set out now, with the whole of its great length still to cross, towards Cape Horn.

There were a few things to be thankful for: we had had no more fever, though the same patients still suffered, now and again, and there had been no hint of a cyclone. We had learned in Samarai that the steamer *Montoro*, a large collier in the New Guinea mail and passenger service, had had to shelter from the blast, the beginnings of which had overtaken us in the Coral Sea. This had been a savage storm: now at least we were gone from the track of such disturbances.

I stood first in the direction of Lord Howe Island to look in there, if I could, without anchoring, and get some potatoes and fresh food. Potatoes had been scarce at Samarai and it was some time since we had had fresh vegetables.

The track of the *Joseph Conrad* out of the Coral Sea.

The life of the ship now went on peaceably — the life and the work. The carpenter had long ago shaped the main topgallant mast and made new trestle-trees for the fore topmast head; he was busy with the ironwork and all that was necessary to make permanent and rapid repairs when the chance came. The ship was a little small to work with the rigging at sea, sending down masts and yards, if it was not absolutely necessary; she was never without motion. Even in the calm she rolled, for something of a swell is rarely absent from the sea, and she rose to everything. For the rest, there was constant employment; the rigging of a full-rigged ship provides infinite labour, and there are the sails, and all the deck-work, and the boats. There was never scarcity of work. Part of the day was given up to lessons — navigation mostly, with seamanship once weekly: the boys had the opportunity to splice and sew canvas and engage in the other niceties of the sailor's calling in their daily work. On Saturdays the quarters were cleaned out fore and aft. The New Zealanders, with the exception of one who had left at Samarai to try his fortune, he said, on the New Guinea gold fields, had settled down very well. Everyone now was well used to the ship, and all were useful, though, perhaps, in varying degrees of usefulness.

One day, I was called upon to draw a tooth, an operation I had secretly long dreaded. I had a fearsome array of dental instruments, forceps, chipping hammers, hypodermic needles, and so forth, and I had a small stock of local anaesthetic for injection. I had, indeed, made it well known about the ship that I had these things, and allowed the view to gain ground that I delighted in them and wished only to have patients. By this means I knew I should scare off any patients there might be, and for more than a year this subterfuge worked. Not that teeth were neglected; but I had always, until then, patched them up, scraped out the nerve, if I could, and filled the cavities temporarily with a mixture of zinc oxide and oil of cloves that set hard. For ordinary toothache I had a good supply of palliatives; the proper dental work was always done by qualified dentists in ports. I hoped to contend only with the aches. But now young Carmichael came marching aft, greatly depressed, with the port side of his jaw like the mizzen truck, and nothing would satisfy him but that I should take the tooth out. My bluff was called.

"It'll hurt," I said; but he was too far gone to mind. He did not even demur when Jim Evans, hastily summoned with Hilgard to act as surgical assistant, suggested in a kindly way that a slight knock on the head with a belaying pin would be a humane preliminary. But the belaying pins were iron, and the effects of a clout with one of them might be permanent. I preferred to try local injections, at least at first. I went ahead: but it appeared soon enough that the strength had gone from my cocaine preparations, from being kept too long at sea. They had no effect at all, though I injected three ampoules. The tooth to be extracted was an old one broken down to the gum. It was no use trying the usual method of getting a lashing on it and heaving away There was nothing to grasp; even with the forceps it was difficult to get a grip. To play round with the forceps, trying to grip that decayed tooth in the boy's aching mouth, would have been agonizing to him; I decided that the best thing I could do was to apply a little of a general anaesthetic, and pass him out. I had a supply of this; I had to have it. I passed him out: he acted a little queerly as he went. He seemed to think he was at the wheel, or somewhere. But out he went, in time — it seemed a long time — and I got a good swing on the forceps.

Yo ho! Heave, and bust her! I ground and scrunched in the approved manner to loosen the roots (or in what I hoped was the approved manner); there was a dreadful rending — and something bust, all right. The forceps came away and something with them; the victim came to, and rubbed his jaw; the assistants relaxed their grip, drank — with the now recovered victim — a bottle of brandy, and the three departed. I noticed then, looking at the forceps, that I had only half the tooth. The other half, I feared, was still in his gum. But I said nothing; somehow, curiously enough, the ache had departed, and the pain was all gone — but I took good care to see that the boy received proper dental attention at Papeete afterwards. It was only in desperation that I touched teeth, or any other part of the human body.

We were forty days out from Samarai when we came to Lord Howe. We had seen it for three days then, and again had had to beat. A presumptuous slump of clod-shaped mountain dumped in the ocean, the island was unprepossessing enough seen from the sea. But ashore we found it a fine place, a quiet spot of lonely beauty inhabited by a kindly group of Australian whites, for Lord Howe is one of the few inhabitable islands of the South Pacific where, so far as is now known, there never have been natives.

The wind had freshened in the middle watch of the night of Sunday, the tenth of May, and had hauled a little fair so that I lay off Lord Howe before the dawn, keeping to windward off the northern end of the island, between the Admiralty Islets and Phillip Bluff, perhaps two miles from the land. Here I backed the main yard and waited for daylight and, at the first lightening of the eastern sky, squared away for the South-west Roads. I conned from aloft — there is coral here, said to be its southernmost Pacific limit, though it is not — and stood carefully towards Goat Island, meaning to stand off and on and not to land, but to get some supplies, and be gone as quickly as possible. I had grown wary and weary of coral reefs, and I did not want to come near this one, for the South-west Roads of Lord Howe are open to most of the ocean's winds, and it was already early winter. But some gentlemen came out from the shore, by motor-boat, to ask if we should like to come ashore to breakfast? And they said the potatoes we needed would have to be dug. So I put the anchor down and stayed, and I was glad. It was an open roads, but the wind was off-shore and the conditions were steady. The glass was high and there was no sea.

"Pigs, goats, poultry, and vegetables are procurable. Wild pigs and goats are numerous, and fish may be caught in abundance," says the admirable, but considerably outdated, *Pilot*, which, being mainly a naval publication, cares little for the passing of time. I announced that we desired these things, and would pay for them in hard cash. But the information is quite wrong; the island, instead of being a place of refreshment for odd sailing-ships and whalers, has become a Gem of the South Seas, a Tourists' Paradise, and the fields where the vegetables once grew are now cleared for tennis courts. The last vessel that had looked in there for provisions, they said, had been a barquentine bound with a cargo of bones from Rockhampton towards New Zealand, twenty-eight years ago. The islanders have long since ceased to keep refreshments for ships, when no ships come. The whalers have gone, and steamers, proceeding on their brief voyages, can carry all they need from the big ports. In the old days, whalers preferred to refresh at Lord Howe, since, if they put in at Australian ports, their crews would desert to the gold fields; the American whalers were accustomed to bring stocks of ploughs and farming implements and all sorts of things that the settlers needed, to barter for their food.

I found an old man resident of the island — a fine old man who had been a sailor once himself — who could recall the Hobart Town whalers by their names, though they have been gone forty years and more — the *Flying Childers*, *Emily Downing*, *Velocity*, *Waterwitch*, and others of the sweet-sounding, smelly wanderers. He had seen nine whale ships in the bay, standing off and on, he said, with their boats ashore for food. They rarely anchored, having a mistrust of the Lord Howe anchorages. In those days there were goats and pigs and all kinds of produce: now there is one captive goat, and those that roam the steep foothills of

Mounts Gower and Lidgbird may be hunted only by the islanders. Progress has come, even to Lord Howe, and the homes — comfortable and well-planned dwellings, beautifully kept — are now "The Pines" and "Ocean View" and "The Bungalow," and they cater for holiday-makers from New South Wales. The main income of the island is, however, not from this source but from the proceeds of the sale of the Kentia palm, found here alone in all the world. The islanders tend the palm and market the seed, through Sydney; all not directly concerned with the tourist business (which is considerable) share in the palms' earnings. Nature is kind to this fair island, not only through its gift of the Kentia palm. Though the appearance of the island from the sea is sullen enough, it is very fertile: here all things might grow and many do — but the tourists, strange folk, prefer to live upon the contents of refrigerators brought from Sydney. The meat and the fruit come this way, and much of the vegetables. It is Progress, I suppose; but I was disappointed — not that my ship came away empty, for by the goodness of the citizens, I was able to get hold of a fine big sheep, a large pig, a bunch of ducks, seven sacks of potatoes, half a ton of very good bananas, and a good supply of some local vegetable, the name of which I forgot to ask.

Here the people, though they no longer till their fields for passing square-rigged ships that never come, know how to live. There is no Collector of Customs, no Magistrate, no Governor, no mumbo-jumbo. You come, and there you are. (You ought, of course, to have pratique from Australia. This I still had. The penalty for not having it is doubtless £500, or some such sum; but the islanders will not collect it.) Here, at last, was a place where white people lived at peace and without pretence. There is no Chief, no Resident, no gaol. (A gaol was sent from Sydney once, to be erected in sections, but the indignant islanders sent it back with the curt message that such things were more needed in New South Wales.) The climate is temperate, and the days are almost invariably pleasant. Money is little used, but there are stores if you want them. Fish abound; there is a fine beach for swimming; mountaineers may try their luck with Lidgbird which has never yet been climbed. The Kentia grows and its seeds are sold, and for little tilling the land gives much. All citizens hold their sections of arable land from the government direct (Lord Howe is under the jurisdiction of New South Wales), and there is neither middleman nor rent. There are no hostelries and no carousals. Behaviour is regulated in accordance with the best interests of the whole community, and a status of material equality is reached more fully here than in most white settlements. It sounds ideal; and yet I don't know. I suppose man lives here as much by brotherly love as elsewhere; but one leaves the island with the pleasant reflection that, after all, the human being at his best, with the usual load of unnecessary economic cares lifted from him, desires to be a decent and friendly animal.

They gave us newspapers, fresh from Sydney, and I saw that Europe seemed determined on a new war, or a continuance of the old at the earliest possible moment. Perhaps a few dictators ought to be banished to Lord Howe.

I ate a glorious breakfast ashore that lasted me for the next three days — a grand feed of bananas and cream and fried eggs and fish, with crisp white toast and coffee and all the trimmings, and I gazed round me benignly. This was a good island! In the afternoon, the islanders came out to the ship lying at anchor with her sails clewed up and ready to be set; and in the evening, with the pig and the sheep and all those things, I hove up and departed, going under easy sail. I did not wish to set too much until we were well clear of Gower Mountain, a great woolpack rock that stands four-square to the west winds, and belches its own squalls. Square Gower is a monstrous berg to rise here precipitous from the Pacific Sea, a brooding mass, cliff-sided, flat-topped, a sullen monument to the implacable forces of Nature that flung it there. Its great height and immense solidity beside the island's low and slender length made distance difficult to judge. We seemed to go with our sails in its very shadow, to head towards it dangerously before the backed head yards canted the ship's head seawards and away: yet we were probably never within four miles of the mountain. An old whaler — he who remembered the Hobart wanderers — came out to the ship and, when we put her under sail, he could not contain himself. He stood by the wheel and burst lustily into "Shenandoah," sweet haunting sea song, and looked aloft at the sheeted sails with shining eyes and an expression like that of a musician, long deaf, suddenly hearing great music again — a mariner of old seeing once again a beautiful ship of a type now nearly lost to the world, seeing her in the glory of her sails at evening, with a mountain behind, and a long beach, and the breakers on the reef flying high, seeing her and feeling once again the life coming to an anchor-free wind ship heading out to sea. He sang. Long may he sing, old mariner: for his kind is as doomed as his ships, and already almost as rare.

So we went away and left the island, and stood to weather the Pyramid south of Gower with the north wind now fresh; and after many days of beating and adversity I felt once again the joy of being there and of sailing this lovely ship for my poor ideals.

XVII

Towards Tahiti

FROM LORD HOWE I hoped to make directly towards Tahiti, going through the Kermadecs north of the Three Kings, off New Zealand. It was the early winter then; in May and June there is usually strength enough in the west winds there without going down to Forty. If I went down to Forty South, I should have to come north again; Tahiti was on 18° South. But again ill fortune dogged my wake, and I could not steer a course to the eastward. The wind persisted from east of north, and I had to go through Cook Strait. From Samarai to Tahiti direct is some 4,000 miles; before I reached Papeete, the ship had sailed more than 9,000. But we did arrive, and that was the main thing: the ghastly beat out of the Coral Sea was the principal cause of the delay. The performance of the ship under the conditions was by no means a poor one; the usual sort of square-rigged vessel would not have been able to accomplish such a passage. Had I been on a commercial voyage I should not have attempted it; had I been at Samarai with the ship bound with cargo either to England or New York, I should have waited until the south-east season set in properly, and then have passed through Torres Straits, going eastwards through the Arafura and the Timor Seas, and across the Indian Ocean with the south-east trade, then onwards round Good Hope. This was the course any vessel would normally have adopted; but I had reasons for wishing to go to Tahiti, and I was determined that, come what might, I would complete the eastwards circumnavigation. Go half-way, and then turn back? That was not to be thought of. So we went on; and in the end were seventy-nine days out of Samarai before we towed in behind the small harbour tug through Papeete Pass.

When I left Lord Howe at the close of the fortieth day from Samarai, I hoped to have at least my longitude towards Tahiti run down in twenty-one more days. This passing mood of optimism was well fostered by a meal of duck and roast mutton from the island, which was greatly enjoyed by all hands. The cook, to make the ducks provide a meal for everyone (for in this ship whatever was received was shared by all), had roasted the sheep's liver and heart in with them. This I did not know and ate only a piece of the liver, thinking it was duck. Though it tasted like queer fowl, I did not notice it. So does salt horse spoil one's taste at sea. When one has become able to eat salt horse under any conditions and even — well, not quite to like it, but not to care whether it is on the board or not, all taste is gone. Once grown accustomed to salt horse, it is no use afterwards to eat turkey. I could not tell the liver from the duck, but was well content, for all that; I still remembered that mighty breakfast on Lord Howe.

The wind continued steadily from the north, and the ship continued to lose latitude. It soon became obvious that I should have to go through Cook Strait, if indeed I was not forced round the southern end of New Zealand. I steered, then, to make a landfall on Mt. Egmont at Cook Strait's western end. A week from Lord Howe this graceful snowcapped cone was in full view, and I stood onwards for the strait. We had gone that way in the ship *Grace Harwar*, bound with wheat from Wallaroo to Queenstown, in 1929, though then also it was not from choice. In all the interval, so completely has sail passed from those waters, no square-rigged ship had gone that way. But now here was I, back again, in another full-rigged ship bound round the Horn. Cook Strait, which separates the north from the south island of New Zealand, is by no means an ideal place for a sailing-ship to navigate. There are strong tides and sudden shifts of wind, usually catching a ship aback with suddenness and force at one end of the strait or the other. If she has a fair wind at the western end, it will, as like as not, fly in her face as soon as she is through; if she is coming from the east, the conditions will be reversed. But difficulties of wind and weather could no longer be allowed to worry; these are always with us, and only constant vigilance — instantly doing the right thing in all emergencies — can get a square-rigged ship round the world. Compared with Bali Strait, Cook Strait was a gentle passage; compared with the Coral Sea, the Tasman was a playground; and the whole of the South Pacific beyond New Zealand was nothing but a further domain of the brave west wind. The wind freshened, and I stood on merrily, and the little ship, with a great bone in her mouth, began to race through the strait.

I had some idea now of going into Wellington, at the eastern end of Cook Strait. Since we had, in any event, to pass close by I thought I might as well go in. I had, in Melbourne, taken provisions and stores for six or seven months, hoping that this would be sufficient to last me to New York; but we were already out nearly six months. Though not then short of anything, it was obvious that quite a few things would be necessary — food, chiefly, and some material for the carpenter. I preferred to err on the side of having too much rather than too little, for a surplus can always be used, whereas a deficiency may be a tragedy. I considered Wellington a better place than Papeete to buy the things I needed; indeed, it would have been sensible to repair the rigging at Wellington and go on round the Horn from there, omitting Tahiti entirely; but I did not wish to leave the Pacific without at least a call at that lovely island. One thing, however, was certain, and that was that if I could not sail into Wellington and out again, it was not worth while to go there. The towage bills would quickly dissipate what small saving might have been possible by purchasing the food there.

Then, when we were off the entrance to Port Nicholson, the wind blew with force right out of the harbour, and, though we could see the city of Wellington, it

The East Indies, Melanesian, and Coral Sea tracks of the *Joseph Conrad*.

was not possible to go in. The wind was fair for continuing the passage towards Tahiti, and I squared away and stood on. We came through Cook Strait with a fine fair wind, bowling through with the tide, and making a good twelve knots. I stood as near as I could to the northern shore, giving the rocks a wide enough berth, and steered towards Pencarrow Head. It was early evening when we were near there: the night was coming down black and threatening, with the glass dropping, and there could be no thought of standing off and on in those dangerous tidal waters. To go in at once, buy provisions, and get out again would take at least two days; if I wasted a day hanging round outside there was no telling when we might arrive at Tahiti, and we had already been long on the way. We saw the gasometers, a radio station, houses, some ships coming out (of which the steamer *Tamahine* spoke us); but I saw no station with which I could communicate by visual signal, at that distance, and we had no radio. I should not in any event have asked for a tug. So we knocked at Wellington's front door and sailed on again; and the good citizens, if they knew about it, must have wondered what the ship was doing. My New Zealanders, who had hoped that night to telephone to their homes in Auckland, were greatly disappointed, and they stood by the main hatch in some dejection.

I sailed on; and no sooner had we come to the eastern end of the strait than the wind dropped utterly, and the set and the tide began to drift the ship dangerously towards Cape Palliser. A calm near the land may be worse than a heavy wind. The difficulty is that the water is too deep to drop an anchor until the vessel is so close in that she must go on the rocks. If the rocks rise sheer or almost sheer from the sea floor, it is of little use to anchor. These were the conditions at Cape Palliser. Steadily, hour after hour, I could see the ship being drifted nearer and nearer in under the light; I could see the black shapes of the rocks waiting; there was no bottom and I could not anchor; there was no wind and I could not sail. I could do nothing. The faintest of airs would give my ship steerage way; but now the calm was so dead she would not answer the helm. It would have been ironical to sail past Wellington, and then drift on Palliser. But the wind came again, in time, after a worrying night: the wind set in fresh from the west with the rocks only a few hundred yards away, and we hurried on. We were across the 180th meridian next day. This was Friday, the twenty-second of May.

On the second Friday the twenty-second of May (for a day must be duplicated on crossing the 180th east-bound), Joseph, the ginger tomcat, fell in the sea from the mizzen channels, and we hove-to and went back for him. Joseph was a good cat; we could not leave him to drown. Joseph had come on board with his brother Conrad from the plantation at Berande, on Guadalcanal in the Solomons, some months before, as a very little kitten. The brothers took happily to the sea life, having known little of any other, and rapidly became favourites on board. One of their chief delights was to climb in the rigging, and at this the ginger one, Joseph, was especially good. He was accustomed to mount to the maintop each morning, springing gaily up the shrouds, and from that height surveying imperiously what he doubtless regarded as his domain. When that palled, he would play on the boat covers or leap on to the cover of the dinghy, which was carried outboard on the port quarter davits as an emergency boat. He was a surefooted little beast, and often sat for hours in the channels, provided no water broke there, staring into the sea. He appeared at a loss to understand where so much water could come from.

On this morning, which was cold with squalls — for we were two degrees south of Forty then, in the west winds zone — he took a leap from the dinghy cover on to the top of the hammock netting, but the ship rolled heavily, and though one small paw found its objective, the others did not, and he slipped into the sea. Here he at once began, very strongly, to swim, looking up only once to give a surprised meow. But he had been seen. It was a fresh wind with quite a sloppy sea. I ordered the helm down at once and backed the main yard. The dinghy was put out in a few seconds, being always ready for just such a service, and two of the best seamen took their places at the oars. These were the sailmaker, Karl Sperling, and the able seaman, Hilgard Pannes, both veterans from the *Parma*. The last glimpse I had had of poor Joseph was when an inquiring albatross, which had been gliding round, came down near him to examine this strange object, but the cat lifted a ginger paw and smote his visitor heartily over the nose, whereupon the startled albatross at once took off again and left him alone. The beak of an albatross would have made short work of poor Joseph! He knew that; but he was not one to be afraid. I could not leave a cat like that to drown. It seemed utterly impossible to find a tiny cat in all that waste of water, for the ship, even hove-to, was still drifting, and the cat was so small. Still, Hilgard and Karl pulled back towards the place where they thought he might be, while many eyes in the rigging kept look-out on the sea for the tiny form. We did not see him again, but I had a rough bearing of where he was and in this direction the dinghy pulled. They were about to give up, after pulling for twenty minutes and searching all the area within two cables of the ship, when, to the astonishment of all hands, there was Joseph, wet and bedraggled, weakly swimming towards the dinghy. The boys hauled him aboard and hurried back to the ship, taking off their jerseys in the cold to wrap round the cat. We hurried him along to the galley, took the dinghy aboard again, squared away and proceeded. That was a fortunate little kitten. He soon recovered from his cold immersion and within two days was happily playing in the rigging again, though he kept away from the channels; and the ungrateful beast snarled at Hilgard.

It was then cold, and we had the old story of the westerly gales again. I kept what sail I could on the ship, and ran on. We had no time to waste. I hoped to be able, after entering the ship inwards at Papeete, to shift across to one of the sheltered bays of Tahiti's sister island, Moorea, to be a little farther from the Papeete saloons while my mariners got on with the complicated task of putting the rigging in good shape for Cape Horn. But it became obvious that, if I were to get round the Horn itself before the break-up of the spring ice of the Weddell Sea and Graham's Island, I could not afford the time to go to Moorea. I should have to stay at Papeete. But for the time being at any rate, the worries of the ports were remote; I was contending with the sea. It blew up a hard gale, and we had eight days of weather as severe as any (with the exception of one Cape Horn storm) through the voyage. It must have been the end of a tropic cyclone which had moved away down there to blow itself out; but it had a long way still to go when it passed over us.

It began in the usual manner — falling glass; threatening sky; heavy, confused swell; and the wind fitful and often falling calm. All the skylights were lashed down, and everything thoroughly secured on deck. I shortened down and waited for what might come, keeping the ship on the port tack, for it looked as if the wind would come from somewhere between north and west. This was unfortunate, but it could not be helped. We had come then to the 150th meridian of westerly longitude near which was Tahiti, some 1,300 miles to the north: we had now to turn toward the north and regain all the latitude lost by going through Cook Strait. If the wind came from the north we could not go that way. I could only hold to what sail the ship would bear and stand on north-eastwards across the wind — but that way lay some reefs.

It blew and blew once the storm began. It lasted for eight days and I had to heave-to three times; but whenever there was a chance to use a let-up in the wind I used it. It was of little avail to heave-to and wait in comparatively safe idleness for the storm to blow itself out. If I had done this we should, in that week, have been driven many hundreds of miles to the eastward of Tahiti. I had to fight it out, to fight the wind for a little progress whenever the chance came. This was difficult. It meant constant sail handling — in sail and set sail, reef and shake out, heave-to and get under way, hour after hour, day after day, without any rest. But the boys did splendidly. Gone entirely now was the passing bickering spirit of the Coral Sea. In eight days we had no less than *eighty* sail-handlings; that is to say, sail was set, changed, reefed, goose-winged, or taken in, eighty times. Such a large number of sail-handlings seems incredible, and I would scarcely have believed it myself, had it not all been recorded in the log; yet it was necessary. I had a small ship, with a lot of rigging — a delicate ship, with two strained masts. She had to be handled carefully. Throughout the whole long storm, I had to gauge accurately the amount of sail she would bear; to know, before they came, the conditions in which she must be hove-to; to keep always at least one sail ahead of the wind; to have one rag of canvas, less than the maximum that might endanger all our lives. The sea grew big, but it was not frightening. I had to be careful and yet make progress; I had to have the ship under control at all times, and yet make headway. And I could not afford any further damage. What had happened in the Coral Sea — the sprung main topgallant and the fractured fore cross-trees — we could repair ourselves; but I could not stand any large bill for repairs at Tahiti. I was cautious then; but I did my best. Three times I hove-to, on each occasion under the goose-winged close-reefed fore tops'l (keeping only the lee clew set), the mizzen staysail, and the fore topmast stays'l. With the helm down she lay-to very well under this canvas. But as soon as there was a chance, I put the helm up again and went on. Some of the squalls were savage.

June came; this was midwinter, and we were still south of Forty. The gale continued from north-west and north-north-west with such savage violence that I had to heave-to again; and she lay so comfortably then that the watch could work dry out on the weather fore channels, lashing the port boat boom which had broken adrift. When this was done I put the helm up and went on, and gave her a little more sail in spite of the sleet squalls and the hail and the tumult of the sea. At night the gale was back worse than ever.

In the middle watch, with the ship under reefed fores'l, close-reefed fore and main tops'ls, foot of the spanker and the two storm stays'ls, she was struck by a sea which carried the dinghy away, and, breaking over the quarter aft, took some of the deck fittings with it — the port poop ladder, a lifebuoy, some capstan bars, and such things. The sea was high! I hove-to again after that; and at daylight went on with some slight abatement. But the abatement was false; there was no cessation. Shortly after midnight the following day the ship was struck by a furious squall which grew rapidly until I had to call all hands and again lie-to until the morning. Then with the wind at north-west, a fresh to strong gale, I gave her back the three close-reefed tops'ls and the foot of the spanker, and faced it once more. We had observations that day, and I saw that we had head-reached nearly a hundred miles towards north-north-east, and we had suffered no further damage. The boys worked splendidly, as they always did in adverse conditions. Even the watch below, summoned from their brief sleep to face the gale again on the reeling yards, perhaps for the fiftieth time, sang in the rain as they fought with the canvas. Karl the sailmaker answered all calls straight from his bunk without clothes, coming up clad only in a Japanese singlet bought at Singapore, a poor thing that, after two minutes' rain, shrank round his neck like a collar. In this he climbed the masts and fought the sails. Looking aloft on the mizzen, I saw him go over the top and thought, for an instant, it was the moon. They all worked splendidly, boys and men; but it was my grain-ship sailors who were the mainstay of the ship as always — the grain sailors and the two Danes who had been so long in the *Georg Stage*.

It was on this, the sixth day of the storm, that some one discovered that the youthful Stormalong, he of the irrepressible grin and the deplorable lack of desire for avoidable toil, had that skull from Bramble Haven on board with him. He had smuggled it on board to take home for the Ipswich "mooseum." Ha! this was what was bringing the long gale. A medicine man's skull in the ship, a long-pig victim! No wonder we had gales! Everybody knew the dire results of having such things in a sailing-ship — parsons, dead bodies, cross-eyed Swedes. The youth was ordered to bring the skull on deck and fling it in the sea. He brought it up, but looked so woebegone that he was given a few hours' respite. If the skull, having brought so hard a gale, could atone now by bringing a fair wind by midnight, the boy was told he might keep it. He leapt at the chance. Making some magic passes over the skull, and at the same time calling upon it to change the wind before midnight, he carried his treasured relic down below. And by midnight, strangely enough, there *was* a fair wind, from the south-west. I set the courses and stormed on; and the small boy kept his skull.

The fair wind lasted only four hours. The wind was soon back from the same old quarter, as hard as ever — a wild, tempestuous day of violent gusts, with the ferocity of the hail-filled squalls sometimes almost frightening, and the sea now running dangerously high. She rode well, though her motion in the cross sea was sometimes violent; I was flung across the deck and broke a rib. In the great gusts the few rags of sodden canvas still set seemed strangely huge; even the mizzen stays'l was enormous with the wind blowing near a hurricane.

The first week of June had gone before the sting finally departed from the gale. With the glass at last surely rising and the savage squalls all gone, I gave her back all sail and hurried on. The wind was from west and I stood towards the north, giving the reefs of Edouard Legouvè and Maria Theresa a wide berth. These apparently, like the reefs of the Coral Sea, bore the names of the unfortunate vessels which had found them, and they had not since been seen. I did not see them, though we passed between. I did not want to see them. If only we had been bound towards Cape Horn before that week of storm, how we could have run! We should have made 1,500 miles. But we had to fight against it, towards Tahiti, and managed only with great labour and infinite toil to wrest a few hundred miles towards the north. The ship had done well. The gear all stood, though it was weakened; she lost no sail; shipped no dangerous water; hurt no one, yielded nothing. We had only the dinghy gone, and a few odds and ends of little moment. Brave little ship! She would do for Cape Horn.

It was the middle of June before we were off Tahiti. After the eight-day gale I stood towards the north at every opportunity, passing through the Austral Islands between Raivavae and Tubai. We saw Raivavae, an interesting island, but passed by night and I did not visit it. There was no moon, and even local schooners have come to grief here. It was on Raivavae reef that the three-master *Maréchal Foch* became a total loss a few years ago. I had a hearty respect for all reefs and took no chances. As soon as Raivavae was out of sight it was dead calm — dropping wind all day and in the evening, lost steerage way. The old, old story! We had then 200 miles to go and were over seventy days out from Samarai; and the ship stopped. Yet in the night she lay so quietly, with all the symmetry of her high sails stilled in the sea's unaccustomed peace, all sound departed from cordage and from block, that I could not feel angry or even dispirited. Let it be calm, since it must be so; let her be at peace if she can. It will not be for long. Yet there are some who moan about the defunct engine, and bewail the outmoded antiquity of the faithful vessel.

It was little better than calm three days later. Then we came upon the island of Mehetia, though we had had Tahiti in sight two days. Tahiti is high and can be seen a great distance in clear weather; we saw it a hundred miles away — and then the wind was ahead, and we could do no better than steer towards Mehetia. Mehetia may be a very interesting place, though I doubt it, for it seems one of the least appealing of this whole Society group: but we were not bound there and I did not look upon it with friendly eyes. The wind was flukey in catspaws from the north, here where we should have had the south-east trade. We were within the tropics again and had arrived, indeed, almost at 19° south. But there was not the slightest sign of the trade wind. The next day it poured with rain and was calm again, and Tahiti had vanished completely from sight. It was not until the seventeenth of June, when we were seventy-eight days out from Samarai, that we were off the fair land of Tahiti at last.

On the morning of that day the weather was so thick with rain that, though I knew the coast of the Taiarapu Peninsula was four miles away, and the mountains there are 4,000 feet high, we could see nothing. I stood onwards, shaping a course to windward of Tahiti round the eastern and northern shores, towards Venus Point and Papeete. Papeete is the port of entry, and this was the sensible way to approach it. I should then come in with the wind and current both favourable. Later it cleared, and we had a light fair wind, and sailed along slowly off the land, gazing with delighted eyes upon this loveliest of the Pacific islands. High peaks, deeply cleft valleys, plantations of a pleasant green nearer the shore, combined with tumbling cascades of water from the abrupt hills to make the whole outline of the land bold and superbly beautiful, with the masses of the serrated hills, contorted and precipitous, rolling upwards and upwards towards the great central cone of Orohena as if raising supplicating arms to this long-dead god. Beautiful and smiling Tahiti lay before us at last, with the curtain of the rain removed by the sun. Against the reef the swells of the blue Pacific washed in contented laziness, as if the very sea was stilled near this lovely land.

By night we drifted in quietness off Venus Point, where the great Cook landed 150 years before to make stellar observations and to cement strong ties of friendship with the great Tahitians of his day. Though many changes have come and gone, and Tahiti has long been largely a white man's island, this same James Cook remains the greatest of all the whites who have set foot on its fertile soil. I thought of him, in his small ships, as we came off Venus Point; and of Bligh, who had anchored there at Matavai Bay with his *Bounty*, the ship that the melancholy Christian seized from him afterwards, off Aitutaki, and sailed to Pitcairn; of Bougainville with his frigate; and Wallis with his *Dolphin*, after he had left behind the inconvenient *Swallow*. It was Wallis who first came to Tahiti after his passage of Magellan Straits: he called the place King George's Island in honour of the unimaginative monarch then on the British throne, but that ill-sounding and unearned name was fortunately little heeded and soon forgotten. The patriot Wallis, though he stayed several months, makes no note in his journals of the island's real name. I thought of these great navigators and all who followed them, and of the story of this island and all these seas, as we drifted quietly that night off Venus Point with no wind and no way, and watched the lights of the white peoples' motor-cars going to the night clubs, and gazed on the background of the mountains against the stars. Now, Papeete has grown to be such a port as I must dread, full of drunkenness and disease, and I looked forward with apprehension to the prospect of remaining two weeks at this fair island. If it had been still a native island I should have loved it.

The surf murmured softly along the reefs; the ship stood erect and graceful in a quietude so deep that no sail slat or block creaked. To the eastward towered the cleft and precipitous skyline of Moorea, and above us rose the grandeur of Tahiti's hills. The stars shone brightly in a cloudless sky as if they delighted in giving their utmost light to this fair scene; but I wondered about the morning.

In the morning the pilot came, and later, a small tug, only about thirty feet long but strong enough to take us through the Pass. We came in and tied up stern-to the waterfront roadway, with lines out to large guns, and the crojack yard mixed up with the foliage of a tree, and a gangway from the poop to the grass sidewalk where a crowd of people stood looking on. And there were some friends who shouted up, Hallo, you're all dead! The ship, it seemed, had been reported in Australia and New Zealand as having gone down with all hands. Well, well. What on earth was this nonsense?

It appeared that we had twice been reported missing, or lost, and were thought to have foundered. The first report was from the south of Tasmania, where some rockets were said to have been seen off the Maatsuyker somewhere. Since no other vessel could be thought of which might have sent up signals of distress (it was possibly the Aurora Australis), it must be the *Joseph Conrad*: a newspaper report mentioned a government lighthouse tender going out to search. Then, about a week later, some wreckage came ashore on the east coast of New Zealand. Nothing was known to be missing; again it must be the *Joseph Conrad*. This time the newspapers mentioned an aeroplane as going out to look. Hang it all! we had shown ourselves plainly in Cook Strait. How any vessel could manage to lose herself almost simultaneously in two places, in both of which she had never been, passed my comprehension. The reports to me seemed so obviously stupid as to be nothing but the most arrant scare-mongering, harmful to the ship and worrying to the friends and relatives of all on board. Had our dinghy been found, or the few things we actually had lost overboard in the storm, the reports might have been more intelligible. But these things had gone 2,000 miles from the New Zealand coast, and were never seen again. But it appeared that the letters of a New Zealander who had left the ship at Samarai lent some semblance of colour to the reports. This worthy youth, who had told me he left to find his fortune on the Bulolo gold fields, had written letters in which he declared, as his considered opinion, that the ship was unseaworthy and would never reach Tahiti! This learned youth, who knew nothing of the sea or of ships, except that he was frightened to sail any farther in this one, had taken some pains to give the impression that the *Joseph Conrad*, which had then sailed under my command close on 40,000 miles, was unseaworthy. So does the quitter justify his leaving, I suppose. But I scarcely felt under any obligation to this particular scaremonger — or to those others of his ilk of whom the vessel from time to time suffered more than enough, who left with mealy mouths and wrote with daggers.

The ship was two weeks at Papeete. She lay moored stern to the sea wall of the waterfront road with her counter so close one could jump ashore. The pretty tropic fish swam lazily among the stones, and the cutters from the Tuamotus discharged their mother-of-pearl and copra close beside us, and the pig-ferries from Moorea came in daily. Across the road were the business houses and, a little way beyond these, the market, where the steward bought our food every morning. Round here were the crowded streets of Chinese stores bearing such legends as "Ah You, Barber," and "Too Fat, Eats," and in all of them the celestial babies played on the floors.

Here and there, near the waterfront, was a tourist hotel, a verandahed club, or a Government office. The streets were full of orientals, hybrids, and motor-cars; the provision stores were stocked with American and Australian canned foods. Beer was cheap in the saloons, and at the indifferent night clubs the curious collection of casual visitors relaxed and sought "island nights" entertainment. The nasal tones of loud Americans being "free" offend an ear that strains for the loveliness of Polynesian speech. But Papeete is a port, and as a port a good one — inexpensive, clean, interesting. The officials I found courteous and obliging: charges are reasonable and facilities good: the services of the one wholly reliable and efficient agent I found on the voyage made the purchasing of ship's stores inexpensive and not difficult. I found that I had wronged Papeete when I thought Wellington would have been a better place for stores. I bought canned New Zealand butter in Papeete more cheaply than I could have got it at Wellington, and, considering freights and import duties, the prices of foodstuffs in general in Papeete were quite reasonable, and fresh food was abundant and low-priced. A few francs, spent judiciously at the market each morning, fed thirty persons very well with three full meals for the day. Fish, fruit, and vegetables were especially good and cheap, compared with other tropic islands. Indeed, we did very well.

The waterfront with its schooners and wandering yachts was always interesting — its firmly moored *Zelée*, complete with gun; the visiting sloop-of-war *Savorgnan de Brazza*, complete with seaplane; the Tuamotuan schooner *Mouette*; the small yawl *Viva* from Los Angeles, which had been ninety-nine days from Fanning Island to the Marquesas (the owner, according to accounts, examining his charts long afterwards, said "Damme, I could have saved nine days on that run"); the Diesel-yacht *Stranger*, also of Los Angeles, whose owner-master was doing his country splendid service by training twenty-eight sturdy Californian boys (who said "Geeze, ten days at sea is enough"); and the big ocean steamers from America with lumber, from Cardiff with coals, from Noumea towards Marseilles with copra and the produce of the islands. Papeete was a busy port in those two weeks. It was quite common for four inter-island schooners — all amply powered and not many now under white command — to arrive or depart within the day, for Huahine, Bora-Bora, Raiatea, the Tuamotus; perhaps the Gambiers, the Australs, or the Marquesas, though communication with these groups is not so frequent. They came in with copra and vanilla and pigs and mother-of-pearl and happy islanders, their rails festooned with the possessions of the passengers (who are carried on deck), and bunches of bananas for their refreshment. The leave-takings of each of them outward bound with lumber and with dry goods and again with people, though they were rarely gone six days, were invariably the occasions of great farewell scenes and crowds. The three-masted steel schooner *Oiseau des Iles*, built in France, was in from Makatea; her master had commanded big Cape Horners — full-rigged ships and barques — and was a good companion in the port. A rum-runner left over from Prohibition days, now sadly gone, had turned respectable cargo-carrier, and brought in produce for the Messageries Maritimes; the big shed on the waterfront reeked of the copra, sickly sweet, that was all for France. The steamer from America worked all night long, discharging canned goods, lumber, petrol, and oil. I liked the schooners, though I saw none under sail, and not one bent a full mainsail: they were good-looking, for all that, bald-headed and powered as they were. White-painted, with mellow-sounding native names and the heavy smell of copra thick upon them, they were sturdy ships, as they need to be in the stormy season of those waters. Sometimes hurricanes sweep over the Tuamotus, and then the schooners must beware.

Every day the pageant of the Papeete waterfront unfolded itself interestingly before the vantage point of our ship's poop. I watched with interest as the Chinamen bargained for hogs beneath the trees on the shore road, and carted them away in motor-trucks to the slaughter. In the cool of the evenings the *wahines* came, graceful and bedecked with flowers, not many of them now with the full blood of their island; and the male Tahitians, citizens of France, paraded by in military uniforms from conscript service at the island's barracks. Ponderous Tuamotuan women, barefoot, black-frocked, waddled erect and heavy-sterned down the road — and there were dogs, dogs, dogs; and little horses, very thin, harnessed in the wagons. The natives of other islands sleep on mats by night on the verandahs of the white men's shops; here in the evenings the pretty *leis* of heavy-scented flowers, not a petal disturbed by the skilled brown hands, are offered quietly for sale. And the Chinamen pad, pad, pad; and procreate abundantly, judging by the numbers of children in their overflowing section: and work, work, work, and gather more trade and business in their hands until, in these days, Papeete is almost a Chinese town, like Boeleleng in Bali. But the Tahitians are not like the Balinese. They have very largely gone.

Beyond the unlovely little town, whose setting would be so beautiful without it, rises the loveliness of the Tahitian hills, abrupt and grand, the summits of the high mountains often hidden in the clouds, as if the gods of Orohena dislike to look too long upon the Tahiti of to-day, remembering what it once has been, thinking, perhaps, what it might have become — not so much Tahiti perhaps as the Tahitians. For Tahiti is still, without doubt, the best tropic island. I did not wonder — I never had wondered — that all the old circumnavigators found good cause to go there and stay indefinitely, omitting to record all the reasons or the happenings in their journals or their log books. The boys said that now they could well understand the mutiny of the *Bounty*, under Captain Bligh.

For climate, for loveliness, and grandeur of scenery, for comparative freedom from disease, for the gentleness of its own people — now so pitifully few — and because it is under the control of the convivial French, Tahiti is the best tropic island in the world. The French have a flair for gaiety that appeals to the Polynesian with his own happiness of heart. Too often, under other jurisdictions, there seems a greater anxiety to see the native with trousers than with a smile. Let him smile, poor devil: let him laugh! If we smiled a little with him it would do us no harm. I like Tahiti. I have always liked Tahiti. I do not know anyone who has been there twice who does not wish to return — some day, somehow. But I do not blind myself to what has happened on this fair island which once was near to Paridise — to what has happened, and is happening still. There is the depression now; there had been, it was vaguely whispered, a financial scandal. Some of the leading citizens had been in jail. But the depression has found out the business men in many lands besides Tahiti. What the French do with the commercial exploitation of the island is their own affair, I suppose; yet Papeete was the one place we were in where the white men of the Pacific were jailing one another.

At the end of two weeks my rigging was repaired, the new topgallant mast and the new crosstrees were aloft, and the sails were bent. I took in my moorings and departed. I should have liked to stay longer in Tahiti, but I had a ship full of people, and I had to think of such distant things as the ice off Cape Horn and in the South Atlantic, and the hurricane season of the West Indies, 10,000 miles away, and the winter of the Western Ocean. I sailed early in the morning of the second of July, 1936, bound direct to New York by way of Cape Horn. The rigging was set up, and everything was in order for the winter passage of the Horn;

and I towed out through the Pass, dipping to the naval schooner *Zelée*, and sailed quietly down the passage between Tahiti and Moorea, bound towards the south. All the well-wishers had gone and the last malcontent had departed; we were twenty-three hands all told. Papeete was my last port, for which I praised God: now nothing was before me but a few more reefs and the road round Cape Horn. And again I was without a cent; I had not a penny to go in anywhere in case of emergency. But I had paid my way, and we had all we needed.

XVIII

In the Wake of the Sailing Gods

O keep from us the Sailing Gods that they bring not
death and disease among us!

THE GOOD wind with which I set out from Papeete
quickly dropped, being nothing but a morning air; and for
a day and a night and the next day, the ship dribbled
onward in baffling catspaws from Tahiti and Moorea's high
hills; the ship out of command and swinging now towards
the sea-smoke of the surf on the Tahitian reefs, and now
towards Moorea. I wished that I could be quickly gone
since I had to go; but we lolled about, and in the evenings
saw again the houses of Punaavia and Paea, and the ship
tossed fretfully with no steerage way, and no wind blew. I
looked again at the heights of Orohena and all the grandeur
of Tahiti and I thought of the people who had died here
not long ago; and of the coming of the Sailing Gods to this
and all the fair Pacific islands, with death and disease and
pestilence in their wake. O keep from us the Sailing Gods!
The words of the old Samoan prayer came unsought to my
mind, the prayer of the head of the family at the evening
meal. It was the practice, in the old days, just before the
evening meal was begun, for one of the older members of
the family to blow upon the fire and bring forth a blaze,
while the head of the family, as a kind of grace, said this
prayer:

> This light is for you, O King, and gods superior
> and inferior! This light is for you all. Be propitious

to this family. Give life to all: and may your presence bring prosperity. Let our children be blessed and multiplied. Remove from us impositions and sicknesses. Regard our poverty; and send us food to eat and raiment for our warmth. O keep from us the Sailing Gods that they bring not death and disease among us! Protect this family by your presence; and may love, health, and long life be given to us all.

There was another old prayer, at the drinking of the ava, when it was customary for the head of the family to throw a little, from a special bowl, on the ground as an offering to the gods, at the same time saying:

Here is ava for you, O Sailing Gods! Come not on shore at this island; but depart along the Ocean towards some farther land.

To the ancient Samoans the sailing gods were perhaps the warriors from Tonga and the Fijis in their big canoes; and the white man sailing in his ships. The white man had been seen at Samoa, sailing by in his ships, sixty years before he first landed, for the Dutch Admiral Roggeveen had sighted the islands in 1722. Then Louis-Antoine de Bougainville, who had fought against Wolfe at Quebec, also sailed by, forty years later; la Perouse in 1787 was the first to land. After the affray with the natives of Tutuila in which de Langlé and ten others of the French were killed, la Perouse also sailed away, later to be lost, and his fate remained a mystery for more than forty years. The grim Edwards in the *Pandora* was next; searching for the renegade Christian and the other mutineers from the *Bounty*; he had no reason to expect to find them there, and sailed by. The prayers of the Samoans were answered for a while; but the white man came, soon enough.

He had come much earlier to Tahiti — come earlier, and finding there more to destroy, had done more harm. He came preaching God, and worshipping money; preaching Christ, and seeking profits. He found a cultured, joyous, and leisured people, and took their culture, their happiness, and their leisure (so far as he could) from them. He took their islands, as he thought he needed them; and he took their lives. The long story of greed and murder in the South Seas is not yet ended, though the murder is now race murder, achieved without guns, but widespread and terrible for all that, recorded in the statistics of increasing death rates, depopulated islands, and dying peoples.

The wind came, and I sailed on; but I looked back and thought of Tahiti and the story of all the South Seas islands.

All kinds of theories have been put forward with regard to the prehistory of the Polynesian peoples, but none has secured universal acceptance, and I, having no claims to competence as an ethnologist, shall not attempt either to expound them, or to decide between them. It seems certain, however, that for many hundreds of years before the coming of the Europeans, the Pacific was undisturbed. If the Chinese, the Arabs, or the more recent Malays were accustomed to sail there, they left no traces of their passage. The wandering Polynesians and the darker Melanesians were left alone until the white races of far Europe developed, and began to stretch out their avaricious hands. The Portuguese opened the sea route to the Far East, and sailed to the Moluccas as early as 1512, by way of Good Hope. The Spaniard Balboa, wandering in the new world Columbus had stumbled upon on his way to the hoped-for East, crossed the Isthmus of Panama in 1513, and saw the Pacific lying becalmed before him. His principal contribution appears to have been to claim the whole place and all its islands for the King of Spain. But now that the Pacific was known to Europeans its penetration quickly followed. Magellan, a Portuguese sailing for Spain, found the straits which bear his name in 1520, and was the first European to sail the Pacific. He sailed westwards, as most of the great navigators did after him for 300 years; he seems to have sighted something of the Tuamotus and to have discovered the Ladrones and the Philippines. He was killed in a fight with the natives, but one of his ships survived to reach Europe, completing the first circumnavigation. The conquest of Peru and the Spanish invasion of Mexico now gave Spain two ports on the eastern shore of the Pacific — Callao in Peru, and Acapulco in Mexico. It was not long before other navigators were pushing on Columbus's track to the East, Saavedra in 1526 being the first to reach the great Spice Islands by this route. The Spaniards colonized the Philippines, and now began regular voyages across the Pacific. They appear to have kept almost entirely to the North Pacific, the Manila galleon crossing once yearly between Manila and Acapulco. She would be able, on this route, to cross westwards before the north-east trade, and to sail back in the variable winds and westerlies beyond the trade belt of the North Pacific, sailing down the California coast after making her American landfall, to Acapulco and so down to Callao.

Soon after the Spaniards came the buccaneers, the pirates, and the marauders, of whom a considerable number were English. How far the unrecorded voyages of these gentry extended into the Pacific is not known, but they certainly, at a very early date, crossed to the Ladrones and to Guam, when they had made things too hot for themselves in Central America. One of these wanderers whose voyages were largely for the good of their health and their fortunes, was William Dampier, who crossed from Lower California to the Ladrones in a vessel called the *Cygnet*, in 1688; he careened his ship on the north-west coast of Australia, but did not think much of that place. The Spaniards having successfully set up the commerce between the Philippines, Mexico, and Peru, soon extended their activities. Odd voyagers, and gentlemen who had been blown out of their way, were continually bringing stories to Callao of great islands and even a continent, which awaited discovery — and exploitation — in the Great South Sea. In 1567, Alvaro de Mendana was sent out from the Peruvian port to look into these things. He discovered the Solomons and the Marshall Islands, returning thence to Mexico and Peru; and the Solomons were promptly lost again for two hundred years. It was not until Bougainville followed Carteret in those waters that they were found again. Mendana had tried to rediscover them himself in the interval, leading an expedition of four ships and 378 people (some of whom were women) from Callao in 1565, to found a colony in the Solomons. On this occasion the Marquesas were discovered and the colony was finally settled on Santa Cruz, which some of the navigators appear to have mistaken for the Solomons. Mendana, however, knew better. He died on Santa Cruz, and the colony was a failure. Santa Cruz, in its turn, was lost for nearly two hundred years until Carteret chanced to sail that way in his leaky *Swallow*.

The chief pilot of Mendana's second voyage was a Portuguese named Pedro Fernandez de Quiros who, after Mendana's death, took the survivors back to Peru, and then set out on a voyage of discovery on his own account. He discovered the New Hebrides, particularly the island still known as Espiritu Santo; this he appears to have imagined to be the great southern continent. It is scarcely probable that he investigated it very far. He, also, was to found a settlement — this was in 1606 — but a mutiny and a few other minor difficulties discouraged him, and he returned to Peru, leaving his second in command, Luis de Torres, to go on, discovering Torres Straits on his way, and eventually to reach Manila. The New Hebrides, the third of the great groups of the South Seas to be discovered by the Spaniards, were then lost for a hundred and sixty years. On this last westward passage from Callao, Torres had called at Anaa in the Tuamotus, some 200 miles to the east of Tahiti; but there is no evidence that he knew of the existence of Tahiti itself. At Anaa, he came across an old native woman wearing a beautiful gold ring apparently of European manufacture, of which she could give no account; this was one of the many mysteries of the early voyages in the Pacific that was never solved.

After Torres' voyage, the Spaniards seem to have devoted their attention to keeping what they had; their decline as a European power had begun and they made no more great voyages of discovery. They then knew New Guinea, the Tuamotus, the Marquesas, the Marshalls, the Ladrones, the Pelews, the Solomons, Santa Cruz, and Espiritu Santo in the New Hebrides. In those days voyages of exploration were designed solely for commercial reasons and the details of them were kept secret by the nations concerned; no charts or descriptions were published. The English had already penetrated the Great South Sea, the pirate Drake raiding up and down the coasts of Peru and Mexico on his round-the-world voyage of 1577–1580; but he added little to the general store of Pacific knowledge. He was followed by Cavendish, an equally resourceful pirate, in 1587, and doubtless many others. Woodes Rogers (with Dampier as his pilot) made a similar voyage in 1709, and Lord Anson in 1744. All these early English voyages were raiding excursions and little else, and though notable as feats of navigation — particularly Drake's — they did not show the European in the best of lights, and they did not contribute particularly to his knowledge of the Pacific.

The Hollanders followed the Spaniards as genuine discoverers. In 1595, the first Dutch fleet under Houtman had sailed to the East, being content with the Good Hope route and the goodly profits of the spice islands. Oliver van Noort entered the Pacific by the Strait of Magellan in 1599, sailed to the Philippines, and home round Good Hope. His objective also was the spice islands. The same year, his countryman, Sebald de Weert, accomplished much the same voyage. In 1615, two more Hollanders, Willem Schouten and Jan le Maire, found the route round the Horn to the Pacific. This, bad as it was, was a great improvement on the old way by the straits. Magellan Straits in these days still worry the navigating officers of big steamships; their successful negotiation in sail was always immensely difficult. So, indeed, was the westward rounding of the Horn, but, there, ships had at least sea room.

Schouten and le Maire crossed the Pacific in the zone of the south-east trade, being the first, since those ambiguous navigators Mendana, Torres, and Quiros, to follow this route. They saw the Tonga group and other islands and, eventually reaching their objective in the East Indies, were promptly flung into jail for infringing the rights of the Dutch East India Company, whose officials refused to believe that they had discovered a new route to the Pacific. This was poor reward for what really was a memorable, and should have been a fruitful, voyage. The Honourable East India Company itself, a few years later — his first voyage was in 1642–1643 — sent Abel Janszoon Tasman, with two ships, the *Heemskirk* and the pink *Zee Haan*, on a voyage from Batavia to the South Seas. Tasman saw Tasmania, New Zealand, and Tonga, and returned to Batavia by way of the north of New Guinea. However, he had found nothing worth exploiting and his achievements were accordingly frowned on. Sent out again to find a route to the islands of Solomon in the South Seas (where there was thought to be gold), he reached a dead end in the Gulf of Carpentaria, missing Torres Straits — which would have brought him to his objective — and returned. He was not sent out again. Admiral Roggeveen made another circumnavigation by way of the Horn and Good Hope in 1721–1722, discovering Easter Island, and some of the Tuamotus, which early became unpopular with navigators. Roggeveen left one of his ships on the reefs of Takapoto, and a hundred ships have followed it on the reefs round those dangerous waters. The Dutch merchants were satisfied with the possessions they now had and the profits they were making, which were considerable. There was an end to Dutch exploration, and the Hollanders devoted their talents and their energies to keeping what they had. In this they have succeeded very well.

It was now the turn of the English, who, during these two hundred years, had steadily risen to a position of dominance in Europe. So far as exploration is concerned, the voyages of Drake, Cavendish, and Anson may be disregarded. The first long voyage explorer actually to reach the Pacific was the buccaneer William Dampier, who was sent out in charge of His Majesty's Ship *Roebuck* — an ancient and decrepit vessel — in 1699. It was Dampier's intention to beat round the Horn to the westward and, crossing the Pacific in the south-east trade, to reach the east coast of Australia. This, however, he was unable to do, because the *Roebuck* was too weak and ancient to stand up to the battle with the storms off the Horn. Dampier would have kept on, but his crew would not; and he had to turn and run eastward with the west winds, going by way of Good Hope. He thus reached Australia's western shore, and achieved little; for he had already a low opinion of that part of Australia. Sailing onwards round New Guinea, he came upon New Britain and New Ireland; but instead of crossing the Pacific and going home round the Horn (which no navigator, apparently, had then done), he returned by way of Good Hope again, and the old *Roebuck* sank beneath him somewhere near the island of Ascension.

For over sixty years after Dampier's voyage, the English

sent no more exploring ventures to the South Seas; then, in 1764, came at last a reawakening of interest in discovery. Commodore Byron was sent out in the ship *Dolphin*, the first vessel to be coppered against the tropic worm; he was followed by Wallis, in the same vessel, and Carteret in the *Swallow*. It was remarkable, however, how these English naval officers were able to sail before the south-east trade leisurely across the South Pacific, where there was so much, and, with the exception perhaps of Carteret, discover so little. The only important new discovery from these three voyages was Wallis's finding of Tahiti; it was left to the great Cook at long last to make the Pacific thoroughly known to European geographers. Beyond scattering the names and titles of English royalty on some rocks here and there, Byron achieved little, and Wallis did not do much better. Carteret, with the rotten *Swallow*, did better than both his superior officers together. Cook's three great voyages — in 1768–1771, 1772–1775, and 1776–1779 — filled in most of the blanks of the Pacific. It was left to his many followers only to add the details. The French, at the same time, had taken a hand in the game. Bougainville, who touched at Tahiti after Wallis, and saw Samoa and several of the Solomons; de Surville, Kerguelen, Marion du Fresne (who was killed by the Maoris in New Zealand), la Perouse (lost at Vanikoro), d'Entrecasteaux, and others made noteworthy voyages. Of Englishmen who followed Cook in the South Seas, Vancouver perhaps achieved the most; Bligh of the *Bounty* added to his country's renown, and his mutineers added to its settlements; Edwards of the *Pandora* lost his ship; Wilson brought missionaries in the *Duff*.

The end of the Pacific paradise was in sight when Cook discovered New South Wales, and the settlement of Sydney in 1787 sounded the death-knell of peace in the Pacific. It had survived the establishment of Callao and Acapulco, but the settlement of the English at Sydney quickly resulted in the complete and final overthrow of the Polynesian peoples, and the utter end of the Pacific idyll. Coming, as it did, simultaneously with the opening of the South Seas to whaling, bringing into the Pacific gangs of desperate and criminal men, it was not long before the fair islands were the abodes of lawlessness and murder, and the great "civilizing" work of death, disease, and debauchery had begun. As early as 1791, two whalers set out from Sydney; one of the first visitors to the port was the American whaleship *Philadelphia* on a South Seas cruise. In 1804 sandalwood was first brought to Sydney by a venturer from the Fijis; in 1847 the redoubtable Ben Boyd first brought Kanaka labourers; and, long before, wandering mariners of slight scruples and great thirst had found the trochus, the trepang, and the pearls. Poor Pacific! It was the end. First there was a great spreading of white bums, beachcombers, and ne'er-do-wells (which has not yet ceased), runaway sailors from the whale ships, and convicts from Botany Bay and Norfolk Island.

At a very early stage in Pacific history, the spread of these debauched drones, as they usually were, had reached surprising proportions, so that on the first official discovery of the island of Rotuma there were no less than forty whites found there, most of whom had escaped from New South Wales. When the mission ship *Duff* first touched at Tahiti in 1797, her people were met on the beach by a Swede who had deserted from some ship. Even before that, when Edwards came in the *Pandora* to apprehend the *Bounty* mutineers, he found the services of one John Brown, deserter from the American whale ship *Mercury*, most useful. When the *Duff* moved on to Tongatabu to land more missionaries, she found three white ne'er-do-wells living there; when John Williams landed first at Samoa there were again several there. There was soon scarcely an island without its quota of renegades and undesirables, for at first the natives thought all white men to be the same, and chiefs were glad to have one of the noble race in their retinue. These men were a great hindrance to the work of the early missionaries; and the recruiting of Polynesians for the crews of visiting vessels, particularly whale ships, quickly began. The returned mariners — if they did return — were rarely improved; what they learned of the white man's ways was generally of little use to them.

It was largely the beauty of the great Arcadia of the South Seas, Tahiti, which turned men's minds towards these gentle isles, and beauty early became the most fatal of the attractions of the islands and their people. The story of Tahiti, though the Tahitians are now so largely gone and their culture with them, is indeed a little better than most — better than that of the Marquesas, ruthlessly depopulated; better than that of Samoa, where a virile and independent people have been turned into a tribe of Polynesian Sinn Feiners; better than that of the New Hebrides, where the remnants of the people labour under a Condominium Government known to the residents as the "Pandemonium," and better, perhaps, also than that of the Fijis, which are gradually becoming Indian.

Wallis, when he discovered Tahiti in the *Dolphin*, does not appear to have been much impressed at first. Perhaps the fact that he got his ship on the Dolphin shoal in Matavai Bay, that he was ill, and that the Tahitians soon gave him a volley of stones, robbed the island of some of its first impression of beauty. Though he found "the face of the whole country picturesque beyond description," the natives were inveterate thieves, and it was not long before muskets were in use to express disapproval of their habits. The *Dolphin* had been at anchor several days in Matavai Bay before an attack was made upon her by the natives, with stones. Their first reception had been good and indeed welcoming, and Wallis does not say what happened to bring about this unfortunate change of attitude. He does, however, state later in his journal that he had a great deal of trouble in controlling his crew while the ship was at Tahiti; and it is more than likely that the attack of the natives was in retaliation for some insult or murder perpetrated on them.

The Polynesian at first regarded the white men as the souls of the departed come to their island for some reason not connected with their good (in this they were right); and, as their gods were usually malevolent, it was natural that they should attempt to frighten them away. However, if this was the Tahitians' view, it is strange that they did not attack the *Dolphin* when she was grounded and at a disadvantage. It seems only too probable that there was good reason for the attack. Wallis, with his guns, made short work of it. However, a few days later, there was a further sally of stone-laden canoes towards the ship, but on this occasion Wallis got in first, and using his ship's full armament, gave the poor natives a mighty "lesson." How many he killed is not known; but he fired on the shore, as well as into the canoes, and must have shot down a considerable number. After this he had the situation under control, though he had so much trouble with his crew that he had to read the articles of war and stop all shore leave. The men found the island go to their heads, particularly after some days of good living and uninterrupted intercourse with the women — they pulled out every hammock nail in the ship to purchase the women's favours — and took badly to discipline. The same thing happened, later, with the *Bounty*'s crew; the delights of Tahitian life and love had far more to do with their mutiny than the tactlessness of the able but somewhat overbearing Bligh. There were some even of my own young gentlemen, in this ship a hundred and fifty years later, who felt inclined to mutiny in Tahiti. Perhaps there is something in the air. Wallis, having lost his hammock nails, shot some natives (probably several hundreds), hoisted the British flag (which the natives pulled down the same night), and called the island King George III's Island, departed. He had met and made friends with the Queen, but considering what it might have been, his account of the island is brief and dull. The whole place, the English agreed, was inexpressibly beautiful, and the way of life of the islanders appealed to them.

There was one dreadful contribution to Tahitian life for which Wallis cannot be blamed. He most certainly did not bring venereal disease, yet, when a few years later Cook arrived in the *Endeavour*, this loathsome scourge was so bad that half his people contracted it. The people of the *Dolphin* had as free an intercourse with the natives, but she had no venereal disease either before or after Tahiti. Wallis, who appears to have been a man strict on this matter, makes careful note of the fact that he had no case either for six months before reaching Tahiti, or for eight months afterwards. He was followed to Tahiti by Bougainville, in the frigate *Boudeuse* and the ship *Etoile*. Bougainville was just from Rio de Janeiro (a good place to contract venereal disorders) and Monte Video. True, he remained at Tahiti only a week, but this was long enough. He says nothing of disease, but he does remark that the sailors were "greatly affected" at the sight of the well-proportioned and splendid limbs of the native goddesses who welcomed them. What they did to the goddesses he does not say; it was not long before they had shot and bayoneted some of the men. Wallis had not been to Rio. Except for brief calls at Madeira and Porto Praya in the Cape Verdes (at neither place did his men have shore leave), he had come direct from England. "We saw no appearance of disease among the natives," he records.

Between the visits of Wallis and Bougainville and the second visit of Cook, two Spanish ships from Callao had twice touched at Tahiti, on the first occasion bringing two priests and a small settlement under Don Domingo de Boenechea. The priests made no converts, and the Don achieved little except to call the English "slaves" and to belittle them, as far as he could, in the eyes of the Tahitians. He then died, and the priests and the settlement were removed. These Spaniards called Tahiti Isla d'Amat; so that, after being neglected, and unknown to Europeans from the dawn of history, the island was thrice visited in five years and given three different names, George III Island, Nouvelle Cythère, and Isla d'Amat, none of which it kept. Beyond the shooting of some natives and the introduction of venereal disease, little else was accomplished. Boenechea did not fail to claim the island for Spain though, as he explained, this was merely out of courtesy to the inhabitants, for Balboa had taken care of the whole Pacific and all its islands 150 years before. Bougainville, in his turn, hoisted the French flag.

What the Tahitians thought of all these strange antics would be difficult to say, but they do not appear to have paid much attention. They were, however, most certainly impressed by Cook. The son of a Yorkshire farm labourer, born obscurely in the cold north country with no advantages beyond his determination and genius, James Cook was, and remains, one of the greatest of British voyagers. Sent to Tahiti to observe the transit of Venus, and to continue thence on a voyage of exploration and discovery, Cook, before his arrival at Tahiti, drew up a list of rules for all hands, the first of which ordered them "to endeavour by every fair means to cultivate a friendship with the natives and to treat them with all possible humanity." He, too, was bothered by the thieving propensities of the lower-class Tahitians and, against his orders, guns were used; but for the most part his relations with all types of people in Tahiti were admirable. He found much to admire in the way of life of the Tahitians, the scene of whose almost idyllic existence "realized the poetical fables of Arcadia." He found Tahiti a garden of Eden, and did all he could to leave it so. He appears to have been one of very few white men who came with this laudable intention, and kept it. The people, he pointed out, "have nothing like money," and in his view the island, beyond being admirably suited for the refreshment of ships, offered small attraction to European commerce. Cook made no secret of the fact that he hoped the white man and his commerce would not come; but he did not know of the Tuamotuan pearls, of copra, vanilla, and all those things.

"Our occasional visits," he wrote, "may in some respects have benefited the inhabitants; but a permanent establishment among them, conducted as most European establishments amongst Indians have unfortunately been, would I fear give them just cause to lament that our ships had ever found them out."

It did, indeed; and it was doubly unfortunate that this first settlement should have been left to the missionaries. Though they were doubtless led by glorious zeal and anxious to do great work for God, the story of their early career in Tahiti and the islands of the South Seas is, in general, lamentable. The name of God and the teachings of Christ have been invoked to cover many malpractices and to cause a great deal of suffering, not only in the South Seas; some of the early collectors of souls for heaven did not pay much attention to the welfare of bodies. It was even urged, at the time of the blackbirding for cheap labour in Australia, that it was better for a native to be taken away from his home, since in Queensland he would have a better chance of "finding God." If he died, he died in God; and to a certain kind of fanatic this seemed to be all that mattered. It is difficult in these days, when most of us are not sure of our own beliefs, to subscribe to this view.

After Cook, who visited Tahiti four times and was loved the more at each visit (this same Cook is still attacked in some quarters in England because he was not in the habit of holding divine service for his men on Sundays), came Bligh, seeking breadfruit for the West Indies. Like Dampier, many years earlier, Bligh also had to turn east at Cape Horn, and had come by way of Good Hope. He collected his breadfruit; sailed; was risen against; set off in the ship's boat with twenty-three men, and sailed with them from off Tonga to Timor (a voyage which remains to this day one of the longest, and certainly most difficult, small-boat journeys ever made); he returned to England, and sailed to Tahiti again to replace the breadfruit the whelps of Christian had thrown into the sea. It has often been urged that Bligh's harshness was entirely responsible for the mutiny, but I find it difficult to believe this. My sympathy is with Bligh. The moody broodings of a melancholy underling who has fallen in love at Tahiti may be hard to put up with, in a small ship; and it is strange that Christian, out of all that ship, gained chiefly only the lowest and the most vile to accompany him. Others stayed in the ship because there was no room in Bligh's boat for them: it is a significant fact that Bligh found the greater part of the ship's people willing to risk their lives with him rather than stay in the *Bounty* with Christian. The early story of the "colonization" of Pitcairn is a grim commentary both on the abilities of this Christian and the calibre of his comrades. Bligh's later career in Australia, though his actions led to the notorious and miserable "rum rebellion," were guided by a firmer sense of justice than many politicians of later days have even dreamed of. In the early days of Australia, Bligh stood pre-eminent as the one strong man upon the side of right, and it is greatly to be regretted that he did not remain in that country.

Between the visits of Bligh to Tahiti came the sadist Edwards, who very well upheld the naval traditions of his day by discovering nothing and poorly recording what he did see. It was this same Edwards who sailed past

Vanikoro later and saw the smoke of the survivors of the la Perouse expedition, but did not bother to investigate. The fate of la Perouse remained a mystery for more than thirty years. In the *Pandora* was a surgeon named Hamilton, who also wrote an account of the voyage. Hamilton mentions that the Tahitians' word for the English, even then, was the "stingy."

"Happy would it have been for these people," he says, "had they never been visited by Europeans; for, to our shame be it spoken, disease and gunpowder is all the benefit they have ever received from us in return for their hospitality and kindness." At that time they spoke of tuberculosis as "English disease" and of venereal complaints as "French disease." The *Pandora's* people also contracted venereal complaints during the ship's stay at Matavai Bay.

In the meantime, the whalers began to call at Tahiti, and the scum of Sydney began to pour over the South Seas. In 1797, the ship *Duff* arrived at Matavai Bay with missionaries from England. The publication of Cook's *Voyages*, which achieved widespread popularity — it is recorded that Marie Antoinette, who had never read a book through in her life previously, asked for this book while she was awaiting execution — and then the great wave of interest which followed the publication of the doings of the *Bounty* and the redoubtable Bligh, directed attention to the South Seas and focused it on Tahiti. The *Duff*, in command of Captain Wilson, a retired officer of the East India Company, sailed from Portsmouth on Friday, September 23, 1796, and made by way of the Cape Verde Islands and Rio de Janeiro towards Cape Horn. Like the *Roebuck* and the *Bounty* before her, she turned back from the Horn and ran towards Tahiti from the west, by way of Good Hope and the south of Tasmania. Tubuai in the Australs was the first land seen, and the *Duff* made the anchorage at Matavai Bay by way of the channel between

Tahiti and Moorea. She would have done better to sail to windward of Tahiti and run down on the bay from the north-east; as it was, she had to beat for several days before finally reaching the anchorage. The day before the land was sighted, the *Duff* passed through a severe electrical storm. Arrived at Matavai, a stay of ten days was made, during which a Swedish ne'er-do-well — forerunner of the considerable number of Scandinavian beachcombers later to drift to the South Seas — was useful as interpreter, though a dictionary of the language prepared by the *Bounty* mutineers had been brought from England. Here the people were very well received, and the majority of the *Duff*'s twenty-nine missionaries landed to begin their work.

The *Duff* then sailed to Moorea to wait a while and then return to Matavai Bay to see if the natives' expressions of goodwill were wholly meant. At Moorea, apparently, the natives did not think so highly of them — particularly the women. Parties of these, "whose gambols in the water were as indecorous as their appearance," swam round the ship. These shameless hussies, in a painfully lascivious and wanton manner, seemed to invite the missionaries to land, "but the piety of the captain and crew steeled their hearts against these Barbarian Syrens and they were obliged to return without success, perhaps," adds the chronicler,[11] "for the first time in their addresses to European seamen." Some of the missionaries went fishing and caught nothing, whereat the natives gave a great howl of derision. They appear to have been thoroughly nasty fellows, and after a shot at a few of them who had been seen thieving, the *Duff* went back to Matavai Bay. Here, for the time being at any rate, all was well, and the ship passed on to the Marquesas and to Tongatabu. On her way back to England, the *Duff* again called at Tahiti, taking off the surgeon, who

---

[11] George Veeson: *An Authentic Narrative of Four Years' Residence at Tongataboo*, London, 1810.

complained that the brethren, apparently considering he had too little to do, had appointed him to be permanent cook, "an indignity to which he would not submit." One of the missionaries from the Marquesas also asked to be taken away. The *Duff* now finally sailed, leaving the Tahitian mission to do what it could. For some time, this was very little. The natives, though interested, found mental effort difficult, and they were content to go on as they were. They could not at first understand the teachings of this new God, though miracles and stories of the marvellous had a great appeal for them. Many of the Biblical accounts, indeed, were similar to their own mythology. However, there were reasons enough — from the native point of view — why the missionaries had scant success. In the first place, venereal disease continued to work great havoc and, though they quickly found some specific whereby the worst of the effects of the secondary stage of syphilis could at least be hidden, the effects themselves remained and mortality was high. Tuberculosis and other diseases increased rapidly. Each whale ship, as she came, left further deserters and some new disease; the whale captains, moreover, were accustomed to pay for what they wanted with firearms and gunpowder, and the introduction of these into tribal wars added to the already heavily increased mortality. The God of the missionaries took the blame for all these ills; within a quarter of a century after Wallis's landing Tahiti, though not at all converted, was already ruined. The inroads of disease, the bad influence of renegade whites, the use of firearms, the recruiting of Tahitians for whaling vessels, and the spread of venereal disease among the women, had brought the great island and the happy islanders to a state of misery they had never known before. In these conditions it was scarcely likely that they would turn to the new God.

An American whale ship, short of provisions, offered firearms to the Tahitian chiefs — especially to the young

King Otu — in return for supplies; but the missionaries supplied the ship free and would not permit the firearms to be landed, nor would they loan their own weapons for an attack on Raiatea. The missionaries also insisted on the round-up and return of some deserters from this whaler, being — very rightly — against any further addition to the numbers of the white refuse already leading lives of utter uselessness and depravity on the island. Feeling against them ran so high on this occasion that there was an attack, and though Pomare, the king's father, promised them immunity, eleven of the missionaries left Tahiti in this whaler. To add to the troubles of the few who remained, the *Duff*, while returning with supplies, was taken by a French privateer, and the mission at Tonga was abandoned. Three of the missionaries there were murdered and the others escaped to Sydney. Shortly afterwards, the missionaries of Tahiti, in their turn, had to flee, following a rising of the natives against the chiefs. The missionaries, being in possession of considerable stores of European manufactures which represented great treasure to the natives, did not scruple to get the chiefs on their side by liberal gifts of ironware, cottons, and the like, reasoning — rightly enough — that since they could not convert the Tahitians by any other means, they might buy the "conversion" of the chiefs and so compel that of the people. Whether this is good Christian practice I will not say; but it was tried, not only in Tahiti, and enforced as well. However, the first Pomare now died, and the missionaries fled first to Moorea and Huahine, and later — most of them — to Sydney. Their houses and property on Tahiti were destroyed and Tahiti was in possession of the rebels. This was in 1804. The rebellion of the people against the chiefs was a direct consequence of the attempt to enforce the new religion on them, and it was felt, further, that the missionaries were using their powers with the chiefs in political as well as spiritual directions. This accusation appears to have been only too well founded.

With the exception of the indefatigable Nott, most of the missionaries retreated to Sydney, to return later when their patron chief, from his refuge at Moorea, regained by intrigue the possession of his kingdom. The missionaries then returned to Moorea and Raiatea, and thence to Tahiti. The return of the second Pomare to Tahiti and the recall of the missionaries led to a long and bitter religious war which continued, off and on, for something like three years, culminating in a pitched battle in which the idolaters were defeated, and their leader slain. This was on November 12, 1815. Thereafter, Christianity was victorious. All temples, altars, and idols were destroyed, and the reign of the missionaries had begun.

Whatever may be said for the missionaries — for the excellence of their motives, their own noble self-sacrifices, the indomitable will they gave to their work, and the glorious conception of a greater living that was behind that work — the fact remains that the dominance of the Tahitians by the missionaries, in the years that followed this religious war, made these the saddest years Tahiti had ever known. Christianity, thus forced upon the people through their chiefs by bloodshed and fighting, was quickly used to give the missionaries entire control of the lives of the Tahitians. From being priests, the missionaries became lawgivers; from being lawgivers, they quickly developed into law enforcers. They drew up a code of laws, eighteen in number, in which the death penalty was prescribed for four offences and of which the whole keynote seemed to be: Thou shalt not smile. They forbade almost all the games in which the Tahitians had indulged, and, as far as possible, set about removing the joy from their lives. It did not seem to them possible that discipline of the flesh could be achieved without the destruction of joy. That this was not their object may be true; but it was their effect. They kept the natives, as far as possible, to their own language, thus seeing that no ideas could be brought to them other than those the missionaries themselves introduced, for they had the printing press. (This idea is still followed in some missions.) Playing on surf-boards, at which the Tahitians used to be as expert as the Hawaiians; innocent diversions such as hide-and-seek and kite flying and even swinging, were alike forbidden, while dancing and such amusements came under a rigid ban. Many of the amusements of the Tahitians had been used to stimulate their amorous passions, the gratification of which had been easy enough. It could scarcely be expected that the missionaries would tolerate this. But many of the sports were forbidden simply because they were sports, and because the people were apt to give too much of their time to fun and too little to study. The new religion, the missionaries left no doubt, was a serious affair. So the Tahitians began to die in larger numbers than ever. Civilization was doing very well.

In Tahiti the missionaries worked through the chiefs and the king or the queen, whoever was in power; in outer islands they did not, at this stage, stop at the usurpation of regal power for themselves. What they did was, they claimed, "for God"; but this is a dangerously inadequate argument. Life was so hemmed in by regulations as scarcely to be worth living; no white community upon earth would have tolerated such conditions for five minutes. At the island of Mangaia in the Cook group — the next group to the Society Islands of which Tahiti is the centre — the code of laws (similar to those of Tahiti and elsewhere) contained such items as these:

> No. 14. For the Village. If a man puts his arm round a woman in the road at night, and he has a torch in his hand, he shall go free. If no torch, he is to be fined $1 cash and $9 trade.
> No. 20. Tattooing Love-marks. The man who does this on a woman, or the woman who does it on a man, is to be fined $2 cash and $13 trade.

No. 21. Sabbath Observance. No one to go to another village on Sunday without good reason. Fine $1 cash and $4 trade.

No. 28. Taking Women Inland. If a man take a woman to the mountains for bad purposes, he is to be fined $15 cash and in addition his other fines for fornication or adultery.

No. 24. Crying after a Dead Woman. If a man do this, and he and the woman were not relations, or if he wear mourning for her, he is to be fined $15. (This is taken to be proof of guilt during life.)

The whole code was framed with the apparently deliberate idea of destroying, or at least suppressing, the natural joy of the race, to bring home to them the better, perhaps, the enormity of their sins. The mission rule was not without its benefits, for doubtless many died in God; and, as the Reverend George Turner of the London Missionary Society pointed out in the 1840's from his station at Samoa, "much had been done to further the commercial interests of civilized countries." The reverend gentleman, while regretting that the Samoans did not "clothe so well as they might do," remarked that they had none the less imported Manchester cotton goods alone "to the value of about £15,000 per annum and is every year increasing."[12] This was of course a desirable state of affairs for Manchester. Further in his discourse, while mentioning casually that the population is declining, Mr. Turner lists "pulmonary affections, paralysis, diseases of the spine producing hunchback, ophthalmia, skin diseases, scrofulous and other ulcers, elephantiasis, and a species of leprosy" as being among the principal diseases, most of which had lately been acquired. This was at Samoa. Much

---

[12] *Nineteen Years in Polynesia*: John Snow, London, 1861.

the same conditions existed at Tahiti. The missionaries, too, were frequently accustomed to expel from the church any who infringed their many regulations, and this was a deadly serious thing to the poor natives.

These conditions could not continue. As in parts of Melanesia to-day, where the congregations of rival sects are encouraged by their "leaders" to interfere with one another, the worthy congregations of the London Missionary Society in Tahiti forcibly ejected some French priests who had gone there to spread their version of the Good Word. This sort of thing led directly to the annexation of Tahiti by the French in 1842, a "protectorate" which was accepted by Queen Pomare in 1846. The rest of Tahiti's history belongs almost to our own day. The traders came, of course — the pearlers, the planters, and all the rest of them. The civil war in the United States gave a temporary fillip to cotton-growing, as it did also in Queensland, with equally serious results, and Chinese labourers were imported to work the cotton fields. It is the descendants of these Chinese who to-day control most of Tahiti's retail trade, and indeed much of the trade throughout French Oceania. The decline of the pure Tahitians continued, but the French attitude of regarding the community as a whole, leading, as it did, to the granting of full citizenship to the Tahitians, was a far better one than its frigid predecessor which may be summed up in the precept, Thou shalt not smile. The Tahitians today have been in contact with the whites for longer than the people of any other Pacific island. If their own civilization has been taken from them, at least they are permitted to fit as well as they can into the scene of what has long become a white man's island.

As in Tahiti, so throughout the Pacific. The nineteenth century was a long holocaust of murder and debauchery. First sandalwood, then blackbirding, then importations of Asiatics to take the place of the dead natives, the alienation of much of their land, the growth of the great copra combine, the war, the depression — so it has gone. Sandalwood, being a profitable commodity, was soon fought for with guns; the whole story of Pacific exploitation is a grim and terrible one of treachery, intolerance, misery, and death. For a hundred years, greed and lust held sway, whatever the missions — many brave and some inspired men worked as missionaries, against heavy odds in these waters — tried to do. The fierce dark Melanesian was a vastly different person from the pleasant and hospitable Polynesian. The Melanesian in some places is still untamed, though the Polynesian has been in trousers a century. In order to ship a cargo of sandalwood, the desperadoes from Sydney thought nothing of wiping out the population of an island; and the natives soon retaliated in kind. The cutting-out of European vessels, the murder of defenceless crews of whalers and merchant vessels, the murders of missionaries — all these led back to the violent brutalities of the whites themselves. The sandalwood was soon exhausted; then the cessation of transportation to Australia and the consequent cutting off of the supply of cheap labour, turned the attention of the Australians to blackbirding. They had the islanders of the Pacific at their back door, so to speak; why not let these heathens have the great benefit of contact with the white man, and perhaps do a little work?

This excellent idea found support so readily that, in the course of a few years, whole islands of Melanesia were denuded of their people, and in the forty-odd years during which blackbirds were brought to Australia, 60,000 entered Queensland alone. Many of them died there, for the death-rate was very high. Others were taken to Fiji, to Samoa, to wherever there might be a market for them, there to be sold like slaves. The Peruvians, even more ungentle in their methods, seized as many as they could from the islands nearer to them — places such as Easter Island and Rapa — for work on the guano fields of their coastal islands.

The poor wretches taken there never returned — never had a chance of returning. It is probable that, from first to last, over 100,000 virile men of the South Seas were forcibly taken off as blackbirds or as slaves, few of whom returned to their own islands. Australia took the Melanesians of the New Hebrides, the Solomons, the Loyalties, and the nearer Papuan islands because they were handiest, and also because the milder Polynesian made a poor slave. The Polynesian did not take kindly to continued and fruitless work for his white masters, naturally enough, and the benefits of "civilized" economics were slow to penetrate to him.

The traders, all this time, were busily teaching the natives to use such luxuries as tinned meat, salmon, soap, cotton lap-laps, and the like, inducing them to pay over as much copra and other products for these great benefits as possible. Plantations grew and thrived; fortunes were made. Then in their turn, the planters themselves began to be caught in the maw of the inexorable machine of their own making — the stamping-out of competitors, the control of markets, the exploitation of the producer. The day of the Copra Combine came, and tin roofs and the profit god reigned in the South Seas. The natives, futile wretches, continued to die (though some communities thrived) and the missions continued with more and more sects and more and more confusion to preach something of the word of Christ. But as in Tahiti to-day the Tahitians share our own bewilderment and do not know what to believe, the value of much of the latter-day "conversion" of the islands' natives is a matter of some doubt. If we could really bring to these people the conception of a nobler living and of a greater, finer way of life; if we knew of these things ourselves and practised them, the white man could hold his head high in the South Seas and face his Maker, when the time comes, with clear eyes. But as it is … We have made of the Pacific a place of fifteen ports and ten radio stations, a delightful cruising ground for the idle and the cranks, of whom wave upon wave has poured over Oceania in these past years — the sexologist (who at least possessed the merit of being fiercely interested in his subject), the alleged psychologist, anthropologist, and whatnot; the seekers of illusion and the plain indolent — and what has become of the Polynesians and their culture has not bothered us very much. All the islands have long been divided among the great powers; administrators, district officers, customs inspectors, gendarmes and the like abound. Flags wave and ships steam; copra dries and the reefs give up their trochus; tourists loiter and advisory councils meet; banks close and jails are filled; and a great deal of good is done in hospitals, in churches, and in schools for the natives of the South Seas. But it will take a long, long time to wash away the blood and the tears from those islands. O keep from us the Sailing Gods!

The Indian community of Fiji is at last flourishing. The Tonkinese of the New Hebrides are doing well. The Annamese of Makatea find conditions to their liking. The Chinese of Nauru are repatriated as their contracts expire. The Chinese of Papeete and Tulagi and Vila and all those places have little cause for complaint. What the Polynesians have to say about all this no one bothers to inquire. After a hundred years of the white man, the Polynesian is at last returning to his old customs, for the white man's world has largely broken down in these days. No more a sailing god! (This title died as soon as the sandalwooders and the blackbirders came: the white men were then renamed the sailing profligates.) The Polynesian, after all the training in the purchase, on credit, of his alleged needs from the trader's store, paying for his corned beef and his salmon with as much copra as he could cut, has found that the ways of his ancestors are better. For corned beef he has pigs; and why should he eat preserved salmon when his lagoons teem with fresh fish? He has poultry, vegetables, and fruit. These things he had before the white man came. For the cotton goods he can revive the native cloth; for his house he has ample material waiting only to be collected; for salt he has sea water, and for lamp oil the coco-nut. The few "contributions" of the white towards his progress and his living can very well be done without; the evening of the sailing gods has come. It is only in the nature of things that they should have destroyed themselves.

The Tahitians have joined the white man in his ambiguous idea of God, and go their ways; and the migratory movements of the latter-day whites come unheeded among them. It is the white now, ill-adjusted in his own world, misled by foolish books and vainly in quest of a better mode of life, who seeks to find solace for himself in the South Seas; no longer does he sail there supreme and triumphant. But the pathos of this last impermanent invasion by the pallid and neurotic who no longer pretend even to be producers, who come in idleness seeking diversion, who thrust flowers in their ears and themselves upon the native maidens — the weak exhibition of this pitiful advance in the fair islands of Oceania is fit enough rearguard for the Sailing Gods, who upon acquaintance turned into profligates, and worshipped only gold.

XIX

The Road Home

FROM TAHITI towards New York the 13,000-mile sea road, by way of the Horn, divides itself naturally into three sections — the run to the Horn first, then from the Horn to the Line, and lastly from the Line to landfall. Until the first of these was behind us we did not think of the others. The far southern headland of all the Americas was, in a sense, the climax of the long voyage, the last turning point, whereafter nothing but the Atlantic remained. To reach it, I stood first towards the south, hoping to come quickly down to the region of the wild west winds, and then to turn south-eastwards and storm towards the Horn. Once south of Forty, I knew we should not be long; but our setting-out was slow, and in the first week the blue Pacific was so quiet that we made scarce 400 miles. I passed again through the Austral Islands, this time having Rurutu in sight throughout a hazy day; near here was Moses Reef — one of the worst of its kind, a mid-ocean blemish showing no sign above the surface, and not breaking in that quiet weather. I gave it a goodly berth, coming by with the full moon of the quiet Pacific night, with the ship heeled gently towards her shadowed sails on the soft foam of her own making, and aloft the three towers of the masts all gracefulness. On deck, the clean sweep of her shone beneath the moon with the dew-covered teak reflecting the light upon the white houses and the boats, where all things, all lines, all gear, were shipshape and trim and in good order.

We stood on very slowly towards the south, losing longitude, for the wind was from the south of east, and I was full-and-by with the yards off the backstays, getting the best speed I could. Once arrived in the stamping ground of the west winds, a little lost longitude would not matter. Day after day now all hands worked steadily at preparing the ship for the winter's rounding of the Horn. She had several danger-spots, being so low-decked, and with the 'tween-decks all accommodation. Every deck opening was a danger-spot — the three big sky-lights, largely made of glass; the doors leading to the main 'tween-decks where the boys lived; the door to the quarters for'ard, on the port side of the deckhouse; and the charthouse doors.

I considered the problem of the skylights for a long time; we had run our longitude down from Good Hope towards the Leeuwin with them, also in mid-winter. But that was on Forty South and we had now to go nearly to Sixty — almost to the Antarctic. The seas that rage down there are the highest and the worst in the world, and I meant to take no chances. We built up wooden breakwaters over the skylights, and then covered them with two stout tarpaulins, of sail canvas, the whole lashed down securely to ringbolts in the deck, and the edges of the tarpaulins battened on the deck and made fast. One of the 'tween-deck doors was closed, caulked, and built up, and the other was fitted with a high washboard; the door to the accommodation for'ard was fitted with a strong canvas screen secured on a frame of steel; the charthouse doors were re-rubbered, and washboards were fitted. Deadlights were screwed down, and everything movable taken from the decks, including the guns. These were stowed in the hold. Everything remaining on deck was securely lashed, including the lifeboats. The royal yards were sent down, the flying jib unbent, the triangular storm try-sail bent in place of the spanker, and the triangular storm mains'l sent to the main yard. New preventer braces were rove at fore and main; the mizzen did not matter so much, since in bad weather the square sail was taken from the mizzen mast soon enough.

The pigs were shifted from the exposed sty on the fore deck to a secure dry place beneath the focs'l head; the cables had been unshackled and taken inboard, so that the hawse-pipes could be plugged and caulked, and no water came in over the decks that way; the capstan and windlass were oiled and covered. The storm fore tops'l of hurricane canvas, which Karl had sewed between Samarai and Tahiti, was bent; it was much smaller than the ordinary tops'ls. It was so small that it had a permanent reef in it; it was the size of the ordinary tops'l, single-reefed. This was a great advantage in a gale. The single tops'ls, while splendid drawing sails and most picturesque, added considerably to the work in bad weather; with double tops'ls the ship would have been three times as handy. However, I liked her as she was, and giving her double tops'ls was too big a job to tackle at that late stage. All the sails we had sewed of strong Scots hemp canvas, and we gave them boltropes of wire; in the Danish days they had been hemp, but the canvas on a long voyage outlasts a rope boltrope if it is good canvas, bravely sewn. We had rove off, too, t'gallant sheets of chain and wire, instead of the Danish hemp; a few minor improvements of that kind better fitted the ship for long-continued hard-weather sailing. After all, the Danes had been accustomed to use the ship only for six months of the year, and to anchor most of the nights. This was different.

All the seizings on the rigging lanyards had been made good. Aloft all the mousings, seizings, and chafing mats had been renewed. The footropes had been over-hauled. New gear was rove off wherever necessary, the fores'l and the three tops'ls were given completely new sets of buntlines and leachlines of new four-stranded manila. It is old gear that causes the loss of half the sails.

I had not been unmindful of the comfort of the crew, so far as that could be looked after; I had built a protection of canvas dodgers, made from old hammocks, on the top of the for'ard house to shelter the lookouts from the worst of the spray and the hail, and I did everything possible to keep the bunks and the quarters dry. The Horn is bad enough in winter without having the quarters flooded and the bunks all sodden. We had no stoves except some oil ones which were unhealthy, but I was of the opinion that a stove is a questionable benefit and can, in a crowd of boys, do more harm than good. We had no heating system; but every one had ample clothing and good oilskins. The whole crew fore and aft was now Nordic and, with one exception, had been born and bred in comparatively cold countries; only the two Americans had been accustomed to winter heat in their homes. The New Zealanders were well used to the cold; to the Danes and the other Scandinavians the run towards the Horn even in July was summery compared with winter sailing in their own Baltic. There was plenty of bedding fore and aft, and a great supply of spare woollen blankets — so many that mittens could be made from them, and caps to fit over the ears under the sou'westers.

I took all the care I could of the comfort of all hands — much more than is customary in merchant vessels; but, after all, I was the guardian of most of them. I was also the physician, and I did not want to have any avoidable ills on my hands. Exposure can be a wretched enemy, and we should have enough to suffer from it. The food was good and ample; such things as milk, jam, sugar, and a few more had to be shared out on allowance, but the allowances were always far more than the Board of Trade scale. No pot ever went on the galley stove the contents of which were not shared by all hands. If the 'tween-decks growled about the stockfish and the dogsbody,[13] they had at least the consolation of knowing that we had the same fare. In this respect I was strictly democratic, always: but there were

---

[13] Dogsbody is rice boiled with raisins in it.

growls enough. To complain about the food — any food, anywhere — seems a general human disposition. But no one in the ship lost any weight: many of the boys, in the two years they were on board, gained a foot in height and twenty pounds in weight. For the actual rounding of the Horn, from Fifty South in the Pacific to Fifty South in the Atlantic, I had a demijohn of rum doled out nightly in boiling hot tea, with supper.

We were two weeks out before the first storm blew and then it was a mild one — hard from the nor'ard first with rain and the glass falling (about twelve hours of this), and then with a slight lift of the glass, the jump to south-south-west. One has to watch these jumps closely so that they do not catch the ship by the lee; but in the South Pacific it is usually possible to see when they are coming, if only with a few minutes' warning. This is enough. There is a hesitant lull, or a heavier rain, or an instant's clearing of the southern sky: then stand from under! With a gust of violence that shakes the ship and scares at once all the tumult from the north wind's sea, the south gale comes! One becomes used to them after a while. After the wind has jumped to the south, it usually blows the sky clear, and settles into a comfortable steady gale from somewhere about the south-west — fair wind, and most helpful to the vessel's progress. But with our first gale we had a high breaking sea and violent squalls of hail, and the parral of the main tops'l yard carried away. This the carpenter and his gang repaired easily; but she was an old ship, I knew, and she had been sailing hard. I hoped that nothing else would carry away; I had done the best I could.

We were lucky on the whole, on the run towards the Horn — luckier than I had ever been before, on a winter's run; luckier, perhaps, than we deserved. We had one determined, heavy gale, a screaming madness of wind to which I dared show no rag of sail, a roaring tumult from the south-west which, even though it was fair wind, I could not use. This was as bad a gale as anyone on board had ever experienced — worse than the storm that sent the sea breaking over the *Parma*'s poop and broached her to, in the grain race of 1932, on the way to Cape Horn; worse by far than anything we had in the *Grace Harwar*, the *Herzogin Cecilie*, the *Lawhill*, or the *Bellands*. But we came through with no very great damage. True, the fore topmast head was discovered sprung next morning, after we had been hove-to twenty hours in the wild sea with the oil-bags out; and we had to send the fore topgallant mast down, with some difficulty, afterwards properly securing the weakened topmast head beneath its wound. The starboard boat was stove in by the sea, and both light brackets were washed away.

A door of the for'ard house was stove in, on the same wild night; the sea rushed in, and some of the rail aft was carried away. But these things, though serious, were relatively unimportant. We were still sound, though weakened; no one was hurt and no one lost; we did not need to go in anywhere, and no water came below. We were thirty-seven days in all, from Papeete strand to beyond Cape Horn, and we sailed in that time something over 4,800 miles. Though it was no "record," this was not bad; after all, we had a small ship and an old one — and if the truth be told, a somewhat weakened vessel by that time, at least aloft.

It was easterly wind that gave me most cause for alarm. On the run towards the Horn, winter is usually more settled than the summer months, though the short days, the long nights, and the intense cold add to the misery; but it is also the season of easterly winds. When, some twenty days out from Tahiti, we had three days of easterly conditions and south-east wind, I was afraid we might have to beat there a long time, as we had had to do in the *Grace Harwar*, once, in June. But we were fortunate. After the

easterlies we had one day of southerly gale with sleet
squalls and savage cold; then hard SSW and SW increasing
almost to a hurricane; and after that, southerly conditions
and good progress right up to Cape Horn.

I broached the demijohn of rum the day we came to
Fifty South, since we then needed it; but I found the stone
jar half full and the rum watered. The miserable cads who
had perpetrated that contemptible theft against a
defenceless ship and a score-odd frozen mariners were
swine indeed; I had bought the thing in Melbourne and it
came on board sealed. It is this sealing of ship's stores that
makes such thieving possible. Give the ship anything! They
cannot check it and they won't be back! Who had stolen
the rum and watered the remnants of it I don't know, but it
was no one in the ship, for the demijohn had borne the
Customs seal unbroken since first it came on board.
Australian rum usually is fiery stuff, but this pallid fluid
tasted like ginger ale: the loss of the rum was serious, for it
was the *only* comfort we had. Used judiciously, served out
nightly in the tea, there would have been enough in a full
demijohn to see us round the Horn; it was as a necessary
medical comfort that we needed it, and not with the
remotest idea of indulging any taste for alcohol we might
have. We had no heat. All was wet where the great sea ran,
and the sprays clouded the driving ship to the topgallant
yards. The decks were open and there was no shelter
anywhere through the long night watches. Life was
existence, a determined hanging-on, with the ship lurching
wildly and plunging, and the hail squalls screaming in the
rigging. And some shore swine, seated comfortably before
his fire, had guzzled our rum! It is not for coming on deck
one needs the stuff, not for any careless tossing down to
gain a momentary illusion; then its effect is brief and,
quickly passing, leaves the cold body worse equipped for
the night-long vigil. But, when one is turning in for a short
sleep, it courses through the blood, quickens the arteries,

enlivens the mind, until one can forget frozen extremities and frostbitten hands and sink quickly into a dreamless slumber that no rolling of the plunging ship can disturb, to turn out a few hours later really refreshed and better able to go on. The unutterable cads ashore could buy more rum; we could not. What was stolen could not be replaced.

Three weeks out from Tahiti we had made only some twenty-one hundred miles.

It was nearing the end of July when we had the great storm. It began to pipe up from the SSW on the Saturday, when we had been at sea twenty-three days, and the glass fell for three days. From noon Saturday to noon Sunday we ran 208 miles in a high sea, which was fairly good going for so small a vessel. Throughout Sunday she ran on well in a high breaking sea with frequent long, hard squalls increasing, with the early coming of the cold night, to a strong gale before which we still ran under the close-reefed fore and main tops'ls and the storm fore topmast stays'l.

This day we sailed over the place where Ronald Walker, aged twenty-one, had been buried from the poop of the ship *Grace Harwar* in 1929, after being killed at his work in the rigging. I flew the Australian ensign at half-mast in his memory. This day, too, we saw a strange and beautiful white bird which was not an albatross; we had none of us seen a sea bird of this kind before, and did not know what it was.

The night brought sleet and snow and greater wind. About daylight next morning, just before nine, a brief lull tempted me to give her the reefed fores'l, for this was fine fair wind and in the great sea her speed had dropped a little. But the lull was illusory, and I could not keep the new sail set half an hour; it came in again without damage. All hands had long grown expert at the handling of recalcitrant square sail even under the most dangerous conditions. Noon of that day — the third day of the blow — brought frequent violent snow squalls blowing fiercely from the WSW, and the sea was now dangerously high. I took in the close-reefed main tops'l and goose-winged the fore, continuing to run under this minimum of canvas, with the fore topmast staysail to help the steering. But by six bells in the afternoon the gale was such that I began to think seriously of the vulnerability of the decks, the skylights, with open ship below; the weak, big doors. If a skylight were stove in, it would be bad. We had done what we could to protect them, but they were still weaknesses; and the charthouse doors fitted ill. The steel charthouse, a welded job from Ipswich, had not been very well made and the doors could not be strengthened. I had the boys to think of; I had to get round the Horn. I could take no undue chances. I could not stand having to take a badly damaged ship in anywhere, for repairs. That would be the end of the voyage. I wished, on the other hand, to make all the progress I could while the wind was fair, because of the probability of easterlies afterwards and because I wanted, naturally enough, to be gone from those cold latitudes as quickly as possible.

But a time came when it was dangerous to run on. The glass still dropped. It became obvious that, bad as it was, the gale itself had not yet begun, though the wind screamed in the rigging. The fierce rolling had caused the compass to swing violently and steering was difficult even by day. The feeling of the wind on their faces was the helmsman's best guide; but by night this is poor substitute for a compass. Though she still ran well in the great seas, she was clearing their ever-rising crests with less and less margin. Sea after sea thundered at her, broke in a wild eruption of spray and spume and murderous noise, and thundered by: she was foam-covered to the trucks. The wet dome of the sky sat heavy on the mast-heads, never lifting to give any light beyond a grey, wintry gloom: now night was coming down.

I put out oil, and ran on: but this was dangerous. I

thought again of the vulnerability of the decks, of all the lives entrusted to my care: should I still run? But if I hove-to, I should drift in the valley of the sea on my way. The headlong rush would cease; no more would the brave ship run down a degree of longitude every four-hour watch, but I should still drift quietly on, and I should lie there in safety, putting out oil. The drift and the scend of the sea would give me two knots. And if I *broached-to*, if I ran too long; if I ran those gigantic breaking seas on board, there would be no morning. Surely the wind would not further increase, the sea not further rise. She had run in safety this long; why not go on? No time to waste! And yet — the safety of all hands was in my keeping. If I made a mistake, I should have a lot to explain before God. Still she ran; I watched. I watched the sea rise, heard the wind increase, suffered the cutting hail. The sweetness of her underwater body was counting now, and she still avoided the weight of the seas with a great cunning in whose contrivance it seemed that man had no part, though she ran drier with some at the helm than for others. Her bluff black bows rode down the hollows and rose upon the crests, and her sweet clean counter dragged no quartering waves to upset the breaking seas and bring them upon us, though she ran at speed.

Now the hail squalls close in, and night is coming down. Heave-to, or run on? Better lie to the night in the trough of the sea, bowing to the storm, than run on and never come to the morning! The squalls march; the wind shrieks; the sea thunders. The ship reels, staggers, lurches, *flings* herself onwards over those high green hills each of which breaks in a flurry of foam as she passes, into the troughs so deep that the wind goes from the sails and screams the louder in the upper rigging. Good helmsmanship alone can guide her now. I have taken in the clew of the fore tops'l and she runs on under the stays'l alone, a rag of wind-stiffened sea-soaked canvas bellied at the bow. The boiling of the foam flying by reeks of murder.

No, no; I shall not run on this night. It is a fair wind; but I cannot go on. If any of those great seas break on me; if for a moment one of the helmsmen so much as fumbles with a spoke; if the ghastly tumult of the maddened sea can come on board — these things in this wind are fatal. Fatal! And I answer for twenty-two lives.

The mizzen stays'l is set, a small sail of stout canvas, to keep her head up when she comes to; I take the wheel, and wait for what smooth, what chance may come. It is the very last of the daylight. The yards which have been squared are braced full-and-by; there is now no sail on them. Off the deck! Off the deck now! The sailors crowd in under the focs'l head, the only sheltered place. I wait: even with only these two rags of stays'ls on her she runs eight knots. If she comes up to the sea at that speed and runs into a wall of breaking water, God help us all. The oil bags are out — have been out a long time: they help, but nothing can stop a real breaking Cape Horn sea if a ship swings into it with speed. The safety of lying-to lies in the fact that the ship then yields; she gives; she does not fight for headway. She lies in the trough of the sea with her shoulder to the breaking water, like an albatross asleep with its head beneath its wing, drifting and yielding. In great storms this is the only safe procedure. But I had now, with the ship still running at speed through the dangerously high sea, to bring her into the trough; to stop her way, without overwhelming her; to bring her up without giving the sea a chance to break on her while she still had way. It was a serious and dangerous proceeding. A chance, now! I had waited long. The wind screamed in all the stays and rose to a mad crescendo as the ship rolled to windward: sea gushed from all the washports: the very spume lifted from the sea flew frightened in the air. But everything still held. A lull, now! Now! A vicious hail squall had just passed; there came a smooth in the wake of a giant sea that, passing under us, had flung us high and rolled the ship as if it had been shaking a swimming dog. This was the chance I awaited. Down helm! I forced the wheel down and she came; the wake subsided and the foam was not now streaking past. At the same moment, while we still had way, I saw the great sea rise to wind'ard — the great sea, the murdering one: a greater sea than any which had roared by that day. I had not been able to see it before; it had swept down savagely out of the murk and the chaos. I could not see far. Nothing now, but to fight it out. Break, then, you accursed sea! See if you can smash us! It seemed to me at the wheel that I could feel the ship stiffen for the meeting, summon up all the reserves of her great hull's strength to take this shuddering blow. It would be bad; I knew. She knew.

Implacable and murderous, the thundering sea rushed on, its pleasure glinting in light from the tumult of its driving foam: up, up, it towered, and the little ship rose valiantly to meet it. But she could not do it. She could not do it. I knew, as soon as I saw that sea. No oil, no anything, could stem that insane onrush. She rose, rose, rose! But not enough. I stood at the wheel clinging with all my strength to the spokes; for I knew the breaking sea would come there, too.

The sea came, flinging the oil bags contemptuously back inboard before it, snarling and roaring, high above the weather rail. An instant it hung there, and I could see the glint of evil in the foam-streaked green water. Then it broke on board. It might very well have been the end of us. But the little ship somehow avoided the worst of its force. We had taken only a glancing blow. It filled the decks, and stormed aft; it swept over me at the wheel; it drove over the saloon skylight, over everything. Would she lift again? Would another come, while the weight of the first still held her down? She began very slowly to lift, to free herself through the washports of the sea's dangerous load. Her way was gone now. She shed the water, in a long, long time — or so it seemed — and afterwards no more came. The skylights had held. There was no water down below. We were in the trough now, and so lay in safety that long, wild night.

In the morning we saw that the starboard boat was badly stove in where the sea had lifted it on the chocks as if the stout manila lashings had been cotton, and had cast it aside. Both light brackets were gone; a door of the for'ard house (fortunately one of slight importance, which gave entrance to the lamp-trimmer's small room) was smashed to splinters, and the sea ran in and out among the lamps; and — worst of all — the fore topmast head was badly sprung from inherent weakness which the storm had brought out. The mast was so badly sprung that the topgallant yard and mast had to come down.

I lay hove-to for twenty hours. It was the worst weather of the whole voyage. The tumult of the implacable sea through that wild night was frightening, even hove-to; she lay rolling heavily, but she rode the seas and shipped no more water. It was noon the next day — the Tuesday — before I dared put up the helm, though the wind all this time had been fair. The conditions had eased a little then, and I ran on under the close-reefed main tops'l and fore topmast stays'l, and still put out oil. In this wild weather the fore topgallant mast was taken down, and preventer stays of iron wire were spliced and set up to the topmast head underneath the place where it was sprung; a new fore topmast stay had also to be set up, of iron wire, double. This was a difficult rigging job to do in those conditions, but all hands worked through until it was done. By that time the weather had moderated considerably, and I was able to set good running sail. The loss of the topgallant mast and the weakening of the headstays was a serious blow, upsetting as it did the sailing balance of the ship (particularly for windward working). I to be more careful now than ever, but we sailed from the scene of the accident — some 2,000 miles westward of Cape Horn — to the end of the voyage without that mast.

I hoped now we should have no more such gales, though that was by no means certain. The little ship made no water and continued to run on, buoyant and brave in the great seas. The skylight coverings had unquestionably brought her through that night of storm. Even after that, only two of the bunks were sodden. So she ran on, from there to the Horn. There was not another great gale, though there were minor storms — trifling things, with the wind only pretending. It often happens in those latitudes in winter that, after a severe storm, the weather is settled, more or less, for a greater or less period, depending upon the ferocity of the storm. The worse the storm, the longer the period of settled conditions afterwards. This is no "law"; but I had noticed it on other voyages. So it proved now. We did not have another really hard blow. We had, instead, a succession of southerly conditions — gloomy at times, with fog, and the clammy moisture weeping from the sails and all the gear; sometimes clear for a time but never bright, and for the most part heavily overcast, with the wind always somewhere between south by east and west by north — not often from the west'ard.

We made good progress. There was not again occasion to consider heaving to. In one week we ran 1,348 miles — from Wednesday, July 29 to Tuesday, August 4. This was an average speed of eight knots for the seven days — not bad for a ship only 100 feet on the waterline, partially dismasted, pretty old, and long in tropic waters with her iron hull gathering the grass. For such a ship to storm at eight knots for a week in the Great West Winds, through high seas the whole time, was, I thought, a credit to her designers and her builders. She was not built for speed, though she was built to sail well; the primary consideration was safety. To sail at eight knots for a week in quiet water would not be anything to cheer; but a high breaking sea is a serious handicap. In eleven days we ran 2,000 miles. I was careful, all this time. I did not try to drive, but to do my best with the ship as she was, and the conditions as I found them. Throughout these eleven days we showed no kites, though I was accustomed to hold to the main topgallant sail which usually did not get becalmed in the troughs. We ran in the ice line, day and night, with double lookouts and the foghorn going, far south of Fifty-five — southernmost ship in the world, then; last full-rigger to make a Cape Horn rounding — staggering onwards with no lights lit, the rust streaks growing on all the paint; the fore topgallant mast below, and only one good boat — that would be useless here if there were real need of it. Nothing now comes to those waters: we were south of the meat ships' track from New Zealand to England. No outward-bounders now thrash round to Chilean ports for nitrate; and I was glad no ship might loom before our path — no ship, and nothing now but icebergs. We ran on unlit through the long nights, for the light brackets were both gone and the lamp room destroyed; had we shown a sidelight we should have lost it.

So we came to the eighth of August, and on that day were off Cape Horn, and by the evening round, and into the Atlantic. Good ocean! All the reefs and all the storms of the great Pacific were behind. How long the tumult of those waters had saved the South Seas from destruction! It seemed almost as if the great belt of the roaring winds had been sent down there by Nature to make the westward rounding of the Horn difficult, and keep the marauding whites from the Pacific isles. For hundreds of years they had succeeded.

We saw nothing of Cape Horn. The day was gloom and all overcast, with strong wind, and I had no observations. I had meant, if I could, to have a look at Diego Ramirez, to check the rating of the chronometer; but I could not risk it. We saw nothing but one piece of kelp, a large piece drifting by, and the obvious ground swell of graying soundings by the Ramirez bank — a swell that stayed all day and was then gone as suddenly as it came, with both its coming and its going as noticeable as name boards on a street. We must have passed pretty close to get on the bank; we ran too fast to take soundings, and I would not stop. We were probably within five miles of Diego Ramirez; we could only see one mile, most of the day.

So we came round, and the next day being clear, saw Staten Island and all the wild snow-covered hills of Tierra del Fuego, and the tide-swept break of the Straits of le Maire. The boys were splendid. True, they had heard so much of Cape Horn's bitterness that, now we were round, they were almost disappointed. What, only one hurricane? Only one lost mast, one stove boat? And Jan, the son of Captain Junker, recalled the mean misery of winter Baltic voyages in tops'l schooners and barquentines, lashed round with chain that they might not burst when their timber cargoes swelled with the sea, which beat and beat in winter gales until they were covered with ice, and there was no food on board — no food, no warmth, no dry spot; and nothing accomplished when the hard voyage at last was done except that a stack of timber had been delivered. And the carpenter, the wild man from Raumo, discoursed on the perils of North Sea winters, and the wretchedness of great schooners and wooden barques bound west round the north of Scotland: but they all of them — the grain-ship sailors, the Baltic mariners, the boys — thanked God that our way, which could have been so hard, had been lightened for us, and the little ship had passed so gently.

They were good boys. What had I as a crew? A small group of grain-ship sailors, aged from nineteen to twenty-one, "veterans" of perhaps two previous Cape Horn roundings: and a handful of British schoolboys from England and the Dominions. Aye, aye; they were pretty good. There was no hanging back, no moaning. There was no need to shout about the decks, and blaspheme: all the malcontents were long departed. For Cape Horn, no moaners! And I thought as I looked round me at the youthful crew, that there are guts and red blood still in youth, still in England.

I looked back now at Staten Island, with the Horn behind, and I hoped to God I should come that way no more in sail. I had hoped that before, perhaps even more fervently on at least two occasions: yet here I was again. And I made no promises and took no oaths, for I knew well that my life, such as it is, is too bound up in these ships for me to make forecasts. If the ships bring me here again I suppose I shall come. But I hope not. It is not sense in these days too often to sail that grim road.

XX

End of the Voyage

WITH the Horn safely rounded, I hoped to stand to the north past Staten Island and to go inside the Falklands, between the Falklands and Patagonia, since the currents favour that way and it possesses the great advantage of avoiding the worst of the ice-fields. The spring ice is generally worse to the east of the Falklands, for some reason, than it is actually off the Horn. But the wind now came from the north-west and I could not head to the westward of the Falklands. I could only stand on to pass them on their eastward side. So I stood on, across the Burdwood Bank, to make towards the south-east trades 3,000 miles away.

The passage of the South Atlantic towards the trades was pleasant enough, though off the Plate we had a hard gale. We saw an ice-island on the Burdwood Bank, probably aground. It was low, long, and much-worn; the sky even in the night was white above it. I would have investigated this a little more closely had I had a fair wind; but the wind was ahead, and I could give nothing away. There was no telling how far the spurs reached from beyond this ice, beneath the surface. I held my course, and kept away and hoped to see no more. On the Atlantic side of the Horn we saw many more sea birds than we had seen on the Pacific side. The albatrosses, which had been almost entirely missing in the Pacific, showed up again though they were never numerous. We saw much kelp for several hundred miles past the Falklands, and later seemed to come into a whales' feeding ground, where the blue whales sported, and the blackfish, and the porpoises, all of them, one morning, were feeding together each in their own herd. In the gale off the Plate I had to heave-to again; the sea once more smashed the light brackets which the carpenter had carefully remade. The squalls blew with fury, and the driving rain was like a horny-handed slap across the face; but it did not last long. Every day brought us then to finer weather and we did not mind an odd gale, though the disturbance off the Plate set up such a sea that the motion of the ship seemed worse than it had ever been before. For the first time, from my place beside the helmsman aft, I saw the jib-boom washed clean and watched the sea rise above the reeling foretop; it was impossible to stand or to stay erect without clinging to some support. It rained a great deal; but after eight hours I could put the helm up, and go on; and that was the last of the really bad weather we had. The conditions were disturbed for a few days, but we made steady northing towards the trade.

The days now passed in peace, and there was warmth in the air. All the Cape Horn lashings could come off; the skylights were opened, and the caulking taken from the doors. The sidelight brackets were again replaced, and the pigs removed to their sty on deck. On the day we reached the south-east trade we killed a pig, as fresh food; in two days he was all gone. The cats began to show themselves on deck, and even to prowl the scuppers when there was no water there on the lookout for flying fish. The carpenter set to work with an axe — his best tool — to shape a new fore topmast from the last of the spars I had shipped in Melbourne. He worked about the decks all day long (for he was dayman again now — he and the sailmaker) with an axe and a broad smile and endless energy. A primitive from the far north, fair skinned and stalwart, he had been at sea in sailing-ships since he was fourteen. He walked to his first ship — the wooden barque *Warma*, loading timber at some port in North Sweden. He walked from Finland, though he knew no word of the Swedish language, using the wild Finnish tongue; and at length after many days he saw the masts of a barque showing above a forest. He went on board. It was the *Warma*. On deck was an old man, rough and tough, sitting sewing sails. He was a very rough-looking man, unshaven and unkempt; he looked more like an old and not very successful farmer than a sailor in a sailing-ship.

"Hallo," he said to the boy, " what do you want?"

"I want to see the captain," said the fourteen-year-old boy, very hungry.

"I'm the captain," said the tough one, spitting in the scuppers.

"Well I'm the new man from Finland," said the boy.

Then they were both surprised. But the boy was signed on, and he became a good sailor. He was at sea two years before he saw soft bread, and four years before he knew that milk could be kept in cans. They don't get condensed milk in the Finnish Baltic sailers. Before he shipped for this round-world voyage he had never seen pickles, tomato sauce, or jam; and he had never eaten toast, or seen curry. He had been master of a barquentine, and mate of several barques. They live hard in the short-voyage ships of Finland.

I stood on quietly towards the Line on the grain-ships' track. I thought of looking in at the island of Trinidad, where there is supposed to be some treasure buried (it is the usual old-pirate-on-his-deathbed-and-secret-plan story), not that we wanted treasure but we could use some firewood, and there is said to be plenty on the beach there. However, there were two insuperable difficulties. In the first place, Trinidad is one of the most difficult islands in the world on which to land and secondly, the wind would not allow me to stand towards it. The wind, when we arrived at those latitudes ought to have been from the south-east; unfortunately it was from the north-west. So I stood on, towards Fernando Noronha, planning to cross the Line farther west than the grain-ships do, since I was bound to New York, and they are always bound to Europe. Crossing the Rio lane a sharp lookout was kept for steamers in order that we might ask for a report, through their radio, to Lloyd's in London. We were out then more than two months and had not seen anything beyond one distant glance at Rurutu and another, a month later, at Staten Island. But we crossed the Rio lane and saw nothing, except one tramp, outward bound in ballast, which passed us in a shower of rain. We were then completely lost to the world and remained so, indeed, for more than ninety days, during which we had no communication with anything, and no one on earth knew where we were. In that time we had sailed over 11,000 miles, but we had crossed only three steamer tracks. Away from steamer lanes the whole ocean is now quieter and more lonely that it has ever been since first man sailed the Western Ocean; except in the trade winds belt of the South Pacific, where there is always the chance of meeting a stray small yacht.

The south-east trade was very quiet, when at last it came. But if the wind was quiet, and we could do no better than 130 or 140 miles a day, we could at least get on with the work. The work in an iron full-rigged ship is endless; all hands were now busily engaged from daylight to dark cleaning off the rust from the run to the Horn — it was curious how everyone forgot so quickly about that place — and getting the metalwork of the ship in good order to be painted; cleaning the boats, chipping, scraping, red-leading, tarring — morning, noon, and night. The topmen, Jan, Hilgard, and Dennis, worked barebacked in their own riggings, Jan the fore, Hilgard the main, and Dennis the mizzen; there were a hundred and one things needing attention on each mast. Keeping up a ship at sea is an art unto itself — an art requiring infinite labour, great patience, good organization, and good workmen. The topmen were the best of the young sailors. Jan and Hilgard were able seamen; Dennis was one of the youngest of the cadets. He came aboard at Ipswich, an insignificant little chap, aged fourteen, from the borders of Wales; and, for a long time, his principal occupations seemed to be to grin and to make a loud noise upon every possible occasion. But Dennis blossomed out quickly into a fine little sailor: he filled out, and grew rapidly, and he took well to the niceties of the sailor's art. He was a first-class sailor but, like most of the other boys, he had no intention of following the sea as a profession. His reason was that life as an officer in a steamship did not attract him.

"I like it here," he said. "This is fun, and it's being alive too. But what is there in a steamer?"

I had no answer for him; but it is a pity that the maritime profession of Great Britain in these days is so unattractive that it cannot keep these boys. Of all the boys who came in the ship, only three left with the intention of following the sea as a profession — John Devlin, whose family had been masters in British sail for generations, and the redoubtable Hard Case and Stormalong. "I'll stay at sea if I have to go in a barge," said the solid-minded Hard Case, who was a surprisingly deep thinker for a boy, and always a youth who knew his own mind. He had a good mind, too. I liked the Hard Case, little harum-scarum as he sometimes was; there was depth to him — depth, spirit, and plenty of character. He will get on. His former schoolmate Stormalong was much the same, except that he was even smaller and, upon occasion, could make more noise. Stormalong had a merry twinkle in his eyes that even hurricanes could not shift; he could smile with the toothache, and that takes spirit. There were many occasions when I was glad this pair had come on board, though, as they said themselves, they had first approached the ship in some alarm and had expected to be thrown off.

They joined with grins that spread from ear to ear, and they never quite lost the sense of pleasure that just being in the ship brought to them. That was the kind of boy I wanted! When that surveyor, who had come down hotfoot to the ship at Harwich before I sailed, was asking the boys about the hell ship allegations (the stupid work of some crazy fellow whose application to join I had refused), young Goodchild up and spoke to him.

"Hell ship, Sir?" he said. "She seems like a bit of heaven to me."

And that was the end of the inquiry.

John was a good lad, too, a year or two older than the younger boys. He knew he was going to follow the sea and realized the value of his opportunity in this ship; he never let a chance to learn anything go by, though much of our seamanship was antiquated, and little of it is now necessary for the modern officers' certificates. But it was still a magnificent groundwork — a foundation in the ancient calling of the sea, a coming-to-grips with the elements upon the ocean, and an experience which would stand the mariner in good stead throughout his life — and not only the mariner. John was from the south of England; Neville, the Yorkshire boy, was from the north. Neville was a quiet little fellow when he came on board, but he did not remain that way very long. A wild mop of long black hair, a rosy face that grinned very easily, a good wit, a lanky form that was — well, sometimes difficult to raise from a recumbent position at the end of watch below; an abundant energy that did not find in toil a sufficient outlet was Master Neville from the Captain Cook country of North Yorkshire. He was a good scout. I liked Neville, liked all the lads. The three New Zealanders who stayed for the Cape Horn passage were good scouts, too. One of them, a youth named Crawford, with his irrepressible humour, his dry repartee, his love of jokes, was a tower of goodwill in the ship. Such a fellow adds tremendously to the harmony of a small community, turning aside the little trials of the day always with a joke.

There was one feature about the boys and about that voyage for which, looking back on it, I feel most grateful; and that was that, when a discontent came and the indolent had been with us too long, it was they who left and the rest never became disaffected. By the natural process of elimination we had a pretty good gang for this last passage. Some who had left would still have fitted in splendidly; we could have done particularly with Ed, Fred, and Tony, and Andrew le Grice from our Western Ocean passage. And if a fellow left because he did not want any more malaria, I could not blame him. Of the eight Americans who had been with the ship at one time or another we had now only one (not reckoning the stalwart Hilgard, from Plandome, who was no freshman in a sailing ship). This was Andrew Lindsay, from St. Louis in Missouri, and a sturdy lad he was. Like the English boys, the Americans also had no intention of following a sea career, though they might have wished to do so. The reason, too, was the same; the profession under their own flag did not appeal to them. Since I knew little of these conditions I could not argue with them, but I could at least point out that, since they now had so excellent a foundation of experience behind them, they ought to find it easier to rise to the top; and, having risen, they could then exert their influence to bring about an improvement in the general conditions for officers in their merchant service. If both merchant services — that of Great Britain and that of the United States — are to continue to have slight appeal for many of the best of the youths of both countries, there cannot fail to be a falling-off in the standard of officer personnel. I had other boys who had joined with some idea of following the sea. I used to encourage them to visit steamships in port, so that they could see something of conditions there, since I knew full well our kind of

seafaring was very different from that of the usual run of
vessels in the Merchant Navy. Except in the cases of the
determined John, Hard Case, and Stormalong, each of
whom in effect said: This is my profession and I will make
my way, they were inclined to think, upon reflection, upon
talking with cadets and young officers in steamers, that
there were better opportunities on the land.

My training-ship scheme did not seem to have achieved
much good. But I venture to believe that the experiences
the boys had in my ship, profound and memorable as some
of them must have been, did help to guide their
development along sound lines, whatever profession or
calling they may later adopt. Even those who left — most
of them — were glad that they had come. Any real training
scheme must extend far beyond one small ship to be of
value in the maritime profession. So far as anything of real
service was concerned, I well knew that I was nothing but
an adventurer on the far outskirts, an onlooker with some
queer ideas, whose only merit was that he had had the
courage to try them.

We were seventy-five days to the Line, crossing on the
longitude of thirty-five West. We had sailed over our
outward track in the South Atlantic twice by then, and had
gone round the world; but New York was still 3,000 miles
away and Ipswich — to us — 6,000. Neptune came on
board to initiate the three New Zealanders with all the old
ceremony, Neptune in the person of wiry Jim with his full
court of barbers, doctor, nurses, police, and so forth, and
Davy Jones, all well made up. This was on a Sunday. On
other days the work went on, and gradually the ship began
to emerge from beneath all the chipping hammers and the
scrapers and the tar and the red lead as a thing of sleek
beauty and freshly-painted grace, until it was a delight to
walk the decks by day and night, and look upon the picture
of her clean and well-kept decks in the shadows of the

trade wind sails. I did not change the fore topmast at sea, since we were able to carry the tops'l and two headsails without difficulty; I carried the studding sails for'ard to help the balance of the canvas. The strong gales we had had and the long hard driving, however, had been a strain on the rigging, stout as it was: things began to go. The foreyard, one of the most important yards in the ship, was found to be badly sprung. It had to be fished, but I thought it prudent to send down the studding sails to relieve the yard; it was a pity, but it could not be helped. We had no piece of timber long enough to make a new foreyard. There was nothing fundamentally wrong with the ship; any small vessel with wooden masts and yards must suffer on such a long voyage, taking the beatings we took from the tropics and the wintry roads of Good Hope and the Horn. We were not, aloft, very different from the *Bounty*, the *Swallow*, the *Duff*, or the *Endeavour*, all of which had carried a full spare mast and yet had frequently to stop while their shipwrights and carpenters cut down trees and shaped new spars. The springing of a yard or two and even a mast must be regarded, in such ships, as at least a predictable accident upon any circumnavigation. A week in a good shipyard would have put us in excellent order again, fit for ten more such voyages; or even another two weeks in Nissan lagoon, if we could have got a spar. The ship was all right; but I knew I had to nurse her now for the sake of the rigging. There could be no thought of overhaul before New York; and we had still something of the West Indies hurricane season before us. It was the middle of September then, and we had at least four weeks of sailing to do.

In these circumstances I found the discourse of the carpenter encouraging, for he had been on a passage in the noble *Warma* of 110 days from the Mediterranean to Copenhagen, in the course of which the vessel sprung six spars, and the jib-boom, and the mizzen topmast. They fished the lot, he said, and they went on.

We also went on, and the doldrums were kind. We had only one day of calm. I put out the starboard lifeboat, which had been repaired, and the boys went rowing, fishing, and swimming. In the watch below they sunbathed on the houses to bring back their coats of tan. The north-east trade came gently to us on 12° North, and I then headed directly for New York, steering for the port for the first time in eighty days of sailing. By night the sea was black with streaks of light where the porpoise played before the bow. There was no noise but the roll of foam, as the rolling cutwater slowly ploughed its way. The sidelights shone on the studding sails full of the fresh soft air of the gentle trade — they and all the sails, swelling above us in the peace of the tranquil night. The lookout leant on the capstan while the tired watch, rolled in their blankets on the focs'l head, slept the sleep of youth, deep and dreamless. And deep and dreamless lay the sea all round; while gently and with silent grace the little ship sailed on.

The lights of New York tinted red upon the clouds showed a hundred miles at sea. After we had first seen them on a cold evening in mid-October we still had to sail two days to make a landfall; for the conditions — as ever — were adverse. The winds were not good and the weather was cold. It blew a little from the north-west, and the Gulf Stream threw up a lumpy and uncomfortable sea in which the little ship plunged and rolled. I was worried about the rigging — about that, and other things, for I knew that I could go no farther. With this port safely made the voyage was done. I knew very well that with threescore thousand miles of sea behind me and the voyage made, my arrival in New York could mean nothing but the climax of my worries — and then? They would be overcome; but it was certain that I could not sail the ship home to England.

We picked up the Fire Island light at long last, after sailing 106 days from Tahiti without seeing anything but the heights of Cape Horn's Staten Island and the hazy outlines of Rurutu a month earlier: yet the sailing had not been monotonous and the voyage was not long. In the morning we were in the liner lanes outside America's great port and the steamers came, all hurrying and very busy, and the pilot was on board bringing with him some newspapers that in a world of chaos shrieked of inconsequential things. The good pilot also gave us a bag of fresh meat that tasted fine. It was almost calm then, but it breezed up with the night and we sailed in to the examination anchorage off Staten Island, and the sound of the cable roaring through the hawse was both welcome and sad, for I knew it was most unlikely that I should ever sail the ship again, and there was more than a chance that no one might. It rained and blew at the anchorage; and at daylight I looked about me at the Shore Road and Bay Ridge, and Manhattan, and those parts, and it seemed to me all anticlimax. I had gone out and was now returned; I had sailed a long way and was now come in again. I had sailed near 60,000 miles and I did not know why; I had crossed the lengths and breadths of four oceans and seven seas; I had passed the Line four times and had rounded Good Hope and the Horn, and beat out of the Coral Sea, and beat by many reefs and anchored in strange places and quiet lagoons; and had brought my collection of youth round the world without accident and without loss. For this I thanked God in humility and devoutly, for I knew that above all I had been sustained throughout that voyage, in whatever manner of vicissitude or near-calamity that arose, by Providence. There had been much in that voyage to sustain my belief; and nothing to shake it.

It rained and blew at the anchorage, and I shifted to a safe berth in the harbour, and tied up at a dock, and the voyage was done.

Epilogue

THE ship was sold at New York, for I had to sell her. The voyage had cost me all I had, and even with the ship sold I had now nothing. I hauled down the British flag and repatriated my crew. I went out from the Tebo yard at the foot of Twenty-third Street in Brooklyn with the American flag flying from the peak of my ship seeming incongruous in my eyes; and I went out into the rain-spattered streets and did not look back again. Brave ship! I remember her now as she lay there with the rich yachts all round, soon to be "converted" to be more fit to join them; and there was such grace and steadfastness and loyalty about that old hull and those tapering spars and all the beauty and sea-kindliness of her as may never be built into a sailing-ship again. The day of all such ships is ended — all such ships, and all such crews. It is unlikely that a crew such as I had will ever again be assembled to circumnavigate a square-rigged ship under the British flag.

My ship was a good ship and no better wind ship will be built; my crew in the end was a good crew though far from angelic, and a better will not be signed upon a Cape Horner's articles again; my voyage was a vague thing and yet it was a voyage not idly begun nor profitably continued, but sailed quietly with resolution and some poor ideals, from the setting out to the end. Now the crew is gone, scattered about the world, and the ship is gone, and over me again the gloomy buildings brood.

Appendix I

The Ship

The *Joseph Conrad* as the *Georg Stage* was designed in 1881 and built by Burmeister and Wain at Copenhagen in 1881–82. By whom she was designed I do not know, but it was most certainly an architect who knew his business thoroughly. Her construction was financed by Frederik Stage, a prominent Danish shipowner of that day, as a memorial to his son Georg, who had died of tuberculosis at an early age in France. Frederik Stage, a man of sturdy and independent character, had begun life as a deckboy and had worked steadily upwards until he became one of the most prominent shipowners in Copenhagen. When his son died he conceived the idea of fitting out a school-ship which would serve both as a memorial to the dead son and as an excellent means of attracting the best of Danish youth to the sea, and giving them a good beginning. He had found his own beginning hard and wished to make that of others easier. At that time and indeed until to-day, the apprenticeship system used in British ships and the cadet system of America were unknown in Denmark, the great majority of Danes who followed the sea having to learn the practical side of their profession in the hard school of the forecastle, where the lot of the deckboy was apt to be hard. Frederik Stage, by the introduction of his school-ship, planned that the early years of boys should be made much easier, since before going out into the merchant ships, the boys would have an opportunity of learning the rudiments of their profession from men who were interested in them, in a ship designed for them, and among their own kind. The ship was designed to train eighty boys, and from the beginning the scheme was a great success. Frederik Stage financed the building and outfitting of the ship, and left a considerable fund the income of which was to be used for her maintenance; but the upkeep costs and the costs of training the eighty boys exceeded the income from his legacy and had to be largely met in other ways, both by private subscriptions and by shipowners' contributions, and — over many years — with the help also of an annual payment from the State. The shipowner Stage was a farsighted man and he saw that the committee which controlled the ship would probably be busier and more efficient if it also had to collect some of the funds; it was for this reason that he made his own contribution insufficient to cover the whole costs. A committee entrusted only with the spending of funds is not always as painstaking or as efficient as the same group when it has to struggle for some of its finance. At any rate, this was the view of the elder Stage, and it seems to me a sound one.

The boys for the ship were chosen from all walks of life, regardless of wealth, social position, or any similar considerations. They had only to be Danish boys of good character and physique who wished to go to sea. They did not have to undertake to do anything. No one paid, or was allowed to pay. Everything was free, except the uniform and outfit, for which the boys were asked to pay 200 Crowns (about £10), but if a boy was chosen and had not this £10, the whole or part was remitted. A special endowment was made for this purpose. No boy was allowed to bring any possessions into the ship; no boy could be sent money from home. All were equal. All received exactly the same treatment. If a boy were sent a hamper for his birthday, he had to share it with his shipmates; so that a poor boy or an orphan would never be made to feel his "inferiority." With their instinctive feeling for true democracy, the Danes had decided that this ship should be run properly. She was; and she was conducted in a thoroughly efficient manner. From the date of her launch until her sale, the little ship secured the services of fine men devoted to her and to the ideals behind her. Quickly the *Georg Stage* became an institution respected and admired not only in the Merchant Service of Denmark. Her boys, thoroughly trained, soon began to make a name for themselves; over many years of splendid service the *Georg Stage* boys became the leading shipmasters and officers of the growing fleets of their native country. On this voyage round the world we met old boys from the ship in most of the ports we came to, and all of them were in good positions. All of them, too, still remembered the ship with affection, and spoke highly of the value of the training they had received on board.

The boys were chosen from among those who applied, and were from 14 to 18 years of age; the average age at entrance was usually about 15 and a half. Between 250 and 300 boys applied each year, so that the committee was able to make a good selection. The ship was laid up over the winter, rigged down to her lower masts, in the Navy Yard at Copenhagen, where she had a snug berth; she was rigged again early in April and went out about the middle of that month, with 80 new boys. These were trained over a five-month summer cruise. No boy ever sailed twice with the ship, as a boy; but it was traditional to choose the officers and petty officers from those who had previously served as cadets on board. The vessel carried a crew of ten, these being the master, first and second mates, teacher, four petty officers (who were both able seamen and instructors); an Admiral Crichton who combined within his efficient person the energy of four men and the capabilities of six — he was engineer, purser, steward, radio operator, carpenter, and store-keeper — and a cook. Of these the cook alone did not need to have begun his career as a cadet. The entire personnel was drawn from the merchant service, though for many of the earlier years it had been customary to use officers and petty officers from the Danish Navy. It was learned, however, that these, though excellent officers, were sometimes not so well accustomed as the merchant service officers to the need for, or the practice of, reasonable economy, particularly in strange ports; and economy was always necessary in the running of the *Georg Stage*. The elimination of sailing training vessels from the navy, moreover, quickly put the younger naval officers out of touch with the older training methods. The permanent officers of the *Georg Stage* were the master, chief mate, and the purser-steward; all others were selected and signed only for one cruise, though it was usual for some of them to return year after year.

As soon as the ship was fitted out and had taken the boys on board, she moved to anchorage in the Sound, and here followed a brief period of intensive training designed to see what the boys were made of, and to fit them to handle the vessel. After three weeks of this, any who wished to leave might do so; the ship then began to cruise through Danish waters, later making a passage through the Baltic to Gefle, Hernosand, or some such port, and later, cruising in the North Sea with a call at Hull, West Hartlepool, or Leith. At the end of the season, in the days when British square-rigged ships were still numerous, it was customary for something like half the boys to find ready berths in the British ships; the others went into their own merchant service, to complete their sea service before going to the navigation school for the year-and-a-half course necessary before they could sit for their mates' certificates. Discipline was strict but never harsh. Corporal punishment could be given only by the Captain, and was always rare. The health of the boys was the first consideration. Seamanship, sail-handling, sending up and down the lighter masts and yards, signalling, Rule of the Road, rowing, swimming, sailing, steering both compass course and by the wind, sail-making, sennet work of all kinds — these were the subjects taught on board, and a high standard of proficiency was insisted upon.

The keynote of the successful training and discipline of the boys was constant and intense physical effort; but the boys were made to feel that the officers were their friends and guardians and not their taskmasters. The running of a school-ship of this kind is one of the most difficult pieces of administration that can well be undertaken, but the success of the *Georg Stage* system over so long a period of years is sufficient commendation. Service on the committee entrusted with their supervision and control of the ship was a high honour; here sat admirals, ship-owners, leading business men, and a representative of the Minister of Marine. The cost of the ship — the actual costs of feeding, keeping, and training 80 boys each summer in the ship — was about £3,000 to £4,000. The annual report of the old school-ship for her last year of Danish service, 1934, gives the actual costs of her running for the year as 53,269 Crowns (about £2,650), but this amount includes nothing for repairs, renewals, or depreciation, since the ship had then been sold. To replace her by a slightly larger vessel cost something over £30,000; the assistance of the government had to be sought for such a large outlay.

The *Georg Stage* was built as a single-topsail full-rigged ship, with a small compound steam engine, which however was even weaker than the internal combustion engine which replaced it. It was never used as a means of propulsion; steam was not kept up. The engine was purely for emergency use and formed no part of the ordinary means of either propulsion or manoeuvring of the vessel. Run down by a steamer and sunk in the Sound outside Copenhagen in 1905 with the loss of twenty-six boys, who were imprisoned below — the ship sank in three minutes — the *Georg Stage* was raised and rebuilt in 1906 with a series of steel watertight bulkheads designed to make her virtually unsinkable. From 1906 to 1916 she had no engine. In 1916 she was given a small Alpha semi-Diesel of fifty-two indicated horse-power, and a bronze adjustable propeller. With this power she could make five knots in a calm; and again it was intended and used only on occasions of real emergency. Even for going to sea from a crowded anchorage, the engine was not used; if she could not go with the sails she could not go, but she was an extraordinarily handy vessel under sail in the comparatively smooth Danish waters

— and indeed, everywhere, though she is small in a sea way. The material used in the construction was Swedish iron, the plates from the garboard strake to the waterline being 11.5 millimetres in thickness, the sheer strake 10.5, and the bulwarks 9.5 millimetres. The main deck was of teak, as also were the fo'c'sle head and the small poop. The 'tween-decks were of pine. The forward house in which were the galley, radio room, lamp-locker, and companions to the 'tween-decks, was of steel; the skylights and companions on deck were heavy teak. The fore and main lower masts were iron; the jib-boom was a piece of larch; the mizzen lower mast, the bowsprit, the three topmasts, the three topgallant masts, and all the yards were of selected pitchpine. The standing rigging was of iron wire, 1¼-in. diameter for the shrouds, and 1-in. diameter for the backstays, all wormed, parcelled, and served, and set up by means of deadeyes to chainplates on the outboard channels (which were part of the main strength of the vessel) with lanyards of 3-in. tarred hemp. The sails were of hemp canvas, No. 2 the courses and tops'ls, spanker, two headsails; No. 3 the topgallants; and No. 4 the flying jib and the royals. The studding sails, of which a full suit was carried for one mast (that is, six sails) were of light duck of exceptionally good quality — so good that at the end of the voyage, in 1936, I was still using the studding sails which had been put on board the ship as part of her original equipment in 1882. The running rigging was of hemp, mainly, and good quality manila; I changed the topgallant and royal sheets to chain in the yardarm sheaves, and the rest wire. The course and tops'l braces were all of 3-in. hemp, as also were the tops'l halliards, course sheets and tacks, etc. The clewlines and buntlines for the tops'l and courses were of 2¼-in. four-stranded manila; for the topgallants and royals, 2½-in. and 2-in. manila was used. The vangs were 2-in. hemp; the jib halliards 2¾-in. hemp, and the jib sheets 3-in. hemp, and served wire. The tops'l sheets were of steel chain the links of which were of steel ½in. in diameter. All footropes and lifts were of iron wire 1in. in diameter, parcelled and served. The steering was by a wheel connected by chains to the quadrant on the rudder post. The windlass was operated by a double-geared hand capstan on the fo'c'sle head. The two Bower anchors weighed about 1,700 pounds each; the port anchor had 135 fathoms of chain and the starboard 120 fathoms. Stream and warp anchors were also carried. As a school-ship the vessel had five boats — two large lifeboats, 23ft. by 6ft. 5in. by 2ft. 10in.; two smaller, 19ft. 6in. by 5ft. 2in. by 2ft. 5in.; and a motor-boat

17ft., by 4ft. 10in. by 20in. with a six horse-power Penta motor. These boats were all of oak, copper fastened. I got rid of the two smaller boats, not thinking it wise to carry them outboard over a long voyage at sea, and lost the motor-boat in New York. The two large lifeboats were rigged with two masts each, with freefooted foresail and mainsail, the peaks of both stretched on adjustable sprits. They were beautiful boats, clinker built, with transom sterns. Each was certified to carry 23 seamen. There was also a small Norwegian pram, carried on the deckhouse, as a workboat.

The main dimensions of the ship herself were:

Length from fore part of stern to after side of the head of the sternpost	110ft. 6in.
Length on waterline	100ft. 8in.
Main breadth to outside plank	25ft. 3in.
Depth in hold from tonnage deck to ceiling amidships	13ft. 1in.
Draft (with full water and stores), aft	12ft.
Draft (with full water and stores), for'ard	11ft. 8in.
Gross tonnage (English measurement)	212.16 tons
Net tonnage (English measurement)	187.8 tons

The vessel, as the *Georg Stage*, carried 103 tons of pig-iron ballast. I reduced this to 83 tons for the ocean voyage. She carried 15 tons of fresh water in ten tanks amidships, in the lower hold, and 8 tons in a reserve tank beneath the fore peak. She had a graceful clipper stern and an old-fashioned counter. The figurehead in her early school-ship days was a representation in wood of the head of *Georg Stage*, but the boys chipped the nose from this, in the well-known manner in which boys of 14 to 16 years of age are apt to behave, and the figure was replaced by one of bronze. This old figurehead was taken out at the sale and set up in the new ship; I replaced it with a figure of Joseph Conrad carved for me by Bruce Rogers in New York. This was made of two pieces of very old seasoned pine.

The foreyard was 49ft. long, the mainyard 50ft., the fore and main tops'l yards 40ft. 6in., the fore and main topgallant yards 28ft. 3in., and the fore and main royal yards 20ft. 9in. The crojack yard was 42ft. 6in., mizzen tops'l yard 35ft., mizzen topgallant yard 25ft., and mizzen royal yard 19ft. long. The bowsprit from the cutwater was 16ft. long and the jib-boom (after the accident off Finisterre) projected 21ft. 6in. beyond the cap, making the total length of bowsprit and jib-boom combined 37ft. 6in. The spanker boom was 27ft. 6in. long, and the gaff 20ft. The diameter of the fore and main yards at their thickest was 13in., of the fore and main tops'l yards 11in., of the topgallant yards 8in.; and of the steel lower masts 17in. The mizzen lower mast had a diameter of 15in. The main mast, keel to truck, was 98ft.; the fore 94ft., and the mizzen 87ft. 6in.

When I took the ship over, my principal alterations were designed to fit the ship keeping the sea over long periods. She had formerly been always near to a port, and in six months of sailing spent more than half the nights at anchorage. In the Danish days, the boys had slept 40 to a 'tween-decks, in hammocks; I built 16 wooden bunks in the for'ard 'tween-decks and put five large cabins—two single and three double — in the after 'tween-decks. These were plain but comfortable. I built a carpenters' shop in the after part of the fore 'tween-decks, built boatskids abaft the for'ard house so that the boats could be carried inboard, put a charthouse over the 'thwartships after companion leading to the saloon, changed the big companion to the after 'tween-decks into a hatch and skylight better suited to keep the sea out, added a galley tank for the rationing of water, dispensed with the radio (the set being a spark transmitter of a type soon to be forbidden), and put in a new galley stove. The lavatories were all beneath the focs'l head, above the main deck — four on each side. I changed two into lockers, one for deck stores and one for paint. There were no bathrooms and I added none. Lighting was by means of oil lamps. The galley stove burned coal and wood; the bunkers held five tons more in sacks, without being in the way of any of the gear. One of the spare cabins aft was kept ready as a hospital, and a full Danish medicine chest, as well as the chest prescribed by the British Board of Trade for deep-sea vessels, was carried. I carried a blacksmith's forge and spare spars, and canvas enough to make a full suit of sails. The provision rooms were sufficient to take stores for thirty people for six months. I added two large iron tanks, for flour, and equipped the galley also as a bakery. There were bunks in the ship for thirty-five persons, and nineteen of these bunks were in single- and double-berth cabins. The total sail area of the ship without the studding sails was between 7,000 and 8,000 square feet; with the studding sails and all kites (a triangular sail on the usually bare crojack yard, a jib tops'l on the fore royal stay, and so on) she could set 10,000 square feet of canvas. The total length of the running rigging was nearly 5,000 fathoms.

The very fastest I was ever able to get the ship to touch was a shade over twelve knots in a fresh squall with a flat sea; she only once averaged ten knots over twenty-four hours. But she came very easily up to eight, without being pushed and without much wind; when she did ten she was moving. I was always pleased when she did nine.

Her displacement was about 400 tons, and if she had been a cargo ship she would have carried about 350 tons of cargo.

The accompanying plans show full details of the vessel.

Appendix II

Extract of the Log of the
Joseph Conrad

Being a résumé of the voyage, giving the dates, ports visited, number of days at sea, unusual occurrences, etc.

1934

August 29	Hoisted the British flag on board the ship *Georg Stage* in the Navy Yard at Copenhagen, and renamed the vessel *Joseph Conrad*, to be registered at Ipswich, England
September 3	Sailed from Copenhagen
September 13	Arrived Harwich
September 16	Shifted to the buoys at Ipswich, off the Cliff Quay
October 16	Sailed down the River Orwell to the anchorage off Harwich
October 22	Sailed from Harwich
November 11	Anchored in Funchal Bay, Madeira. Sailed same evening

19 *Days from Harwich*

December 12	Sighted Watling Island (San Salvador)
December 16	Anchored off Nassau, Bahamas

35 *Days from Madeira*

December 19	Sailed from Nassau for New York
December 30	Arrived New York

11 *Days from Nassau*
Sailed from Harwich 6,766 miles

1935

January 2	Vessel driven ashore on rocks off the Shore Road at Bay Ridge, New York Harbour
January 4	Salvaged and dry-docked at the Todd yard, Brooklyn, where the vessel repaired
January 31	Sailed from New York for Rio de Janeiro in continuance of circumnavigation
March 7	Sighted St. Paul Rocks
March 9	Crossed the Equator for the first time

37 *Days from New York*

March 15	Landed on Brazilian coast near Itamaraca, north of Pernambuco

March 28	Sighted Cape Frio
March 29	Hove-to at night outside Rio
March 30	Anchored at Rio

58 *Days from New York*
Sailed 6,000 miles

April 6	Sailed from Rio towards Cape Town
April 25	Hove-to off Tristan da Cunha and received the islanders on board
May 7	Berthed at Cape Town

31 *Days from Rio de Janeiro*
Sailed 3,400 miles

May 14	Sailed from Cape Town towards the East Indies
June 30	Sighted south-eastern point of Java
July 1	Sailed through Bali Strait
July 2	Anchored off Boeleleng, Bali

49 *Days from Cape Town*
Sailed 6,450 miles

July 10	Sailed from Bali
July 11	Passed through Sapudi Strait
July 17	Crossed the Equator for the second time
July 19	Arrived at Singapore

9 *Days from Bali*
Sailed 950 miles

July 24–26	In dry dock at Singapore
July 31	Sailed 11p.m. towards Sydney, north-about
August 11	Anchored on reef off Balabac Island
August 12	Anchored off Dalawan Bay, Balabac Island

From Singapore 940 miles

August 14	Sailed from Dalawan Bay through Sulu Sea
August 16	Passed Kagayan Sulu: landed on Mambahenauhan
August 21	Anchored in Chongos Bay, Tawi Tawi

From Dalawan Bay 312 miles

August 21–25	Landed at Bongao, Malasa, Lapid-lapid, Balimbing, Parangan, etc.
August 26	Sailed from Chongos Bay
September 2	Entered the Pacific south of Mindanao
September 5	Sighted Sonsorol of the Carolines
September 18	Crossed the Equator for the third time; 49 days out from Singapore
September 24	Off the Nuguria Islands
September 25	Sighted Feni, Tanga, New Ireland, etc.
September 27	Anchored in Nissan Lagoon, Bismarck Archipelago

From Chongos Bay 2,831 miles

September 28 –	Heaving down the ship in Nissan Lagoon

Appendix II – extract of the log of the *Joseph Conrad*

October 4
October 5 Sailed from Nissan
October 13 Anchored near Losuia, Kiriwina, in the Trobriand Islands
October 17 Sailed from Trobriands
November 1 Arrived Tulagi, Solomon Islands
November 7 Sailed from Tulagi
November 8–11 At anchor off Berande, Guadalcanal
November 11 Sailed from Berande
November 18 Anchored at Owa Raha
November 21 Sailed from Owa Raha towards Sydney
November 22 – Malaria outbreak on board
December
December 9 Anchored in Double Bay, Sydney

> 131 *Days from Singapore*
> Sailed 7,800 miles

December 18 Sailed from Sydney
December 21 Hove-to in gale for first time on voyage
December 30 Backed mainyard off Melbourne Heads awaiting tide
December 31 Arrived Melbourne: alongside at Williamstown

> 13 *Days from Sydney*
> Sailed 700 miles

1936
January 31 Sailed from Melbourne towards Samarai via Auckland
February 21 Arrived Auckland, New Zealand

> 23 *Days from Melbourne*
> Sailed 2,000 miles

February 27 Sailed from Auckland
March 18 Sighted Uluma Reef: driven back by gale
March 23 Anchored at Bramble Haven
March 25 Left Bramble Haven; arrived Samarai

> 26 *Days from Auckland*
> Sailed 2,500 miles

March 31 Sailed from Samarai towards Tahiti: anchored off Bell Rock
April 1 Anchored in the lagoon, Wari Island
April 3 On Wari Reef; hove off again, and sailed
April 4–May 5 Beating out of Coral Sea
May 11 Arrived at and left Lord Howe Island
May 19 Sighted Mount Egmont, Cook Straits
May 20 Sailed past Wellington
May 22 Ginger cat overboard and rescued
May 31–June 7 Heavy gales; lost dinghy; minor deck damage
June 11 Sighted Raivavae in the Australs

June 15	Sighted Tahiti
June 16	Off Mehetia
June 18	Arrived in Papeete Harbour

79 *Days from Samarai*
Sailed 8,000 miles

July 2	Sailed from Papeete towards Cape Horn
July 6	Sighted Rurutu in the Australs
July 27	Very hard gale: hove-to
July 28	Gale continued: fore topmast head sprung; starboard boat stove in; minor deck damage
August 8	Rounded Cape Horn

37 *Days from Papeete*
Sailed 4,820 miles

August 9	Sighted Staten Island
August 22	Heavy gale in South Atlantic: hove-to
August 26	Crossed outward-bound track between Rio and the Cape
September 6	South-east trade on 18° South
September 15	Crossed the Equator for the fourth time

75 *Days from Papeete*
Sailed 9,331 miles

September 23	Picked up North-east trade on 12° North
October 16	Arrived New York

106 *Days from Tahiti*
Sailed 13,000 miles

November 10	Hauled down the British flag: the American flag hoisted by Mr. Huntington Hartford, to whom the ship was sold.

The vessel sailed 57,800 miles and was at sea 555 days.

Appendix III

The Crew of the *Joseph Conrad*

The following is a list of all persons on board the ship *Joseph Conrad* on her passage round Cape Horn, together with their ages, nationalities, and their port of embarkation for the voyage.

Name	Age	Capacity	Nationality	Joined
Alan Villiers	32	Master	Australian	Copenhagen
Alan Chapman	26	Mate	Australian	Auckland
Hans Christian Pedersen	22	2nd Mate	Danish	Copenhagen
Frank Villiers	28	3rd Mate	Australian	Ipswich
Horst de Wolff	22	Boatswain	German	Copenhagen
Karl Heinz Sperling	21	Sailmaker	German	Copenhagen
Usko Into Österman	22	Carpenter	Finnish	Ipswich
James Evans	29	Leading Seaman	Australian	Melbourne
Jan Junker	18	Able Seaman	Danish	Copenhagen
Hilgard Pannes	18	Able Seaman	American	Ipswich
John Devlin	17	Cadet	English	Ipswich
Neville Twynam	17	Cadet	English	Ipswich
Dennis Leech	15	Cadet	English	Ipswich
Vernon Harcourt	18	Cadet	English	Ipswich
James Fuller ("Hard Case")	15	Cadet	English	Ipswich
Stanley Goodchild ("Stormalong")	15	Cadet	English	Ipswich
C. J. Carmichael	18	Cadet	S. African	Cape Town
Andrew Lindsay	18	Cadet	American	New York
Bruce McDougall	20	Cadet	N. Zealander	Auckland
Raby Crawford	20	Cadet	N. Zealander	Auckland
Peter Henley	20	Cadet	N. Zealander	Auckland
Knut Wilhelms	22	Steward	Finnish	Copenhagen
W. A. Catchpole	36	Cook	English	Ipswich

GLOSSARY

The complications of square-rig sailing are not to he explained away by any glossary, no matter how exhaustive. The reader is recommended to study the sail plan and deck and hull plans of the vessel in the Appendices, on which the various sails and the more important sections of the ship are named. The sail plan may help to show the manner in which the masts of a full-rigged ship are constructed in three sections, and supported by their tracery of shrouds and backstays with the fore-and-aft stays taking the pitching stresses. In the compilation of this Glossary, Admiral Smyth's *Sailor's Word Book*, published in 1867 (a copy of which was loaned to me by Mr. C. R. Patterson), has been of value, many of the terms used in the description of the *Joseph Conrad*'s rigging being out of date.

Afteryards. The yards on the main and mizzenmasts.

Anti-cyclone. An area of high atmospheric pressure and generally good weather.

Ballast, in. A vessel is in ballast when sailing without cargo, and stone, gravel, iron, water, or similar material is stowed in the hold to give the ship stability.

Barquentine. A vessel square-rigged on the foremast and fore-and-aft on the other two, three, four, or five masts — a common type of vessel on the west coast of America a few years ago.

Beat, to. To work a sailing vessel to windward, i.e., making a series of tacks or "boards" with the vessel lying close to the wind on opposite boards, alternately, thus forcing the ship to progress against the direction of the wind.

Bêche-de-mer. (Trepang), a sea slug found on reefs and used by the Chinese as an article of food.

Bilge. That part of the floor in a ship — on either side of the keel — which approaches nearer to a horizontal than to a perpendicular direction, and begins to round upwards.

Bitts. A frame composed of two strong pieces of straight oak timber, fixed upright in the forepart of a ship, and bolted securely to the beams, whereon to fasten cables as she rides at anchor; a similar frame of iron on a ship's deck, or on quays, for making fast mooring lines.

Boards, to make. To tack; to work to windward.

Bollard. Technically a thick piece of wood on the head of a whaleboat, round which the harpooner gives the line a turn, in order to veer it steadily, and check the whale's velocity; also a mooring-post on a wharf.

Boltrope. A rope sewed all round the edge of the sail, to prevent the canvas from tearing. The bottom of it is called the foot-rope, the sides leech-ropes, and if the sail be oblong or square the upper part is called the head-rope; the stay or weather rope of the fore-and-aft sails is termed the luff.

Bower. Bower-anchors are those at the bows and in constant working use. They are called best and small, not from a difference of size, but as to the bow on which they are placed; starboard being the best bower, the port the small bower.

Bowline. A rope leading forward which is fastened to a space connected by bridles to cringles on the leech or perpendicular edge of the square sails. It is used to keep the weather-edge of the sail tight forward and steady when the ship is close hauled to the wind; and which, indeed, being hauled taut, enables the ship to come nearer to the wind. Not now in use.

Boom. A long spar run out from different places in the ship, to extend or boom out the foot of a particular sail, as jib-boom, flying jib-boom, studding-sail booms, driver or spanker-boom, etc. A ship is said to come booming forwards when she comes with all the sail she can make.

Braces. The braces are ropes belonging to all the yards of a ship; two to each yard, rove through blocks that are stropped to the yards, or fastened to pendants, seized to the yardarms. Their use is either to square or traverse the yards horizontally.

Braces, preventer. Extra lines of stout rope rove off to assist the braces in checking in the yards; used only in heavy weather. See *Braces.*

Bulkheads. Partitions built up in several parts of a ship to form and separate the various cabins, etc., from each other. Some are particularly strong, as those in the hold; others are light, and removable at pleasure. Indeed, the word is applied to any division made with boards, to separate one portion of the 'tween-decks from another. It is also applied to steel partitions.

Buntlines. Ropes attached to the foot-ropes of topsails and courses, which,

passing over and before the canvas, turn it up forward, and thus disarm the force of the wind. By aid of the clewlines, reef tackles, and buntlines, a topsail is taken in or quieted if the sheets carry away, but more especially by the buntlines, as the wind has no hold then to belly the canvas.

Capstan. A mechanical arrangement for lifting great weights. There is a variety of capstans, but they agree in having a horizontal circular head, which has square holes around its edge, and in these long bars are shipped, and are said to be "swifted" when their outer ends are traced together. Beneath is a perpendicular barrel, round which is wrapped the rope or chain used to lift the anchor or other great weight, even to the heaving a ship off a shoal. Capstan bars are long pieces of wood of the best ash or hickory, like the spokes of a wheel. They are used to heave the capstan round by the men setting their hands and chests against them and walking round.

Cat's-paw. A light air perceived at a distance in a calm by the impressions made on the surface of the sea, which it sweeps very gently and then passes away, being equally partial and transitory. Old superstitious seamen are seen to scratch the backstays with their nails, and whistle to invoke even these cat's-paws, the general forerunner of the steadier breeze.

Cay. The term was introduced by the buccaneers as meaning small insular spots with a scant vegetation; without the latter they are merely termed sandbanks. Key is especially used in the West Indies, and often applied to the smaller coral shoals produced by zoophytes.

Chain sheet. A length of chain used to set a sail, made fast by a shackle in the clew-iron and leading down on deck.

Channel. A general term signifying the outside plates which receive the bolts of the chain-plates and carry the deadeyes, and serve to spread and to support the rigging. Not used in modern square-rigged ships.

Clew, the. The corners of the sail to which the sheets are made fast. The lower corners of a square sail.

Clew to the bunt. To take in square sail by hauling the clews — the corners — to the quarters of the yards instead of to the yardarms, which is the more modern practice.

Clew up, to. To haul up the clews of a sail and thus take it in. Sails are always clewed up from the deck before the sailors go aloft.

Cockbill, to. The situation of the anchor when suspended from the cat-head ready for letting go. Also said of a cable when it hangs right up and down. To cockbill the yards is to top them up by one lift to an angle with the deck.

Course. The direction taken by anything in motion, shown by the point of the compass toward which it runs, as water in a river, tides, and currents; but if the wind, as similarly indicated by the compass point from which it blows. Course is also the ship's way. In common parlance, it is the point of the compass upon which the ship sails, the direction in which she proceeds, or is intended to go. Also means the lower sails, such as the foresail and mainsail.

Cringle-making. A cringle is a short piece of rope worked grommet-fashion into the bolt-rope of a sail to hold a metal thimble to which the shackles or hooks of blocks are made fast. Making these and fitting the thimbles is a fine art.

Crojack yard. The lower or principal yard on the mizzenmast of a square-rigged ship.

Cutwater. The foremost part of a vessel's prow, or the sharp part of the knee of a ship's head below the beak. It cuts or divides the water before reaching the bow, which would retard progress.

Davit. A steel gallows-like stanchion to which the boat falls are made fast, by means of which lifeboats are swung out and in.

Deadeye. A round wooden block cut with three holes, held fast to the channels by the chain-plate, and used to hold the lanyards which support and set up the shrouds and backstays. The term *dead* signifies that there is no revolving sheave.

Deadlight. Strong shutters made exactly to fit the cabin windows and ports inboard. They are fixed on the approach of bad weather.

Ditty-bag. A handy canvas bag used by seamen for containing their smaller necessaries. Often lavishly ornamented with sennet-work and fine sewing of sail-twine.

Fid. A square bar of wood or iron used to support the weight of the topmast or topgallant mast; also (and now more generally) a conical pin of hard wood used in splicing rope and for grommets and cringle-making. A marline-spike is a metal *fid.*

Fiferail. The wooden rails forming the upper fence of the bulwarks each side of the quarter-deck and poop. Also, the rail round the mainmast, and encircling both it and the pumps, furnished with belaying pins for the running rigging.

Flukes. The broad triangular plates on the arms of a bower anchor, which enter the ground and hold the ship.

Focs'l head. Forecastle head; the forepart of the upper deck at a vessel's bow; the raised section of a vessel forward.

Glossary

Fore-and-aft rigs. Implies jibs, stay-sails, and gaff and boom sails; in fact, all sails which are not set to yards. Schooners are fore-and-aft rigged, having no yards. A ship is square-rigged.

Fores'l. The foresail or forecourse, the principal sail on the foremast. (See the sail plan.)

Goose-wing, to. Means to reduce the set area of a sail until only one clew remains sheeted. This is usually done only in heavy gales.

Hammock nettings. Hammocks are swinging seabeds. Hammock nettings are the places where hammocks are stowed when not in use, and extend along the rail.

Hawse. A term of wide meaning. Strictly, it is that part of a vessel's bow which is pierced for her cables to run through. It also denotes any small distance between a vessel's head and the anchors employed to ride her, thus "the sloop fell athwart our hawse," "she anchored in our hawse," etc.

Hawsepipe. A cast-iron pipe in the hawseholes to prevent the cable from cutting the wood or chafing the metal.

Headsail. A general name for all those sails which may be set on the foremast and bowsprit, jib, and flying jib-boom, and employed to influence the fore-part of the ship.

Headstay. A fore-and-aft stay of iron wire from the foremast to the jib-boom. A general term signifying any of the fore-and-aft wires supporting the foremast, as distinct from the backstays.

Heave-to, to. To put a vessel in the position of lying-to, by adjusting her sails so as to counteract each other, and thereby check her way or keep her perfectly still. In a gale, it implies to set merely enough sail to steady the ship; the aim being to keep the sea on the weather bow whilst the rudder has but little influence. The sail is chiefly set on the main and mizzenmast; as hove-to under a close-reefed main topsail, or main trysail, or driver. It is customary in a foul wind gale, and a last resource in a fair one.

Jib, flying. Formerly a light sail set before the jib, on the flying jib-boom. The third jib in large ships, as the inner jib, the jib, and the flying jib, as in the *Joseph Conrad*.

Jib-boom. A continuation of the bowsprit forward, being a spar run out from the extremity in a similar manner to a topmast on a lower-mast, and serving to extend the foot of the jib and the stay of the fore topgallant mast, the tack of the jib being lashed to it. It is usually attached to the bowsprit by means of the cap, and the heel comes in to the knightheads.

Kedge anchor. A small anchor used to keep a ship steady and clear from her bower-anchor while she rides in harbour, particularly at the turn of the tide. The kedge anchors are also used to warp a ship from one part of a harbour to another. They are generally furnished with an iron stock, which is easily displaced for the convenience of stowing.

Kedge out, to. To warp a ship ahead, though the tide be contrary, by means of the kedge anchor and hawser; to get out of a bad place by continually shifting a small anchor ahead and warping the vessel up to it.

Kite. Sailor's term for light sails set usually only in fine weather, such as the royals, studding-sails and flying-jib.

Lanyard. A short piece of rope made fast to anything to secure it, or as a handle; more especially the tarred hempen lines rove in the deadeyes, setting up the shrouds, backstays, etc.

Leadline. A line attached to the upper end of the sounding-lead, used for making soundings in shoal water.

Main. A continent or mainland. Also, figuratively, the ocean; also short term for the mainmast.

Marrying. At sea means the joining of the ends of two ropes so that they will pass through a block.

Mat, chafing. A mat worked in rope or of sennet sewn on canvas placed aloft to prevent undue wearing of blocks or running rigging on the canvas. Chafing is a serious problem in all sailing-ships.

Mizzen. The spanker or driver is often so named. The third of three masts in a sailing vessel.

Mizzen stays'l. a fore-and-aft sail of various shapes set on the mizzen stay.

Mousing. A term used aboard ship to denote a turn or two of wire strand or marline round the point of a tackle-hook at its neck to prevent its unhooking; also used on shackle pins to prevent them from working loose.

Overfall. A rippling or race in the sea where, by the peculiarities of the bottom, the water is propelled with immense force, especially when the wind and tide, or current, set strongly.

Overhangs. That part of a ship's hull projecting beyond her waterline length — the counter and the bow.

Parrals. Those bands of rope, or sometimes iron collars, by which the centres of yards are fastened at the slings to the masts, so as to slide up and down freely when requisite.

Pawls, capstan. A stout but short set of bars of iron fixed close to the capstan-whelps, to prevent them from recoiling and over-powering the men. For capstans they are horizontal, bolted to the whelps, and butting to the deck-rim. They prevent the barrel of the capstan from slipping backwards under a strain. (See *Capstan*.)

Peak. The upper outer corner of those sails which are extended by a *gaff*.

Pintle. The rudder is hung on to a ship by pintles and braces. The braces are secured firmly to the stern-post by jaws, which spread and are bolted on each side. The pintles are hooks which enter the braces, and the rudder is then wood-locked; a dumb pintle on the heel finally takes the strain off the hinging portions.

Pratique. Formerly a Mediterranean term, implying the licence to trade and communicate with any place after having performed the required quarantine, or upon the production of a clean bill of health. Now in general use to signify the same thing. A vessel from beyond the sea must first have *pratique* to enter a port.

Racking. The operation of fastening two lines or sections of a tackle together with a seizing, so as to prevent the tackle from rendering through the blocks. Racking denotes also the spunyarn or other stuff used to rack two parts of a rope together.

Reef, to. Means to reduce the area of a sail while still leaving some of the sail set. A common practice in increasing winds. *Close-reefed* is when all the reefs (usually three) in the topsail are taken in.

Rope yarn. The smallest and simplest part of any rope, being one of the large threads of hemp or other stuff, several of which being twisted together form a strand.

Royal. The name of a light sail spread immediately next above the topgallant sail, to whose yardarms the lower corners of it are attached. It used to be termed topgallant royal, and is never used but in comparatively fine weather.

Royal yard. The fourth yard from the deck, on which the royal is set.

Scarf, to (or **scarph**). Is to join wood such as a fractured or sprung yard or boom by sloping off the edges and maintaining the same thickness throughout the joint. Such joints are usually strengthened by means of lashings, or bolted iron bands.

Scuppers. Round apertures cut through the water ways and sides of the ship at proper distances, in order to carry the water off the deck into the sea.

Seize, to. To fasten any two ropes, or different parts of one rope, together with turns of small stuff such as marline or spunyarn, or sometimes ropeyarn.

Seizing. Fastening any two ropes, or different parts of one rope together, with turns of small stuff. Also wire.

Set. The direction in which a current flows, or of the wind. Also applied to the direction of the tide. Also, when applied to sails, implies loosing and spreading them, so as to force the ship through the water on weighing.

Skids. Raised stanchions over the main deck, parallel to the poop and forecastle beams, for stowing the boats and booms upon.

Skys'l yarder. A ship setting skysail yards, that is, carrying square sails above the royals.

Spanker. A fore-and-aft sail, setting with a boom and gaff, frequently called the driver. It is the after-most sail of a ship or barque.

Spike. Short for marline-spike, a pointed instrument of high quality steel used in splicing.

Square, to. To square in or square up means to haul the yards more squarely

'thwartship, with the wind hauling aft. As the wind becomes fairer — that is, more directly behind the vessel on her course — the yards are trimmed until the after-yards are square.

Stand from under, to. To keep out of the way; a sailor's call of warning.

Stay, preventer. An extra stay of wire rigged to relieve a strained piece of standing rigging and to assist in supporting the mast.

Stays'l. A triangular sail hoisted upon a stay. A stay is a strong wire extending from the upper end of each mast toward the stem of the ship, as the shrouds are extended on each side. The object is to prevent the masts from springing, when the ship is pitching deep, and to support them.

Sternway. The movement by which a ship goes stern foremost. The opposite of headway.

Studding-sails. Fine-weather sails set outside the square sails; the term scudding-sails was formerly used. Topmost and topgallant studding-sails are those which are set outside the topsails and topgallant sails. They have yards at the head, and are spread at the foot by booms which slide out on the extremities of the lower and topsail yards, and their heads or yards are hoisted up to the topsail and topgallant yardarms.

Stuns'l. A corruption of studding-sail.

Stuns'l booms. A spar rigged out for the purpose of setting a studding-sail, and taking its name from the sail it belongs to.

Tide rip. Those short ripplings which result from eddies or the passage of the tide over uneven bottom; also observed in the ocean where two currents meet, but not appearing to affect a ship's course.

Topgallant. The topgallant mast is the third mast above the deck, the mast of a square-rigged ship being in three pieces, each called masts — the lower-mast, topmast and topgallant mast. Also an abbreviation for topgallant sail, the sail set on the topgallant mast. (See the sail plan of the *Joseph Conrad*.)

Topmast head. The top or uppermost section of the topmast, the second mast above the deck. The "head" is the section of the mast above the rigging.

Tops'l, single. The deep sail on the topmast, which for many years has been cut into two sails, the lower and upper topsails. The *Joseph Conrad* had only one topsail on each mast.

Trade-winds. Currents of air moving from about the 30th degree of latitude towards the equator. The diurnal motion of the earth makes them incline from the eastward, so that in the northern hemisphere they are from the north-east and in the southern hemisphere from the south-east. Their geographical position in latitude varies with the declination of the sun. In some parts of the world, as the Bay of Bengal and the China Sea, the action of the sun on the neighbouring land has the power of reversing the trades; the winds are there called monsoons.

Trestle-trees. Two strong bars of timber fixed horizontally fore-and-aft on each side of the masthead, to take the weight of the cross-trees and the section of the mast above.

Triple reefed. Close-reefed, having all three reefs taken in the topsail. Signifies heavy weather.

Trysail. A reduced sail used by small craft in lieu of their mainsail during a storm. Used generally to denote a jib-headed fore-and-aft sail set in bad weather from a boom, instead of the full spanker.

Wash-board. A movable upper strake which is attached by stud-pins on the gunwales of boats to keep out the spray. Wash-boards are also fitted on the sills of the lower-deck ports for the same purpose, and in companion-ways and galley doors, etc., to keep out something of the sea.

Washport. Swinging sections of the bulwarks which open when a sea comes on board to permit the water to run off the deck. They are usually too small to permit a man being swept out through them, or are protected by iron bars.

Waterspout. A large mass of water collected in a vertical column, and moving rapidly along the surface of the sea. Seen frequently in the China Sea and the Doldrums.

Wear ship, to. To put a sailing-ship on the other tack — that is, to bring her close to the wind on the other beam — by running off before the wind and coming up again on the other tack, trimming the yards as she comes. A ship thus manoeuvred keeps the wind in the sails, and for that reason it is usual to *wear* a square-rigged ship in bad weather rather than to *tack* her. In *tacking* it is necessary to come head-to-wind.

Windlass. (from the Ang. Sax. windles). A machine erected in the fore-part of a ship which serves her to ride by, as well as heave in, the cable. Worked by the capstan or by levers.

Afterword

When Alan Villiers sold the *Joseph Conrad* to an American millionaire in 1936, his mission was, it seemed, at an end. He had sailed the former Danish sail-training ship 57,000 miles around the world, and had managed to do so without losing either the ship itself or any of her crew. What did he leave to show for it?

An idea: and ideas are more important than facts, as any real leader knows. Purposeful, versatile and superbly gifted as a writer, Alan Villiers was a pioneer. In choosing to spend his life in sailing ships – to *sail* them as well as photograph and record their passing – he brought both knowledge and pleasure to millions who might never go to sea themselves, but could share his enthusiasm for the sea and its international community. He inspired a generation of sailors, conservationists and environmentalists before 'green' issues reached the political agenda; for was the wind not free?

Perhaps ironically, given its emphasis upon tradition, the Royal Navy no longer practises training in sail: but the vast majority of nations still recognise the value of such training, and the Royal Navy is in the minority. Sail transcends boundaries. The forecastle of the old commercial sailing ship was a thoroughly international affair, and the brotherhood – and sisterhood – of the sea lives on, whether for the round-the-world sailor or Sunday yachtsman. In 1956, the Sail Training Association was formed – later chaired by Sir Robin Knox-Johnston – and today there are thousands of vessels across the globe, putting into practice what Alan Villiers believed in and brought to life on the *Conrad*.

Sail-training is no longer confined to the able-bodied, a development my father would have welcomed. A lover of sail, he was never an opponent of change *per se*. Where progress *was* progress, he supported it. New designs for engineless sailing ships were of particular interest to him, and he welcomed developments like the Jarvis brace-winch that made the work of the sailor both less laborious and less dangerous. Those ideas could be taken further, without destroying the essential purpose of training in sail.

What is that purpose? Those who have read this book will have grasped it for themselves. In the end is the beginning.

Peter Villiers
North Devon, 2006